Mathematics
for Modern Economics

Mathematics
for Modern Economics

CHRIS BIRCHENHALL
University of Manchester
and
PAUL GROUT
University of Birmingham

Philip Allan
Barnes & Noble Books

First published 1984 by

Philip Allan Publishers Limited
Market Place
Deddington
Oxford OX5 4SE

and in the USA by
Barnes and Noble Books
81 Adams Drive
Totowa
New Jersey 07512

British Library Cataloguing in Publication Data

Birchenhall, Christopher Roger
Mathematics for modern economics.
1. Economics. Mathematical
I. Title   II. Grout, Paul
510'.2433   HB135

ISBN 0–86003–023–7
ISBN 0–86003–124–1 Pbk

Library of Congress Cataloging in Publication Data

Birchenhall, Chris.
Mathematics for modern economics.

1. Economics, Mathematical. I. Grout, Paul.
II. Title.
HB135.B525   1984   510   84–12464
ISBN 0–389–20521–4
ISBN 0–389–20522–2 (pbk.)

Typesetting by Activity Ltd., Salisbury
Printed and bound in Great Britain by
Billing and Sons Ltd., Worcester

Contents

v

Contents

viii   Contents

Preface

This book is intended for students who wish to acquire an intuitive understanding of the basic mathematical techniques of modern economic analysis. For this reason the text makes no attempt to treat the mathematics as a separate and abstract subject. Instead the mathematics is presented as an extension to and formal expression of familiar fundamental economic intuitions and theories. Indeed the main prerequisite for the text is not mathematical — it is assumed the reader has no more than a small acquaintance with mathematics — but economic: it is assumed the reader has, or is in the process of acquiring, some understanding of basic economics as presented in texts such as P. A. Samuelson's *Economics*. Assuming only a knowledge of basic algebra, the text develops the requisite ideas and techniques of differential calculus up to and including modern duality.

The presentation is in four parts. The main body of the book is in three parts dealing with differential calculus, constrained optimisation, and the theory of the firm and consumer respectively. An Appendix covers matrix algebra, second order difference equations and some of the more formal background of calculus.

Part 1 begins with a brief statement, in Chapter 1, of the concepts that are likely to be familiar to the student and puts this existing knowledge into context. Chapter 2 introduces the essential concept of a function — the basic building block of the majority of economic models, as functions are used to represent formally the relationships between economic variables. A critical tool in the analysis of functions is differential calculus which is introduced in Chapters 3 and 4. Students familiar with such economic ideas as *marginal* cost or *marginal* utility will find they have implicitly been using the ideas of differential calculus. Chapter 3 deals with differentiation of functions of one variable and Chapter 4 deals with differentiation of functions of several variables. Two novel features of Chapter 4 are the introduction of partial functions and the use of directional derivatives. Economics students who have met the *ceteris paribus* assumption will find that the notion of a partial function is a natural introduction to partial differentiation. Similarly the concept of a directional derivative simplifies the understanding of total differentiation. Chapter 5 discusses the use of calculus in identifying unconstrained optima. Chapter 6 is something of a digression, albeit an important one, from the main theme of the text, in that it is an introduction to the analysis of dynamic models. In particular it discusses first order difference and differential equations, and also covers integration while developing first order differential equations. The final chapter of Part I consists of a discussion of concave and convex functions which form the foundation of Part II. Indeed unless it is stated otherwise, all functions in Chapters 8 to 12 are assumed to be concave or convex. Such functions are immensely powerful in the analysis of constrained and unconstrained maximisation and, in conjunction with Chapter 13, simplify the analysis considerably.

Part II deals with the central problem of economic analysis, namely the analysis of the rational choice of agents faced with economic constraints, the two prime examples being the utility-maximising choices of consumers facing a budget constraint, and the profit-maximising choices of a firm facing technological constraints. Chapter 8 offers an informal introduction to constrained optimisation by translating the familiar analysis of indifference curves and isoquants into the formal language of calculus. In so doing, the student will meet for the first time the idea of a Lagrangian function associated with a constrained optimisation problem, the essential idea of the Lagrangian being to convert a constrained into an unconstrained optimisation problem. This chapter finishes with a discussion of a very simple one-variable example which serves as a bridge between Chapters 8 and 9. The key to obtaining an intuitive understanding of the Lagrangian method is the concept of the shadow price of an economic constraint. Informally speaking, the shadow price tells us how much the decision maker is willing to pay for a marginal relaxation of a constraint. The appropriate vehicle for the formal discussion of shadow prices is the envelope function introduced in Chapter 9, where a constructive 'proof' of the Lagrangian theorem is presented. Although the Lagrangian method remains a vital instrument in an economist's tool-kit, modern economics makes extensive and growing use of the so-called dual approach — Chapters 10, 11 and 12 introduce the most popular forms of this approach. Chapter 10 presents an informal, geometric discussion of the indirect utility function and Roy's Identity. This provides an introduction to the fundamental ideas of duality in economics, namely that there are alternative ways of expressing the structure of optimisation problems, and that these indirect alternatives are often more convenient. Chapter 11 discusses three other dual structures — the expenditure function of a consumer, and the cost and profit functions of a firm. Chapter

12 introduces the envelope theorem and uses this to derive Roy's Identity, Shephard's Lemma and Hotelling's Lemma.

The final chapter of Part II gives a brief discussion of the extension of the Lagrangian theorem to several constraints, including the Kuhn–Tucker theorem as a special case. A novel feature of Chapter 13 is the use of indirect concavity. It is common in economic analysis to use quasi-concave functions, particularly in consumer theory, but while we mention this notion in passing, we concentrate on the concept of indirect concavity which is far simpler and covers virtually all the economists' requirements.

Part III of the text brings together the answers to problems set in the text and each answer is embodied in an economic commentary which relates the relevant problem to the theory of the consumer or the theory of the firm. The answers are not presented in the order that the problems appear in the text but are structured to form a systematic analysis of the behaviour of consumer and firm, the solutions being linked together to form a text. This section is an integral part of the text, giving the student a coherent store of worked examples that they have initially tackled as problems. Inevitably because of this dual purpose the presentation is occasionally somewhat uneven. The main reason for setting the basic theory of consumer and firm behaviour as a series of problems is to give the student insight into the relationship between mathematics and modern economics, but Part III of the book serves two other important roles. Firstly, it motivates students who may have reservations about the role of mathematics. The process of mastering the mathematical methods in the text guarantees that the student has also obtained a deeper understanding of economic analysis and extended his knowledge of economic theory. Secondly Part III contains some cases where the mathematical manipulation is straightforward in comparison to the conceptual difficulties of the economic problem. Having worked through this part of the book, students should be fully aware that mathematical manipulation alone is of no use in economics, and must be combined with a strong intuitive grasp of the essence of the problem to have any use.

A note on the use of Chapters 14 to 16 is in order. As indicated above, these chapters contain solutions to the problems set in earlier chapters. Each problem is followed by a page reference indicating that the solution to that problem starts on that page. When looking up the solution to a problem you will thus refer to the indicated page. On that page you then scan down the left-hand margin until you find a number matching the number of the problem. For example, in looking for the solution to Problem 4.3 you should refer to page 322 and look for the number 4.3 in the left margin. The solution to the problem starts on the line containing the problem number and continues until the box symbol next appears in the right-hand margin. Clearly when reading Chapters 14 to 16 as stand-alone discussions of the consumer and firm you can ignore these references.

When writing a text of this nature the authors draw heavily on their own training and research, and it is doubtful whether one can be truly original in presenting widely understood and familiar ideas. Hence we would like to thank those who have either taught us or whose written work has helped our understanding of our topic. Equally we must thank those numerous students whose probing questions have increased that understanding. Finally, we must thank those colleagues who have directly or indirectly assisted our work. Our special thanks must go to Paul Madden, who has read the whole text, indeed several drafts of key chapters, and has been responsible for a great improvement in style and the removal of error. Unfortunately we cannot guarantee that we have met the high standards of clarity or precision that characterises this valuable colleague. Particular thanks go also to Ian Walker who read earlier drafts of our chapters on duality and made valuable suggestions, particularly the four quadrant diagrams that appear in Chapter 10. Again we cannot claim to have completely satisfied Ian's criticism nor to have exactly reproduced his diagrams. Our thanks also to the following who have read parts of earlier drafts and whose constructive criticisms have been welcomed: Maurice Peston, David Laidler, Mick Wilkes, Roger Backhouse and Mervyn King.

As with any publication the efforts of the editorial staff have been vital and we extend our thanks to Philip Cross and Mary Robinson for their work on our manuscript. Last, but not least, we must publicly thank the efforts of the following secretaries, without whom much, in particular this text, would be impossible: Rita Kushner, Marie Waite and Marilyn Mansell.

Finally the book contains an Appendix. This covers matrix algebra of which most economists will require some familiarity. The use of concavity and convexity have enabled us to avoid alternative statements of second order conditions which require matrix algebra. Our reliance on concavity and convexity follows the practice of almost all modern economics, but some knowledge of other methods of checking second order conditions is useful and this is covered in the Appendix. Similarly some of the formal background of calculus that is implicit or omitted in the body of the text is covered in the Appendix for those interested in greater rigour. Finally the use of second order difference equations may be necessary for some students. Such a discussion goes beyond the basic coverage of Chapter 6, and so it is included in the Appendix.

PART I

Differential Calculus

1

Algebra: The Language of Mathematics

1 Introductory Remarks

The purpose of economic analysis is to clarify the main determining or causal relationships between economic variables, and to generate qualitative and quantitative conclusions about these relationships. Our aim in this text is to introduce the reader to some aspects of the use of mathematics in modern economic analysis. In particular we shall develop the role of differential calculus in the analysis of the decisions made by rational economic agents. Consider the following statement: a household will demand less of a normal good if the household income falls. This is a qualitative rather than a quantitative statement in that it does not attempt to say how much the household demand will fall, only stating that the change in demand will be negative, without reference to the specific quantitative measure of this change. It is the task of economic analysis or theory to offer such qualitative statements and increasingly modern economists require such statements to be logically derived from explicit assumptions. Hence it is not surprising that economists are using mathematical models to give expression to their theories, for, by adopting the rigours of mathematical deduction, the chances of logical inconsistency are reduced, while at the same time we can draw upon the work of mathematicians to simplify the deductive process. For example, we shall show that the use of differential calculus allows us to produce a fruitful analysis of rational economic decisions, this analysis drawing on the work of mathematicians who have clarified and validated the logic of the calculus.

3

As might be expected, these advantages are not costless in that economists have to learn the language and methods of mathematics. Fortunately this is not such a horrific task as some readers might fear; indeed the use of differential calculus in economics has a long history and many of the formal ideas have been absorbed into the more informal language of economics. Corresponding to the mathematician's idea of differential calculus, economists use marginal analysis; for example we shall see that marginal cost corresponds to the derivative of a cost function. A second related fact that facilitates the translation between our economics and mathematics is the universal use of geometric arguments in economic analysis, and in this text we shall make extensive use of diagrams to intermediate between the formal results and their economic counterparts. The key to this translation between the formal mathematical models and the more familiar geometric models is the observation that the curves in our diagrams can be interpreted as the graph of an appropriate function. Hence the demand curve that appears in the traditional cross-diagram analysis of a single market can be viewed as the graph of the associated demand function.

While functions are the basic building blocks of our mathematical models, the language of those models is algebra and it is the aim of this chapter to review some of the main elements of this topic. While this review will refresh the reader's memory of some of the details, it will hopefully deepen his understanding of the role of algebra in mathematics in general and economic analysis in particular.

2   Sets

2.1 Introduction

A *set* is a collection of distinct and well defined objects. A set can be defined in two ways, namely by enumeration of its members or by specifying a criterion of membership. For example, we can write (1,2,3) to represent the set made up of the numbers 1, 2 and 3. Often defining a set by listing its members is inconvenient, indeed sometimes it is impossible. Consider the set of all residents of the UK. While it would be extremely difficult to list all the members of this set, we can define it readily as the set of all objects for which it is true that the object is a person and is resident in the UK.

As we have indicated, much of this text will be concerned with the analysis of the choice of rational economic agents. In discussing such decisions we need to specify the *opportunity set* of the decision maker, that is to say the set of alternative actions which are feasible for that agent. For example the opportunity set of a consumer is taken to be the set of all *combinations* of goods which the consumer can buy with the available budget. If we know the consumer's budget and the prices of all goods, the opportunity set is well defined in that we can check whether any given combination is feasible for the consumer, i.e. we can check whether or not he can afford to buy that combination of goods.

2.2 Real Numbers

Throughout this text we shall assume that economic variables are real variables, i.e. their values are real numbers. It is worth pausing temporarily to clarify what this means and why we make this assumption. The set of *natural numbers* are those numbers we use to count distinct objects, i.e. (0,1,2,3,...), while the set of *integers* is the set of signed natural numbers, i.e. (0, +1, −1, +2, −2, +3, −3, ...). A *rational number* is the ratio of an integer and a natural number, e.g. — 3/2; note a rational number has a sign, namely the sign of the integer forming the numerator. While natural numbers are well named and integers and rational numbers seem to be 'natural' extensions of integers, we need to go beyond rationals to real numbers. For example, it can be shown that the square root of 2, i.e. $\sqrt{2}$, is not a rational number. Equally the constant π that appears in our geometry, for example the area of a circle with radius r is πr^2, is not a rational number. Although these numbers are not rational, the magnitudes are very real, e.g. the area of a circle of radius 1. For this reason we concentrate on the set of real numbers, which includes both the above examples. A precise definition of real numbers need not concern us here, let us simply point out that they can be viewed as the set of all decimal numbers, the decimals possibly being of infinite length. Hence, we write $\sqrt{2} = 1.414...$ where the dots indicate that the decimal part of the number continues indefinitely and without recurrence.

Finally, if we imagine an infinitely long straight line on which we choose an 'origin' then there is a one to one correspondence between the set of real numbers and the points on this line. For every real number there is a unique point on this line whose distance from the origin is equal to that real number, negative and positive being associated with the 'left' and 'right' side of the line. In this way we can identify the set of real numbers with this line, in which case we refer to the latter as the *real line* (see Figure 1.1).

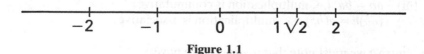

Figure 1.1

3 Basic Algebra

3.1 Introduction

Analysis of economic decisions usually falls into two phases, namely the formulation and the solution phases. The former phase involves us in formulating the opportunity set as well as the preferences of the decision maker. While doing this, we invariably introduce decision variables which may or may not be required to satisfy certain restrictions, for example in the case of the consumer we refer to the quantities of the goods he may purchase. The important point is that these quantities are variable and do not have any specific value, even though they may be restricted. In the second phase of our analysis we aim to solve our model of the decision maker by identifying that choice which the model implies to be 'best' for the agent. In this phase we will be searching for a characterisation of the agent's optimum choice, and more often than not the optimal values of the decision variables will be specific but unknown.

Defining algebra to be the study of the properties of numbers in general, rather than specific numbers, we can begin to appreciate the value of algebra in the study of decisions, for it facilitates the manipulation and investigation of unspecific or unknown numbers in both the specification and solution phases. In the remaining sections of this chapter we scan some of the basic algebra which will be particularly useful in subsequent chapters.

3.2 Operations

Adding, subtracting, multiplying and dividing numbers are familiar enough operations, but it is worthwhile just emphasising some of the differences between them. First we can note that the order in which we add or multiply a set of numbers is not significant in the sense that we will always end up with the same answer. Yet this is not true for subtraction and division, for example the subtraction of 2 from 3 is not the same as the subtraction of 3 from 2.

Putting this observation formally we can assert that the following are true for all real numbers a,b,c.

   (i) $a + b = b + a$, i.e. addition is commutative;
  (ii) $(a + b) + c = a + (b + c)$, i.e. addition is associative;
 (iii) $ab = ba$, i.e. multiplication is commutative;
 (iv) $(ab)c = a(bc)$, i.e. multiplication is associative.

In contrast we must note that in general we have:

(v) $\quad a - b \neq b - a$
(vi) $\quad (a - b) - c \neq a - (b - c)$
(vii) $\quad a \div b \neq b \div a$
(viii) $\quad (a \div b) \div c \neq a \div (b \div c)$

3.3 $\sum$ and $\prod$ Notation

The fact that we can refer unambiguously to the sum and the product of a set of numbers has led to the introduction of a succinct notation to represent such sums and products. Thus let $x_1, x_2, \ldots, x_n$ be a set of n numbers for some natural number, n, then we write $\sum_{i=1}^{n} x_i$ to denote the sum of these numbers and $\prod_{i=1}^{n} x_i$ to represent their product. The first of these expressions can be read as 'the sum of the x_i as i ranges from 1 to n', and the second expression reads 'the product of the x_i as i runs from 1 to n'.

For example, consider a consumer who spends his budget on 15 different commodities, and let e_i, $i = 1,2,3,\ldots,15$, be the amount he expends upon the i'th good. Then his total expenditure $e_1 + e_2 + e_3 + \ldots + e_{15}$ can be denoted by $\sum_{i=1}^{15} e_i$. Hence, if his budget or income is m, then he will face the constraint that his total expenditure cannot be greater than m, i.e. $\sum_{i=1}^{15} e_i \leqslant m$.

As a second example we can imagine our having a sample of individuals and a record of each individual's income. The sample mean of the incomes is the sum of the individual incomes divided by the number of individuals in the sample. Hence if we have n individuals in the sample and their incomes are y_i, $i = 1,2,3,\ldots,n$, then the sample mean income is $1/n \sum_{i=1}^{n} y_i$.

A further property of addition and multiplication is the fact that if we multiply two numbers by the same third number and then add up those products we will get the same answer given by adding the two numbers then multiplying by the third. More formally we have

(ix) $\quad a(b + c) = ab + ac$, i.e. multiplication and addition are
distributive.

More generally we will have

$$c\left(\sum_{i=1}^{n} x_i \right) = \sum_{i=1}^{n} cx_i$$

i.e. common multiplicative terms can be taken outside the summation sign.

To give an economic illustration of this statement, interpret the x_i as the quantity of a good purchased by the i'th customer and let c be the price of the good. The sum $\sum_{i=1}^{n} x_i$ is thus the total quantity of the good purchased by the customers while $\sum_{i=1}^{n} cx_i$ is the total expenditure of the customers on that good. Hence the above expression simply states that the customer's total expenditure will equal the cost of the total quantity of the good they purchase.

One feature of the use of the summation sign which often causes problems is illustrated by the following statement:

$$\sum_{i=1}^{n} (x_i + c) = \sum_{i=1}^{n} x_i + nc$$

On the left-hand side (LHS) of this expression we have the sum of n numbers of the form $x_i + c$, that is to say the i'th number in the sum is itself the sum of two numbers namely x_i and c. The second number in the i'th term is independent of i, that is to say it is common to all terms in the sum. On the right-hand side (RHS) of our equation, we separated out that common term, note that the number c appears n times on the LHS and thus we have nc on the RHS.

As an illustration of this last equation, we can interpret $x_i + c$ as the total cost of a household's quarterly use of its telephone, with c being the fixed charge or rental and the x_i being the variable charge dependent upon the number of units used by the household. On the LHS we then have the total cost of all households' use of the telephone while on the RHS we have the sum of total variable charge $\sum_{i=1}^{n} x_i$ and the total fixed rental nc.

A somewhat more general statement is

$$\sum_{i=1}^{n} (x_i + y_i) = \sum_{i=1}^{n} x_i + \sum_{i=1}^{n} y_i$$

which says if we have a set of numbers, each of which is itself the sum of two numbers x_i and y_i, then their sum is equal to the sum of the separate sums of the x_i's and y_i's.

3.4 Powers of a Number

Given a real number r and a natural number n, we write r^n to indicate the n'th power of r, i.e. r multiplied by itself n times, so that $r^2 = rr$ and $r^3 = rrr$. Note that $r^1 = r$, and we usually define r^0 to be equal to 1, unless $r = 0$ in which case $r^0 = 0^0$ is undefined. We define r^{-1}, r raised to the power of minus one, to be the reciprocal of r, i.e. $r^{-1} = 1/r$. Equally r^{-n} is defined to be the reciprocal of r^n, i.e. $r^{-n} = 1/r^n$ or equivalently as the n'th power of r^{-1}, i.e. $r^{-n} = (r^{-1})^n = (1/r)^n = (1/r^n)$. If r is a positive number, we can also define $r^{1/n}$, i.e. r raised to the power of $1/n$, as being that number which raised to the power n gives r, i.e. $r^{1/n}$ is such that $(r^{1/n})^n = r$. That is to say $r^{1/n}$ is the n'th root of r, in particular $r^{1/2} = \sqrt{r}$, is the square root of r, and $r^{1/3} = \sqrt[3]{r}$ is the cube root of r. Given a rational number $p = m/n$ where m is an integer and n a natural number we can define $r^p = r^{m/n} = (r^{1/n})^m = (r^m)^{1/n}$, thus $r^{3/2} = (\sqrt{r})^3 = \sqrt{r^3}$. Having given meaning to r raised to the power of a rational number, we can extend the idea of powers of a real number. We shall not pursue this notion here, but simply indicate that we can manipulate r^p, where p is real, as if p were rational.

In particular we have the following general results. For all real $r > 0$ and real p, q we have

(i) $r^p \times r^q = r^{p+q}$ i.e. when multiplying powers of the same factor we add up the powers;

(ii) $r^p \div r^q = \dfrac{r^p}{r^q} = r^{p-q}$ i.e. when dividing powers of the same factor we subtract the powers;

(iii) $(r^p)^q = (r^q)^p = r^{pq}$ i.e. powers of powers is given multiplying the powers.

For examples of (i)–(iii) we have

(a) $r^2 \times r^3 = r^5$
(b) $r^3/r^2 = r$
(c) $(r^2)^3 = r^6$

3.5 Inequalities

It is useful to distinguish between *weak* and *strict* inequalities. Hence we write $a \geqslant b$ to indicate a weak inequality and read this notation as saying a is no less than b or a is greater than or equal to b, while we write $a > b$ to indicate a strict inequality, namely that a is strictly greater than b. Equally $a < b$ says a is strictly less than b and $a \leqslant b$ says a is no greater than b.

Note first that when we say a is *positive* we mean $a > 0$, i.e. a is strictly greater than zero, while b being *non-negative* means $b \geqslant 0$ which allows b to be zero. Similarly $a < 0$ is read as a is *negative* and $b \leqslant 0$ as b is *non-positive*.

Inequalities have the following properties:

(i)   If c is a positive number then $ac > bc$ if and only if $a > b$ and $ac \geqslant bc$ if and only if $a \geqslant b$. Note this tells us that we can multiply or divide inequalities by positive numbers without changing those inequalities.

(ii)   If c is a negative number then $ac > bc$ if and only if $a < b$ and $ac \geqslant bc$ if and only if $a \leqslant b$. Hence dividing or multiplying an inequality by a negative number reverses the inequality.

(iii)   For *any* number c, $a + c > b + c$ if and only if $a > b$ and $a + c \geq b + c$
         if and only if $a \geq b$. Hence adding or subtracting numbers across an
         inequality does not alter the inequality.

Given any non-zero number, $b \neq 0$, it follows that $b^2 > 0$. For if b is
positive then $b > 0$ which, multiplied by b, tells us $b^2 > b0 = 0$, while if b is
negative then $b < 0$ and multiplying by b gives $b^2 > b0 = 0$. Note the
reversal of the sign in this last case because b is negative. We can thus
conclude that the square of any number is non-negative and that the square
is zero only if the number is zero, i.e. for all b, $b^2 \geq 0$ and $b^2 = 0$ if and only
if $b = 0$. This in turn implies that there is no real number whose square is
negative and thus no negative number has a real square root.

Our interest in inequalities arises largely from our interest in optimisation. Given a set of numbers S, we say x is the maximum member of S if x is
a member of S and x is not less than any member of S, i.e. $x \geq y$ for all
members y of S; we write $x = \max S$ to indicate this property. Symmetrically
the minimum member of S is such that it is no greater than any member of S,
i.e. $z = \min S$ if $z \leq y$ for all y in S. Consider now two sets S and T such that
every member of T is the negative of some member of S and vice versa. For
example we might have $S = (-1, 2, 3)$ and $T = (+1, -2, -3)$. We could
denote this relation between S and T by writing $T = -S$, the minus sign in
front of S indicating that T is generated by multiplying each element of S by
minus one.

If $T = -S$ then $\min T = -\max S$, i.e. the minimum member of T is minus
one times the *maximum* member of S. For if $a = \min T$, then $a \leq t$ for all t in
T, multiplying this inequality by minus one tells us $-a \geq -t$ for all t in T. But
as every t in T is equal to $-s$ for some s in S and vice versa, we can conclude
$-a \geq s$ for all s in S. That is to say $-a = \max S$ or $a = -\max S$ as asserted. If
you consider our simple example $S = (-1, 2, 3)$, $T = (+1, -2, -3)$ we can
see that $\min T = -3$ while $\max S = 3$, so that we do indeed have $\min T =
-\max S$. This is a very important observation because it shows we can
always convert a maximisation problem into a minimisation problem and
vice versa, an idea we will pick up and develop later in the text.

3.6 Equations in One Unknown

In the main body of the text we shall develop the use of calculus in the
identification of optimum, where typically we are able to state that the
optimal values of decision variables must satisfy certain equations. Insofar
as we can solve those equations, we are then able to identify the optimal
choice. We need to be clear what it means to solve an equation and to
develop techniques of solution.

As an illustrative example, consider the statement that a profit-maximising competitive firm will choose its output so as to equate marginal cost with price. Let us assume marginal cost varies with quantity as follows

$$MC = a + bq$$

where q is output and a,b are known constants, and if p is price, then the profit-maximising output q^* must satisfy

$$a + bq^* = p$$

In this expression we are taking a,b and p as known and we wish to *solve* the equation for q^*, by which we mean that we wish to express the unknown, namely q^*, in terms of the knowns a, b and p. In this case our task is straightforward. By subtracting a from both sides of the equation and then dividing both sides by b, which we assume is not zero, we obtain

$$bq^* = p - a$$

and thus

$$q^* = \frac{p - a}{b}$$

This example is an illustration of a linear equation which generally does not generate any particular technical problem of solution. The only technicality worth noting is that if we had $b = 0$ then either $p - a = 0$, in which case *all* q^* satisfy the equation, or $p - a \neq 0$, in which case the equation is inconsistent and there is no solution, for it requires $p - a$ to be simultaneously equal to but not equal to zero.

A second class of equations which commonly arise and for which we can readily find solutions are quadratic equations, a typical example of which is

$$ax^2 + bx + c = 0$$

Here a, b and c are the 'knowns' and x is the 'unknown'. First we note that if $a = 0$, then the equation is linear and the above discussion is relevant; hence let us assume now $a \neq 0$. It can be shown (see Chapter 2, Section 3) that this quadratic equation has a solution if and only if the 'knowns' satisfy the inequality $b^2 - 4ac \geqslant 0$; furthermore if this condition is satisfied, remembering $a \neq 0$, then the solutions of the equations are given by

$$x = \frac{-b \pm \sqrt{(b^2 - 4ac)}}{2a}$$

Here the use of $\pm$ indicates we can use either $+$ or $-$ to generate a solution. Hence in general there will be two solutions, unless $b^2 - 4ac = 0$, in which case there is only one solution.

Once we move away from linear and quadratic equations, solution procedures become unclear if not extremely difficult. For example, for cubic equations of the form

$$ax^3 + bx^2 + cx + d = 0$$

there is no simple procedure that will tackle all possibilities. Should $d = 0$ then the equation can be rewritten as

$$(ax^2 + bx + c)x = 0$$

in which case either $x = 0$ or $ax^2 + bx + c = 0$, and we can find the solutions. But if $d \neq 0$, then in general we will be unable to write down an analytic solution for x. In practice we may adopt numerical methods to solve general cubic equations based perhaps on a computer, rather than look for a universal formula such as we have for quadratic equations.

It is not traditional for an introductory text to emphasise problems such as this, but as we shall argue in the text it is such problems that have in part led to economists adopting the 'dual' approach to optimisation.

In summary, we have illustrated the fact that an equation may or may not have solutions and we may or may not be able to find those solutions by 'mechanical' procedures.

2
Functions of One Variable

1 Functions and their Graphs

Functions are the formal counterpart of the familiar diagrammatic concepts used in economics (e.g. demand curves, supply curves), and are the basic building block of formal economic models. A demand curve represents diagrammatically the relationship between the quantity demanded of a good and the price of that good, and the formal algebraic representation of the demand curve is the demand function, i.e. a demand curve is the graph of a demand function. Similarly a supply curve is the graph of a supply function. Occasionally in economics it is common to refer, rather loosely, to both the function and its diagrammatic representation as functions, e.g. when we talk of consumption functions. In this opening section we classify what is meant by a function and its graph, and we will see that it is possible to interpret most of the curves of theoretical diagrams as graphs of functions. Thus the relationship between functions and their graphs allows us to translate between the geometric and mathematical arguments.

We can think of a demand function as mapping out the relationship between price and quantity. For any given price the demand function identifies (maps onto) the unique quantity that will be demanded at that price. In general we think of functions mapping one variable onto another. If we denote price by p, quantity by q and the demand function by f we write:

$$q = f(p) \tag{2.1}$$

13

or

$$f:p\rightarrow q \tag{2.2}$$

The first notation is the most common but the second has the advantage of explicitly suggesting the interpretation of mapping p onto q. In this example p is the argument (or independent variable) of the function and q is the value (or dependent variable) of the function. When defining a function we should also indicate the set of possible values of the argument; this set is called the *domain* of the function. The set of possible values of the function is known as the *range* of the function. For a relationship to be a function, each element in the domain must define (map onto) a *unique* value in the range. If we do not have a unique value then we do not have a function mapping the one variable onto the other. Hence whenever we refer to a demand function we imply that the quantity demanded at any price is unique.

Often we wish to use an explicit analytic expression for a function, that is to say we write down an algebraic expression indicating how we calculate the value of the function for any given value of the argument. For example, our demand function may take the explicit forms

$$q = a - bp \tag{2.3}$$

or

$$q = ap^{-b} \tag{2.4}$$

where a and b are positive constants, i.e. they do not vary as the independent variable price p varies. For example, we might have $a = 10$ and $b = 0.5$. Given that we usually think of price as non-negative, we normally restrict the domain of our demand function to the set of non-negative numbers. Also note that we would normally consider the quantity demanded to be non-negative, hence in the case of (2.3) we would need to restrict price p to be such that $a - bp \geqslant 0$, i.e. $bp \leqslant a$ or $p \leqslant a/b$. Hence (2.3) has a domain equal to the set of non-negative numbers satisfying $p \leqslant a/b$. In the case of (2.4) we do not have the possibility of negative values as long as p is positive. However, we face the difficulty that the reciprocal of zero is undefined ($a\,0^{-b}$ is not defined). Hence we restrict the domain of the function to strictly positive numbers.

In most of this text we will not concern ourselves unduly with defining the domain of our functions and will take as understood that they are chosen such that the value of the function is well defined and the domain and range are economically meaningful.

Given a function, its graph is a geometric representation of the relationship embodied in the function.

In Figure 2.1 we have drawn part of the graph of a function mapping the variable x onto y. Here we measure the independent variable, or argument of the function, along the horizontal axis (abscissa) and the dependent variable,

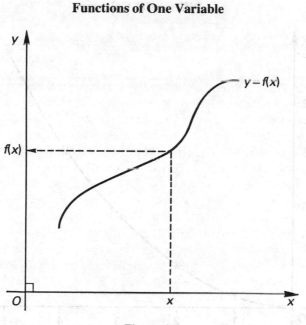

Figure 2.1

or value of the function along the vertical axis (ordinate). The solid curve in the diagram is the graph of the function $y = f(x)$. For every x in the domain of the function we can read off the corresponding value $f(x)$ of the function by drawing broken vertical and horizontal lines as illustrated. Thus the height of the graph above x, as measured from the origin, indicates the value $f(x)$ of the function at x.

If we have an explicit function we can attempt to construct its graph by plotting specific points on that graph. For example, let us attempt to plot the graph of the function

$$y = 0.1x^2 \qquad\qquad (2.5)$$

Concentrating on the values of x between 0 and 5, we can tabulate the integer values of x and corresponding values of y as in Table 2.1.

Table 2.1

x	y
0	0
1	0.1
2	0.4
3	0.9
4	1.6
5	2.5

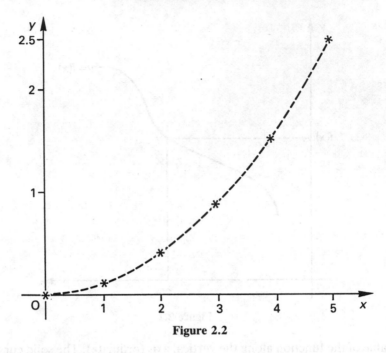

Figure 2.2

Figure 2.2 plots these six pairs of numbers as the six points marked with a 'star'. We have also sketched in a line passing through these six points, i.e. we have interpolated between these six references points on the graph of equation (2.5), with the hope that this will act as an approximate graph of (2.5). Clearly, the more reference points we plot, the more accurate the interpolation.

While interpolation is of value, particularly when done by a computer, we do not have to resort to its use to any large extent in this text as we tend to concentrate on standard functions, and are mainly concerned with the qualitative features of functions, rather than their precise quantitative structure. Rather than being concerned with the precise value of a function or precise position of its graph, we are more concerned with the general shape of its graph, e.g. whether it slopes up or down, whether it is bending up or down, etc. We shall see in subsequent chapters that slope is not always easy to define carefully; indeed, we shall need to introduce differential calculus to clarify this concept. However, before we do that, we discuss a short menu of types of function and investigate two single types, linear and quadratic functions.

2 Linear Functions

Although relatively simple in nature, linear functions are sufficiently important to warrant our reviewing their properties in full.

Definition 2.1: A function $y = f(x)$ of a single variable is *linear* if it takes the form

$$f(x) = ax + b \qquad (2.6)$$

where a,b are constants, i.e. a,b do not vary as x varies.

The graphs of linear functions are straight lines, and conversely almost all straight lines in two-dimensional diagrams can be considered to be the graph of some linear function. Hence we can usually translate freely between linear functions and straight lines in diagrams. If $a = 1$ and $b = 0$ in (2.6) then $f(x)$ is called the identity function.

As the graph of a linear function is a straight line, it is possible to construct it as follows. Identify two distinct points on the graph and then draw the straight line passing through those two points. For example, we can consider the two points representing the values $x = 0, y = a$ and $x = 1, y = a + b$ as in Figure 2.3. The point where the graph meets the y-axis or ordinate is called the y-intercept and this occurs at $x = 0, y = a$. Equally, if $a \neq 0$ the graph will meet the x-axis at $y = 0, x = -b/a$ and this is known as the x-intercept. Note if $a = 0$, then the value of the function is constant, i.e. $y = b$ for all x. In this case, if $b \neq 0$ then the graph is a horizontal straight line which never meets the x-axis, see Figure 2.4. Should $a = 0$ and $b = 0$ for all x and the graph coincides with the x-axis. This feature of the x-intercept reflects the

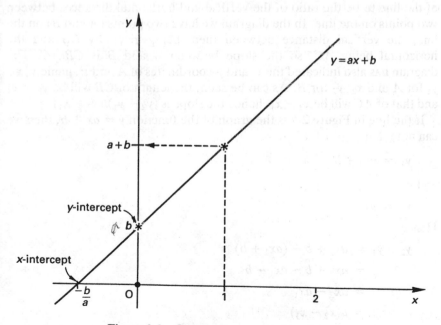

Figure 2.3   Graph of $y = ax + b$, $a,b > 0$

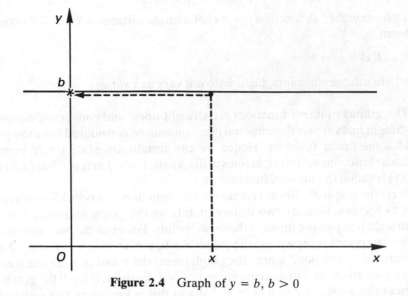

Figure 2.4   Graph of $y = b$, $b > 0$

fact that the equation $ax + b = 0$ has (i) a unique solution $x = -b/a$ if $a \neq 0$, (ii) no solution if $a = 0$, $b \neq 0$, (iii) an infinite number of solutions if $a = 0$ and $b = 0$. One way of characterising a straight line is that it has a constant slope. Given a straight line, such as that drawn in Figure 2.5, we define *the* slope of the line to be the ratio of the vertical and horizontal distances between two points on the line. In the diagram we have two points (A and B) on the line, the vertical distance between them being given by CB and the horizontal being AC, so the slope between A and B is CB/AC. The diagram has also indicated the x- and y-coordinates of A and B, namely, x_1, y_1 for A and x_2, y_2 for B. As can be seen, the length of CB will be $y_2 - y_1$ and that of AC will be $x_2 - x_1$, hence the slope is $(y_2 - y_1)/(x_2 - x_1)$.

If the line in Figure 2.5 is the graph of the function $y = ax + b$, then we can note that

$$y_1 = ax_1 + b$$

and

$$y_2 = ax_2 + b$$

Hence

$$
\begin{aligned}
y_2 - y_1 &= ax_2 + b - (ax_1 + b) \\
&= ax_2 + b - ax_1 - b \\
&= ax_2 - ax_1 \\
&= a(x_2 - x_1)
\end{aligned}
$$

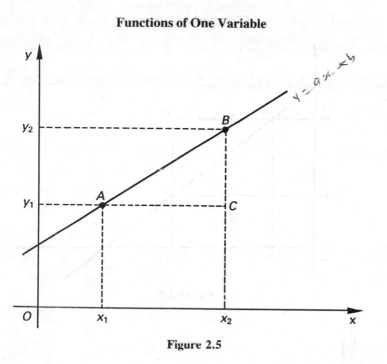

Figure 2.5

Therefore the slope is

$$\frac{y_2 - y_1}{x_2 - x_1} = a$$

That is to say the slope of the graph of $y = ax + b$ is equal to the coefficient a of x. Figure 2.6 illustrates the situation where we have a negative slope. Note that as B lies below C, we consider CB to have the negative length $y_2 - y_1$.

The interesting feature of linear functions and their graphs which we exploit later in the text is the following. Given one point on the graph of a linear function, together with the slope of that graph, we can construct the algebraic form of the function. In Figure 2.7 we have a straight line with slope equal to a and which passes through the point P which has coordinates $\bar{x}, \bar{y}$ as illustrated. Knowing the slope of the line to be equal to a allows us to assert that we can view this line to be the graph of a linear function whose coefficient on x is equal to a, i.e. a function of the form $y = ax + b$ for some yet unknown b. To find b we use the fact that the graph passes through the point P, hence b must be such that

$$\bar{y} = a\bar{x} + b$$

Hence

$$b = \bar{y} - a\bar{x}$$

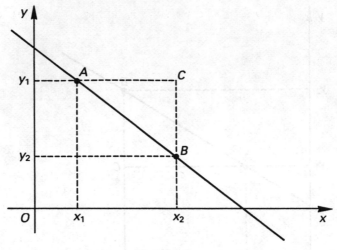

Figure 2.6

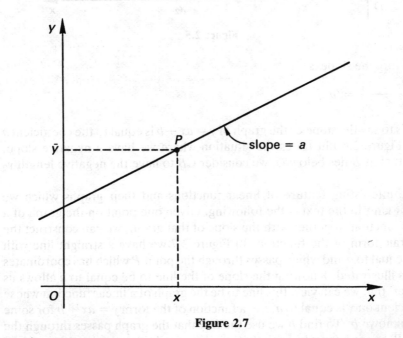

Figure 2.7

and

$$y = ax + (\bar{y} - a\bar{x})$$

or

$$y = \bar{y} + a(x - \bar{x})$$

It is this sort of expression which we will use in subsequent chapters.

3 Quadratic Functions

3.1 Introduction

$$x = \frac{-b \pm \sqrt{b^2 - 4ac}}{2a}$$

A function $y = f(x)$ of the form

$$y = f(x) = ax^2 + bx + c \tag{2.7}$$

is called a quadratic function. Here as usual a, b, c are constants, i.e. they do not vary as x varies. Quadratic functions are the simplest of non-linear functions and they act as a useful introduction to the more general approach of subsequent chapters which is based on differential calculus.

The following cost function is a simple economic example of a quadratic function. Imagine a firm producing a quantity q of a single good such that the total cost, TC, of producing that output is given by

$$TC = \alpha q^2 + \beta q + \gamma \tag{2.8}$$

where α (alpha), β (beta) and γ (gamma) are positive constants. If the firm sells its output in a competitive market at a price p, then the total revenue, TR, obtained from selling its output q will be TR $= pq$. Hence the profit, which we denote by π (pronounced pi), will be

$$\pi = TR - TC = pq - (\alpha q^2 + \beta q + \gamma)$$

i.e.

$$\pi = -\alpha q^2 + (p - \beta)q - \gamma \tag{2.9}$$

3.2 Graphs of Quadratic Functions

Let us consider the graphs of quadratic functions. As usual for given values of a, b, c in (2.7) we could plot specific points on the graph by choosing a set of values for x, calculating the corresponding values of y and plotting these pairs of values in our diagram. This procedure will show that the graphs of all quadratic functions with $a \neq 0$ will either be U-shaped or an inverted U shape, i.e. $\cap$-shaped. If the coefficient of x^2 in (2.7) is positive, then the graph is U-shaped; see a typical example in Figure 2.8, which implies that the slope of the graph (in some sense of the term) is increasing as x increases. Conversely, if the coefficient of x^2 is negative, then the graph looks like that in Figure 2.9 and the slope is decreasing as x increases.

Consider the slope of the graph of equation (2.7) between two values, x_1, x_2, of the argument so that the corresponding values of y will be

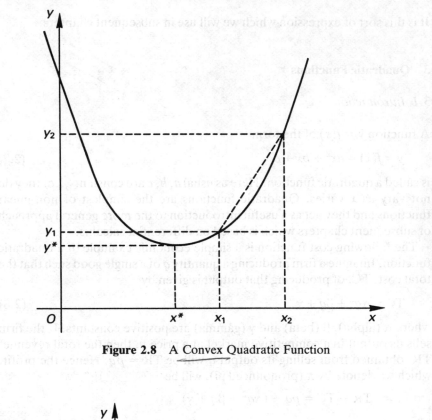

Figure 2.8   A Convex Quadratic Function

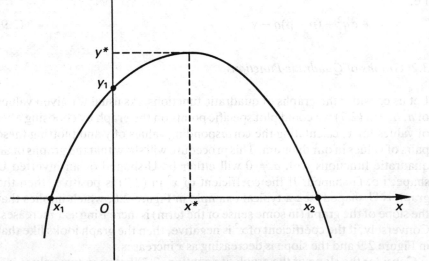

Figure 2.9   A Concave Quadratic Function

$$y_1 = ax_1^2 + bx_1 + c$$

and

$$y_2 = ax_2^2 + bx_2 + c$$

Therefore

$$y_2 - y_1 = ax_2^2 - ax_1^2 + bx_2 - bx_1$$
$$= a(x_2^2 - x_1^2) + b(x_2 - x_1)$$

Note that $x_2^2 - x_1^2 = (x_2 - x_1)(x_2 + x_1)$, which can be confirmed by multiplying out the two brackets. Hence we have

$$\frac{x_2^2 - x_1^2}{x_2 - x_1} = x_2 + x_1 \quad \text{and the slope} \quad = \frac{y_2 - y_1}{x_2 - x_1} = a(x_2 + x_1) + b$$

(2.10)

Note that unlike the case of a linear function, the slope between two points depends upon the particular pair, x_1, x_2, of chosen values. Nevertheless, we can say that if $a > 0$ then the slope increases whenever x_1 or x_2 increases, while if $a < 0$ then the slope decreases as x_1 or x_2 increases. Thus, in a very real sense, we can say that the slope of the graph increases or decreases respectively. If the graph of a function is such that the slope is increasing everywhere on the graph, we say the function is *convex*, while if the slope is decreasing everywhere, we say the function is *concave*. Hence (2.7) is convex if $a > 0$ and is concave if $a < 0$; thus Figures 2.8 and 2.9 are basic examples of graphs of convex and concave functions respectively. We shall develop these crucial concepts of concavity and convexity later in the text.

In Figure 2.9 we have indicated the points where the graph cuts the two axes, i.e. the intercepts of the graph. The y-intercept is readily identified from the function because it is that point on the graph which is on the y-axis. Since it is on the y-axis, the associated value of x, i.e. its x-coordinate, will be zero. Putting zero in (2.7) yields $y = c$, that is to say the y-intercept occurs where the value of the function is equal to the constant term in the function. The x-intercepts are also characterised in a similar fashion; given that they lie on the x-axis, it must follow that they occur when the value of the function is zero. Hence x_1, x_2 in Figure 2.9 must satisfy

$$ax^2 + bx + c = 0 \qquad (2.11)$$

Before we develop a method of solving such quadratic equations, observe that although the graph in Figure 2.9 has two x-intercepts, in Figure 2.8 there are none. It is possible for there to be just one 'x-intercept'. In fact in this latter case the graph does not cut or intercept the x-axis but just touches it, e.g. Figure 2.10. In this case the x-axis is *tangential* to the graph.

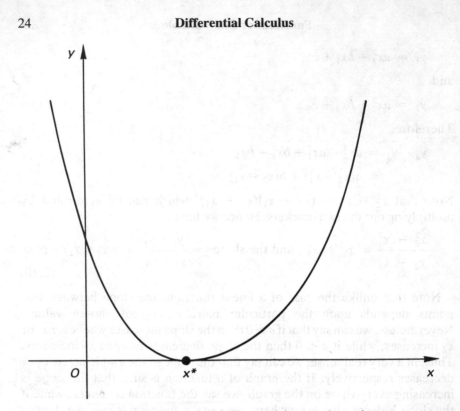

Figure 2.10   Graph Tangential to x-axis at x^*

A formal procedure of searching for a solution to the quadratic equation (2.11) is to 'complete the square', i.e. we rewrite the LHS of the equation so that it takes the form of the square of a linear function of x, plus some term involving only the constants.

Note that if $a = 0$ then (2.11) becomes a linear equation which we know how to solve, hence the discussion will be restricted to the case $a \neq 0$. To simplify subsequent algebra we rewrite (2.11) as

$$\frac{1}{4a} (4a^2x^2 + 4abx + 4ac) = 0$$

i.e. we have multiplied *and* divided by 4a. Removing the 1/4a gives

$$4a^2x^2 + 4abx + 4ac = 0$$

Now

$$(2ax + b)^2 = 4a^2x^2 + 4abx + b^2$$

hence

$$4a^2x^2 + 4abx = (2ax + b)^2 - b^2$$

and our equation becomes

$$(2ax + b)^2 - b^2 + 4ac - 0$$

or

$$(2ax + b)^2 = b^2 - 4ac \qquad (2.12)$$

Here we have 'completed the square' and can proceed to a solution. The next step is to take the square root of both sides of (2.12), because we know that if x is a solution of (2.11), then $2ax + b$ will be a square root of $b^2 - 4ac$. It should be stressed at this point that $b^2 - 4ac$ has no square root if it is negative, one square root if it is zero and two square roots if it is positive, i.e. if $\sqrt{(b^2 - 4ac)}$ is a square root of $b^2 - 4ac$ then so is $-\sqrt{(b^2 - 4ac)}$. We thus conclude that if $b^2 - 4ac \geqslant 0$ then the roots of (2.11) are given by

$$2ax + b = \pm\sqrt{(b^2 - 4ac)}$$

or

$$2ax = -b \pm \sqrt{(b^2 - 4ac)}$$

or

$$x = \frac{-b \pm \sqrt{(b^2 - 4ac)}}{2a} \qquad (2.13)$$

Note (2.13) covers the case when $b^2 - 4ac = 0$, giving $x = -b/2a$. Hence, given a quadratic function such as (2.7), we can say that its graph has no x-intercepts if $b^2 - 4ac < 0$, otherwise they are given by (2.13).

3.3 Maximum and Minimum Points of Quadratics

The completion of the square has a second major usage, namely, in identifying optima (maxima or minima) of quadratic functions. Referring again to Figures 2.8 and 2.9, we can see the convex function of Figure 2.8 has a minimum, while the concave function of Figure 2.9 has a maximum, both indicated by the starred values of x and y. These optima can be identified by rewriting the function (2.7) using our 'completion of the square' ideas as follows.

$$y = f(x) = \frac{1}{4a}(4ax^2 + 4ab + 4ac)$$

i.e.

$$y = \frac{1}{4a}[(2ax + b)^2 - b^2 + 4ac] \qquad (2.14)$$

Consider the term in the square brackets, which contains the square of the number $2ax + b$ and the constant $-b^2 + 4ac$. The squared term will always be non-negative, i.e. greater than or equal to zero, and thus has a minimum value of zero which is attained when $2ax + b = 0$, that is when $x = -b/2a$. As the constant term in the bracket does not vary as x varies, we can conclude the square bracket has a *minimum* value of $-b^2 + 4ac$ which is attained when $x = -b/2a$. It follows that if $a > 0$, so that $1/4a > 0$, then the minimum value of the function is $y^* = (-b^2 + 4ac)/4a = c - b^2/4a$, attained when $x = -b/2a$. That is to say, the convex quadratic function illustrated in Figure 2.8 has a minimum at $x^* = -b/2a$ and a minimum value of $y^* = c - b^2/4a$. In contrast, if $a < 0$ so that $1/4a < 0$, then we conclude that the function has a *maximum* value of $(-b^2 + 4ac)/4a$, attained when $x = -b/2a$, i.e. the concave quadratic function illustrated in Figure 2.9 has a maximum at $x^* = -b/2a$ and a maximum value of $y^* = c - b^2/4a$.

3.4 Polynomial Functions

To complete this section we can note that linear and quadratic functions are examples of *polynomial* functions whose general form is

$$y = f(x) = a_n x^n + a_{n-1} x^{n-1} + \dots + a_1 x + a_0$$

where n is a positive integer and the a_i's, $i = 0,1,\dots,n$ are constants. That is to say, a polynomial is a linear combination of positive powers of the argument. We shall not attempt to give a discussion of such functions at this stage; indeed, we shall usually restrict discussion to linear, quadratic and cubic functions. A *cubic* function is a polynomial with $n = 3$, i.e. of the form

$$f(x) = a_3 x^3 + a_2 x^2 + a_1 x + a_0$$

Figure 2.10 illustrates the cubic $y = x^3 - 3x$. Note this function is neither convex nor concave, although it is concave for $x < 0$ and convex for $x > 0$.

4   Logarithmic and Exponential Functions

4.1 Logarithmic Functions

If we take any positive real number, say a, it is possible to find a number r such that a is equal to 10 to the power of r, i.e. $a = 10^r$. This number r is called the logarithm to the base 10 of a and is denoted by $\log_{10} a$. Hence we have

$$r = \log_{10} a \text{ if and only if } a = 10^r$$

Let r, s be the logarithms to base 10 of positive real numbers a, b respectively, so that $r = \log_{10}a$ and $s = \log_{10}b$. As $a = 10^r$ and $b = 10^s$, it follows that $a \times b = 10^r \times 10^s = 10^{r+s}$, hence $\log_{10}(a \times b) = r + s$, i.e.

$$\log_{10}(a \times b) = \log_{10}a + \log_{10}b$$

This is the fundamental property of logarithms that forms the basis of multiplication and division by use of log tables. With the rise of calculators, logarithmic tables are no longer in common use and our interest in logs arises from the common use of logarithmic functions in economic models. For reasons that will become clearer later in the text, it is not usual to use logarithmic functions with the base of 10, but rather to use logarithms to the base of a curious number called Napier's constant. This number is invariably denoted by the letter e and has an approximate value of 2.718, in fact e is the limiting value of the function

$$f(x) = \left(1 + \frac{1}{x}\right)^x$$

as x approaches plus infinity. Hence if we consider the values of this function for $x = 1,2,3,4,5...$ we obtain values $f(x) = 2, 2.250, 2.370, 2.441, 2.488...$, which slowly increase and converge onto the number e. Formally speaking then, e is the limit of the sequence $(1 + 1/x)^x$ as x approaches plus infinity. Logarithms to base e are known as *natural logs*.

Definition 2.2: The *natural* logarithmic function is denoted by $\ln(x)$ and is such that

$$y = \ln(x) \text{ if and only if } x = e^y$$

Note the domain of this function is the set of positive real numbers.

As with logarithms to base 10 natural logarithms possess the following properties:

(1) $\ln(a \times b) = \ln(a) + \ln(b)$
(2) $\ln(a/b) = \ln(a) - \ln(b)$
(3) $\ln(a^n) = n\ln(a)$
(4) $\ln(e) = 1$
(5) $\ln(1) = 0$

The argument establishing the first three properties are based on the manipulation of indices. If we let $r = \ln(a)$ and $s = \ln(b)$, then $a = e^r$ and $b = e^s$ hence $a \times b = e^r \times e^s = e^{r+s}$ and $a/b = e^r/e^s = e^{r-s}$ hence $\ln(a \times b) = r + s = \ln(a) + \ln(b)$ and $\ln(a/b) = r - s = \ln(a) - \ln(b)$. Note in particular that $\ln(b^{-1}) = \ln(1/b) = \ln(1) - \ln(b) = -\ln(b)$, i.e. the logarithm of a reciprocal is minus the logarithm of the number. Property (3) follows in similar fashion for $a^n = (e^r)^n = e^{rn}$ so that $\ln(a^n) = rn = n\ln(a)$. Property (4) follows directly from the definition because $e^1 = e$, hence $\ln(e) = 1$; similarly as $e^0 = 1$ we have $\ln(1) = 0$.

Values of the natural logarithm function can be found in standard mathematical tables, but such specific details are not important in most applications. We shall be concerned mainly with the qualitative properties of the natural logarithm function, these being summarised in Figure 2.11. As can be seen, the graph of $\ln(x)$ exhibits the concavity of the function in that it has a decreasing slope.

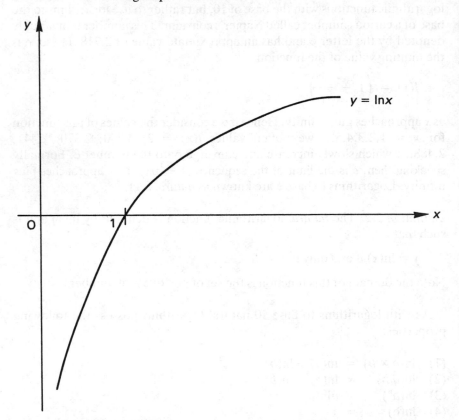

Figure 2.11　The Natural Log Function

4.2 Exponential Functions

The general form of an exponential function is

$$y = f(x) = a^x \tag{2.15}$$

where a is some positive constant. That is to say, an exponential function maps the argument x onto the xth power of the constant a (note it is *not* the ath power of x). For example, if $a = 2$ then we have the function $y = 2^x$ which takes the values 1, 2, 4, 8 as $x = 0, 1, 2, 3$ respectively, while $y = x^2$ would take the values 0, 1, 4, 9 as $x = 0, 1, 2, 3$ respectively. As with logarithm functions we shall be primarily interested in the exponential function based on Napier's constant e.

Definition 2.3: When we refer to *the* exponential function we shall mean the function

$$y = e^x \qquad\qquad (2.16)$$

which is often written as $y = \exp(x)$.

A graph of the exponential function is drawn in Figure 2.12 and we can note that it is a convex function in that the slope of its graph is increasing everywhere.

We can note that the natural logarithm and exponential functions are the inverse of each other, given that we restrict ourselves to positive numbers. That is to say, we have

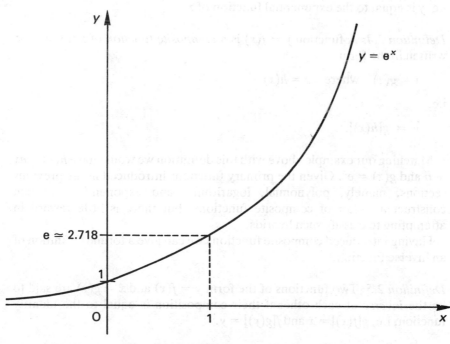

Figure 2.12 The Exponential Function

$\ln(e^x) = x$ and $\exp[\ln(x)] = x$

for all positive x. Both of these results follow from our definition of the natural logarithm function — think about it!

5   Composite Functions and Inverses

Consider the function

$$y = \exp(ax + b)$$

where a, b are constants. This is neither an exponential nor a linear function of x, it is a composite of both exponential and linear functions. In other words, it is a function of a function of x, or more specifically, it is an exponential function of a linear function of x. To clarify this we can introduce a new variable, z say, defined by

$$z = ax + b$$

We see that z is a linear function of x while we have

$$y = \exp(z) = e^z$$

i.e. y is equal to the exponential function of z.

Definition 2.4: A function $y = f(x)$ is a *composite function* of x if it can be written in the form

$$y = g(z) \quad \text{where} \quad z = h(x)$$

i.e.

$$y = g[h(x)].$$

Matching our example above with this definition we would have $h(x) = ax + b$ and $g(z) = e^z$. Given the primary functions introduced in the previous sections, namely, polynomial, logarithmic and exponential, we can construct a welter of composite functions, but there is little reward in attempting to classify such hybrids.

Having introduced composite functions we can give a formal definition of an inverse function.

Definition 2.5: Two functions of the form $y = f(x)$ and $x = g(y)$ are said to be the *inverse* of each other if their composition is equal to the identity function, i.e. $g[f(x)] = x$ and $f[g(y)] = y$.

We have already met an example of this idea in our assertion that the exponential and logarithm functions are the inverse of each other. As a second example we can note that if $a \neq 0$, then

$$y = ax + b \quad \text{and} \quad x = (y - b)/a$$

are the inverse of each other.

Not all functions have an inverse. For example, the function $y = f(x) = x^2$ does not have an inverse. It might seem that $x = g(y) = +\sqrt{y}$ is such an inverse, but if x is negative then the composite function $g[f(x)] = +\sqrt{x^2}$ will have a positive value and thus cannot be equal to x.

Note also the distinction between an inverse function and the reciprocal of a function. Given a function $f(x)$ where $f(x) \neq 0$ for all x in its domain, the reciprocal function is one divided by $f(x)$, i.e. $1/f(x)$. We can note also the notation distinction between the inverse of $f(x)$, which we write as $f^{-1}(x)$, and the reciprocal of $f(x)$, which we write as $[f(x)]^{-1}$. For example, if $f(x) = \exp(x)$ then $f^{-1}(x) = \ln(x)$ while $[f(x)]^{-1} = 1/\exp(x) = 1/e^x = e^{-x} = \exp(-x)$.

6 Limiting Values of Functions

Consider the sequence of numbers 1, 1/2, 1/3, 1/4,... i.e. the values of $1/n$ as n runs over the set of natural numbers. Hopefully it is intuitively reasonable to say that this sequence approaches zero or *converges* to zero as n goes off to infinity, so that we can say that the *limit* of this sequence as n goes to infinity is zero. In contrast the sequence $+1, -1, +1, -1, +1...$, i.e. the values of $(-1)^n$ as n runs over the natural numbers, do not approach any value and thus we can say it does not converge. Furthermore, the sequence 1, 2, 3, 4...,n,... does not converge as n goes to infinity, indeed, it *diverges* to infinity.

A little more formally we could say that a sequence of numbers x_1, x_2, x_3,...,x_n,... converges to a value $\bar{x}$ if we can make the absolute difference $x_n - \bar{x}$ between x_n and $\bar{x}$ as small as we like by choosing n to be sufficiently large. For example, if the sequence has $x_n = 1/n$ then we can say that it converges to zero because the absolute difference $|(1/n) - 0| = 1/n$ can be made as small as we like by choosing a sufficiently large n. In particular, if we require the difference to be less than 1 per cent or 0.01, then we would choose n to be greater than 100, so that $|(1/n) - 0| < 1/100 = 0.01 = 1$ per cent.

Definition 2.6: A sequence of numbers x_1, x_2,...,x_n... is said to *converge* to the *limit* $\bar{x}$ if for any real number $\varepsilon > 0$ we can say there is a sufficiently large N such that if for all $n > N$ we have $|x_n - \bar{x}| < \varepsilon$. The limit of such a converging sequence can be denoted by $\lim\limits_{n \to \infty} x_n$.

If we consider the function $f(x) = 1/x$ defined for all positive real numbers, then again it seems reasonable to say that $f(x)$ converges onto zero as x goes to infinity. Similarly, it seems clear that $f(x)$ converges onto the number 1 as x approaches 1. In contrast, we would say $f(x)$ diverges to infinity as x approaches 0 because $1/x$ becomes indefinitely large as x gets closer to 0. To illustrate this last point, consider the following sequence of values for $x = 1, 1/2, 1/3,...,1/n,...$ so that the function $f(x) = 1/x$ takes on the values $1, 2, 3,...,n,...$ respectively. This last sequence can be seen to diverge as asserted.

Definition 2.7: A function $f(x)$ is said to converge to the value $\bar{y}$ as x approaches $\bar{x}$ if for every sequence $x_1,x_2,...,x_n,...$ converging onto $\bar{x}$ the sequence of values $f(x_1), f(x_2),...,f(x_n),...$ converges onto $\bar{y}$. We denote such a limit by $\lim_{x \to \bar{x}} f(x)$.

7   Linear Simultaneous Equations

The solutions of simultaneous equations are required frequently in economics, notably in optimisation and market equilibrium problems; therefore this issue will be discussed in some detail. This section will consider only linear equations — the case of non-linear simultaneous equations is left to Chapter 5.

The simplest case occurs when there are two unknowns and two equations. Denoting the unknowns as x and y, the general form of the two linear equations is written

$$ax + by + e = 0 \qquad (2.17)$$

and

$$cx + dy + f = 0 \qquad (2.18)$$

where a, b, c, d, e and f are constants that will be known in specific contexts. The process we follow is to eliminate one of the unknowns; let us eliminate y.

The simplest way is to multiply (2.17) by d and to multiply (2.18) by b, obtaining

$$adx + bdy + ed = 0 \qquad (2.19)$$

and

$$bcx + bdy + bf = 0 \qquad (2.20)$$

Now subtract equation (2.10) from (2.19) which gives

$$(ad - bc)x + ed - bf = 0 \tag{2.21}$$

(2.21) can be rearranged to give

$$(ad - bc)x = bf - ed \tag{2.22}$$

There are now several possible outcomes:

(1) $ad - bc \neq 0$. If $ad - bc$ is not equal to zero, we can divide (2.22) by $ad - bc$ and obtain

$$x = (bf - ed)/(ad - bc) \tag{2.23a}$$

Using this value of x, y can be found from either (2.17) or (2.18). This gives

$$y = (ec - af)/(ad - bc) \tag{2.23b}$$

The quantity $ad - bc$ is called the determinant of the equations, and if it is non-zero, the equations will have a unique solution given in equations (2.23).

(2) $ad - bc = 0$, $ed - bf = 0$. If the determinant is zero, then equation (2.21) says that $ed - bf$ must be equal to zero. If this is true, the equations are said to be consistent and will have an infinite number of solutions (see below).

(3) $ad - bc = 0$, $ed - bf \neq 0$. If the determinant is zero and $ed - bf$ is not equal to zero, then the equations are said to be inconsistent. Equation (2.21) was drawn up on the assumption that there exist x and y that satisfy the two equations. However, if $ed - bf$ is not zero and $ad - bc$ is zero, then equation (2.21) cannot be true and the assumption that there exist x and y that satisfy both equations simultaneously must be wrong.

There may appear to be a fourth possibility here, i.e. the case of $ad - bc = 0$ and $ec - af \neq 0$. If this case holds, then we must have inconsistency because we can rewrite (2.23b) as

$$(ad - bc)y - ec + af = 0$$

which clearly cannot be true. However it is easy to see that if $ec - af \neq 0$, then $f \neq ec/a$ (with $ad - bc = 0$ i.e. $c/a = d/b$) must imply $f \neq ed/b$, i.e. $ed - fb \neq 0$. So if the determinant is zero then $ec - af \neq 0$ is the same condition as $ed - bf \neq 0$.

Earlier in the chapter we discussed the concept of the slope of a linear function and this will help in our understanding of the solution of simultaneous linear equations. The slope of a function $y = ax + b$ was shown to be a. We have seen that we can rewrite equations (2.17) and (2.18) as

$$y = \frac{-c - ax}{b} = -\frac{a}{b}x - \frac{e}{b} \qquad (2.24)$$

and

$$y = \frac{-f - cx}{d} = -\frac{c}{d}x - \frac{f}{d} \qquad (2.25)$$

The slope of (2.24) is $-a/b$ and the slope of (2.25) is $-c/d$. If the functions have different slopes, i.e. $a/b \neq c/d$, then they must intersect at some point and since they are linear functions they will intersect only once. The condition $a/b \neq c/d$ can be written $ad \neq bc$ or $ad - bc \neq 0$ which is the statement that the determinant is non-zero. Figure 2.13(a) shows the graphs of two functions which give equations with a non-zero determinant.

Obviously if $a/b = c/d$, then the slopes of the two functions are identical. There are two possibilities here. One is that the two graphs lie on top of each other. Setting $x = 0$ in both (2.24) and (2.25) we obtain $y = -c/b$ and $y = -f/d$ respectively. If the two graphs lie on top of each other we must have $-e/b = -f/d$, i.e. $ed - bf = 0$. This of course is the consistency condition and we have an infinite number of solutions. If $ed - bf$

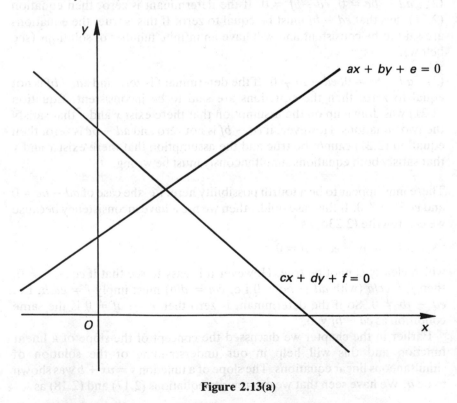

Figure 2.13(a)

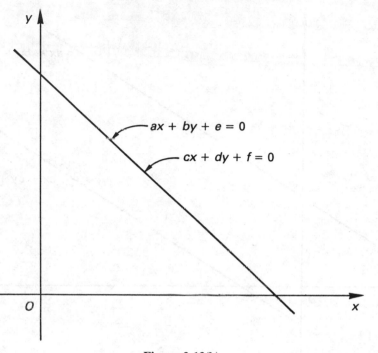

Figure 2.13(b)

is not zero, then the two graphs cut the vertical axis at different points which, since they have identical slopes, implies they can never meet. Figure 2.13(b) shows the graph of two functions which give consistent equations with a zero determinant and Figure 2.13(c) shows the case when the equations are inconsistent.

The above is a reasonably complete discussion of the solution of pairs of linear equations in two unknowns. Should we wish to tackle problems involving more than two unknowns, then similar considerations of determinants and consistency are involved. However, it is convenient to use matrix algebra to discuss the more general problem and we refer the reader to the Appendix for a discussion of the problem.

Exercises

2.1   Given a linear consumption function of the form

$$C = a + bY$$

where C is consumption and Y is disposable income, we can define

Differential Calculus

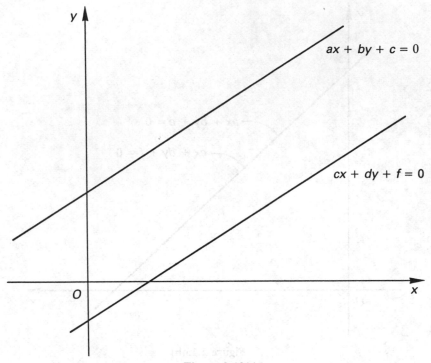

Figure 2.13(c)

the marginal propensity to consume (MPC) to be the change in consumption due to a unit change in disposable income. Show MPC = b. The average propensity to consume (APC) is the ratio of consumption to disposable income. Show that MPC differs from APC for all disposable incomes unless $a = 0$. Draw the graph of the function mapping Y onto APC.

2.2 Draw the graphs of the following functions:

    (i) $y = 2^x$ for all x;
    (ii) $y = \log_2 x$ (i.e. log to base 2) for $x > 0$.

(*Hint*: in (ii) consider $x = 1,2,4,8$, etc. and $x = 1/2,1/4,1/8$, etc.).

2.3 Draw the graph of the following profit function:

$$\pi = -q^2 + (p - 5)q - 2$$

for (i) $p = 8$, and (ii) $p = 7$, indicating the intercepts. Is this function convex or concave? Does it have a maximum or a minimum? If so, where?

2.4 A function $f(x)$ is said to be one to one if for every y in its range there is a *unique* x such that $y = f(x)$. Show that $y = f(x)$ has an inverse function $x = f^{-1}(y)$ if and only if it is one to one.

2.5 For the following supply and demand equations, find the equilibrium price and quantity exchanged:

$$\text{demand:} \quad q = a - bp$$

$$\text{supply:} \quad q = -c + dp$$

where a, b, c and d are known positive parameters. For what values of these parameters are your solutions economically meaningful?

2.6 For the following pairs of simultaneous equations, indicate whether they are consistent and find all the solutions if consistent:

(i) $x_1 + x_2 = 1$
$\quad\,\, x_1 + x_2 = 2$
(ii) $3x_1 + 6x_2 = 9$
$\quad\,\,\, 2x_1 + 4x_2 = 6$
(iii) $x_1 + 3x_2 = 4$
$\quad\,\,\,\, 2x_1 - 5x_2 = 10$

2.7 Solve the following equations for x_1, x_2 and λ:

$$x_2 = 2\lambda$$

$$x_1 = 3\lambda$$

$$2x_1 + 3x_2 = 7$$

2.8 What are the values of the following limits?

(i) $\displaystyle \lim_{x \to \infty} \left(\frac{x + 1}{x} \right)$

(ii) $\displaystyle \lim_{x \to 0} \left(\frac{x}{x + 1} \right)$

3

Differentiation of Functions of a Single Variable

1 The Derivative

1.1 Introduction

In this chapter we shall introduce the notion of derivative functions, these being the formal expression of the marginalist concepts used in economics and a crucial tool in our analysis. Indeed the 'marginalist school', as initiated by Marshall and others at the end of the last century, arose in part as an informal interpretation of their mathematical analysis of microeconomic phenomena. Consequently the translation of these informal concepts and intuitive ideas into the formal language of mathematics is straightforward.

As an example, let us consider the marginal propensity to consume (MPC). In Figure 3.1 we have drawn the graph of a non-linear consumption function. In this case we have drawn the relationship so that the graph is turning down. Intuitively this must mean that the MPC is also falling, i.e. as income increases, the proportional increase in consumption decreases. However, there are two points we should note, given that the consumption function is non-linear. Firstly, the MPC will vary as the level of income varies, thus we cannot refer to *the* marginal propensity to consume without reference to the level of income. We must now view MPC as a function of income; hence we might draw a second graph, Figure 3.2, illustrating the relationship between MPC and income. However in drawing Figure 3.2 we are immediately confronted with the following question. What do we mean by the MPC at a particular level of income? Recalling the conventional textbook definition, we could say that the MPC is the proportional change in

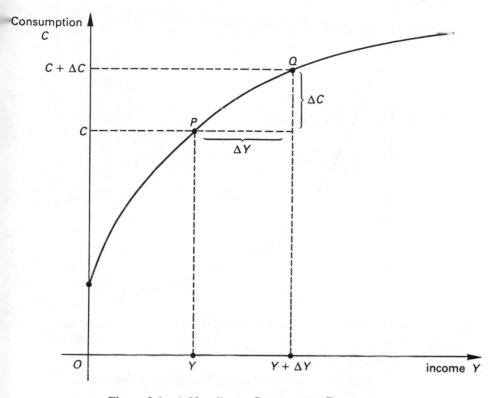

Figure 3.1 A Non-linear Consumption Function

consumption given a marginal change in income. Unfortunately, without being precise in the notion of marginal change there is still ambiguity to this answer and the issue requires clarification.

Let us return to Figure 3.1 which illustrates a change in income ΔY and a corresponding change in consumption ΔC, the proportional change in consumption being $\Delta C/\Delta Y$ which is equal to the slope of the line PQ. The ambiguity arises from the fact that the slope of the line PQ will depend on the size and sign of the change in income, i.e. the closer Q is to P the greater will be this slope. One cannot avoid the ambiguity by defining MPC as the proportional change in consumption for a unit change in income, because this will depend on the definition of a unit of income.

Some progress can be made if we recall that marginal changes are usually thought to be small and noting that Figure 3.1 indicates that, as long as we concentrate on small changes in income, then the ratios $\Delta C/\Delta Y$ will all be *approximately* equal to each other. While the ambiguity remains, its

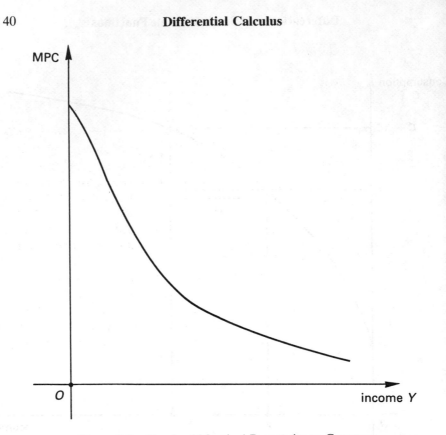

Figure 3.2   Graph of Marginal Propensity to Consume

significance is diminished. Pursuing this idea we might hope that as we make ΔY smaller and smaller, the differences in $\Delta C/\Delta Y$ will become smaller and, *in the limit*, will go to zero. Indeed this will be the solution to the puzzle and we can define the MPC at Y as the limit of $\Delta C/\Delta Y$ as ΔY approaches zero. The following subsection explores this concept in a specific example and subsection 1.3 outlines the concept in general terms.

First let us briefly relate this discussion to the tangent to the graph at P in Figure 3.1. Consider what happens to the straight line through P and Q, as Q approaches P. Obviously the straight line will get closer and closer to the tangent at P and in the limit will converge onto this tangent. For any Q, the slope of the line through P and Q is $\Delta C/\Delta Y$; therefore defining the MPC at Y as the limit of $\Delta C/\Delta Y$ as ΔY approaches zero turns out to be equivalent to defining the MPC at Y as being the slope of the tangent at P. Tangents will play an important role in subsequent chapters and we shall develop these points further in later chapters.

1.2 A Marginal Cost Example

Consider a total cost function of the form

$$C = 100 + Q^2$$

where Q is quantity produced. Suppose we wish to determine the marginal cost of production when output is equal to 10. Using a similar argument to that used in the previous subsection, we can define the marginal cost (MC) as the limit of $\Delta C/\Delta Q$ as ΔQ approaches zero. Table 3.1 gives us values of ΔC and $\Delta C/\Delta Q$ for different values of ΔQ. For example, the first row has $\Delta Q = (20 - 10) = 10$, $\Delta C = (100 + 20^2) - (100 + 10^2) = 300$ and $\Delta C/\Delta Q = 30$. As ΔQ approaches 0, i.e. as Q approaches 10, the ratio $\Delta C/\Delta Q$ seems to approach 20 and thus we can tentatively conclude that the MC at $Q = 10$ is 20. We could in principle obtain the MC in a similar fashion for any output and thus build up the relationship between MC and Q. This is obviously a very tedious, inefficient and somewhat imprecise method of deriving the MC curve. A more sensible procedure is to attempt to derive an algebraic expression which allows us to derive the MC as a function of Q. To do this let us consider any output Q, and any change, ΔQ, in output. The associated change, ΔC, in cost will be

$$\Delta C = [100 + (Q + \Delta Q)^2] - (100 + Q^2)$$
$$= 100 + Q^2 + 2Q\Delta Q + (\Delta Q)^2 - 100 - Q^2$$
$$= 2Q\Delta Q + (\Delta Q)^2$$

Hence

$$\frac{\Delta C}{\Delta Q} = \frac{2Q\Delta Q + (\Delta Q)^2}{\Delta Q} = 2Q + \Delta Q \tag{3.1}$$

Clearly as ΔQ approaches zero $\Delta C/\Delta Q$ will tend to $2Q$, i.e. we can

Table 3.1

Q	ΔQ	ΔC	$\Delta C/\Delta Q$
20	10	300	30
15	5	125	25
13	3	69	23
12	2	44	22
11	1	21	21
10½	½	4¼	20½
10⅓	⅓	6⅑	20⅓
.	.	.	.
.	.	.	.

conclude that MC $= 2Q$. In particular we can confirm that when $Q = 10$ we have MC $= 20$. We denote the limit of $\Delta C/\Delta Q$ as ΔQ tends to zero as $\lim_{\Delta Q \to 0} \dfrac{\Delta C}{\Delta Q}$, therefore from (3.1) we know

$$\lim_{\Delta Q \to 0} \frac{\Delta C}{\Delta Q} = 2Q$$

If you check through the argument used to derive (3.1) you will see that (3.1) is true whether the change in Q is positive or negative. As a result, whether ΔQ approaches zero through a series of small positive changes, or approaches zero through a series of small negative changes, $\Delta C/\Delta Q$ approaches $2Q$. In such cases we say $\lim_{\Delta Q \to 0} \dfrac{\Delta C}{\Delta Q}$ exists. Although we will concentrate on cases when this limit exists, there are some economic cases when this limit does not exist (see Problem 5.4).

1.3 The Derivative Function

Let us briefly summarise the process we have followed in the previous subsection, but now using a general function $y = f(x)$. We denote by Δy the change in the value of y induced by a change Δx in the value of x. The value of the independent variable has changed from x to $x + \Delta x$ and function f will change its value from $f(x)$ to $f(x + \Delta x)$. Therefore

$$\Delta y = f(x + \Delta x) - f(x) \tag{3.2}$$

Definition 3.1: A function $y = f(x)$ is differentiable if for all x, $\lim_{\Delta x \to 0} \dfrac{\Delta y}{\Delta x}$ exists.

If $f(x)$ is a differentiable function, we have the following definition:

Definition 3.2: The limit of $\Delta y/\Delta x$ as x approaches zero is called the derivative of y and is written dy/dx, i.e.

$$\lim_{\Delta x \to 0} \frac{\Delta y}{\Delta x} = \frac{dy}{dx} \tag{3.3}$$

we read dy/dx as 'dee y by dee x'. As we observed in the previous subsection with the MC example, the derivative will depend on the value of x, i.e. if $y = f(x) = x^2$ then $dy/dx = 2x$. Therefore for each function $y = f(x)$ there will be a function relating the derivative of the function to x.

Definition 3.3: The function relating dy/dx to x is called the derivative function and is denoted by $f'(x)$, i.e. if $y = f(x)$ then $dy/dx = f'(x)$.

We read $f'(x)$ as 'f prime of x'. Using (3.2) and (3.3) we obtain

$$\frac{dy}{dx} = \lim_{\Delta x \to 0} \frac{\Delta y}{\Delta x} = \lim_{\Delta x \to 0}\left[\frac{f(x + \Delta x) - f(x)}{\Delta x}\right] \tag{3.4}$$

Example 3.1
Let $y = f(x) = 1/x$

$$\frac{dy}{dx} = \lim_{\Delta x \to 0} \frac{f(x + \Delta x) - f(x)}{\Delta x}$$

$$= \lim_{\Delta x \to 0}\left[\frac{\frac{1}{x + \Delta x} - \frac{1}{x}}{\Delta x}\right]$$

$$= \lim_{\Delta x \to 0}\left[\frac{x - (x + \Delta x)}{x(x + \Delta x)} \div \Delta x\right]$$

$$= \lim_{\Delta x \to 0}\left[\frac{-\Delta x}{(x^2 + x\Delta x)}\frac{1}{\Delta x}\right]$$

$$= \lim_{\Delta x \to 0}\left[\frac{-1}{x^2 + x\Delta x}\right]$$

$$= -\frac{1}{x^2}$$

Thus the derivative function of $f(x) = 1/x$ is $f'(x) = -x^{-2}$. $f(x)$ and $f'(x)$ for this case are drawn in Figure 3.3.

Example 3.2
Let $y = nx, n \neq 0$

$$\frac{dy}{dx} = \lim_{\Delta x \to 0}[n(x + \Delta x) - nx]/\Delta x$$

$$= \lim_{\Delta x \to 0}\frac{n\Delta x}{\Delta x}$$

$$= \lim_{\Delta x \to 0} n$$

$$= n$$

Thus the derivate function of $y = nx$ is $f'(x) = n$. If n is positive (i.e. $f(x)$ has positive slope) $f'(x)$ must be positive, and if n is negative the derivative function must be negative. Figure 3.4(a) and (b) draw $f(x)$ and $f'(x)$ for $n = 2$ and $n = -2$ respectively.

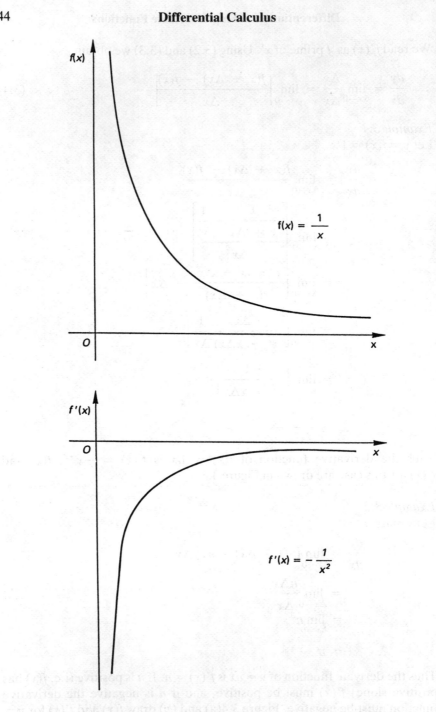

Figure 3.3

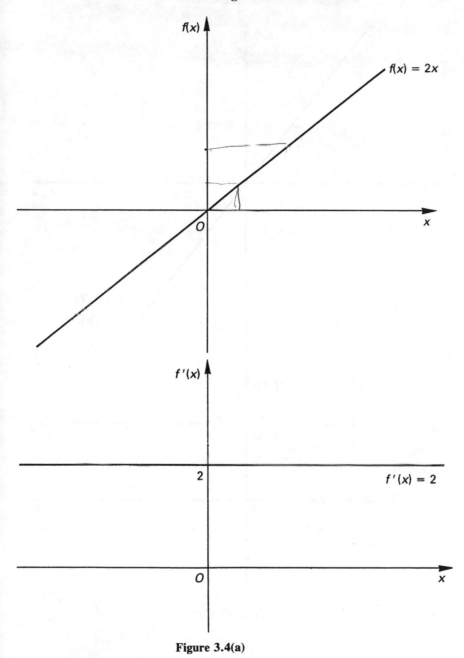

Figure 3.4(a)

We can use the definition in (3.4) to differentiate all functions of one variable, but the process would be very time consuming. Fortunately, there

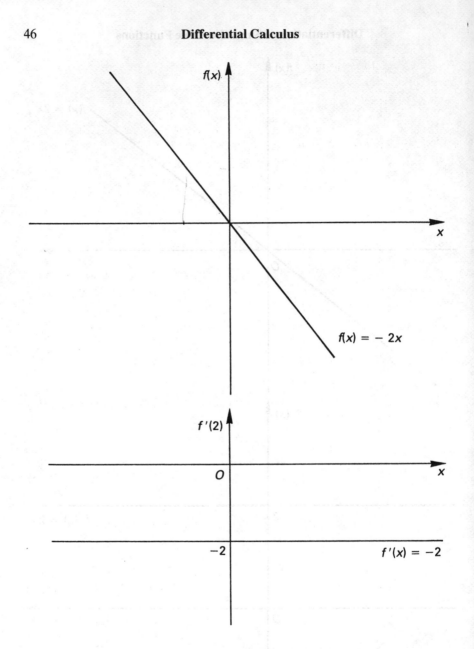

Figure 3.4(b)

exists a series of rules which can be employed to differentiate the most common functions. The process of generating the derivative function is called differentiation and these rules are called the rules of differentiation.

2   Rules for Differentiation

2.1 Constant Rule

Suppose we have a function $y = f(x) = a$ where a is a constant. Obviously y does not change its value: hence Δy must be zero for all Δx, and so must be zero in the limit giving the following rule:

The Constant Rule: If $y = f(x) = a$ where a is a constant, then $dy/dx = 0$.

2.2 Power Rule

Suppose we have a function $y = f(x) = ax^n$ where a is constant. We have already seen that if $a = 1$ and $n = 2$, then $f'(x) = 2x$. More generally if n is a non-zero integer we have

$$\lim_{\Delta x \to 0} \frac{a(x + \Delta x)^n - ax^n}{\Delta x}$$

$$= \lim_{\Delta x \to 0} \frac{a(x^n + nx^{n-1}\Delta x + ...) - ax^n}{\Delta x} \tag{3.5}$$

The remaining terms in the numerator of (3.5) all have Δx to a power greater than or equal to 2. Therefore (3.5) becomes

$$\lim_{\Delta x \to 0} (anx^{n-1} + ...)$$

where all the remaining terms have Δx in them. This gives the following rule:

The Power Rule: If $y = f(x) = ax^n$ where a is a constant and n is a non-zero integer, then $dy/dx = nax^{n-1}$.

As we shall see the rule is true for all real powers of x. The function $y = f(x) = x^n$ is called a power function because it involves only a power of x, hence the name of the rule. Verbally the rule says that for a power function we can construct the derivation function by 'multiplying by the power and reducing the power by one'. We have already seen one case of this, i.e. if $y = f(x) = x^2$ then $f'(x) = 2x$.

Example 3.3
   (i)   If $y = 3x^2$, then this rule tells us that

$$\frac{dy}{dx} = 2 \times 3x^{2-1} = 6x^1 = 6x$$

(ii)   If $y = ax$ then

$$\frac{dy}{dx} = 1ax^{1-1} = ax^0 = a$$

(Recall that any number raised to the power of zero is equal to one.)

(iii)   If $y = x^{1/2}$ then

$$\frac{dy}{dx} = \frac{1}{2}x^{1/2-1} = \frac{1}{2}x^{-1/2} = \frac{1}{2x^{1/2}}$$

2.3 Addition Rule

If a function can be written as the sum of two functions, e.g. $f(x) = v(x) + u(x)$ then the following is true:

$$\frac{f(x + \Delta x) - f(x)}{\Delta x} = \frac{v(x + \Delta x) + u(x + \Delta x) - v(x) - u(x)}{\Delta x}$$

$$= \frac{v(x + \Delta x) - v(x)}{\Delta x} + \frac{u(x + \Delta x) - u(x)}{\Delta x}$$

so

$$\lim \frac{f(x + \Delta x) - f(x)}{\Delta x} = \lim_{\Delta x \to 0} \frac{v(x + \Delta x) - v(x)}{\Delta x} + \lim_{\Delta x \to 0} \frac{u(x + \Delta x) - u(}{\Delta x}$$

This gives the following rule:

The Addition Rule: If $y = f(x)$ can be written as the sum of two functions, i.e. $y = u(x) + v(x)$, then the derivative of y is the sum of the derivatives of the two functions, i.e.

$$\text{if } \quad y = u + v \quad \text{then} \quad \frac{dy}{dx} = \frac{du}{dx} + \frac{dv}{dx}$$

The rule obviously extends to the sum of n functions. Note also that $f(x) = u(x) - v(x)$ is a special case and $\dfrac{dy}{dx} = \dfrac{du}{dx} - \dfrac{dv}{dx}$.

Example 3.4

(i)   If $y = 100 + x^2$, then with $u = 100$ and $v = x^2$ we have

$$du/dx = 0 \text{ by the constant rule}$$
$$dv/dx = 2x \text{ by the power rule}$$
$$\text{hence } dy/dx = 0 + 2x = 2x \text{ by the addition rule}$$

(This is our cost function in the previous subsection.)

(ii)   If $y = x^3 + 5x^2 + 2x + 10$, we then proceed by differentiating term by term. The derivative of x^3 by the power rule is $3x^2$, that of $5x^2$ is $10x$, while those of $2x$ and 10 are 2 and zero respectively. Hence

$$dy/dx = 3x^2 + 10x + 2$$

2.4 Chain Rule

Consider the two following functions:

$$y = (1+x^2)^{1/2} \qquad\qquad (3.6)$$

$$y = 1/(1+x^2) \qquad\qquad (3.7)$$

Neither of these functions can be differentiated using the power and addition rules directly. However both are composite functions and can be viewed as functions of the function $1 + x^2$. If we write $u = 1 + x^2$ then they can be written as

$$y = u^{1/2}$$

and

$$y = u^{-1}$$

respectively. Observe that we can differentiate y with respect to u in both cases, and also we can differentiate u with respect to x, i.e.

$u = 1 + x^2$ gives $du/dx = 2x$

$y = u^{1/2}$ gives $dy/du = \tfrac{1}{2}u^{-1/2}$

and

$y = u^{-1}$ gives $dy/du = -u^{-2}$

That is, we know $\Delta y/\Delta u$ and $\Delta u/\Delta x$ and can calculate the limit in each case to obtain the derivative. Multiplying $\Delta y/\Delta u$ by $\Delta u/\Delta x$ the Δu's cancel and we obtain $\Delta y/\Delta x$. In the limit this gives

$$\frac{dy}{dx} = \frac{dy}{du}\frac{du}{dx}$$

and we are able to find the derivative of y with respect to x by using these links on the chain. Finally, we have:

The Chain Rule: If a function $y = f(x)$ can be written as composite function $y = g(u)$ where $u = h(x)$, then the derivative of y with respect to x is equal to product of the derivative of y with respect to u and the derivative of u with respect to x, i.e. if $y = g(u)$ and $u = h(x)$ then

$$\frac{dy}{dx} = \frac{dy}{du}\frac{du}{dx}$$

In the case of (3.6) we have

$$\frac{dy}{dx} = \frac{dy}{du}\frac{du}{dx} = \tfrac{1}{2}u^{-1/2}\,2x = \frac{x}{u^{1/2}} = \frac{x}{(1 + x^2)^{1/2}}$$

and for (3.7)

$$\frac{dy}{dx} = \frac{dy}{du}\frac{du}{dx} = -u^{-2}\,2x = \frac{-2x}{u^2} = \frac{-2x}{(1 + x^2)^2}$$

2.5 Logarithm Rule

Suppose we wish to differentiate $y = f(x) = \ln(x)$. In this case

$$\frac{dy}{dx} = \lim_{\Delta x \to 0} \frac{\ln(x + \Delta x) - \ln(x)}{\Delta x}$$

$$= \lim_{\Delta x \to 0} \frac{\ln\left(\dfrac{x+\Delta x}{x}\right)}{\Delta x}$$

$$= \lim_{\Delta x \to 0}\left[\frac{1}{\Delta x}\ln\left(1 + \frac{\Delta x}{x}\right)\right] \qquad (3.8)$$

If we denote $x/\Delta x$ as b we can rewrite the term inside the bracket in (3.8) as

$$\frac{b}{x}\ln\left(1 + \frac{1}{b}\right)$$

or

$$\frac{1}{x}\ln\left(1 + \frac{1}{b}\right)^b \qquad (3.9)$$

Notice that as $\Delta x \to 0$, b becomes infinitely large. Consequently, (recalling Chapter 2 Section 4) as Δx approaches zero $\left(1 + \dfrac{1}{b}\right)^b$ approaches e and in the limit as Δx approaches zero $\left(1 + \dfrac{1}{b}\right)^b$ is e. In the limit (3.9) is $\dfrac{1}{x}\ln(e)$, which, recalling $\ln(e) = 1$, gives the following rule:

The Logarithm Rule: The derivative of the logarithm function is the reciprocal function, i.e. if $y = f(x) = \ln(x)$ then

$$\frac{dy}{dx} = \frac{1}{x}$$

Note that to obtain the derivative of $y = \ln(f(x))$ we need to combine the chain rule and the logarithm rule. If we write $y = \ln(u)$ where $u = f(x)$ then we know that $dy/dx = (dy/du)(du/dx)$. This gives us a generalised logarithm rule:

The Generalised Logarithm Rule: If $y = \ln f(x)$ then $\dfrac{dy}{dx} = \dfrac{f'(x)}{f(x)}$

The logarithm rule also helps us to differentiate functions of the type $y = f(x) = a^x$. We can write this function as

$$\ln y = x \ln(a)$$

and (since $\ln(a)$ is a constant)

$$d \ln(y)/dx = \ln(a)$$

Yet the generalised logarithm rule tells us

$$d \ln(y)/dx = \frac{1}{y}\frac{dy}{dx}$$

hence

$$\frac{1}{y}\frac{dy}{dx} = \ln(a)$$

therefore

$$\frac{dy}{dx} = y \ln(a)$$

This gives the general rule:

$$\text{if } y = a^x \text{ then } \frac{dy}{dx} = a^x \ln(a)$$

The logarithm rule allows us to confirm that the power rule applies for all real powers. Let $y = f(x) = x^r$ where r is a real number and x is restricted to the set of positive reals, it being understood that x^r is also positive.

As

$$y = x^r$$

then

$$\ln(y) = \ln(x^r)$$

or

$$\ln(y) = r \ln(x)$$

Differentiating with respect to x, we obtain

$$\frac{1}{y}\frac{dy}{dx} = \frac{r}{x}$$

therefore

$$\frac{dy}{dx} = r\,\frac{y}{x} = r\,\frac{x^r}{x} = rx^{r-1}$$

Hence the power rule is valid for all power functions involving any real power as long as the dependent variable is restricted to be positive and the value of the function is interpreted to be positive.

Example 3.5

For a demand function $q = f(p)$ the (arc) elasticity is defined as $\dfrac{\Delta q}{q} \Big/ \dfrac{\Delta p}{p}$ however to remove the dependence on the size of the change Δp we can define the point elasticity to be $\dfrac{p}{q}\dfrac{dq}{dp}$.

It is possible to view this last term as being equal to $\dfrac{d\,\ln(q)}{d\,\ln(p)}$, the derivative of $\ln(q)$ with respect to $\ln(p)$. For we have

$$\frac{d\,\ln(q)}{d\,\ln(p)} = \frac{d\,\ln(q)/dp}{d\,\ln(p)/dp}; \quad \text{yet} \quad \frac{d\,\ln(p)}{dp} = \frac{1}{p}$$

and $\quad \dfrac{d\,\ln(q)}{dp} = \dfrac{1}{q}\dfrac{dq}{dp}$; $\quad$ hence $\quad \dfrac{d\,\ln(q)}{d\,\ln(p)} = \dfrac{p}{q}\dfrac{dq}{dp}$.

For instance, if we have $q = kp^{-\alpha}$ then taking logs of both sides we obtain

$$\ln(q) = \ln(k) - \alpha\,\ln(p)$$

therefore elasticity $= \dfrac{d\,\ln(q)}{d\,\ln(p)} = -\alpha.$

Such demand functions are called iso-elastic.

2.6 Exponential Rule

In the last subsection it was shown that if $y = a^x$ then $dy/dx = a^x\ln(a)$. If we apply this to the special case of $y = e^x$, then we can differentiate the exponential function. The crucial point is that because $\ln(e) = 1$, the exponential has a very special derivative, namely $dy/dx = e^x$, i.e. the derivative of the exponential function is the exponential function!

The Exponential Rule: The derivative of the exponential function is the exponential function, i.e. if $y = e^x$ then

$$dy/dx = e^x$$

The above rule goes some way towards explaining why the number e is so useful in economics, as the following example shows.

Example 3.6
Suppose the size of income, y, at time t is given by the function

$$y = e^{\lambda t}$$

If we write $u = \lambda t$ we have $y = e^u$ and can use the chain rule and exponential rule to differentiate the function. We know

$$\frac{dy}{dt} = \frac{dy}{du}\frac{du}{dt}$$

$$= e^u \lambda$$

$$= \lambda e^{\lambda t}$$

The proportionate rate of growth of income is given by $\dfrac{1}{y}\dfrac{dy}{dt}$

In this case it is

$$\frac{\lambda e^{\lambda t}}{e^{\lambda t}} = \lambda$$

i.e. the proportionate rate of growth is constant. For this reason exponential functions are frequently employed to model the growth of variables.

2.7 Product and Quotient Rules

Consider a function $y = f(x)$ where $f(x)$ is the product of two functions $u(x)$, $v(x)$, i.e. $f(x) = u(x)v(x)$. Given a change Δx in x the associated change in y will be given as follows:

$$\Delta y = \Delta f(x) = f(x + \Delta x) - f(x)$$

$$= u(x + \Delta x)\, v(x + \Delta x) - u(x)\, v(x)$$

This can be rewritten by adding and subtracting the term $u(x)v(x + \Delta x)$, which gives

$$\Delta y = u(x + \Delta x)v(x + \Delta x) - u(x)v(x + \Delta x)$$

$$+ u(x)v(x + \Delta x) - u(x)v(x)$$

or

$$\Delta y = [u(x + \Delta x) - u(x)]v(x + \Delta x)$$

$$+ u(x)[v(x + \Delta x) - v(x)]$$

hence

$$\frac{\Delta y}{\Delta x} = \left[\frac{u(x + \Delta x) - u(x)}{\Delta x}\right] v(x + \Delta x)$$

$$+ u(x)\left[\frac{v(x + \Delta x) - v(x)}{\Delta x}\right]$$

If we now let Δx go to zero, the terms in the square parentheses will converge onto $u'(x)$ and $v'(x)$ respectively. Furthermore $v(x + \Delta x)$ will approach $v(x)$ hence we obtain

$$\frac{dy}{dx} = \lim_{\Delta x \to 0} \frac{\Delta y}{\Delta x} = u'(x)v(x) + u(x)v'(x)$$

The Product Rule: If $y = f(x)$ can be written as the product of two functions $u(x)$ and $v(x)$ so that $y = u(x)v(x)$, then the derivative of y with respect to x is:

$$\frac{dy}{dx} = u(x)\frac{dv}{dx} + v(x)\frac{du}{dx}$$

Example 3.7
Let $y(x) = x^2(1 + x)$.
Denoting $u(x) = x^2$ and $v(x) = (1 + x)$, we have

$$\frac{dy}{dx} = u(x)\frac{dv}{dx} + v(x)\frac{du}{dx}$$

$$= x^2 + (1 + x)2x$$

$$= x^2 + 2x + 2x^2$$

$$= 3x^2 + 2x$$

This rule generalises to the product of n functions, e.g. if $n = 3$, $y = u(x)\,v(x)\,w(x)$ then

$$\frac{dy}{dx} = uv\frac{dw}{dx} + uw\frac{dv}{dx} + vw\frac{du}{dx}$$

A special case of the product rule occurs if the functions are of the form $y = f(x) = \dfrac{v(x)}{u(x)} = v\,u^{-1}$. Applying the product rule and the chain rule we have

$$\frac{dy}{dx} = \frac{dv}{dx} u^{-1} - 1 u^{-2} \frac{du}{dx} v$$

$$= \left(\frac{dv}{dx} u - \frac{du}{dx} v\right)\Big/ u^2$$

This special case is frequently called the quotient rule·

The Quotient Rule: If $y = f(x)$ can be written as $y = \dfrac{v(x)}{u(x)}$ then

$$\frac{dy}{dx} = \left(\frac{dv}{dx} u - \frac{du}{dx} v\right)\Big/ u^2$$

Example 3.8
Consider $y = x/(1 + x^2)$ so that $y = v(x)/u(x)$ where $v(x) = x$ and $u(x) = 1 + x^2$. As $dv/dx = 1$ and $du/dx = 2x$ we have by the quotient rule

$$\frac{dy}{dx} = \frac{1(1 + x^2) - 2x\,x}{(1 + x^2)^2}$$

$$= \frac{1 + x^2 - 2x^2}{(1 + x^2)^2} = \frac{1 - x^2}{(1 + x^2)^2}$$

2.8 The Inverse Function Rule

Suppose we have a function of the form $x = f(y)$ which has inverse of $y = f^{-1}(x)$ but $f^{-1}(x)$ is difficult to derive explicitly. How do we find dy/dx?

Let us differentiate both sides of $x = f(y)$ with respect to x. The derivative of x with respect to x is 1 and

$$\frac{df(y)}{dx} = \frac{df(y)}{dy}\frac{dy}{dx}$$

hence we have

$$\frac{df(y)}{dy}\frac{dy}{dx} = 1$$

If $df(y)/dy \neq 0$ we can rewrite this as

$$\frac{dy}{dx} = 1\Big/ \frac{df(y)}{dy}$$

This gives us the following rule:

The Inverse Function Rule: The derivative of an inverse function is the reciprocal of the derivative of the original function, i.e.

$$\frac{dy}{dx} = 1 \bigg/ \frac{dx}{dy}$$

This is a special case of an implicit function rule which we will meet in the next chapter.

Example 3.9
Consider $y = f(x) = x^3 + x$ for which $dy/dx = f'(x) = 3x + 1$. As $f'(x) > 0$ for all x we can show that $f(x)$ does have an inverse, even though it is difficult to write down in an explicit form.
    Writing $x = f^{-1}(y)$ we have from the above rule

$$\frac{dx}{dy} = 1 \bigg/ \frac{dy}{dx} = \frac{1}{f'(x)} = \frac{1}{3x^2 + 1}$$

Note here the derivative of $f^{-1}(y)$ is expressed in terms of x.

Problems

3.1   If $y(p)$ is the quantity demanded for a good with price p then the (own price) elasticity of demand η is defined as follows:

$$\eta = \frac{p}{y} \frac{dy}{dp}$$

If the demand price function (= inverse of the quantity demanded function) is given by

$$p = a - by$$

a,b being positive constants, find the (own price) elasticity of demand as a function of quantity y. (*Hint*: use the inverse function rule.)
Solution on p. 345.

3.2   If the demand price function is

$$p = ay^\varepsilon$$

where a,ε are constants, show that the elasticity of demand is constant.
Solution on p. 345.

3.3   If $y(p)$ is the quantity supplied when the price of a good is p, then the elasticity of supply η is defined as with demand to be

$$\eta = \frac{p}{y} \frac{dy}{dp}$$

If

$$y = Ap$$

where A is constant, show that $\eta = 1$.
Solution on p. 342.

3.4 Consider a firm whose total cost $c(y,w,r)$ of producing output y when the prices of inputs are w and r. Assume this function can be written in the form

$$c(y,w,r) = y^{\gamma}\phi(w,r)$$

where $\gamma > 0$ is a constant and $\phi(w,r)$ is the cost of producing unit output. Discuss the shape of the average cost function, i.e. the function mapping output onto average total costs (= total costs ÷ output).
Solution on p. 327.

3.5 Given a utility function $u(x)$ of a single variable in the context of uncertainty, we are interested in the following related functions (see Chapter 14, Section 8):

$$\rho^A(x) = -\frac{u''(x)}{u'(x)}$$

and

$$\rho^R(x) = -\frac{u''(x)x}{u'(x)}$$

Here $u'(x)$ is the derivative function of $u(x)$, while $u''(x)$ is the derivative of the derivative function, i.e. the second order derivative of $u(x)$ (see Chapter 5). Find $\rho^A(x)$ and $\rho^R(x)$ when

$$u(x) = \frac{\alpha + \beta x^{1-\rho}}{1 - \rho},$$

α, β and ρ being constants.
Solution on p. 316.

3.6 Consider a monopolist firm with demand price $p(y)$ for its output y so that its total revenue function is

$$TR = p(y)\, y$$

Show that the marginal revenue function MR (= derivative function of TR) can be written as follows:

$$MR = p\left(1 + \frac{1}{\eta}\right)$$

where η is the elasticity of demand.
Solution on p. 345.

3.7 As noted in the Appendix, the following is valid for a real x less than 1 in absolute size:

$$\ln(1 + x) = x - \frac{x^2}{2} + \frac{x^3}{3} - \frac{x^4}{4} + \ldots$$

$$= \sum_{r=1}^{\infty} \frac{(-1)^{r+1}x^r}{r}$$

Consider $y_n = \left(1 + \frac{r}{n}\right)^{nt}$ so that

$$\ln(y_n) = nt \; \ln\left(1 + \frac{r}{n}\right)$$

$$= nt\left[\frac{r}{n} - \frac{1}{2}\left(\frac{r}{n}\right)^2 + \frac{1}{3}\left(\frac{r}{n}\right)^3 - \ldots\right]$$

Conclude that as n goes to infinity $\ln(y_n)$ approaches rt and thus y_n approaches e^{rt}.
Solution on p. 298.

Exercises

3.1 Find the derivative of the following functions:

(i) $y = 3$ i.e. for all x,y takes the value 3
(ii) $y = -2x + 5$
(iii) $y = 6x^2 - 3x + 4$
(iv) $y = 1/x^2 = x^{-2}$
(v) $y = x + 1/x = x + x^{-1}$

3.2 Using the chain rule, differentiate the following:

(i) $y = (1 + x)^2$
(ii) $y = \ln(1 + x^2)$
(iii) $y = \exp(\sqrt{x}) = e^{\sqrt{x}}$

3.3 Using the product rule differentiate the following:

(i) $y = x \ln(x)$
(ii) $y = \ln(x)/x = x^{-1} \ln(x)$

3.4   If the amount of capital k required to produce output q is given by $k = q^2 + q$, use the inverse function rule to find the marginal product of capital.

3.5   Find the marginal cost function given the following total cost function:

$$TC = \alpha + \beta q - \gamma q^2 + \delta q^3$$

where α, β, γ and δ are constants and q is output.

3.6   Given a function $f(x)$ is the product of two positive valued functions $g(x), h(x)$, then

$$\ln[f(x)] = \ln[g(x)] + \ln[h(x)]$$

Use the generalised logarithmic rule of differentiation to confirm that the derivative of $f(x)$ is given by the product rule.

3.7   If a firm's average cost of producing output q is given by

$$AC = \alpha q^n$$

where α, n are constants, show that marginal cost is $n + 1$ times average cost.

3.8   Show that average *fixed* costs are always declining as output increases, i.e. show that the derivative of the average fixed cost function is negative.

4

Differentiation of Functions of Several Variables

1 Vectors

1.1 Vectors and Vector Notation

Economic decisions are invariably complex in that they involve the simultaneous choice of several quantities, e.g. a household has to choose a whole pattern of consumption and not just how much meat or bread to buy; a firm has to choose its combination of inputs, as well as output, when attempting to maximise its profit. To analyse these situations we make use of functions of several variables. For example we introduce a utility function which tells us the level of utility for every pattern of consumption, or a production function which tells us how much output can be produced from every combination of inputs. In the case of two goods we can write x_1 and x_2 to represent the quantities of the first and second good respectively. Thus we can write $u(x_1,x_2)$ to indicate the level of utility a household attains when it consumes the quantities x_1,x_2 of the two goods and write $f(x_1,x_2)$ to indicate the maximum output a firm can produce using the quantities x_1,x_2 of the two inputs.

We have already seen that a pair of quantities (x_1,x_2) can be represented by a point in a two-dimensional diagram; thus we can consider the choice of these two quantities as the choice of a single point. A more concrete terminology might be to say that the choosing of (x_1,x_2) is the choosing of a 'basket' or 'bundle' of goods, this 'basket' containing a quantity x_1 of the first good and quantity x_2 of the second good. Clearly such notions of 'baskets' or 'bundles' can readily be extended to the case of many goods; thus we may have a 'basket' containing the quantity x_i of the i'th good where i runs over the values $1,2,\ldots,n$ for some n. In this way we can in principle represent very complex decisions such as those faced by consumers and firms in reality. Corresponding to the idea of the consumer or firm choosing a single, complex object, i.e. a 'basket' of goods, we have the mathematical notion of a *vector*. An n-dimensional vector or n-vector $\mathbf{x}$ is an ordered set of n numbers; here n may be any positive integer, i.e. $1,2,3,\ldots$ The numbers in an n-vector x are referred to as the components or elements, and can be represented by $\mathbf{x}_i$, $i = 1,2,\ldots,n$. Now there are two ways we can write an n-vector in full, namely as a row of numbers, i.e. $\mathbf{x} = (x_1,\ldots,x_n)$ or as column

of numbers $\mathbf{x} = \begin{bmatrix} x_1 \\ \vdots \\ x_n \end{bmatrix}$. The most common notation is that of a column

vector, but in the main body of this text we shall not be concerned with this distinction. The reader is referred to the Appendix for a more formal discussion of linear algebra and matrices where the distinction is important. Finally we can note that while two-dimensional vectors are readily represented geometrically, the geometric representation of three-dimensional vectors is somewhat more tricky, while that of higher dimensions is impossible. Nevertheless it is not uncommon to refer to the vector $\mathbf{x}$ as if it were a point in an abstract n-dimensional space.

1.2 Operations on Vectors

Having introduced the use of the vector notation to represent the 'basket' of goods, we can readily proceed to think of sets of vectors. For example the set of possible 'baskets' a consumer is able to purchase can be represented by the set of vectors $\mathbf{x}$ whose value does not exceed the consumer's budget. Geometrically this set can be represented in the usual way as in Figure 4.1. If the prices of the goods are denoted by p_i, $i = 1,\ldots,n$, then the value or cost of the basket $\mathbf{x}$ is $p_1x_1 + p_2x_2+\ldots+p_nx_n$ and the consumer can purchase $\mathbf{x}$ if this cost does not exceed his budget m. Now just as we can represent a basket of goods by a vector, so we can represent the corresponding set of prices by a vector $\mathbf{p}$. The value of the basket $\mathbf{x}$ given price vector $\mathbf{p}$ corresponds directly to the mathematical idea of *inner* or *dot product* of two vectors. The inner product of two vectors is the sum of the products of corresponding elements of the two vectors; thus the inner or dot product of $\mathbf{p}$ and $\mathbf{x}$ is $p_1x_1 + p_2x_2+\ldots+p_nx_n$ and can be denoted by $\mathbf{p}\ \mathbf{x}$. Hence our consumer can afford to buy $\mathbf{x}$ if $\mathbf{p}\ \mathbf{x} \leqslant m$.

Definition 4.1: Given two n-vectors $\mathbf{x}$ and $\mathbf{y}$, then their dot or inner product $\mathbf{x}\ \mathbf{y}$ is defined by

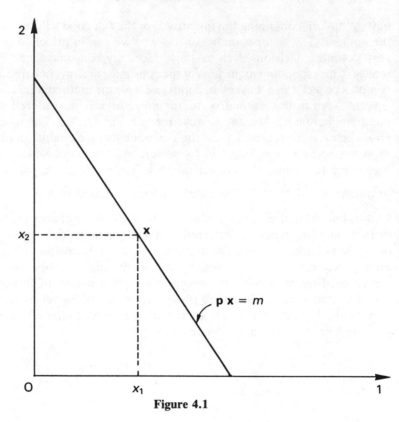

Figure 4.1

$$\mathbf{x}\ \mathbf{y} = x_1 y_1 + \ldots + x_n y_n = \sum_{i=1}^{n} x_i y_i$$

Note that the inner product is not defined for two vectors of different dimensions. Furthermore we can emphasise that the value of the inner product $\mathbf{x}\ \mathbf{y}$ is a single number whatever the dimensions of $\mathbf{x}$ and $\mathbf{y}$.

Should a consumer obtain two 'baskets' $\mathbf{x},\mathbf{y}$ of goods then the total quantity of the i'th good obtained from the joint basket will be $x_i + y_i$; hence the following is a natural definition.

Definition 4.2: Given two n-vectors $\mathbf{x},\mathbf{y}$ their sum $\mathbf{x} + \mathbf{y}$ is defined to be that vector whose i'th component is $x_i + y_i$, i.e. $(\mathbf{x} + \mathbf{y})_i = x_i + y_i$.

Equally if the customer obtains two identical baskets $\mathbf{x}$, then the total quantity of the i'th good will be $2x_i$, hence we can define $2\mathbf{x}$ to be the vector whose i'th component is $2x_i$.

Definition 4.3: Given an n-vector $\mathbf{x}$ and a real number α we define $\alpha\mathbf{x}$ to be that vector whose i'th component is αx_i, i.e. $(\alpha \mathbf{x})_i = \alpha x_i$.

If we write $\mathbf{x} = (x_1,\ldots,x_n)$ and $\mathbf{y} = (y_1,\ldots,y_n)$ as row vectors, then these last two definitions can be summarised in the following formal statement.

For any real α,β we have

$$\alpha \mathbf{x} + \beta \mathbf{y} = (\alpha x_1 + \beta y_1,\ldots,\alpha x_n + \beta y_n)$$

These definitions imply the following properties (see Exercise 4.1):

(1)   If $\mathbf{p},\mathbf{x}$ and $\mathbf{y}$ are n-dimensional vectors then

$$\mathbf{p}\,(\mathbf{x} + \mathbf{y}) = \mathbf{p}\,\mathbf{x} + \mathbf{p}\,\mathbf{y}$$

(2)   If $\mathbf{p}$ and $\mathbf{x}$ are n-vectors and α is a real number, then

$$\mathbf{p}\,(\alpha \mathbf{x}) = \alpha(\mathbf{p}\,\mathbf{x})$$

These two properties can be summarised in the statement

$$\mathbf{p}\,(\alpha \mathbf{x} + \mathbf{y}) = \alpha(\mathbf{p}\,\mathbf{x}) + \mathbf{p}\,\mathbf{y}$$

2 Functions of Several Variables and Partial Functions

2.1 Introduction

Having introduced the idea and notation of vectors, we can succinctly represent a function of several variables by considering the variables entering the function as forming a vector. Hence $f(\mathbf{x})$ will represent a function of the variables x_i, $i = 1,\ldots,n$, the dimension of $\mathbf{x}$ being understood in any particular circumstance. Hence, when discussing the choice of consumption goods, we can write $u(\mathbf{x})$ to represent the consumer's utility when the 'bundle' $\mathbf{x}$ is consumed. Equally in the context of production we can write $f(\mathbf{x})$ to indicate the maximum output that can be produced given the 'bundle' of inputs $\mathbf{x}$.

An immediate problem we face when discussing functions of several variables is to give a concrete interpretation of the graph of a function. If we have a function $f(x_1,x_2)$ of two variables, we can in principle imagine constructing its graph in three dimensions. Thus we could measure x_1 and x_2 along a *pair* of horizontal axes and plot the values of f against a vertical axis. In this way we will generally obtain a 'surface' suspended in our three dimensional space. Unfortunately it is not often practical to represent such surfaces in two-dimension diagrams; nevertheless it is recommended that the reader attempt to imagine such surfaces and graphs. Going a step further by considering a function of three or more variables, we face the problem that we cannot imagine what the graph might look like because it would involve a four-dimensional space.

2.2 Partial Functions

Fortunately we can largely sidestep the difficulty outlined above by 'breaking down' a function of several variables into what we shall call its partial functions, this in turn leading into partial differentiation. Below we offer a formal definition of partial functions and will develop the idea for special classes of functions in subsequent sections.

Definition 4.4: Given a function $f(x_1,...,x_n)$ of n variables, we can introduce for each variable x_i a family of partial functions where each partial function treats all other variables x_j, $j \neq i$, as constants. This can be represented as

$$x_i \rightarrow f(\bar{x}_1,...,\bar{x}_{i-1}, x_i, \bar{x}_{i+1},...,\bar{x}_n)$$

where the 'bars' over x_j, $j \neq i$, indicate we are treating them as constants in this mapping.

The reader will appreciate that this notion of treating all other variables as constant corresponds to the economist's use of the phrase 'all other things being the same' or *ceteris paribus*. This is no accident, for the convenience of the *ceteris paribus* assumption in our informal arguments is matched by the convenience of considering partial functions in our mathematics. Just as we consider 'shifts' in demand curves, etc. due to changes in some other variable, so we must recognise that the partial function will 'shift' as we consider different values of the other variables, thus we have a family of partial functions for each variable.

2.3 Linear Functions of Many Variables

As in the case of functions of one variable, the simplest and perhaps the most important class of functions of several variables is the set of linear functions.

Definition 4.5: A function $f(\mathbf{x})$ of n variables x_i, $i = 1,...,n$, is *linear* if it can be expressed in the form

$$f(\mathbf{x}) = r + \mathbf{v}\,\mathbf{x}$$

for some constant real number r and some constant n-vector $\mathbf{v}$. Here constant means that the number does not vary as $\mathbf{x}$ varies.

For example, if we interpret $\mathbf{x}$ as a basket of inputs for a firm's production, and introduce a vector $\mathbf{p}$ of prices of inputs, then the function $f(\mathbf{x}) = \mathbf{p}\,\mathbf{x}$ is linear in $\mathbf{x}$ if we treat prices as constants, i.e. independent of $\mathbf{x}$. Thus the firm's costs will be a linear function in the quantities of inputs.

For a function of the form

$$f(x_1, x_2) = r + v_1 x_1 + v_2 x_2$$

the partial functions of f associated with the variable x_1 are represented

$$x_1 \rightarrow f(x_1, \bar{x}_2) = r + v_1 x_1 + v_2 \bar{x}_2$$

there being one partial function for each value $\bar{x}_2$. For any given $\bar{x}_2$ we can plot the graph of the partial function, as in Figure 4.2. Note that the intercept with the ordinate is at the point $r_1 + v_2 \bar{x}_2$, this being the value of the partial function at $x_1 = 0$. Furthermore it is readily confirmed that the slope of the partial function is v_1 and thus this slope is independent of $\bar{x}_2$.

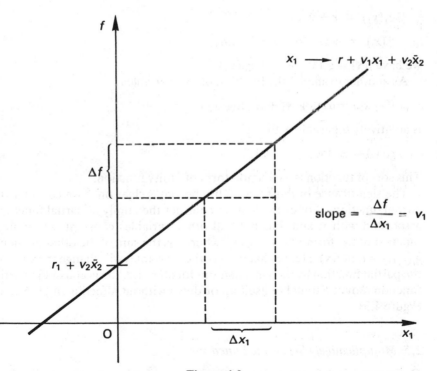

Figure 4.2

Indeed changes in $\bar{x}_2$ shift the graph of the partial function bodily up or down. Clearly the partial functions associated with x_2 are defined in a similar fashion, i.e. for a given $\bar{x}_1$ the partial function is defined by $x_2 \rightarrow f(\bar{x}_1,x_2) = r + v_1\bar{x}_1 + v_2x_2$. Again the slope v_2 of this partial function is independent of $\bar{x}_1$, and changes in $\bar{x}_1$ effectively shift the intercept $r + v_1\bar{x}_1$ with the vertical axis.

2.4 Additive Separable Functions

Definition 4.6: A function $f(\mathbf{x})$ of n variables x_i, $i = 1,\ldots,n$, is said to be *additively separable* if it can be written in the form

$$f(\mathbf{x}) = g_1(x_1) + \ldots + g_n(x_n)$$
$$= \sum_i g_i(x_i)$$

i.e. it is the sum of separate functions of the n variables.

Note that all linear functions are additively separable; thus if $f(\mathbf{x}) = r + \mathbf{vx}$, then writing

$$g_1(x_1) = r + v_1x_1$$
$$g_i(x_i) = v_ix_i \quad \text{for} \quad i = 2,\ldots,n,$$

we have $f(\mathbf{x}) = g_1(x_1) + \ldots + g_n(x_n)$.

As another example, the function of two variables

$$f(x_1,x_2) = \alpha_1 \log x_1 + \alpha_2 \log x_2$$

is additively separable with

$$g_i(x_i) = \alpha_i \log x_i; \quad i = 1,2$$

This sort of function is a common form of utility function.

The significance of this separability becomes clear once we consider the partial functions. For example if we consider the family of partial functions associated with x_i and thus hold all other variables constant we obtain a function of the form $x_i \rightarrow r + g_i(x_i)$ where r is the sum of the other elements $g_j(x_j), j \neq i$, of $f(\mathbf{x})$. Hence changes in other variables will change the value of the partial function by the same amount for all x_i, i.e. the graph of the partial function moves parallel to itself up or down without affecting its slope (see Figure 4.3).

2.5 Multiplicatively Separable Functions

Definition 4.7: A function $f(\mathbf{x})$ of n variables x_i, $i = 1,\ldots,n$, is *multiplicatively*

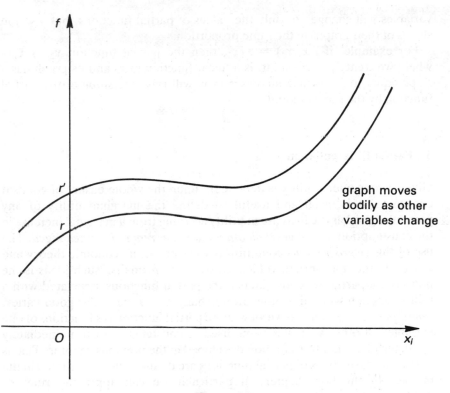

Figure 4.3

separable if it can be written in the form

$$f(\mathbf{x}) = g_1(x_1) \times g_2(x_2) \times \ldots \times g_n(x_n)$$

$$= \prod_{i=1}^{n} g_i(x_i)$$

The most common example of such a function would be

$$f(\mathbf{x}) = x_1^{\beta_1} \times x_2^{\beta_2} \times \ldots \times x_n^{\beta_n}$$

i.e. the product of power functions of the x_i. If the β_i's are positive and add up to one we refer to this as a Cobb–Douglas function.

The partial functions here take the form

$$x_i \rightarrow rg_i(x_i)$$

where r is the product of the other $g_j(x_j)$, $j \neq i$. In this case changes in other variables will change not only the values of partial functions, but also the slopes of their graphs in the same proportion.

For example, if $f(x_1,x_2) = x_1x_2$, then the partial function $x_2 \rightarrow \bar{x}_1x_2$ where we treat $\bar{x}_1$ as constant, is a linear function in x_2 and its graph has a slope equal to $\bar{x}_1$! Hence increases in $\bar{x}_1$ will raise the *slope* of the partial function by the same amount.

3 Partial Differentiation

Given a consumer's utility is dependent upon the whole basket of goods it consumes, it is usual and useful to define the marginal utility of any particular good as the increase in utility accruing from a marginal increase in the consumption of that good *all other quantities remaining unchanged*. The use of this *ceteris paribus* condition is widespread in economic theory and obviously the appropriate vehicle in which to formalise such ideas is the notion of a partial function. Hence the partial functions associated with a utility function will tell us how utility changes as a particular good varies, *ceteris paribus*. Given that we view these partial functions as functions of one variable, all other variables being used as constants, we can immediately apply the ideas of differentiation developed in the previous chapter. That is to say, the derivatives of partial functions are defined and constructed in the manner of the last chapter; in particular we can apply the rules of differentiation, remembering to treat all other variables as constants. The derivatives of the partial functions are known as the partial derivatives of the original function.

Definition 4.8: Given a function $f(\mathbf{x})$ of n variables x_i, $i = 1,...,n$, the derivatives of its associated partial functions are known as the *partial derivatives* of f and are denoted by $\partial f/\partial x_i$ or $f_i'(\mathbf{x})$.

The notation $\partial f/\partial x_i$ makes use of the curly dee (∂) and is thus read as 'dee f by dee x_i'. The notation $f_i'(\mathbf{x})$ is useful in that it stresses that in general these partial derivatives will be functions of all variables entering into the original function $f(\mathbf{x})$.

Example 4.1

(a)   If $f(x_1,x_2) = p_1x_1 + p_2x_2$, the partial function is

$$f(x_1,\bar{x}_2) = p_1x_1 + p_2\bar{x}_2$$

and the partial derivative of $f(x_1,x_2)$ with respect to x_1 is the derivative of $f(x_1,\bar{x}_2)$, i.e.

$$\frac{\partial f}{\partial x_1} = f_1'(x_1, \bar{x}_2) = p_1$$

Similarly

$$\frac{\partial f}{\partial x_2} = f_2'(\bar{x}_1, x_2) = p_2$$

(b)   If $f(x_1, x_2) = x_1 x_2$, then

$$\frac{\partial f}{\partial x_1} = x_2$$

$$\frac{\partial f}{\partial x_2} = x_1$$

(c)   If $f(x_1, x_2) = \ln x_1 + \ln x_2$, then

$$\frac{\partial f}{\partial x_1} = \frac{1}{x_1}; \quad \frac{\partial f}{\partial x_2} = \frac{1}{x_2}$$

(d)   If $f(x_1, x_2) = x_1^{1/2} x_2^{1/2}$, then

$$\frac{\partial f}{\partial x_1} = \frac{1}{2} \frac{x_2^{1/2}}{x_1^{1/2}}$$

$$\frac{\partial f}{\partial x_2} = \frac{1}{2} \frac{r_1^{1/2}}{x_2^{1/2}}$$

(e)   If f is additively separable, i.e. $f(\mathbf{x}) = \sum_i g_i(x_i)$, then

$$\frac{\partial f}{\partial x_i} = \frac{dg_i}{dx_i}$$

because the derivatives of $g_j(x_j), j \neq i$, with respect to x_i will be zero!

Given a function $f(\mathbf{x})$ of n variables there will be n partial derivative functions $f_i'(\mathbf{x})$ which we can 'stack up' into a vector which we denote by $\mathbf{f}'(\mathbf{x})$, i.e.

$$\mathbf{f}'(\mathbf{x}) = \begin{bmatrix} f_1'(\mathbf{x}) \\ f_2'(\mathbf{x}) \\ \vdots \\ f_n'(\mathbf{x}) \end{bmatrix}$$

While partial functions give a clear conceptual basis to partial differentiation it is useful to draw out a formal definition involving only the original function. We can thus state that:

$$\frac{\partial f}{\partial x_i} = f_i'(\mathbf{x}) = \lim_{\Delta x_i \to 0} \left[\frac{f(x_1,\ldots,x_i + \Delta x_i,\ldots,x_n) - f(\mathbf{x})}{\Delta x_i} \right]$$

4   Implicit Functions and Implicit Differentiation

4.1 Indifference Curves, Isoquants and Level Surfaces

The standard geometric means of analysing the choice of a consumer or a firm is the use of indifference curves and isoquants. Using indifference curves we draw out the principles·governing a consumer choice by arguing that utility is maximised where the indifference curve is tangential to the budget constraint (see Figure 4.4). Equally a firm's cost minimising input vector is typically characterised by the tangency of isocost lines with the isoquant. These tangency conditions can be restated by saying that the marginal rate of substitution (MRS), in the case of the consumer, or the marginal rate of technical substitution (MRTS), in the case of the firm, will be equal to relative price. Our aim in the next section is to indicate how we can find the MRS and MRTS, given the utility and production function respectively. However, before we do, let us clarify the relationship between

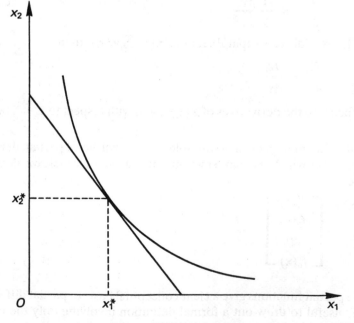

Figure 4.4

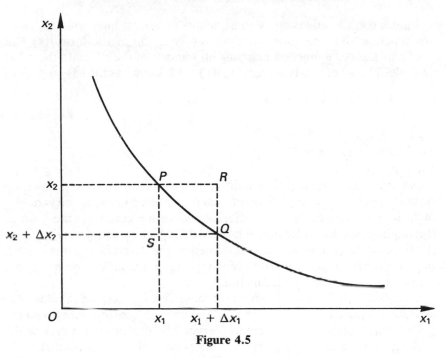

Figure 4.5

these functions and our standard diagrams, and introduce the idea of an implicit function.

Consider first an indifference curve such as that drawn in Figure 4.5. By definition all the points on this curve generate the same level of utility; let $\bar{u}$ denote this common level of utility. If $u(x_1,x_2)$ is the associated utility function it follows that for all $\mathbf{x}$ on this curve we have $u(x_1,x_2) = \bar{u}$. Now look again at Figure 4.5 and, forgetting the origins of the diagram, view the curve as the graph of some function. For any value of x_1 we can 'read off' an associated value for x_2. This mapping from x_1 to x_2 induced from the indifference curve tells us, for each x_1, the x_2 required to make $u(x_1,x_2)$ equal to $\bar{u}$. The formal counterpart of this mapping would view the equation $u(x_1,x_2) = \bar{u}$ as determining the 'unknown' x_2 given the values of x_1 and $\bar{u}$. For example if $u(x_1,x_2) = x_1x_2$, then we characterise the indifference curve by the equation $x_1x_2 = \bar{u}$, from which we deduce $x_2 = \bar{u}/x_1$. In this way we can see that the equation $u(x_1,x_2) = \bar{u}$ can be viewed as implicitly defining a function mapping x_1 onto x_2. Indeed this function $u(x_1,x_2) = \bar{u}$ mapping x_1 onto x_2 is called an implicit function. Until this section we have always dealt with functions written in explicit form, i.e. $y = f(x)$, but many functions are most easily dealt with in implicit form. For example, the function $ax + by + (ax)^3 + (xy)^{1/2} = 0$ has no simple explicit formulation and is best dealt with in its implicit form.

Similar considerations apply to isoquants or isocost lines. Indeed, given any function $f(\mathbf{x})$ of several variables, an equation of the form $f(\mathbf{x}) = k$ implicitly defines a function mapping all but one of the x_i's onto the other variable. The set of points $\mathbf{x}$ satisfying $f(\mathbf{x}) = k$ is known as the *level surface* of f.

4.2 Implicit Differentiation

As we have seen, we can view indifference curves, isoquants or any level surface as inducing an implicit functional relationship between the variables of the function. If we view the indifference curve in Figure 4.5 as the graph of this implicit function, it follows that the MRS, which by definition is equal to the slope of this graph, will be determined by the derivative of this implicit function. Given a general utility function $u(x_1,x_2)$ what can we say about the derivative of this implicit function?

Consider again Figure 4.5, where we show a change Δx_1 in the value of x_1 and the associated change Δx_2 in x_2, these changes moving us between the points P and Q on the indifference curve. The derivative we seek is the limiting value of $\Delta x_2/\Delta x_1$ as Δx_1 approaches zero. Now we know that

$$u(x_1 + \Delta x_1, x_2 + \Delta x_2) = u(x_1,x_2)$$

i.e. the utility at P and Q are the same. It follows that

$$u(x_1 + \Delta x_1, x_2 + \Delta x_2) - u(x_1,x_2) = 0$$

hence

$$u(x_1 + \Delta x_1, x_2 + \Delta x_2) - u(x_1,x_2 + \Delta x_2)$$
$$+ u(x_1,x_2 + \Delta x_2) - u(x_1,x_2) = 0$$

To obtain this last equation we have simultaneously added in and subtracted out the term $u(x_1,x_2 + \Delta x_2)$. If we now write

$$\Delta_1 u = u(x_1 + \Delta x_1, x_2 + \Delta x_2) - u(x_1, x_2 + \Delta x_2)$$

and

$$\Delta_2 u = u(x_1, x_2 + \Delta x_2) - u(x_1,x_2)$$

we can say

$$\Delta_1 u + \Delta_2 u = 0$$

$\Delta_2 u$ indicates the change in utility as we go from P to S, while $\Delta_1 u$ indicates the change as we go from S to Q in Figure 4.5. Let us now divide our last equation by Δx_1 to obtain

$$\frac{\Delta_1 u}{\Delta x_1} + \frac{\Delta_2 u}{\Delta x_1} = 0$$

which implies

$$\frac{\Delta_1 u}{\Delta x_1} + \frac{\Delta_2 u}{\Delta x_2}\frac{\Delta x_2}{\Delta x_1} = 0 \qquad (4.1)$$

We now let Δx_1 go to zero, noting that as we do so Δx_2 will also go to zero. The limit of $\Delta x_2/\Delta x_1$ as Δx_1 goes to zero is the derivative dx_2/dx_1 of the implicit function which we seek. Consider then

$$\lim_{\Delta x_1 \to 0} \frac{\Delta_1 u}{\Delta x_1} = \lim_{\Delta x_1 \to 0} \frac{u(x_1 + \Delta x_1, x_2 + \Delta x_2) - u(x_1, x_2 + \Delta x_2)}{\Delta x_1}$$

$$= u_1'(x_1, x_2) = \frac{\partial u}{\partial x_1}$$

(note $x_2 + \Delta x_2 \to x_2$ as $\Delta x_1 \to 0$)

$$\lim_{\Delta x_2 \to 0} \frac{\Delta_2 u}{\Delta x_2} = u_2'(x_1, x_2) = \frac{\partial u}{\partial x_2}$$

Hence, from (4.1) we obtain:

$$\frac{\partial u}{\partial x_1} + \frac{\partial u}{\partial x_2}\frac{dx_2}{dx_1} = 0$$

therefore

$$\frac{dx_2}{dx_1} = -\frac{\partial u/\partial x_1}{\partial u/\partial x_2}$$

i.e.   MRS = ratio of the marginal utilities.

More generally, given a function of two variables $f(x_1, x_2)$, we can view the equation $f(x_1, x_2) = k$ as defining implicitly x_2 as a function of x_1, a function whose derivative dx_2/dx_1 satisfies

$$\frac{\partial f}{\partial x_1} + \frac{\partial f}{\partial x_2}\frac{dx_2}{dx_1} = 0$$

or

$$\frac{dx_2}{dx_1} = -\frac{\partial f/\partial x_1}{\partial f/\partial x_2}$$

In particular the MRTS for a firm will be equal to the ratio of marginal products of the inputs. We can summarise the result of this subsection in the following rule:

The Implicit Function Rule: If x_1 is an implicit function of x_2 to x_n of the form $f(\mathbf{x}) = k$ then

$$\frac{\partial x_1}{\partial x_i} = - \frac{\partial f/\partial x_i|}{\partial f/\partial x_1}$$

Example 4.2
Find dx_1/dx_2 when $f(x_1,x_2) = x_1^2 + x_2^2 = 9$, $x_1 > 0$, $x_2 > 0$. Using the implicit function rule

$$\frac{dx_1}{dx_2} = - \frac{\partial f/\partial x_2}{\partial f/\partial x_1} = - \frac{2x_2}{2x_1} = - \frac{x_2}{x_1}$$

For this particular case we can write the function in explicit form to check the result:

$$x_1 = g(x_2) = (9 - x_2^2)^{1/2}$$

giving

$$\frac{dx_1}{dx_2} = \frac{1}{2}(9 - x_2^2)^{-1/2} 2x_2 = \frac{x_2}{(9 - x_2^2)^{1/2}} = \frac{x_2}{x_1}$$

5   Direction and Total Derivatives

5.1 Directional Derivatives

Consider a firm, with production function $f(x_1,x_2)$, being offered the prospect of buying a 'package' of inputs $\mathbf{v}$, where $\mathbf{v}$ is some vector of quantities of inputs. In assessing the desirability of the offer it needs to identify the marginal productivity of the 'package'. Imagine it can buy various 'quantities' δ of the 'package', i.e. it can buy in the inputs $\delta\mathbf{v}$. A marginal increase in use of $\mathbf{v}$ can thus be viewed as a marginal increase in δ. In Figure 4.6 we have drawn an isoquant passing through the current position P of the firm's input vector $\mathbf{x}$. The point T represents the vector $\mathbf{x} + \mathbf{v}$ which involves a unit purchase of the 'package' $\mathbf{v}$, while Q can be viewed as representing a 'small' purchase $\Delta\mathbf{x} = \delta\mathbf{v}$ of the 'package'. The increase in production made possible by the purchase of $\delta\mathbf{v}$ is given by the difference in the value of f at P and Q. Associated with the change $\Delta\mathbf{x} = \delta\mathbf{v}$ in inputs, we have the change

$$\Delta f = f(\mathbf{x} + \delta\mathbf{v}) - f(\mathbf{x})$$

in production. We can thus define the marginal productivity of the 'package' $\mathbf{v}$ as being the limit of the ratio $\Delta f/\delta$ as δ goes to zero. Let us investigate this marginal product. Proceeding in a fashion similar to that in our discussion of

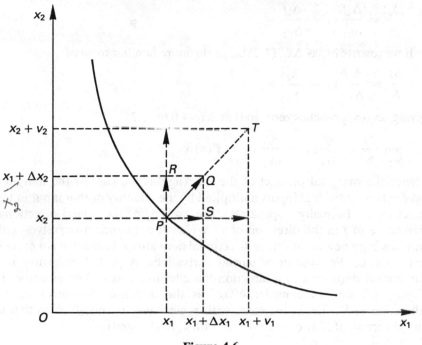

Figure 4.6

MRS in the previous section, we can view the movement from P to Q as being broken up into the movements from P to R and from R to Q. We thus proceed as follows:

$$\Delta f = f(x_1 + \delta v_1, x_2 + \delta v_2) - f(x_1, x_2)$$
$$= f(x_1 + \delta v_1, x_2 + \delta v_2) - f(x_1, x_2 + \delta v_2)$$
$$+ f(x_1, x_2 + \delta v_2) - f(x_1, x_2)$$

and writing

$$\Delta_1 f = f(x_1 + \delta v_1, x_2 + \delta v_2) - f(x_1, x_2 + \delta v_2)$$
$$\Delta_2 f = f(x_1, x_2 + \delta v_2) - f(x_1, x_2)$$

we have

$$\Delta f = \Delta_1 f + \Delta_2 f$$

Hence

$$\frac{\Delta f}{\delta} = \frac{\Delta_1 f}{\delta} + \frac{\Delta_2 f}{\delta}$$

and finally we have

$$\frac{\Delta f}{\delta} = \frac{\Delta_1 f}{\delta v_1} v_1 + \frac{\Delta_2 f}{\delta v_2} v_2 \qquad\qquad (4.2)$$

If we rewrite δv_i as Δx_i, (4.2) takes the more familiar form of

$$\frac{\Delta f}{\delta} = \frac{\Delta_1 f}{\Delta x_1} v_1 + \frac{\Delta_2 f}{\Delta x_2} v_2$$

giving, as δ approaches zero, so that $\Delta x_i \to 0$ $i = 1,2$

$$\lim_{\delta \to 0} \frac{\Delta f}{\delta} = \frac{\partial f}{\partial x_1} v_1 + \frac{\partial f}{\partial x_2} v_2 = \mathbf{f}'(\mathbf{x})\, \mathbf{v}$$

Hence the marginal product of the 'package' is the sum of the marginal products of individual inputs multiplied by the quantity of that input in the 'package'. Formally speaking $\lim_{\delta \to 0} \Delta f/\delta$ is the directional derivative of f in the direction of $\mathbf{v}$. We shall not concern ourselves with introducing a new notation for directional derivatives, because it is a natural extension of the concept of partial derivatives. A partial derivative is a directional derivative in a direction 'parallel to an axis'. For example, in Figure 4.6 we can consider $\partial f/\partial x_1$ as the direction derivative in the 'direction of S', (i.e. x_1 increases with x_2 unchanged) and $\partial f/\partial x_2$ as that in the 'direction of R' (i.e. x_2 increases with x_1 unchanged).

5.2 Euler's Theorem

An application of the directional derivative concept is the important result known as Euler's Theorem.

Definition 4.9: A function $f(\mathbf{x})$ of n variables x_i, $i = 1,\ldots,n$, is *homogeneous of degree k* if for all $\alpha > 0$ we have

$$f(\alpha \mathbf{x}) = \alpha^k f(\mathbf{x})$$

In particular it is homogeneous of degree 1 if

$$f(\alpha \mathbf{x}) = \alpha f(\mathbf{x})$$

and of degree 0 if

$$f(\alpha \mathbf{x}) = f(\mathbf{x})$$

Euler's Theorem
If $f(\mathbf{x})$ is homogeneous of degree k then

$$\mathbf{f}'(\mathbf{x})\, \mathbf{x} = k f(\mathbf{x})$$

or

$$\sum_{i=1}^{n} \frac{\partial f}{\partial x_i} x_i = kf(\mathbf{x})$$

The proof of this theorem involves considering the marginal change in $f(\alpha\mathbf{x})$ for a marginal change in α away from the value $\alpha = 1$. Hence consider $\alpha = 1 + \delta$ for a 'small' number δ. As f is homogeneous of degree k we have

$$f(\alpha\mathbf{x}) = \alpha^k f(\mathbf{x})$$

hence the change in f as α goes from 1 to $1 + \delta$ is

$$f[(1 + \delta)\mathbf{x}] - f(\mathbf{x}) = (1 + \delta)^k f(\mathbf{x}) - f(\mathbf{x})$$

or

$$f(\mathbf{x} + \delta\mathbf{x}) - f(\mathbf{x}) = [(1 + \delta)^k - 1]f(\mathbf{x})$$

Dividing throughout by δ gives

$$\frac{f(\mathbf{x} + \delta\mathbf{x}) - f(\mathbf{x})}{\delta} = \frac{[(1 + \delta)^k - 1]}{\delta} f(\mathbf{x})$$

Now let δ go to zero. On the left-hand side we have the directional derivative of f in the direction of $\mathbf{x}$! We know this is equal to $\mathbf{f}'(\mathbf{x}) \, \mathbf{x} = \sum_{i=1}^{n} \partial f/\partial x_i \, x_i$. On the right-hand side we have the derivative of the k'th power function evaluated at 1, i.e.

$$\lim_{\delta \to 0} \frac{(1 + \delta)^k - 1}{\delta} = \lim_{\delta \to 0} \frac{(1 + k\delta + \ldots) - 1}{\delta} = k$$

where the ... indicate terms involving higher powers of δ.
Hence

$$\mathbf{f}'(\mathbf{x}) \, \mathbf{x} = kf(\mathbf{x})$$

as stated in the Theorem.

Example 4.3
The function $y = f(l,k) = l^\alpha k^\beta$, $\alpha + \beta = 1$, has the property that if inputs are paid their marginal product, they receive a constant proportion of output and these shares exactly account for total output. The function is

homogeneous of degree 1 since

$$(\gamma l)^\alpha(\gamma k)^\beta = \gamma^{\alpha+\beta}l^\alpha k^\beta = \gamma l^\alpha k^\beta$$

therefore we know

$$\frac{\partial f}{\partial l}l + \frac{\partial f}{\partial k}k = f(l,k)$$

To check in this case

$$\frac{\partial f}{\partial l} = \alpha l^{\alpha-1}k^\beta$$

and

$$\frac{\partial f}{\partial k} = \beta l^\alpha k^{\beta-1}$$

therefore

$$l\frac{\partial f}{\partial l} = \alpha l^\alpha k^\beta$$

$$k\frac{\partial f}{\partial k} = \beta l^\alpha k^\beta$$

and

$$l\frac{\partial f}{\partial l} + k\frac{\partial f}{\partial k} = (\alpha + \beta)l^\alpha k^\beta = l^\alpha k^\beta$$

5.3 Total Derivatives

Consider a consumer purchasing and consuming a basket $\mathbf{x}$ of goods which yields a utility $u(\mathbf{x})$. The choice of $\mathbf{x}$ will depend upon the prices of the various goods and the budget m available to the consumer. Here we assume prices are fixed and ask what happens to $u(\mathbf{x})$ as the budget m increases? Viewing the components of $\mathbf{x}$ as functions of the budget m we can say that a marginal change in m will lead to marginal changes $\partial x_i/\partial m$ in the quantities consumed. Writing $\partial \mathbf{x}/\partial m$ for the vector of partial derivatives $\partial x_i/\partial m$, we can say that a marginal change in m will induce a change of $\mathbf{x}$ *in the direction* $\partial \mathbf{x}/\partial m$. We can apply our result on directional derivatives to conclude that a marginal change in m will induce a change $u'(\mathbf{x})\partial \mathbf{x}/\partial m$ in $u(\mathbf{x})$, i.e.

$$\frac{\partial}{\partial m} u(\mathbf{x}) = u'(\mathbf{x}) \frac{\partial \mathbf{x}}{\partial m}$$

$$= \sum_{i=1}^{n} \frac{\partial u}{\partial x_i} \frac{\partial x_i}{\partial m}$$

This is a particular example of a general result known as the total derivative rule. Let $f(\mathbf{x})$ be a function of n variables x_i, $i = 1,...,n$, where each x_i is in turn a function of a variable t. Then a change in t will induce a change of $\mathbf{x}$ in the direction $d\mathbf{x}/dt = (dx_1/dt,...,dx_n/dt)$ and thus the directional derivative result establishes the following.

The Total Derivative Rule: If $y = f(\mathbf{x})$ is a function of n variables x_i, $i = 1,...,n$, and each x_i is a function of a variable t, then the total derivative of y with respect to t is given by

$$\frac{dy}{dt} = \frac{\partial f}{\partial x_1} \frac{\partial x_1}{\partial t} + ... + \frac{\partial f}{\partial x_n} \frac{\partial x_n}{\partial t}$$

$$= f'(\mathbf{x}) \frac{dx}{dt}$$

Example 4.4
If $y = f(x_1,x_2) = x_1 x_2$, $x_1 = t^3$ and $x_2 = a + bt$ then

$$\frac{dy}{dt} = \frac{\partial f}{\partial x_1} \frac{dx_1}{dt} + \frac{\partial f}{\partial x_2} \frac{dx_2}{dt}$$

$$= x_2 3t^2 + x_1 b$$

$$= (a + bt)3t^2 + t^3 b$$

$$= 3at^2 + 4bt^3$$

On this occasion we can easily write y as a direct function of t to check the above solution, i.e.

$$y = t^3(a + bt)$$
$$= at^3 + bt^4$$

therefore

$$\frac{dy}{dt} = 3at^2 + 4bt^3$$

Problems

4.1   Consider the following utility functions

(i) $u(x_1,x_2) = x_1^{1/2}x_2^{1/2}$

(ii) $v(x_1,x_2) = x_1^2 x_2^2$

For each find the marginal utility of the first good (= partial derivative with respect to x_1) and then partially differentiate these marginal utilities again with respect to x_1. These 'second order' partials tell us how the marginal utilities change as x_1 increases. Show that for u in (i) the marginal utility decreases while for v in (ii) the marginal utility increases as x_1 increases.
Solution on p. 279.

4.2   Consider a production function $y = Al^\alpha k^\beta$ where y is the output, l the labour input and k the capital input of a firm.
(a) Find the average productivity of labour (= y/l) as a function of l and by considering the partial derivative of this function, conclude that average productivity is falling if $\alpha < 1$.
(b) Show the marginal product of labour $\partial y/\partial l$ is proportional to the average productivity.
Solution on p. 320.

4.3   Consider a production function $f(k,l)$ which is homogeneous of degree α so that

$$f(\lambda k,\lambda l) = \lambda^\alpha f(k,l)$$

for all k,l and $\lambda > 0$. Partially differentiate both sides of this equation with respect to k or l, using the chain rule on the left-hand side, and conclude that these partials, and thus the marginal products of k and l, are homogenous functions of degree $\alpha - 1$. In particular conclude that the marginal products associated with homogenous of degree 1 production functions are independent of the level of production.
Solution on p. 322.

4.4   Given a production function $f(k,l)$ we define the elasticity of substitution σ as follows

$$\sigma = \frac{\text{MRS}}{(l/k)} \frac{\partial(l/k)}{\partial \text{MRS}}$$

where

$$\text{MRS} = \frac{f_k}{f_l}$$

Find σ when

(a) $f(k,l) = Al^\alpha k^\beta$

(b) $f(k,l) = [\alpha l^\rho + (1 - \alpha)k^\rho]^{1/\rho}$

where A, α, β and ρ are constants.

(*Hint*: find MRS and its derivative with respect to l/k and then use the inverse function rule).

Solution on p. 323.

Exercises

4.1 Confirm the properties stated at the end of Section 1 for the two dimensional case, i.e. where $\mathbf{x} = (x_1, x_2)$, $\mathbf{y} = (y_1, y_2)$ and $\mathbf{p} = (p_1, p_2)$.

4.2 Draw the graphs of the partial functions of the function

$$f(x_1, x_2) = 5 + 2x_1 - 3x_2$$

How do these graphs shift as the other variable increases?

4.3 Find the partial derivatives of the following function

$$f(x_1, x_2) = x_1^{1/4} x_2^{3/4}$$

How do the graphs of the partial functions change as the other variable increases?

4.4 If $f(x_1, x_2) = g_1(x_1) g_2(x_2)$, i.e. f is multiplicatively separable in x_1, x_2, show that

$$\frac{x_i}{f} \frac{\partial f}{\partial x_i} = \frac{x_i}{g_i} \frac{\partial g_i}{\partial x_i} \qquad i = 1,2$$

i.e. the (partial) elasticities are independent of the other variable. (Note that the $\ln[f(\mathbf{x})]$ is additively separable in x_1, x_2.)

4.5 Given $f(x_1, x_2) = (x_1 + x_2)^2 = k$, where k is a constant, find the derivative dx_2/dx_1 of the implicit function mapping x_1 onto x_2.

4.6 If $f(x_1, x_2) = x_1 x_2$ find the directional derivative of f at (x_1, x_2) in the direction of $v = (v_1, v_2)$.

4.7 If $f(\mathbf{x}) = \mathbf{p} \, \mathbf{x}$ where $\mathbf{p}$ is a vector of constants, what is the directional derivative of f at $\mathbf{x}$ in the direction of $\mathbf{v}$?

4.8 Given a function $f(\mathbf{x})$ of several variables show that the directional derivative of f at $\mathbf{x}$ is zero for *all* directions $\mathbf{v}$ if and only if all the partials of f at $\mathbf{x}$ are zero.

4.9   Given a production function $f(x_1,x_2)$ which is homogenous of degree k, confirm the following:

    (i)   If $k > 1$ then a doubling of both inputs x_1,x_2 will more than double output, i.e. there are increasing returns to scale.

    (ii) If $k = 1$ then a doubling of inputs doubles output, i.e. there are constant returns to scale.

    (iii) If $k < 1$ then a doubling of inputs will less than double output, i.e. there are decreasing returns to scale.

4.10   Consider a production function $f(x_1,x_2)$ homogenous of degree k and let inputs have (real) prices (p_1,p_2) equal to their marginal product ($=$ partial derivative). Use Euler's Theorem to show that the total (real) cost of inputs $p_1x_1 + p_2x_2$ is greater than, equal to, less than output as k is less than, equal to, greater than 1.

4.11   If a consumer has utility function $u(x_1,x_2) = \ln(x_1) + \ln(x_2)$ and $x_1 = \alpha m$, $x_2 = \beta\sqrt{m}$ where m is the consumer's income, find the total derivative of utility with respect to m.

5

Unconstrained Optimisation

1 Functions of One Variable

1.1 Stationary Points

Identifying optima plays a major role in the mathematical analysis of economic behaviour because most economic analysis is based on the principle that economic agents are rational and choose their actions to optimise their objectives, e.g. we usually assume that a firm will choose its output to maximise profits. Economic analysis tells us that a necessary condition for a firm to be maximising profits is that its marginal revenue, MR, should equal its marginal cost, MC. This specific case provides an excellent introduction to the results of this chapter if we think of this condition in terms of marginal profit. Given that profit is total revenue minus total cost, then marginal profits, MPR, will be marginal revenue minus marginal cost, i.e.

MPR = MR − MC

The condition MR = MC is equivalent to the statement that marginal profits must be zero. If we view profits as a function of output, then marginal profits will be equal to the derivative of this function. Consequently the condition that MPR must be zero translates into the condition that the function is maximised at the point where its derivative is equal to zero.

Figure 5.1(a) illustrates a demand and cost relationship for a firm giving the level of profit as a function of output illustrated in Figure 5.1(b). As can be seen from the figure, the profit-maximising output is $\hat{q}$ and at this output

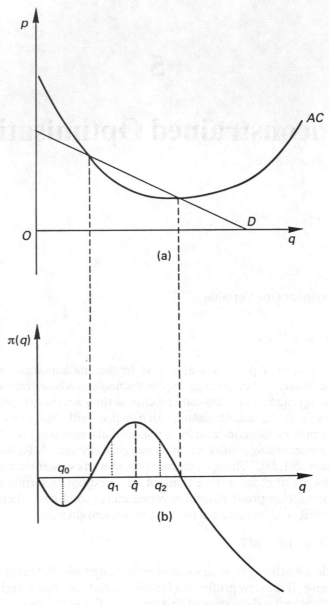

Figure 5.1

level the slope of the profit graph is zero in line with our suggestion that it is necessary for the function to have a zero derivative at the maximum. However, the figure also illustrates the fact that profit reaches a minimum at q_0 and that at this output level, the slope of the graph is zero. Indeed we shall argue that it is necessary to have a zero derivative at a minimum. Thus, this illustration shows that, although a zero derivative is necessary, it is *not* sufficient for the identification of a maximum nor a minimum.

Let us now run through the argument that a zero derivative is necessary for a maximum and a minimum. The procedure is to argue that any output where the derivative is non-zero cannot be a maximum nor a minimum. Consider then the output level q_1 illustrated in Figure 5.1(b), where the gradient of the function is positive. At this point a small increase in output will increase profits, while a small decrease in output will decrease profits, hence q_1 cannot be a maximum nor a minimum. A similar argument holds for output q_2. In this way we can argue that any output at which the derivative of profits is non-zero cannot be a maximum nor a minimum; hence a maximum or a minimum must be associated with a zero derivative.

Although the condition we have established is not sufficient, it is nevertheless very powerful, because it allows us to say that when we seek a maximum or a minimum, we can restrict our attention to those points whose derivative is zero, i.e. in this particular context, to those outputs with zero marginal profitability (there is a slight qualification to this statement below). As we shall see in the next section, this means that the first step in identifying optima is to construct the derivative function, set it equal to zero and solve the equation. In this way identifying optima is reduced to the problem of solving an equation.

At this point we ought to distinguish between types of optima. In Figure 5.1(b) q_0 is a minimum, but if we increased output sufficiently, then profits will be lower than they are at q_0. Thus although q_0 is a minimum relative to the other points in the locality of q_0, it is not the minimum for the function as a whole. It is important to make a distinction between these points so we refer to local maximum or minimum and global maximum or minimum.

Definition 5.1: A point x^* is a global maximum of $f(x)$ if $f(x^*) \geq f(x)$ for all x in the domain of the function. A point x^* is a local maximum if $f(x^*) \geq f(x)$ for all x in the neighbourhood of x.

The equivalent definitions for global and local minima are obvious. Using this definition, q_0 is a local minimum but is not a global minimum of the function, while $\hat{q}$ is both a local and a global maximum. In this chapter we will concentrate on identifying local maximum and minimum points. Generally in economics we wish to identify the global maximum and minimum points, but this is best left until we have discussed concavity and convexity in Chapter 7.

Earlier in this subsection we suggested we would need to qualify the statement that, to find local maxima or minima, we need only look at points where the derivative is zero. An example that does not fit this rule is given in

Figure 5.1(b), at the point $q = 0$. This point is a local maximum but we do not have a zero derivative. However, we can say that, if the function is differentiable (see Problem 5), any local maximum or minimum that lies in the *interior* of the range of the function (i.e. not at the end points) must have a derivative equal to zero. We refer to the set of points in the domain of the function that have zero derivatives as stationary points.

Definition 5.2: x is a stationary point of $f(x)$ if $f'(x) = 0$.

Notice that in the example we have discussed the domain of the function is restricted to $q \geqslant 0$, because negative output has no meaning in this context. Strictly speaking, we are saying that this profit-maximisation problem is a constrained optimisation problem. This point highlights the fact that the techniques we are using to find unconstrained local optima will not directly apply to constrained optimisation. This is an issue we consider in detail in Chapters 8 and 9.

1.2 Identifying Optima

Given a differentiable function $y = f(x)$, we wish to establish necessary and sufficient conditions for a point to be a local optima of $f(x)$. Consider the function drawn in Figure 5.2. We have argued in the previous section that a necessary condition for a point to be an optimum point of $f(x)$ is that f is stationary at that point, i.e. $f'(x) = 0$. Let us briefly restate the argument in terms of Figure 5.2. If, for a given point, say x_0, the derivative, $f'(x_0)$, is not zero, then it is possible to increase or decrease the value of the function by moving to the right or left as appropriate. It is intuitively obvious, although we will not formally prove it, that the sign of the change in the value of the function, $\Delta f(x)$, for a sufficiently small *increase* in x, Δx, will be the same as the sign of $f'(x)$, i.e. for sufficiently small Δx:

$$\text{sign of} \quad \Delta f(x) = \text{sign of} \quad f'(x)$$

For a sufficiently small *decrease* in x we have

$$\text{sign of} \quad \Delta f(x) = \text{sign of} \quad -f'(x)$$

Hence, any point of $f(x)$ which is not stationary cannot be a maximum or minimum of $f(x)$.

The important point to notice is that this argument does not apply to stationary points. This is important because it is intuitively tempting to say that small changes in x will not change the value of $f(x)$ if $f'(x) = 0$. However, x^* in Figure 5.2 shows that this is incorrect. In general the value of the function will change no matter how small the movement away from x^*, and

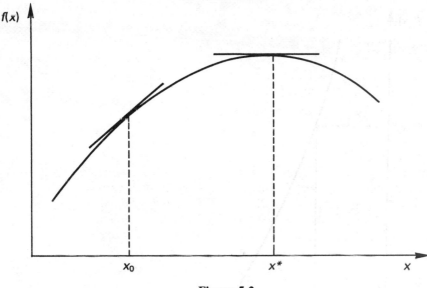

Figure 5.2

we require further analysis to identify the change in the value of a function at stationary points.

The point x^* in Figure 5.2 is not only stationary but is also a turning point in the sense that the sign of the derivative $f'(x)$ at points immediately to the left of x^* is opposite to the sign of $f'(x)$ at points immediately to the right of x^*. To illustrate this idea we have drawn, in Figure 5.3, the graph of the derivative function associated with the function whose graph we have drawn in Figure 5.2. The domain of $f(x)$ is represented on the horizontal axis of Figure 5.3, as in Figure 5.2, but the vertical axis gives the value of $f'(x)$ and not $f(x)$, i.e. the height of the graph at x_0 represents the derivative of $f(x)$ at x_0. Obviously the graph of $f'(x)$ cuts the horizontal axis at x^*, because x^* is a stationary point and a turning point of $f(x)$. This illustrates the general proposition that if at a point, x^*, the derivative function cuts the horizontal axis, then x^* is a turning point of the function. More usefully it illustrates the fact that the combination of x^* being a stationary point of f and the graph of $f'(x)$ having a negative gradient at x^* ensures that the graph of $f(x)$ turns down at x^*, i.e. x^* is a local maximum. How do we know if the gradient of $f'(x)$ is negative? Obviously, since the derivative of $f(x)$ is the gradient of $f(x)$, the derivative of $f'(x)$ will give the gradient of $f'(x)$. Not surprisingly, the derivative of the derivative of $f'(x)$ is called the second order derivative.

Definition 5.3: Given a differentiable function $y = f(x)$ with derivative function $dy/dx = f'(x)$, the second order derivative of $f(x)$ is defined to be

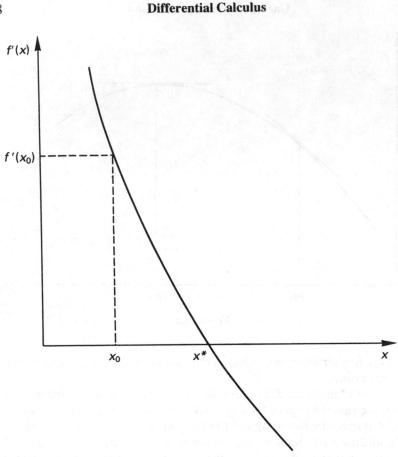

Figure 5.3

the derivative of the derivative function and denoted by $d^2y/dx^2 = f''(x)$.

The second order derivative d^2y/dx^2 is read as 'dee two y by dee x squared' and $f''(x)$ is read as 'f double prime of x'. If $f''(x^*)$ is negative, then the graph of $f'(x)$ must be downward sloping at x^*. Therefore, if x^* satisfies $f'(x^*) = 0$ and $f''(x^*) < 0$, as in Figure 5.3, we can conclude that $f'(x)$ changes sign from positive to negative at x^*, and thus x^* is a turning point of $f(x)$ and a local maximum. Similarly if $f''(x^*) = 0$ and $f'(x^*) > 0$, then the same type of argument allows us to conclude x^* is a local minimum. Putting this more formally, if x^* is a stationary point of $f(x)$, and the second order derivative at x^* is non-zero, then for sufficiently small changes in x, Δx, we have

$$\text{the sign of} \quad \Delta f(x^*) = \text{the sign of} \quad f''(x^*) \qquad (5.1)$$

Notice that the sign of $\Delta f(x)$ is independent of the sign of the change in x, i.e.

(5.1) is true whether Δx is positive or negative. Therefore, if $f''(x) > 0$, a small change in x, at a point where $f'(x) = 0$, will increase the value of $f(x)$ whether x is increased or decreased. Similarly if $f''(x) < 0$, a small change in x, at a point where $f'(x) = 0$, will decrease the value of the function. We can summarise this in the following result:

Theorem 5.1
(a)   A necessary condition for x^* to be a local optimum of $f(x)$ is that x^* be a stationary point of $f(x)$, i.e. $f'(x) = 0$.
(b)   A sufficient condition for a stationary point, x^*, to be a local maximum (minimum) is that $f''(x^*) < 0$ $[f''(x^*) > 0]$.

   Thus to find a maximum or a minimum we solve the equation $f'(x) = 0$ and check the sign of $f''(x)$ at the solutions of this equation. This only establishes local maxima or minima. To investigate whether we have a global maximum (minimum), and to find whether it is unique, we need to evaluate $f(x)$ at the local maxima (minima). If there are several local maxima (minima) the one with the highest (lowest) $f(x)$ is the global maximum (minimum).

Example 5.1
Let $y = f(x) = -2x^3 + 9x^2 - 12x - 6$. Here

$$\frac{dy}{dx} = f'(x) = -6x^2 + 18x - 12$$

Hence the stationary points of the function satisfy

$$-6x^2 + 18x - 12 = 0$$

or

$$-6(x^2 - 3x + 2) = 0$$

or

$$-6(x - 2)(x - 1) = 0$$

Therefore, the stationary points of f are $x = 1$ and $x = 2$.
   To obtain the second order derivative, we simply differentiate $f'(x)$ using the same rules of differentiation; hence we have

$$\frac{d^2y}{dx^2} = f''(x) = -12x + 18$$

It can be seen that when $x = 1$, $d^2y/dx^2 = +6 > 0$ and thus the graph of $f'(x)$ cuts the x-axis at $x = 1$ from below, i.e. $f'(x)$ changes from negative to positive as x increases through $x = 1$. Hence, the graph of f must be turning up at $x = 1$ and this point must be a local minimum. In a similar fashion, given that $d^2y/dx^2 = -6 < 0$ at $x = 2$, we can conclude the latter is a local maximum.

This function provides a good example of why we need to evaluate the function at stationary points before we can identify whether we have a global or local maximum and minimum. Evaluating the function at $x = 1$ and $x = 2$ we obtain

$$f(x) = -2 + 9 - 12 - 6 = -11$$

and

$$f(x) = -16 + 36 - 24 - 6 = -10$$

respectively. Although $x = 1$ is a local minimum if we evaluate the function at $x = 10$, we obtain

$$f(x) = -2000 + 900 - 120 - 6 = -984$$

therefore $x = 1$ is not a global minimum. Similarly evaluating the function at $x = -10$ we obtain

$$f(x) = 2000 + 900 - 120 - 6 = 2,784$$

therefore $x = 2$ is not a global maximum.

In this particular case we cannot identify the global maximum or minimum because $f(x)$ is always decreasing for all $x > 3$ and increasing as x becomes a large negative number.

2 Functions of Several Variables

2.1 Stationary Points

Consider a firm with production function $f(\mathbf{x})$, which purchases inputs at prices $\mathbf{p}$ and can sell output at price p_0. Using inputs $\mathbf{x}$, the firm's revenue is $p_0 f(\mathbf{x})$, and the cost of purchasing $\mathbf{x}$ is $\mathbf{p}\,\mathbf{x}$, i.e. $p_1 x_1 + p_2 x_2 + \ldots + p_n x_n$. The firm's profits, π, are given by

$$\pi = p_0 f(\mathbf{x}) - \mathbf{p}\,\mathbf{x} \tag{5.2}$$

Which vector of inputs will maximise the firm's profits? Let us suppose $\mathbf{x}^*$ maximises (5.2). For this to be true the i'th partial function, defined holding $x_j = x_j^*$ $(j \neq i)$, must be at a maximum at $x_i = x_i^*$. The partial function is a function of one variable and the stationary point is defined as in Section 1, i.e. the derivative of the partial function must be zero. Therefore a necessary condition for $\mathbf{x}^*$ to maximise (5.2) is that the i'th partial derivative is zero, $\partial\pi/\partial x_i = 0$. A similar argument holds for each variable; therefore a necessary condition for $\mathbf{x}^*$ to maximise (5.2) is $\partial\pi/\partial x_i^* = 0$ for all i:

$$\frac{\partial\pi}{\partial x_i} = p_0 f_i'(\mathbf{x}) - p_i = 0$$

Therefore the necessary condition can be stated as

$$p_0 f_i'(\mathbf{x}) = p_i \qquad \text{for all } i \tag{5.3}$$

$f_i'(\mathbf{x})$ is the marginal (physical) product of the i'th input and $p_0 f_i'(\mathbf{x})$ is the marginal revenue product. Condition (5.3) translates into the well known statement that a necessary condition for profits to be maximised is for the marginal revenue product of each input to equal its price.

Let us now state this more formally. We define a function $y = f(\mathbf{x})$ as stationary in the following way.

Definition 5.4: A function $y = f(\mathbf{x})$ is stationary at $\mathbf{x}^*$ if each partial function is stationary at $\mathbf{x}^*$, i.e. $f(\mathbf{x}^*)$ is stationary if $\partial f/\partial x_i = 0$ for all i.

If we draw the graphs of the partial functions (e.g. Figure 5.4) then they look almost identical to Figure 5.2. Thus we can use the argument for single variable functions to show that a necessary condition for the partial function to have an interior maximum or minimum is for the partial derivative to be zero (i.e. it must be stationary). Obviously $f(\mathbf{x})$ cannot be at a maximum (minimum) point if the partial functions are not at maximum (minimum) points, therefore we have the following result.

Theorem 5.2
A necessary condition for a point $\mathbf{x}^*$ to be a local unconstrained maximum or minimum of $f(\mathbf{x})$ is that $f(\mathbf{x})$ is stationary at x^*, i.e. $f_i'(\mathbf{x}^*) = 0$ for all i.

Again, as in the single variable case, identifying optima reduces to solving equations. However, if $\mathbf{x}$ is an n-dimensional vector we must now solve n simultaneous equations to find $\mathbf{x}$. Although, in principle, this can always be done, in practice it can prove difficult (see the following section).

Example 5.2
Consider a competitive firm using capital, k, and labour, l, with production function $y = l^{1/2} + k^{1/2}$. If labour costs w per unit and capital r per unit, profits are

$$\pi = p(l^{1/2} + k^{1/2}) - wl - rk$$

We have

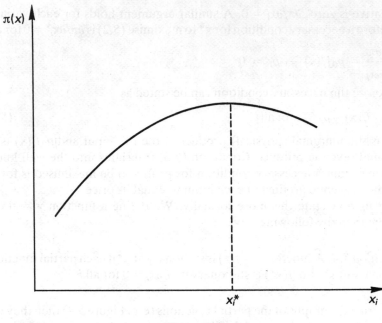

Figure 5.4

$$\frac{\partial \pi}{\partial l} = \frac{1}{2}pl^{-1/2} - w$$

and

$$\frac{\partial \pi}{\partial k} = \frac{1}{2}pk^{-1/2} - r$$

Setting these equal to zero and solving we obtain

$$l = \left(\frac{p}{2w}\right)^2$$

and

$$k = \left(\frac{p}{2r}\right)^2$$

2.2 Identifying Optima

While the extension to functions of several variables of the first order condition for optimality (i.e. stationarity) is straightforward, this is not the case when we consider second order conditions. The reason for this difficulty is that the partial functions and their derivatives are not adequate. The reason is that they do not adequately illustrate what might happen if we simultaneously change two or more of the variables. Discussion of this problem is left to Chapter 7 and the Appendix. However, we can note one feature that arises from the extension of our partial analysis to second order derivatives, namely if the graph of the i'th partial function turns up (down) at $\mathbf{x}$, i.e. the second order partial derivative with respect to x_i is positive (negative), then x *cannot* be a maximum (minimum). Hence a necessary condition for $\mathbf{x}^*$ to be a maximum (minimum) is that all second order partial derivatives with respect to each variable must be non-positive (non-negative). Note here, we are referring to the second order partials, $\partial^2 y/\partial x_i^2 = f''_{ii}(x)$, involving the twice partial differentiation with respect to x_i. It does *not* include the cross partials of the form $\partial^2 y/(\partial x_i \partial x_j)$ where $i \neq j$. Hence we can conclude a necessary condition for x^* to be a maximum (minimum) is $f''_{ii}(x^*) \leq 0$ (≥ 0) for all i.

Example 5.3

Suppose a firm's profit level is given by

$$\pi = p(l^\alpha + k^\beta) - wl - rk, \qquad \alpha > 1, \beta < 1$$

where p is price (fixed), l is labour and k capital. If we equate the marginal revenue product of capital and labour to the rate of interest and the wage respectively do we maximise profit?

$$\frac{\partial \pi}{\partial l} = p\alpha l^{\alpha-1} - w = 0$$

and

$$\frac{\partial \pi}{\partial k} = p\beta k^{\beta-1} - r = 0$$

are the first order conditions for a maximum or a minimum. These conditions imply the marginal revenue product of capital equals the rate of interest and the marginal revenue product of labour equals the wage rate. However,

$$\frac{\partial^2 \pi}{\partial l^2} = p\alpha(\alpha - 1)l^{\alpha-2}$$

which is positive for $\alpha > 1$ and

$$\frac{\partial^2 \pi}{\partial k^2} = p\beta(\beta - 1)k^{\beta-2}$$

which is negative for $\beta < 1$. Therefore we do not maximise profit nor minimise profit by setting the marginal revenue product of capital and labour equal to the rate of interest and the wage rate respectively.

3 Non-linear Simultaneous Equations

The underlying theme of this text is the use of unconstrained and constrained optimisation techniques to analyse economic decision making. The traditional method requires the solution to a set of non-linear simultaneous equations (Example 5.4 is a simple example). Although we place a great deal of emphasis on non-traditional approaches in this text, we still consider traditional methods and a student will have to come to terms with non-linear equations, to some extent, to follow the literature. Unfortunately there is no simple universal method for finding solutions in the non-linear case and each case will have to be tackled individually. Here we shall illustrate one aspect of the traditional technique that we shall meet later, the elimination of the so-called Lagrange multiplier, λ (one unknown amongst several in a series of non-linear equations).

Example 5.4
Consider the equations:

$$x_2^2 = 3\lambda \qquad (5.4)$$

$$2x_1x_2 = 4\lambda \qquad (5.5)$$

$$3x_1 + 4x_2 = 15 \qquad (5.6)$$

Here we have three equations in the three unknowns x_1, x_2 and λ, the latter being the Lagrangian multiplier. To eliminate λ from the first two equations we *divide* equation (5.4) by equation (5.5), that is to say we divide the LHS of (5.4) by the LHS of (5.5) and the RHS of (5.4) by the RHS of (5.5). Given the equations (5.4) and (5.6) these two ratios must be equal, hence we obtain

$$\frac{x_2^2}{2x_1x_2} = \frac{3\lambda}{4\lambda} \qquad (5.7)$$

Cancelling the x_2's on the LHS and the λ's on the RHS of (5.7) we obtain

$$\frac{x_2}{2x_1} = \frac{3}{4}$$

or

$$x_2 = \frac{3}{4} 2x_1 = \frac{3}{2} x_1 \qquad (5.8)$$

We now substitute (5.8) into (5.6) to obtain

$$3x_1 + 4\frac{3}{2}x_1 - 15$$

therefore

$$9x_1 = 15 \qquad (5.9)$$

or

$$x_1 = \frac{5}{3}$$

From (5.8) and (5.9) we now obtain

$$x_2 = \frac{5}{2} \qquad (5.10)$$

while from (5.4) (or (5.5)) we obtain

$$\lambda = \frac{1}{3}\left(\frac{5}{2}\right)^2 = \frac{25}{12} \qquad (5.11)$$

To obtain the above solution we divided (5.4) by (5.5). This cannot be done if x_1, x_2 or λ are zero. They cannot all be zero but λ and x_2 can, which gives $x_1 = 5$ (from (5.6)). Checking $x_1 = 5$, $x_2 = \lambda = 0$ with (5.4) and (5.5) we see this is also a solution.

Most of the examples we shall use in this text are very similar to this problem (but usually with a unique solution) simply because it is difficult to generate examples which comply with our basic assumptions of economic theory and yet are relatively simple to solve. To illustrate the problems that can arise, consider the following example which could easily be generated by an optimisation problem.

Example 5.5

$$\frac{1}{2}x_1^{-1/2} = \lambda \qquad (5.12)$$

$$\frac{1}{3}x_2^{-2/3} = 2\lambda \qquad (5.13)$$

$$x_1 + 2x_2 = 5 \qquad (5.14)$$

Eliminating λ gives

$$\frac{1}{3}x_2^{-2/3} = x_1^{-1/2}$$

or

$$x_2 = 3^{-3/2} x_1^{3/4} \qquad (5.15)$$

Substituting this into (5.14) gives

$$x_1 + \frac{2}{3^{3/2}} x_1^{3/4} = 5 \qquad (5.16)$$

which is not readily solved. We might try putting $x_1 = r^4$ for some r to give $x_1^{3/4} = r^3$ then (5.16) would become an equation in r, namely

$$r^4 + \frac{2}{3^{3/2}} r^3 = 5 \qquad (5.17)$$

As we said in Chapter 1 there are no simple procedures for solving equations of this form.

The difficulties encountered when solving a set of non-linear simultaneous equations have been a major impediment, particularly for applied economic modelling. Increasingly the profession has turned to other techniques which attempt to side-step these problems. These techniques use the concepts of dual analysis and form the largest proportion of our discussion of constrained optimisation techniques.

4   Tangents and Tangent Functions

4.1 Tangents

In our discussion of derivatives we pointed out that geometrically the derivative of a function gives the slope of that function, defined as the slope of the tangent to the function. This was useful as an introduction to a derivative because the concept of a tangent is familiar. However, in a formal analysis of tangents we do not use the tangent to define the derivative but use the derivative to define the tangent! Given a function $y = f(x)$ we can find the derivative and the gradient at any point, e.g. the gradient at $\bar{x}$ is $f'(\bar{x})$. The tangent to the graph at $\bar{x}$ is that *straight line* which meets the graph at $x = \bar{x}$ and which has a gradient equal to $f'(\bar{x})$ (see Figure 5.5).

4.2 Tangent Functions

A tangent is a straight line and can be viewed as the graph of a linear function. We call this the tangent function and denote it by $t(x)$. Because the tangent function is linear it can be written in the form

$$t(x) = m\,x + c \qquad (5.18)$$

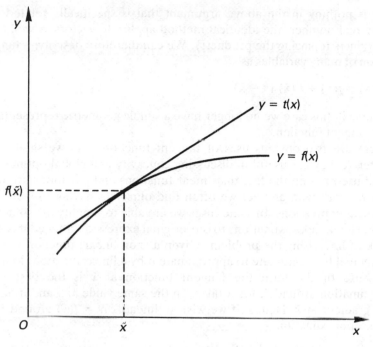

Figure 5.5

for some m and c. The tangent function has a derivative of m. Hence if this tangent function is tangential to $y - f(x)$ at $\tilde{x}$ we must have $m = f'(\tilde{x})$, i.e.

$$t(x) = f'(\tilde{x})x + c \qquad (5.19)$$

We also know that the graphs of $f(x)$ and $t(x)$ meet at $\tilde{x}$, i.e. the value of $f(x)$ at $\tilde{x}$ must equal the value of t at $\tilde{x}$:

$$t(\tilde{x}) = f(\tilde{x})$$

or (substituting into (5.19) and putting $x = \tilde{x}$):

$$f(\tilde{x}) = f'(\tilde{x})\,\tilde{x} + c$$

therefore

$$c = f(\tilde{x}) - f'(\tilde{x})\,\tilde{x} \qquad (5.20)$$

Replacing c from (5.20) in (5.18) gives

$$t(x) = f'(x)\,x + f(\tilde{x}) - f'(\tilde{x})\,\tilde{x}$$

Rearranging this we obtain:

$$t(x) = f(\tilde{x}) + f'(\tilde{x})\,(x - \tilde{x})$$

There is nothing in the above argument that is specifically related to x being a real number; the identical method applies to vectors as well (with dot products replacing the products). We can therefore describe a tangent function of many variables as

$$t(\mathbf{x}) = f(\bar{\mathbf{x}}) + f'(\bar{\mathbf{x}}) \, (\mathbf{x} - \bar{\mathbf{x}})$$

Of course in this case we no longer have a simple geometric representation of the tangent function.

There are two obvious uses of tangent functions. As we shall see in Chapter 7, they are useful in discussing concavity and global optima. The second use rests on the fact that linear functions and equations are much easier to work with and yet we often find ourselves having to work with non-linear expressions. In some cases we are able to simplify life somewhat by using linear approximations to our original expression. Indeed it is usual to talk of linearising the problem. Given a (non-linear) function $y = f(x)$ we may feel it is legitimate to approximate it by a linear function. In a very real sense of the term the tangent function at $\bar{x}$ is the best linear approximation around $\bar{x}$, for it takes on the same value at $\bar{x}$ and it has the same gradient at $\bar{x}$. Hence, if we wish to linearise $y = f(x)$ around $\bar{x}$, we use the approximation

$$y = f(x) \simeq t(x) = f(\bar{x}) + f'(\bar{x}) \, (x - \bar{x})$$

Note that if $f'(\bar{x}) \neq 0$ then the error in this approximation is less (in absolute size) than $f'(x) \, (x - \bar{x})$ for x sufficiently near to $\bar{x}$. We ought to mention, but will not pursue the idea, that higher order approximations can be generated. Thus the corresponding quadratic approximation to $y = f(x)$ about $\bar{x}$ is

$$y = f(x) \simeq f(\bar{x}) + f'(\bar{x}) \, (x - \bar{x}) + \tfrac{1}{2} f''(\bar{x}) \, (x - \bar{x})^2$$

the error being less in absolute size than $\tfrac{1}{2} f''(x) \, (x - \bar{x})^2$ for x sufficiently close to $\bar{x}$. The linear and quadratic approximations are special cases of a result known as Taylor's Theorem, which is discussed in the Appendix.

Example 5.6

To show that the linear approximation is reasonable, we take an example of a linear function and show the approximation is exact. Consider then $y = f(x) = 3x + 2$ which we can try to approximate around $x = 1$ by its tangent function. At $x = 1$, $y = r$ and the derivative $dy/dx = f'(x) = 3$. Hence the tangent function at $x = 1$ is $t(x) = 5 + 3(x - 1) = 5 + 3x - 3 = 3x + 2$. As we might have expected the tangent function is identical to the original.

Example 5.7

Contrast this with a quadratic function $y = f(x) = x^2 - 4$ which we approximate around $x = 3$. When $x = 3$, $y = 5$ and $dy/dx - f'(x) = 2x - 6$, hence the tangent at $x = 3$ is $t(x) = 5 + 6(x - 3) = 5 + 6x - 18$, i.e. $t(x) = 6x - 13$. Compare the values of f and t at $x = 4$, which are 12 and 11 respectively.

We might anticipate that a quadratic approximation to $f(x)$ would be exact in the present case. When $x = 3$, $d^2y/dx^2 = f''(x) = 2$. Hence our quadratic approximation would be

$$y = 5 + 6(x - 3) + \tfrac{1}{2} 2 (x - 3)^2$$

$$= t + 6x - 18 + x^2 - 6x + 9$$

i.e.

$$y = x^2 - 4$$

confirming our anticipation.

Problems

5.1 Using Problem 3.6, conclude that the total revenue function has a stationary point if the elasticity of demand is -1.
Solution on p. 346.

5.2 Given a production function $f(k,l)$, show that the average product of labour function

$$AP_l = \frac{f(k,l)}{l}$$

has a stationary point when the average product of labour is equal to the marginal product of labour.
Solution on p. 320.

5.3 Given total cost $C(y)$ viewed as a function of output y, then the average total cost is given by

$$AC = \frac{C(y)}{y}$$

and marginal cost MC is equal to the derivative $C'(y)$ of $C(y)$. Show that AC has a stationary point when $AC = MC$.
Solution on p. 328.

5.4 Consider a firm whose demand price p for its output y is given by the conditional function

$$p = \begin{cases} 250 - y & \text{if } y \leqslant 50 \\ 400 - 4y & \text{if } y > 50 \end{cases}$$

Draw the demand curve for this firm and illustrate the respective marginal revenue curve (note p is not differentiable at $y = 50$). If the firm's total costs are given by

$$C(y) = \tfrac{1}{2}Y^2$$

find the profit-maximising level of output, i.e. that output which maximises

$$\prod = p(y)\, y - C(y)$$

(*Hint*: compare marginal revenues and costs at different outputs). Solution on p. 361.

5.5   Find the stationary point of the following functions of y_1 and y_2:

(i) $\prod = y_1(a - by_1) + (y_1 + y_2)[a - b(y_1 + y_2)]$
(ii) $\prod = y_1(a - by_1) + y_2(a - by_2)$

a and b being constants.
Now reconsider the function in (i) when y_2 is viewed as a function of y_1, namely

$$y_2 = \frac{a - by_1}{2b}$$

Hence considering $\prod$ as a function of y_1 alone find its stationary point.
Solution on p. 351.

 5.6   Consider two firms producing quantities q_1, q_2 of homogenous outputs, i.e. their outputs are perfect substitutes, such that the demand price for their total output $q = q_1 + q_2$ is given by

$$p = a - bq$$

a,b being constants. Both firms have common total cost functions of the form

$$c(q_i) = \phi q_i; \quad i = 1,2$$

where $\phi > 0$ is a constant. Find the level of output q_1 which maximises the profit of firm 1 *given* the output q_2 of the second firm. (You may assume this q_1 is the stationary point of profits viewed as a function of q_1 alone.) In this way we obtain firm 1's profit-maximising output as a

function of firm 2's output, this being known as firm 1's reaction function. In a similar manner you can find firm 2's reaction function. Finally viewing these two functions as a pair of simultaneous equations in y_1 and y_2, find the solution to these equations, i.e. find the pair of outputs that lie on both reaction functions. This pair is known as the Cournot–Nash equilibrium.
Solution on p. 355.

5.7 Reconsider the situation in problem 5.6 but now consider the situation where firm 1 chooses its output q_1 and then firm 2 chooses q_2. As firm 2 knows q_1 he will choose q_2 according to its reaction function obtained in 5.6. But firm 1, in choosing q_1, will know what q_2 will be for every q_1 and will choose q_1 so as to maximise its profits viewed as a function of q_1, remembering q_2 is also a function of q_1. Find this profit-maximising output q_1 and corresponding value of q_2. This is known as the Stackelberg equilibrium with firm 1 as leader and firm 2 as follower.
Solution on p. 360.

5.8 A consumer in allocating income m_0 across two periods saves a proportion s_0 in period zero, that is to say he consumes $(1 - s_0)m_0$ in the initial period and $s_0 m_0$ in the next period. His total utility from this allocation is given by

$$u[(1 - s_0)m_0] + u(s_0 m_0)$$

where u is such that its second order derivative $u''(x)$ is negative everywhere. It follows that the derivative function $u'(x)$ is strictly monotonically decreasing in x. Conclude that the consumer optimal choice of s_0 is $\frac{1}{2}$.
Solution on p. 301.

5.9 Given two firms producing a homogenous product collude and choose their outputs so as to maximise the sum of their profits, show that their marginal costs will be equal.
Solution on p. 362.

5.10 Consider a monopolist supplying two distinct markets with the same good. Show that the profit-maximising combination of sales to each market will be such that the marginal revenues from both markets are equal to each other. Conclude that prices will tend to be higher in the market with the higher elasticity of demand. Solution on p. 350.

Exercises

5.1 Find the local (and global if possible) maximum and/or minimum of:

(a) $y = x^2(x + 1)$

(b) $y = x^2 - 2$

(c) $\dfrac{3x}{(x - 1)(x - 4)}$

5.2 A competitive firm has average cost

$$AC = 2Q + 3 + F/Q$$

(F = fixed costs) and faces a price of £2,003. How many units will the firm produce and does the firm make losses or gains if fixed costs are (a) £1 million, (b) £250,000? At what level must fixed costs be for the firm to be in long-run equilibrium? What can be said about AC at this output? If price falls to £1,003 what is optimal output? If price falls to 103 what is optimal output? Draw diagrams to illustrate.

5.3 Most economic optimisation problems will have at least one solution and thus we rarely have to worry about inconsistency, but we may face problems of indeterminacy, i.e. an infinite number of solutions. For example, profit maximisation for a firm producing under constant returns to scale may produce the following equations in the unknown inputs x_1, x_2 and output q:

$$\tfrac{1}{2}x_1^{-1/2} x_2^{1/2} = 1 \qquad (1)$$

$$\tfrac{1}{2}x_1^{1/2} x_2^{-1/2} = 2 \qquad (2)$$

$$x_1^{1/2} x_2^{1/2} = q \qquad (3)$$

Confirm that (1) and (2) imply $x_2 = \tfrac{1}{2}x_1$, and thus (3) implies $x_1 = \sqrt{2q}$, which in turn gives $x_2 = q/\sqrt{2}$.

5.4 (i) Find the function whose graph is tangential to the logarithmic function at $x = 1$.

(ii) Find the tangent function to $y = e^x$ at $x = 0$.

Note it can be shown that for all x, $\ln(x) \leqslant x - 1$, hence conclude the tangent at $x = 1$ lies everywhere above the graph of $y = \ln(x)$. Equally it can be shown that $e^x > 1 + x$ for all x, hence conclude the tangent at $x = 0$ lies everywhere below the graph of $y = e^x$.

5.5 Consider the function $y = f(x) = -x^2$. Show that the tangent function $f(x)$ at $\bar{x}$ is given by

$$t(x) = \bar{x}^2 - 2\bar{x} x$$

Hence conclude

$$t(x) - f(x) = (\bar{x} - x)^2 \geqslant 0$$

and thus the tangent lies everywhere above the graph.

6

Difference and Differential Equations

1 Introduction

The previous chapters have assumed that the consumer or producer can instantaneously achieve the optimal consumption or production point given the constraints he faces. However, in many cases, a consumer or firm facing a new economic environment is unlikely to come to equilibrium instantaneously; that is to say it is likely that the actions of the consumer or firm would undergo systematic adjustment to the new environment. For example, imagine a firm which experiences a significant shift in the relative prices of its inputs and outputs. Even if the prices remain constant at their new relative levels, we would expect the firm's pattern of production to change systematically for some time after the price change. We would not normally expect the firm instantaneously to reorganise its plant, material supplies and employment of labour; rather we would expect it to run up against constraints on the speed at which it can adjust the productive activities to their new equilibrium levels. Such adjustments imply that we would observe changes in agents' actions which are not caused by a contemporaneous change in the environment. Therefore, in modelling such adjustments it is useful to proceed as if the agent's environment is fixed; thus the associated equilibrium actions can be treated as fixed.

In this chapter we consider various simple models where there is some delay in the response of supply or demand, solving for an equilibrium if it exists and analysing whether or not the system eventually reaches an equilibrium level. We require different, but closely related, techniques depending on whether time is discrete or continuous. Time is a discrete variable if it is restricted to take integer values 0, ±1, ±2, etc., while it is a

continuous variable if it is allowed to take any real value. Difference
equations are used to analyse discrete time models and differential
equations are used in continuous time models. Although we concentrate on
the concept of time to introduce those concepts, their use is not restricted to
intertemporal economics; there are many models which are not intertemporal but where difference or differential equations are useful tools (see, for
example, the last section of Chapter 14).

2   Difference Equations

2.1 Introduction

Let us begin with a partial adjustment model of production where the
change in the quantity produced between two periods is proportional to the
difference between the desired or equilibrium quantity and the actual
quantity produced in the first period. Denoting the quantity produced in
period t by Q_t and the desired or equilibrium quantity by Q^*, the partial
adjustment model takes the following form:

$$\Delta Q_t \equiv Q_t - Q_{t-1} = \alpha(Q^* - Q_{t-1}) \tag{6.1}$$

On the left-hand side of this equation we have the change in actual output
ΔQ_t or $Q_t - Q_{t-1}$; thus (6.1) says that the change in Q_t is α times the
difference $Q_{t-1}^* - Q_{t-1}$ between equilibrium and actual quantities
in period $t - 1$. It should be stressed that (6.1) does not in itself determine
output Q_t in the sense that output at time t is conditional on the output level
in the previous period. However, if we know the value of output at any given
time period, say we know Q_0 where $t = 0$, then we can, in principle, calculate
the value of all subsequent values of Q_t. Thus it is the combination of an
initial value of Q_t together with (6.1) that determines the values of all the Q_t.
This relationship between initial and subsequent values of variables
governed by dynamic equations such as (6.1) is one of the ideas to be
developed in this chapter.

Taking Q_{t-1} to the right-hand side of (6.1), and expanding out the
bracket on the right-hand side we obtain

$$Q_t = Q_{t-1} + \alpha Q^* - \alpha Q_{t-1} \tag{6.2}$$

Hence

$$Q_t = (1 - \alpha)Q_{t-1} + \alpha Q^* \tag{6.3}$$

We have written the difference equation (6.1) such that we can view the
current value Q_t as being a linear function of its value in the preceding

period. It is common to refer to Q_{t-1} in equations such as (6.3) as the _lagged_ value of Q_t. This draws out explicitly the relationship between current and past values of the variable, suggesting the following definition.

Definition 6.1: A general difference equation in a variable y specifies the value of y at period t as a function of preceding or lagged values of y, i.e.

$$y_t = f(y_{t-1},...,y_{t-n})$$

A difference equation is said to be of the n'th order if y_t depends upon lagged values up to and including y_{t-n} but not on lagged values preceding y_{t-n}. A difference equation is said to be _linear_ if y_t is a linear function of its lagged values, while it is linear with constant coefficients if we have

$$y_t = \beta_0 + \beta_1 y_{t-1} + ... + \beta_n y_{t-n}$$

where β_i, $i = 0,1,...,n$, are constants, i.e. they do _not_ vary as t varies.

In this chapter we concentrate on first order linear difference equations with constant coefficients, i.e. we shall be interested in difference equations of the form

$$y_t = \beta_0 + \beta_1 y_{t-1} \tag{6.4}$$

and, in the Appendix, $y_t = \beta_0 + \beta_1 y_{t-1} + \beta_2 y_{t-2}$

We can see that the form of the partial adjustment model in (6.3) is an example of the first order equation in (6.4) with Q_t replacing y_t, $(1 - \alpha)$ replacing β_1 and αQ^* replacing β_0.

If the intercept term, i.e. β_0, is zero in (6.4) we say the equation is _homogenous_, otherwise it is _non-homogenous_. The example (6.3) is generally non-homogenous because we normally have a non-zero equilibrium value Q^*.

2.2 A Geometric Approach to First Order Equations

Viewing difference equations as functions mapping lagged values onto current values of a variable, we can consider the graph of this function. In the case of a first order equation we have a function of only one variable, thus we can draw two-dimensional diagrams with the current value measured on the vertical axis and the lagged value measured along the horizontal axis. The unbroken line in Figure 6.1 illustrates the graph of the partial adjustment model (6.3), which has an intercept with the vertical axis at αQ^*. In this figure we have also drawn a broken line through the origin at an angle of 45° to the axes, this line indicating those points where $Q_t =$

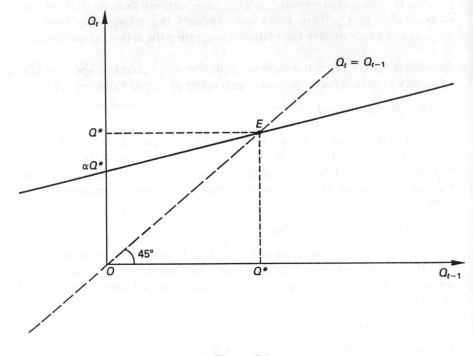

Figure 6.1

Q_{t-1}. The point E where the graph of the difference equation crosses this 45° line represents the equilibrium of the difference equation, in the sense that at this point Q is unchanging. In the case of (6.3) this equilibrium occurs when $Q = Q^*$, confirming the interpretation of Q^* as the equilibrium value. This idea of equilibrium is developed in the next section.

Figure 6.2 illustrates how we can use such diagrams to investigate the development of a variable governed by a first order difference equation. Given an initial value Q_0 at $t = 0$ of the variable, we can readily identify Q_1, the value of Q at $t = 1$, by drawing the vertical line from Q_0 up to the graph at the point A, then reading Q_1 from the Q_t axis. To proceed further we plot this value Q_1 down onto the Q_{t-1} axis by using the 45° or $Q_t = Q_{t-1}$ line. Having done this we construct Q_2 from the point B on the graph and, proceeding iteratively in this manner, we illustrate the evolution of Q_t. In this case we can anticipate that Q converges onto equilibrium as t increases indefinitely. Note that in drawing Figure 6.2 we have made the slope of the graph of (6.3) less than one, i.e. we have assumed $(1 - \alpha)$ is positive and less than one. To emphasise the importance of this assumption, Figure 6.3 illustrates the case where $(1 - \alpha)$ is less than minus one, i.e. α is greater than

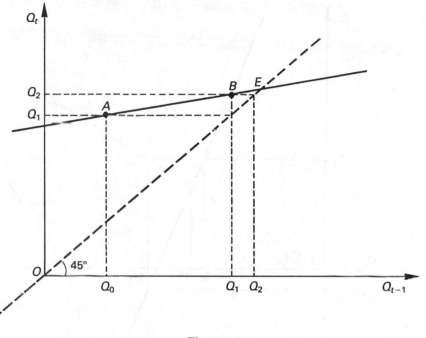

Figure 6.2

two. Using the same procedure to construct Q_1, Q_2, etc., we find that the situation is unstable; even with Q_0 quite close to equilibrium Q^*, we find Q_t diverging away from equilibrium. If we have the rather odd situation of α being negative, so that $1 - \alpha$ is greater than one, we also find Q_t diverging away from equilibrium. As we shall see, to ensure that Q_t converges onto an equilibrium we shall require $(1 - \alpha)$ to be greater than minus one and less than plus one, i.e. to be less than one in absolute size.

Clearly similar diagrams can be drawn for the more general difference equations (6.4) and a similar story will emerge. The only point to be stressed is that the equilibrium associated with (6.4) is where $y_t = y_{t-1}$, i.e. where y is not changing. As in Figures 6.2 and 6.3 this will occur where the graph of the difference equation cuts the 45° line. There is only one circumstance where this notion of equilibrium breaks down, namely where the graph also has a slope of one, i.e. cuts the axes at an angle of 45°. In this case the graph is parallel to the 45° line and thus either never cuts the 45°, as in Figure 6.4, or is coincidental with it, as in Figure 6.5. This suggests we shall have to treat the case where $\beta_1 = 1$ separately.

2.3 Non-homogenous First Order Equations

In the next section we shall see that the analysis of homogenous first order

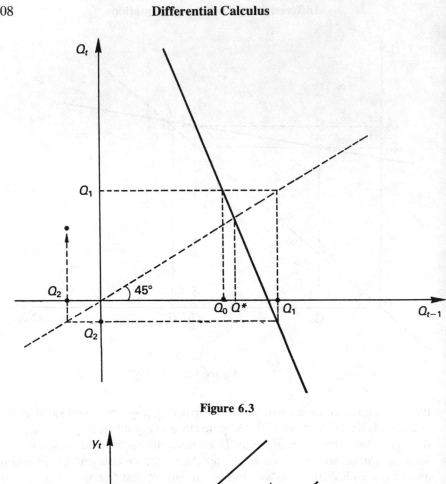

Figure 6.3

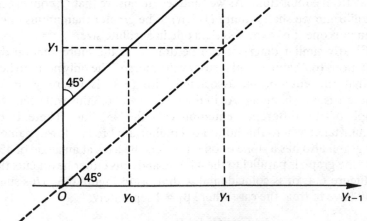

Figure 6.4 *No equilibrium*

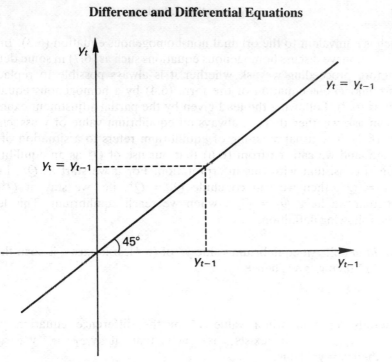

Figure 6.5 All Values are Equilibrium Values

difference equations is reasonably straightforward, but before that we show that we can nearly always replace a non-homogenous equation by an equivalent homogenous equation. Hence solutions of the latter will implicitly give us solutions of the former.

To proceed let us consider the partial adjustment model in (6.3) again. By subtracting Q^* from both sides of (6.3) we obtain

$$Q_t - Q^* = (1-\alpha)Q_{t-1} + \alpha Q^* - Q^* \qquad (6.5)$$
$$= (1-\alpha)Q_{t-1} - (1-\alpha)Q^*$$

hence

$$Q_t - Q^* = (1-\alpha)(Q_{t-1} - Q^*) \qquad (6.6)$$

We can now see that the deviation $Q - Q^*$ of Q from Q^* is reduced by a factor α every period. If we introduced a new variable $z_t = Q_t - Q^*$, so that z_t measures output as a deviation from its equilibrium value, then (6.6) becomes

$$z_t = (1-\alpha)z_{t-1} \qquad (6.7)$$

That is to say, by shifting to measuring our variables as deviations from equilibrium, we have been able to construct a homogenous equation (6.7) which is equivalent to the original non-homogenous equation (6.3). In the next section we discuss homogenous equations such as (6.7) in some detail.

Before proceeding we ask whether it is always possible to replace a non-homogenous equation of the form (6.4) by a homogenous equation such as (6.7). Following the lead given by the partial adjustment example we can ask whether there is always an equilibrium value of y associated with (6.4). The usual meaning of equilibrium refers to a situation of 'no change' and we can see from (6.6) that our use of Q^* as an equilibrium value is consistent with this interpretation. For if we start at Q^*, i.e. if $Q_{t-1} = Q^*$, then we can conclude $Q_t = Q^*$, i.e. we stay at Q^*; in particular we have $Q_t = Q_{t-1}$ when we reach equilibrium. This leads to the following definition.

Definition 6.2: An equilibrium value y^* of (6.4), if it exists, is such that if $y_{t-1} = y^*$ then $y_t = y^*$; hence

$$y^* = \beta_0 + \beta_1 y^*$$

Generally an equilibrium value y^* of the difference equation $y_t = f(y_{t-1},...,y_{t-n})$, if it exists, is such that if $y_{t-1} = y^*,...,y_{t-n} = y^*$ then $y_t = y^*$, hence

$$y^* = f(y^*,...,y^*)$$

We have been careful to qualify the definition with the phrase, 'if it exists', to ensure that the reader does not assume that equilibrium always exists. In the case of (6.3) we can say that *if* there is an equilibrium, then

$$y^* = \beta_0 + \beta_1 y^*$$

thus

$$(1 - \beta_1)y^* = \beta_0$$

Now if $\beta_1 \neq 1$ so that $1 - \beta_1 \neq 0$ then we can conclude

$$y^* = \frac{\beta_0}{1 - \beta_1} \tag{6.8}$$

but if $\beta_1 = 1$ so that $1 - \beta_1 = 0$ then if there is to be an equilibrium we require $\beta_0 = 0$. Hence if $\beta_1 = 1$ and β_0 is *not* zero, we must conclude there is no equilibrium. Note if $\beta_1 = 1$ and $\beta_0 = 0$ then the equation becomes $y_t = y_{t-1}$, as in Figure 6.5, and *all* values of y are equilibria!

Theorem 6.1

With reference to the first order equation (6.4) we have:
(i) if $\beta_1 \neq 1$ then there is a unique equilibrium value y^* of y given by (6.8);

(ii) if $\beta_1 = 1$ and $\beta_0 \neq 0$ then there is no equilibrium;
(iii) if $\beta_1 = 1$ and $\beta_0 = 0$ then all y are equilibria.

Proceeding towards a solution, i.e. identifying the relationship between initial and subsequent values, we remove the case $\beta_1 = 1$ first. If $\beta_1 = 1$ and $\beta_0 = 0$ so that $y_t = y_{t-1}$ then we can immediately conclude that $y_t = y_0$ for all t, i.e. the variable does not change regardless of its initial value. In the case $\beta_1 = 1$ and $\beta_0 \neq 0$ then $y_t = y_{t-1} + \beta_0$ so that y is increased by β_0 every period and we can immediately conclude $y_t = y_0 + \beta_0 t$ where y_0 is the initial value of y at $t = 0$. Solutions for these two cases are illustrated in Figures 6.6 and 6.7 respectively.

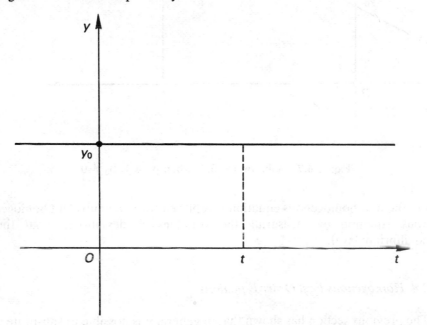

Figure 6.6   Solution to (6.4) when $\beta_1 = 1$, $\beta_0 = 0$

Let us now consider the case $\beta_1 \neq 1$ so that the equation (6.4) has an equilibrium y^* given by (6.8). Subtract y^* from both sides of (6.4) to obtain

$$y_t - y^* = \beta_0 + \beta_1 y_{t-1} - y^*$$
$$= \beta_0 - (1 - \beta_1)y^* + \beta_1 y_{t-1} - \beta_1 y^*$$

But $(1 - \beta_1)y^* = \beta_0$; hence

$$y_t - y^* = \beta_1(y_{t-1} - y^*) \tag{6.9}$$

Writing $z_t = y_t - y^*$, (6.9) can be written as

$$z_t = \beta_1 z_{t-1} \tag{6.10}$$

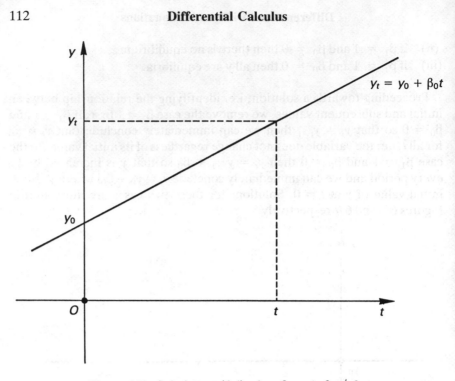

Figure 6.7   Solution to (6.4) when $\beta_1 = 1$, $\beta_0 \neq 0$

i.e. the non-homogenous equation is replaced with an equivalent homogenous equation by measuring the variables as deviations about the equilibrium level.

2.4 Homogenous First Order Equations

The previous section has shown that in general it is possible to substitute a homogenous (6.10) for a non-homogenous equation (6.4). We now solve (6.10), i.e. find an expression for z_t in terms of z_0, the initial value of z at $t = 0$.

Applying (6.10) for $t = 1,2,3$ we obtain

$$z_1 = \beta_1 z_0$$

$$z_2 = \beta_1 z_1 = \beta_1^2 z_0$$

$$z_3 = \beta_1 z_2 = \beta_1^3 z_0$$

These suggest that the general solution will take the form

$$z_t = \beta_1^t z_0 \qquad\qquad (6.11)$$

this being plausible because z is multiplied by β_1 each time period.

Theorem 6.2
The solution to (6.10) is given by (6.11).

While this result may seem relatively obvious, we can note that it can be formally proved by the *principle of induction.*

Let $P(n)$ be a proposition that depends on an integer n; for example it might be 'if z is governed by (6.10) then z_n is given by $\beta_1^n z_0$'. The principle of induction says that if $P(0)$ is true, and $P(k)$ implies $P(k + 1)$ then $P(n)$ is true for all n. We know that (6.11) is valid for $t = 0$; furthermore if (6.11) is true for $t = k$, then (6.10) tells us that

$$y_{k+1} = \beta_1 y_k = \beta_1 \beta_1^k y_0 = \beta_1^{k+1} y_0$$

i.e. (6.11) is true for $t = k + 1$; hence the principle of induction tells us that (6.11) is true for all t.

Theorem 6.3
If, in the difference equation

$$y_t = \beta_0 + \beta_1 y_{t-1}$$

we know $\beta_1 \neq 1$, then

$$y_t = y^* + \beta_1^t(y_0 - y^*) \tag{6.12}$$

where

$$y^* - \frac{\beta_0}{1 - \beta_1}$$

This proposition follows directly from Theorem 6.2 by substituting $z_t = y_t - y^*$ and $z_0 = y_0 - y^*$, with y^* given by (6.8).

In particular we are able to conclude that the partial adjustment model implies that

$$Q_t = Q^* + (1 - \alpha)^t(Q_0 - Q^*)$$

Having found the solution to the general first order difference equation in Theorem 6.3, we can immediately proceed to the following conclusion concerning stability of equilibria.

Theorem 6.4
If y is governed by the difference equation

$$y_t = \beta_0 + \beta_1 y_{t-1}$$

then if $-1 < \beta_1 < +1$, y_t converges onto y^* as t increases to infinity. Furthermore, if $\beta < -1$ or $\beta > +1$ then y_t diverges away from equilibrium.

Inspection of the solution (6.12) establishes this proposition, for if β_1 is less than one in absolute size, i.e. $-1 < \beta_1 < +1$ then β_1^t gets smaller and smaller and approaches zero as t tends to infinity. Conversely if β_1 is greater than one in absolute size, then β_1^t becomes larger and larger tending to infinity in absolute size as t tends to infinity. In particular we can conclude that the partial adjustment process is stable if $0 < \alpha < 2$.

3 Integration

3.1 Introduction

In expressing our partial adjustment model in continuous time we introduce a function q of the continuous time variable t, such that $q(t)$ tells us the *rate* of production at the instant t. (Section 4 below discusses this in more detail.) The partial adjustment model then specifies the derivative of this function as follows:

$$\frac{dq}{dt} = \gamma_1(q^* - q) \tag{6.13}$$

Given an initial value for q, say $q = q_0$ at $t = 0$, a solution of (6.13) is a function of time $q(t)$ such that it satisfies (6.13) for all t and $q(0) = q_0$.

We can see that the essential problem of finding the solution to (6.13) is that of finding the nature of a function, given that we start with its derivative function. While the rules of differentiation allow us to construct derivative functions, given the function, we now wish to reverse this process. The process that reverses differentiation is known as *integration*; thus we say that we need to integrate (6.13) to find its solution.

Definition 6.3: Given a function $f(x)$ of a continuous variable x, $F(x)$ is an *indefinite integral* of $f(x)$ if the derivative function $F'(x)$ of F is equal to $f(x)$, i.e.

$$F'(x) = f(x)$$

for all x.

To emphasise the relationship between $F(x)$ and $f(x)$ we usually use the following notation. If F is an indefinite integral of f, then we write

$$F(x) = \int f(x)dx$$

the symbol ∫ being an elongated S and the right-hand side being read simply as the 'indefinite integral of f with respect to x'.

Viewing integration as the reverse of differentiation suggests there are potentially numerous circumstances where we may be interested in integrating a function. For example, we might ask whether we can reconstruct a firm's total cost function $TC(q)$ given its marginal cost $MC(q)$ function. Given that we consider $MC(q)$ as the derivative of $TC(q)$, then we can view $TC(q)$ as an indefinite integral of $MC(q)$. The reader can reconsider all the usual 'marginal' concepts and interpret the corresponding 'total' concepts as indefinite integrals.

Before attempting to solve equations such as (6.13) we shall consider the more general idea of integration. To close this section, the use of the adjective 'indefinite' in the definition is explained. Let $F(x)$ be an indefinite integral of $f(x)$ so that the derivative of F is equal to f. Now consider a function $G(x)$ constructed by adding some constant, C say, onto $F(x)$, i.e. $G(x) = F(x) + C$. As the derivative of a constant is zero we can conclude that the derivative of G is equal to that of F and hence $G'(x) = f(x)$ and G is also an indefinite integral of $f(x)$. Hence there is a degree of 'indefiniteness' in the integral of a function in that we can always add on an arbitrary constant to any given indefinite integral. Indeed we can go further and say that if we have two indefinite integrals $F(x)$, $G(x)$ of a function $f(x)$, then the difference between them, $F(x) - G(x)$, is constant. To see this let us write $H(x) = F(x) - G(x)$ as that difference, so that $H'(x) = F'(x) - G'(x) = f(x) - f(x) = 0$, i.e. the difference $H(x)$ has a zero derivative for all x. This implies that H does not vary as x varies or equivalently that the graph of $H(x)$ is horizontal, i.e. the value of $H(x)$ is constant. In summary we can say that the indefinite integral is determined up to an arbitrary constant.

This indefiniteness is matched by equivalent considerations in economic examples. For example, given a firm's marginal cost function we may well expect to be able to 'integrate out' its total variable cost, TVC, but marginal cost tells us nothing about fixed costs, FC. As total costs TC = TVC + FC and we can see that integrating marginal costs leaves total cost indefinite in that it does not determine fixed costs.

3.2 A Geometric Interpretation of Integration

In this section it will be demonstrated that we can interpret the indefinite integral of a function as being the area under its graph. In Figure 6.8 we have drawn the graph of a function $f(x)$ and shaded the area under that graph to the left of the point A. When we refer to the 'area under the graph' we are, strictly speaking, referring to the area between the graph and the abscissa or horizontal axis. Hence the area to the left of the point B, where the graph

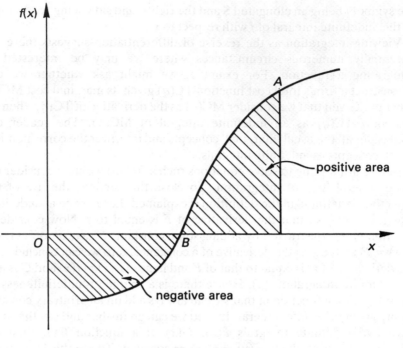

Figure 6.8

lies below the axis, lies above the graph. It is convenient to consider areas
lying below the axis, such as that to the left of B, as having a negative sign.

Given a function $f(x)$ we can introduce a function $A(x)$ defined informally
as follows:

$A(x) = $ total area 'under' the graph of f lying to the left of x.

Using Figure 6.9 we can argue that the derivative of $A(x)$ is equal to $f(x)$,
i.e. that $A'(x) = f(x)$ and thus $A(x)$ is an indefinite integral of $f(x)$. In this
figure we have considered a change Δx in the variable x and illustrated the
corresponding change ΔA in the area below the graph. Using the points as
marked

$\Delta A = $ area of $ABFE$

We can also see from the diagram that

area of $ACFE \leq \Delta A \leq$ area of $DBFE$

Yet $ACFE$ and $DBFE$ are rectangles; hence

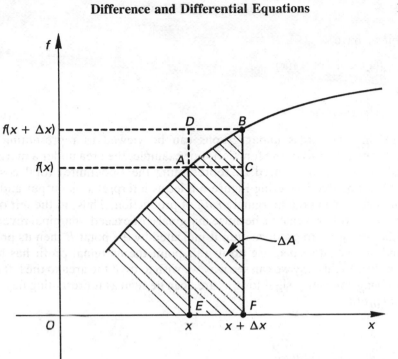

Figure 6.9

$$\text{area of } ACFE = \text{height} \times \text{width}$$
$$= AE \times EF$$
$$= f(x)\Delta x$$

and

$$\text{area of } DBFE = \text{height} \times \text{width}$$
$$= DE \times EF$$
$$= f(x + \Delta x)\Delta x$$

Hence we have the following inequalities

$$f(x)\Delta x \leqslant \Delta A \leqslant f(x + \Delta x)\Delta x$$

Dividing through by Δx, assumed to be positive, we obtain

$$f(x) \leqslant \frac{\Delta A}{\Delta x} \leqslant f(x + \Delta x)$$

Finally if we let Δx approach zero the middle term $\Delta A/\Delta x$ approaches $dA/dx = A'(x)$ while the right-hand term approaches $f(x)$; hence in the limit we have

$$f(x) \leqslant A'(x) \leqslant f(x)$$

i.e.

$$A'(x) = f(x) \tag{6.14}$$

In this way areas under graphs can be viewed as representing the indefinite integrals of the function. For example, the area under a marginal cost curve can be viewed as representing the (indefinite) total cost of production. Reconsidering Figure 6.8 let us interpret x as output and the function as being the marginal *profit* of production. Thus, to the left of B, marginal profit is negative because marginal cost exceeds marginal revenue. If the firm were to produce output indicated by the point B then its profits would be negative because up to this point the marginal profit has been negative. In this way we can see why we wish to treat the area to the left of B as having a negative sign, for this area can be seen as representing negative total profit.

3.3 Rules of Integration

To generate rules of integration we need simply to invert the rules of differentiation, remembering that we always need to include an arbitrary constant implicitly or explicitly onto our indefinite integrals. This constant, usually called the *constant of integration*, will be included explicitly in the following rules and invariably denoted by C.

Constant Rule: The indefinite integral of a constant valued function $f(x) = k$, where k is a constant, is $kx + C$, i.e.

$$\int k dx = kx + C \tag{6.15}$$

The term appearing with an integral, i.e. appearing between the symbols $\int$ and dx, is known as the *integrand*; thus the integrand in (6.15) is k. To confirm that the integral, i.e. the term on the right-hand side, is correct we can show that the derivative of the integral is equal to the integrand. In the case of (6.15) we can see that the integral $kx + C$ does have a derivative equal to the integrand k.

Alternatively we can use the geometric interpretation of an integral to generate (6.15). In Figure 6.10 we have drawn the graph of the constant function $f(x) = k$. The shaded area can be viewed as *an* integral of f; this being a rectangle, it has area equal to height × width, which is kx; hence the indefinite integral of f can be written as $kx + C$ as in (6.15).

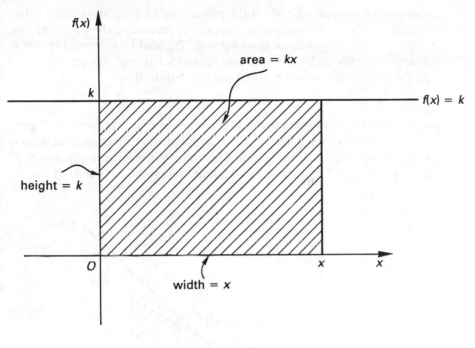

Figure 6.10

Yet a third way to confirm (6.15) is to note that if $F(x)$ is an indefinite integral of $f(x) = k$, then the graph of F will have a constant slope of k, i.e. it is a straight line of slope k, hence $F(x)$ must be a linear function with a coefficient of k on x.

Power and Reciprocal Rules: The indefinite integral of $f(x) = x^n$, where $n \neq -1$, is $1/(n + 1) x^{n+1} + C$, while the indefinite integral of $f(x) = x^{-1} = 1/x$ is $\ln (x)$.

$$\int x^n dx \;\; = \;\; \frac{1}{n + 1} \; x^{n+1} + C \;\; \text{if} \;\; n \neq -1 \tag{6.16(i)}$$

$$\int 1/x \; dx = \ln (x) + C \tag{6.16(ii)}$$

Again, to confirm these assertions we only need to confirm that the derivatives of the integrals are equal to the integrands. As regards (6.16) (i) the power rule of differentiation will confirm that $1/(n + 1) x^{n+1} + C$ has a derivative equal to the integrand x^n. Note that the integral in (6.16) (i) is *not* well defined for $n = -1$. The log rule of differentiation immediately confirms (6.16) (ii).

Apart from the case of $n = -1$ the power rule of integration tells us that the integral of a power function is obtained by increasing the power by one and then dividing by that increased power. It should be stressed that n is *not* restricted to be an integer, the rule applies for all real powers of x.

In the particular case where $n = 1$ the rule tells us that

$$\int x dx = \tfrac{1}{2}x^2 + C$$

and this can be established using the geometric interpretation. In Figure 6.11 we have drawn the graph of $f(x) = x$, the identity function, and shaded the triangular area under the graph. This triangle has an area equal to $\tfrac{1}{2} \times$ height $\times$ width $= \tfrac{1}{2}x^2$; hence an indefinite integral of x is indeed $\tfrac{1}{2}x^2 + C$.

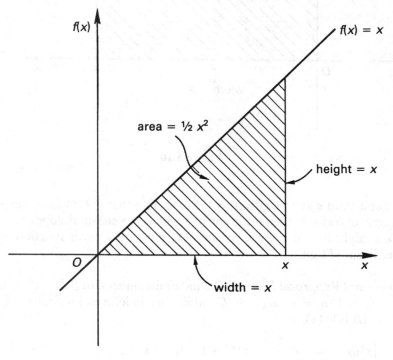

Figure 6.11

Note also that the power rule implicitly tells us that the integral of $x^0 = 1$ is x.

Exponential Rule: The integral of the exponential function e^x is the exponential function e^x, i.e.

$$\int e^x dx = e^x + C \tag{6.17}$$

This is readily confirmed by the exponential rule of differentiation.

Addition Rule: The integral of a sum of two functions is equal to the sum of their individual integrals.

$$\int [u(x) + v(x)]dx = \int u(x)dx + \int v(x)dx \tag{6.18}$$

Applying the addition rule of differentiation to the right-hand side of (6.18) shows that the derivative is equal to the sum of the derivatives of the two integrals. Yet the derivatives of the integrals are, by definition of an integral, equal to $u(x)$ and $v(x)$ respectively. Hence the right-hand side indeed has derivative $u(x) + v(x)$ which is equal to the integrand of the left-hand side.

Example 6.1

(a) $\int x + 3dx \quad = \int x dx + \int 3dx \qquad$ by addition rule

$\qquad = \frac{1}{2}x^2 + 3x + C \qquad$ by power rule

(b) $\int \frac{1}{x} + e^x dx = \int \frac{1}{x} dx + \int e^x dx \qquad$ by addition rule

$\qquad = \ln (x) + e^x + C \qquad$ by exponential and reciprocal rules

Multiplicative Constant Rule: If we multiply a function by a constant k then its indefinite integral is also multiplied by k.

$$\int kf(x)dx = k\int f(x)dx \tag{6.19}$$

By the definition of integrals both sides of (6.19) have derivatives equal to $kf(x)$ and hence they are both integrals of $kf(x)$ as required.

Example 6.2

$\int 3x^2 - 5x + 4dx = \int 3x^2 dx + \int -5x dx + \int 4dx \qquad$ by (6.18)

$\qquad = 3\int x^2 dx - 5\int x dx + 4\int 1 dx \qquad$ by (6.19)

$\qquad = x^3 - \frac{5}{2} x^2 + 4x + C \qquad$ by (6.16)

Integration by Parts: The counterpart of the product rule of differentiation is known as integration by parts and is usually written as follows:

$$\int u \frac{dv}{dx} dx = uv - \int \frac{du}{dx} v dx \tag{6.20}$$

Recalling that the product rule of differentiation says

$$\frac{d(uv)}{dx} = u \frac{dv}{dx} + \frac{du}{dx} v$$

we can conclude

$$u \frac{dv}{dx} = \frac{d(uv)}{dx} - \frac{du}{dx} v$$

If we now integrate both sides of this equation we obtain

$$\int u \frac{dv}{dx} dx = \int \left[\frac{d(uv)}{dx} - \frac{du}{dx} v \right] dx$$

$$= \int \frac{d(uv)}{dx} dx - \int \frac{du}{dx} v dx \quad \text{by addition rule}$$

$$= uv - \int \frac{du}{dx} v dx$$

This last step established (6.20) and follows because uv is clearly *an* integral of $d(uv)/dx$ by definition of an integral.

To illustrate the use of integration by parts we offer the following example.

Example 6.3

In $\int xe^x dx$ we write $u = x$ and $dv/dx = e^x$. It follows that $du/dx = 1$ and $v = \int dv/dx \ dx = \int e^x dx = e^x$. Hence, using (6.20) we have

$$\int xe^x dx = uv - \int \frac{du}{dx} v dx$$

$$= xe^x - \int 1 e^x dx$$

$$= xe^x - e^x + C$$

Integration by Substitution: The counterpart of the chain rule of differentiation is integration by substitution. If the integrand $f(x)$ can be written as a composite function of the form $g(u)(du/dx)$ where u is some function of x, then

$$\int f(x)dx = \int g(u) \frac{du}{dx} dx = \int g(u)du \tag{6.21}$$

To confirm (6.21), differentiate the right-hand side with respect to x (to carry this through we use the chain rule of differentiation). Hence the derivative of $\int g(u)du$ with respect to x is its derivative with respect to u times the derivative of u with respect to x. Hence

$$\frac{d}{dx} \int g(u)du = \frac{d}{du} \int g(u)du \frac{du}{dx} = g(u) \frac{du}{dx} = f(x)$$

as required.

Example 6.4

(a) $\int \dfrac{1}{x-a}\,dx$, a being a constant. Let $u = x - a$; then $\dfrac{du}{dx} = 1$, and the integrand can be written as $\dfrac{1}{u}\dfrac{du}{dx}$

Applying (6.21) with $f(x) = 1/(x - a)$ and $g(u) = 1/u$ we have

$$\int \frac{1}{x-a}\,dx = \int \frac{1}{u}\,du = \ln(u) + C$$

$$= \ln(x - a) + C$$

(b) $\int e^{\lambda x}dx$ where λ is a constant. Let $u = \lambda x$ then $\dfrac{du}{dx} = \lambda$ and we can

say $e^{\lambda x} = e^u \dfrac{1}{\lambda}\dfrac{du}{dx}$; thus applying (6.21) with $f(x) = e^{\lambda x}$,

$g(u) = \dfrac{1}{\lambda} e^u$ we have

$$\int e^{\lambda x}dx = \int \frac{1}{\lambda} e^u du = \frac{1}{\lambda} \int e^u du$$

$$= \frac{1}{\lambda} e^u + C$$

$$= \frac{1}{\lambda} e^{\lambda x} + C$$

4   First Order Differential Equations

4.1 *Introduction*

While relationships such as (6.1) which model the change in a variable from one period to the next are very common, particularly in applied work, it may be felt that the process of adjustment takes place continuously. Although the basic concept of adjustment remains the same, a proper appreciation of the shift from discrete to continuous time requires a careful interpretation of variables such as 'output' in continuous time. A non-economic analogy is useful here. Consider a car travelling between two towns. While we may ask how far it travels within any given time period, say one hour, we ask at what *speed* it is going at any one instant, say at twelve o'clock precisely. To say the car has a speed of 50 miles per hour means that if it maintains this speed for an hour it will travel a distance of 50 miles. Building on this analogy we may ask how much a firm produces within any given time period, say one year, while asking what is its *rate* of production at one instant. To say that a firm's rate of production is $q(t)$ per year at time t means that if this rate were maintained for a year it would produce a quantity $q(t)$. Hence the relationship between output within a period and the rate of production is matched by the relationship between distance travelled and speed of a car. Similarly if we view a firm continually adjusting its production, then we may view it as choosing rates of changes in the *rate* of production. Denoting by $q(t)$ the rate of production we can consider the firm chooses the rate of change of $q(t)$, i.e. dq/dt. Hence in continuous time the partial adjustment model of Section 2 may now be expressed as

$$\frac{dq}{dt} = \gamma[q^* - q(t)] \tag{6.22}$$

where q^* is the equilibrium rate of production. This can be rewritten in the form

$$\frac{dq}{dt} = -\gamma q + \gamma q^* \tag{6.23}$$

This equation draws out the fact that the partial adjustment model implicitly specifies the time derivative of q as a linear function of q.

Definition 6.4: A first order (autonomous) differential equation in a variable y specifies the derivative of y, with respect to the independent variable t, as a function of y.

$$\frac{dy}{dt} = f(y)$$

If this function f is linear in y the differential equation is linear, i.e.

$$\frac{dy}{dt} = \beta_0 + \beta_1 y \tag{6.24}$$

β_0, β_1 being constants. The equation is homogenous if $\beta_0 = 0$, otherwise it is non-homogenous.

Note a differential equation is non-autonomous if the function f depends upon time t; for example a non-autonomous linear equation could take the form

$$\frac{dy}{dt} = \beta_0(t) + \beta_1(t)y$$

where now β_0, β_1 are functions of time. We concentrate only on autonomous equations.

4.2 A Geometric Viewpoint

Given that a differential equation expresses dy/dt as a function of y, we can draw the graph of this function in the usual way, measuring y along the abscissa and dy/dt along the ordinate. Figures 6.12 and 6.13 illustrate two linear differential equations, with negative and positive slopes respectively. In both cases we have indicated the intercept y^* of the graph with the y-axis at which point dy/dt will be zero. Hence y^* will be the equilibrium value of y, i.e. once $y = y^*$ then y will not change. Furthermore we have indicated two points A,B on the graph corresponding to values of y less and greater than y^* respectively. At these points we have drawn arrows indicating in which direction y and dy/dt will change. For example, at point A in Figure 6.12, where the graph lies above the y-axis, we can conclude that at A dy/dt will be positive and thus y will increase, which in turn implies dy/dt will decrease. Similar arguments apply to B in Figure 6.12 and A,B in Figure 6.13. With these arrows we can see that in the case of Figure 6.12 the equilibrium y^* will be stable, in the sense that y always tends towards y^*. In contrast the equilibrium y^* in Figure 6.13 is unstable in the sense that y always tends away from y^*. Obviously, if a linear differential equation has an equilibrium then that equilibrium will be stable if the 'slope coefficient' is negative. The size of the coefficient is not important in contrast to the case of difference equations.

4.3 Non-homogenous Equations

As with difference equations we can in general convert a non-homogenous differential equation into an equivalent homogenous equation by measuring the variable as a deviation from equilibrium. To illustrate this idea we use the partial adjustment equation (6.22), where

$$\frac{dq}{dt} = \gamma(q^* - q)$$

Writing $z = q - q^*$ and noting that $dz/dt = dq/dt$ because q^* is a constant, we can conclude

$$\frac{dz}{dt} = -\gamma z \tag{6.25}$$

Definition 6.5: An equilibrium y^* of the first order differential equation $dy/dt = f(y)$ is such that $dy/dt = 0$ when $y = y^*$, hence

$$f(y^*) = 0$$

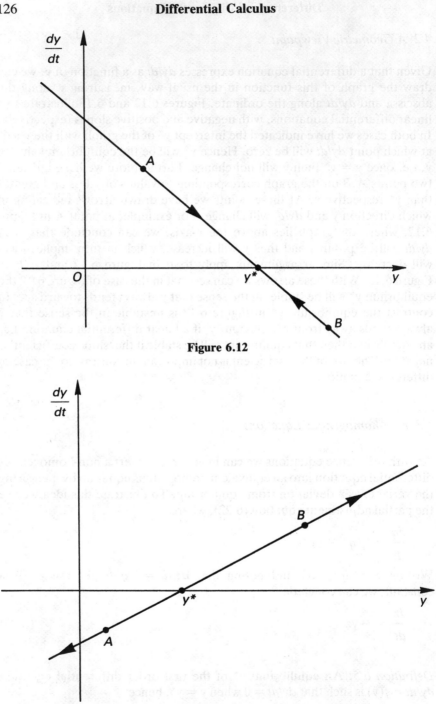

Figure 6.12

Figure 6.13

In the case of the linear equation $dy/dt = \beta_0 + \beta_1 y$ the equilibrium y^*, if it exists, will satisfy

$$\beta_0 + \beta_1 y^* = 0$$

Clearly if $\beta_1 \neq 0$ the equilibrium is given by

$$y^* = -\beta_0/\beta_1 \qquad (6.26)$$

If $\beta_1 = 0$ and $\beta_0 \neq 0$ then there is no equilibrium, while $\beta_1 = 0$ and $\beta_0 = 0$ imply all y are equilibria.

Let us now consider the linear differential equation (6.24) when $\beta_1 \neq 0$ which has an equilibrium y^* given by (6.26). Let us then define $z = y - y^*$ so that $dz/dt = dy/dt$ giving

$$\frac{dz}{dt} = \beta_0 + \beta_1 y$$

$$\frac{dz}{dt} = \beta_1\left(y + \frac{\beta_0}{\beta_1}\right) = \beta_1(y - y^*)$$

i.e.

$$\frac{dz}{dt} = \beta_1 z \qquad (6.27)$$

In this way the non homogenous (6.24) can be converted into the equivalent homogenous (6.27). We discuss the solutions of equations such as (6.27) in the next section but before we proceed we deal with the case where $\beta_1 = 0$, i.e.

$$\frac{dy}{dt} = \beta_0 \qquad (6.28)$$

Integrating both sides of (6.28) with respect to t gives

$$\int \frac{dy}{dt} \, dt = \int \beta_0 dt$$

and hence

$$y = \beta_0 t + C \qquad (6.29)$$

If we know $y = y_0$ when $t = 0$ we can also conclude $C = y_0$; hence

$$y = y_0 + \beta_0 t \qquad (6.30)$$

This solution can be illustrated by viewing y as a function of t and plotting the graph of this function, this being done in Figure 6.14 which can be compared with Figure 6.7.

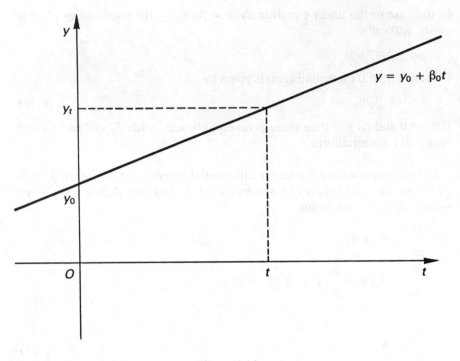

Figure 6.14

4.4 Homogeneous Equations

Having shown that non-homogeneous equations can usually be replaced by an equivalent homogeneous equation of the form (6.27) we now solve this homogeneous equation. The first step is to rewrite (6.27) as

$$\frac{1}{z}\frac{dz}{dt} = \beta_1$$

and integrate both sides with respect to t to yield

$$\int \frac{1}{z}\frac{dz}{dt}\ dt = \int \beta_1 dt \tag{6.31}$$

The right-hand side of (6.31) is readily obtained from the constant rule of integration, it being $\beta_1 t + C$. Furthermore we can apply the substitution rule, (6.21) to the left-hand side by replacing x by t, u by z and $g(z) = 1/z$ to yield

$$\int \frac{1}{z}\frac{dz}{dt}\ dt = \int \frac{1}{z}\ dz = +\beta_1 t + C$$

We now apply the reciprocal rule of integration (6.16) (ii) to the left-hand side to conclude

$$\ln (z) = +\beta_1 t + C \tag{6.32}$$

The reader can recall that the exponential function is the inverse of the natural log function; that is to say if we raise the Napier constant e to the power $\ln (z)$ we will obtain z. Hence

$$z = e^{\ln(z)} = e^{+\beta_1 t + C}$$

or

$$z = e^{+\beta_1 t} e^{C}$$

or

$$z = A e^{+\beta_1 t} \tag{6.33}$$

where $A = e^{C}$. Furthermore if we know $z = z_0$ at $t = 0$ then we can conclude $A = z_0$ giving the final solution to (6.27), namely

$$z = z_0 e^{+\beta_1 t} \tag{6.34}$$

This in turn implies that the solution to (6.24) is given by

$$y - y^* = (y_0 - y^*)e^{+\beta_1 t}$$

or

$$y = y^* + (y_0 - y^*)e^{+\beta_1 t} \tag{6.35}$$

where $y = y_0$ at $t = 0$. Equally the solution to the partial adjustment model can be written as

$$q - q^* = (q_0 - q^*)e^{-\gamma t}$$

or

$$q = q^* + (q - q^*)e^{-\gamma t} \tag{6.36}$$

Problems

6.1 The net present value, NPV, of a *constant* continuous stream of income flow y over a period $t = 0$ to $t = T$ is given by the following integral:

$$\text{NPV} = \int_0^T y e^{-rt} dt$$

where r is the rate of discount or rate of interest used for discounting. Evaluate this definite integral. (See Exercise 6.4 for definite integrals.)
Solution on p. 299.

6.2   The following differential equation appears in a wage setting problem presented in Chapter 14, Section 8. Here we view the wage w as a function of the level of academic achievement y. Given

$$\frac{dw}{dy} = \frac{1}{w}$$

find an expression for w in terms of y. You may assume $w = 0$ if $y = 0$.
(*Hint*: rewrite equation as $w(dw/dy) = 1$ and integrate with respect to y.)
Solution on p. 317.

Exercises

6.1   Find solutions for the following difference equations:

(i) $y_t = y_{t-1} - 1, y_0 = 5$
(ii) $y_t = 2y_{t-1}, y_0 = 1$
(iii) $y_t = 0.5y_{t-1}, y_0 = 1$
(iv) $y_t = -0.5y_{t-1} + 4, y_0 = 1$

Which of these equations have equilibria and which of the equilibria are stable?

6.2   Find expressions for the following indefinite integrals:

(i) $\int 2dx$

(ii) $\int \dfrac{x}{2}\, dx$

(iii) $\int \dfrac{x+1}{x^2}\, dx$ — note integrand $= \dfrac{1}{x} + \dfrac{1}{x^2}$

(iv) $\int e^{-x}dx$

(v) $\int xe^{-x^2}dx$ — note integrand $= -\frac{1}{2}e^u \dfrac{du}{dx}$ where $u = -x^2$

(vi) $\int \dfrac{1}{x-a}\, dx$ — note integrand $= \dfrac{1}{u}\dfrac{du}{dx}$ where $u = x - a$

6.3   Find the solution to the following differential equations:

(i) $\dfrac{dy}{dt} = 2; y = 1$ at $t = 0$

(ii) $\dfrac{dy}{dt} = 0.5(y - 1); y = 2$ at $t = 0$

(iii) $\dfrac{dy}{dt} = 2(y - 1); y = 2$ at $t = 0$

(iv) $\dfrac{dy}{dt} = -0.5y + 4; y = 1$ at $t = 0$

6.4   Given an indefinite integral $F(x)$ of a function $f(x)$, the *definite integral* of $f(x)$ from $x = a$ to $x = b$, which is denoted by $\int_a^b f(x)dx$, is equal to the quantity $F(b) - F(a)$, i.e.

$$\int_a^b f(x)dx = F(b) - F(a)$$

Note this quantity is independent of the indefinite integral used, i.e. the indefinite constant of integration cancels out.

Interpret definite integrals in terms of areas under graphs and find the definite integrals, as x runs from $x = 1$ to $x = 2$, corresponding to the indefinite integrals in Exercise 6.2.

7

Concave and Convex Functions

1 Introduction

We have seen that it is fairly easy to identify a point which may be a maximum or a minimum of a function. It is also clear that the process of finding whether the point is a maximum or a minimum, and then checking whether it is a global or a local maximum or minimum, and if it is unique, can be tedious. This problem also holds when we look for a constrained maximum and minimum, a process we have yet to consider. Fortunately there are classes of functions for which these problems disappear. For example, suppose we know that the function we are dealing with is a strictly concave function. Then, as we shall see in Section 2, if we have a point where the first derivatives are zero, then we do not need to check to see whether this point is a maximum or a minimum. Neither do we need to check whether the point is a global or local maximum or minimum. Finally we do not even need to check if the point is a unique global maximum or minimum. Simply by knowing that the function belongs to the class of strictly concave functions we know immediately that if a point has all the first derivatives zero then it must be the unique, global maximum point of the function. In this chapter we will concentrate on two classes of functions — concave and convex functions. The above example is one of the many properties of these functions we will consider.

When discussing a particular class of functions there are two immediate types of questions to consider. Firstly, what properties does this class of functions have? Secondly, how do we identify whether a specific function is in this class or not? In dealing with concave and convex functions the first question is the one to which we will give most consideration. There are two reasons for this. One is that it is relatively easy to consider the properties of these functions and one gains a great deal of insight by doing so. The second reason is that the typical approach in economic theory is to follow an argument through in a general class of cases rather than use a specific algebraic function. It is usual for authors to assume that the functions they use belong to a special class, e.g. an article or text will leave the exact form of the utility function unspecified throughout and simply identify a class (it will frequently be assumed that utility functions are strictly concave, for example). Consequently when reading economic texts one is rarely called upon to check that a particular function belongs to a certain class but will need to know the useful properties of concave and convex functions. This is important because the process of identifying that a specific function belongs to a certain class can be difficult and tedious. We do identify special cases in Sections 2 and 3, those which are most common, but leave the general discussion to the Appendix.

2   Concave Functions of a Single Variable

2.1 A Definition of Concave Functions

In Figure 7.1 we have drawn the graph of a function of one variable, $y = f(x)$. This particular function has the property that it bends downwards as x increases. Unfortunately this is not a very formal description of this property, and we will begin this section with a more formal description which is based on the fact that the 'chord' PQ lies below the graph. Consider the point R which lies on the line PQ exactly halfway between P and Q. The point R has a horizontal coordinate $(y + x)/2$ and a vertical coordinate $\frac{1}{2}f(y) + \frac{1}{2}f(x)$. Now consider the point S which has the same horizontal coordinate as R, i.e. $(y + x)/2$, but is the point where the vertical line above $(y + x)/2$ cuts the function. The vertical coordinate of S is $f[(y + x)/2]$ and the function has the property that the vertical coordinate of S is greater than the vertical coordinate of R, i.e.

$$f\left(\frac{y + x}{2}\right) > \frac{1}{2}f(y) + \frac{1}{2}f(x) \tag{7.1}$$

We can repeat this argument for any point along the line PQ and see that a similar inequality to (7.1) holds. Pick a point at random, e.g. T. This will have horizontal coordinate $z = \alpha x + (1 - \alpha)y$ and vertical coordinate $\alpha f(x) + (1 - \alpha)f(x)$ for some α between zero and one (point R is simply the special case of this where $\alpha = \frac{1}{2}$). If we compare T to the point U we see that U has

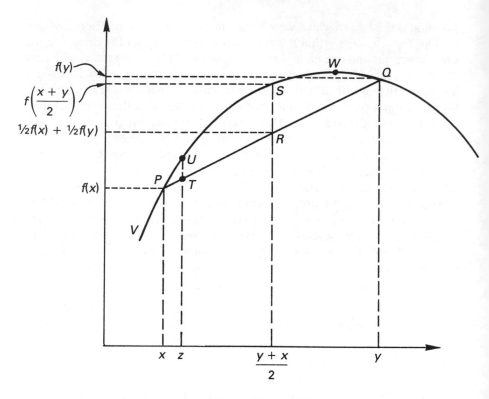

Figure 7.1

vertical coordinate $f(z)$ i.e. $f(\alpha x + (1 - \alpha)y)$ and that the vertical coordinate of U is greater than T, i.e.

$$f[\alpha x + (1 - \alpha)y] \geq \alpha f(x) + (1 - \alpha)f(y) \qquad (7.2)$$

The point T was picked at random and the argument given above holds for all such points. Since each point on the line PQ corresponds to an α between zero and one, this is the same as saying that inequality (7.2) holds for all α between zero and one. Furthermore there is nothing special about the initial two points P and Q which define x and y. If we had started with any other two points, e.g. V and W, the same inequality would hold, where x and y would now be the horizontal coordinates of V and W. Thus the fact that (7.2) holds for all α between zero and one and for all x and y in the domain of the function, is sufficient to guarantee that the function either 'bends down' or is a linear function. Functions that satisfy (7.2) for all $0 < \alpha < 1, x$ and y are called concave functions.

Definition 7.1: A function f is concave if for every pair, x,y, and every α

between zero and one we have

$$f[\alpha x + (1 - \alpha)y] \geqslant \alpha f(x) + (1 - \alpha)f(y)$$

We now have a formal definition of a concave function which does not require the function to be differentiable. However, if $f(x)$ is differentiable we can characterise concave functions in other ways.

2.2 An Alternative Characterisation when f(x) is Differentiable

In Figure 7.2 we have drawn a concave function f together with a tangent at the point P. Notice that the tangent to the point P lies everywhere above or on the graph. This is a general property of concave functions and serves as an alternative characterisation when the function is differentiable. Specifically a differentiable function is concave if and only if every tangent to its graph lies above or on that graph. Of course this property does not depend on differentiability but is particularly useful in this case. To produce a formal statement of this property remember that the tangent itself can be viewed as

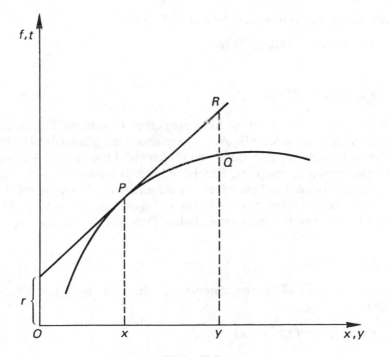

Figure 7.2

a function where the slope of the tangent is equal to the derivative of the function, $f(x)$, at the point of tangency. Hence the tangent function in Figure 7.2 is of the form

$$t(y) = r + f'(x)y \tag{7.3}$$

where $f'(x)$ is the derivative of $f(x)$ at x and r is the intercept of the tangent function. It is important to stress that in this context the tangent function is a function of y and $f'(x)$ is a constant. Consequently the derivative of $t(y)$ with respect to y is equal to $f'(x)$ for all y, i.e. the slope of the tangent function is equal to the slope of $f(x)$ at x. Also the value of $f(x)$ and $t(x)$ must be equal, i.e.

$$f(x) = t(x)$$

or, if we replace $t(y)$ from (7.3) and set $y = x$,

$$f(x) = r + f'(x)\, x$$

This gives

$$r = f(x) - f'(x)x$$

which we can use to substitute for r in (7.3) giving

$$t(y) = f(x) - f'(x)x + f'(x)y$$

or

$$t(y) = f(x) + f'(x)(y - x) \tag{7.4}$$

We can use (7.4) to describe the properties of concave functions. We have said the tangent must lie everywhere above the graph but to be totally correct we should say that a function is concave if the tangent does not lie below the graph at any point. Referring back to Figure 7.2, when we say the tangent does not lie below $f(x)$ at y we mean that R does not lie below Q. The vertical coordinate of R is $t(y)$ and the vertical coordinate of Q is $f(y)$ so the statement R does not lie below Q means $f(y)$ does not lie below $t(y)$, i.e.

$$f(y) \leqslant t(y)$$

Replacing $t(y)$ by (7.4), the statement R does not lie below Q can be written

$$f(y) \leqslant f(x) + f'(x)(y - x) \tag{7.5}$$

As P is an arbitrary point on $f(x)$ and R is an arbitrary point on the tangent, concavity requires that (7.5) holds for all x and y. Stating this formally:

Theorem 7.1

A differentiable function, $f(x)$, is concave if and only if for all x,y inequality (7.5) holds.

Our basic definition of a concave function is given in Definition 7.1. For Theorem 7.1 to follow from this, it must be the case that a function $f(x)$ satisfies (7.5) if and only if it satisfies Definition 7.1. To show this we need to show that if $f(x)$ is differentiable and satisfies Definition 7.1, it satisfies (7.5), and if $f(x)$ satisfies (7.5), it must satisfy Definition 7.1. We begin by showing that if $f(x)$ is differentiable and satisfies Definition 7.1 it must satisfy inequality (7.5). Beginning by replacing α in Definition 7.1 by $1 - \delta$ where δ is a small positive number, we obtain:

$$f[(1 - \delta)x + \delta y] \geqslant (1 - \delta)f(x) + \delta f(y)$$

We can rewrite this as

$$f[x + \delta(y - x)] \geqslant f(x) + \delta[f(y) - f(x)]$$

or

$$\delta[f(y) - f(x)] \leqslant f[x + \delta(y - x)] - f(x)$$

Dividing this by the positive δ we obtain

$$f(y) - f(x) \leqslant \frac{f[x + \delta(y - x)] - f(x)}{\delta} \tag{7.6}$$

As we have already seen in Chapter 4, as δ goes to zero (7.6) becomes (since the left-hand side of (7.6) is constant for all δ)

$$f(y) - f(x) \leqslant f'(x)(y - x) \tag{7.7}$$

which is equivalent to inequality (7.5).

We can now show that if $f(x)$ satisfies inequality (7.5) it must satisfy the inequality in Definition 7.1. Let us write $z = \alpha x + (1 - \alpha)y$ so that inequality in Definition 7.1 can be written

$$f(z) \geqslant \alpha f(x) + (1 - \alpha)f(y) \tag{7.8}$$

If $f(x)$ satisfies inequality (7.5) for all pairs, then the following two inequalities must be true:

$$f(x) \leqslant f(z) + f'(z)(x - z)$$
$$f(y) \leqslant f(z) + f'(z)(y - z)$$

If we multiply the first by α and the second by $(1 - \alpha)$ and add these together we obtain

$$\alpha f(x) + (1 - \alpha)f(y) \leqslant \alpha f(z) + (1 - \alpha)f(z) = f(z) \tag{7.9}$$

which is (7.8), the inequality in Definition 7.1, with z replacing αx

$+ (1 - \alpha)y$. Note that we obtain $\alpha f(z) + (1 - \alpha)f(z)$ in the middle of (7.9) because the other components on the right-hand side sum to zero, i.e.

$$\alpha(x - z) + (1 - \alpha)(y - z) = \alpha x - \alpha z + (1 - \alpha)y - (1 - \alpha)z$$
$$= \alpha x + (1 - \alpha)y - z$$
$$= z - z = 0$$

2.3 Concavity and the Maximisation of f(x)

In Chapter 5 we considered the stationarity conditions that allow us to identify maximum points of a function. These did not differentiate between global or local maxima and we needed to evaluate these points to identify global maxima. One of the attractions of concavity and one of the main reasons why we are studying concave functions, is that there is a basic relationship between concavity and the sufficiency of stationarity for a global maximum. This relationship is as follows:

Theorem 7.2
Given a differentiable concave function, $f(x)$, a necessary and sufficient condition for x^* to be a global maximum of $f(x)$ is $f'(x^*) = 0$, i.e. x^* is a stationary point of $f(x)$.

We already know that when $f(x)$ is differentiable we must have $f'(x^*) = 0$ if x^* is to be a local maximum, which a global maximum must obviously be. This was shown in Chapter 5. Therefore we need only to show here that $f'(x^*) = 0$ is sufficient for x^* to be a global maximum. That is we need to show that if $f(x^*) = 0$ and $f(x)$ is a differentiable concave function, then $f(x^*) \geq f(x)$ for all x. Applying inequality (7.5) to x^* and x we have

$$f(x) \leq f(x^*) + f'(x^*)(x - x^*)$$

which, since $f'(x^*) = 0$ implies

$$f(x) \leq f(x^*)$$

as required.

The attraction of concave functions should now be clear. If we know that a function is concave, then the identification of a global maximum is far easier than for a function that is not concave. If $f(x)$ is concave then we are sure we have a global maximum if we have a stationary point. We do not need to investigate whether this is a global or a local maximum, nor do we need to investigate whether it is a maximum or a minimum, since concavity implies it must be a maximum. It will obviously be helpful if there exist simple methods of identifying whether a function is concave and we now turn to this problem.

2.4 Identification of Concave Functions

Looking at the examples given in Figures 7.1 and 7.2, notice that both these functions have the property that the slopes of the functions did not increase as we move to the right. If we draw a graph of the derivative $f'(x)$ for these functions they will be like that in Figure 7.3, i.e. $f'(x)$ does not slope upwards. The slope of $f'(x)$ is given by the second derivative of $f(x)$, i.e. $f''(x)$. If $f'(x)$ does not slope upwards, then it must be true that $f''(x) \leqslant 0$, i.e. the slope of $f'(x)$ must either be negative or zero. Not only is this property true for the two concave functions drawn in Figures 7.1 and 7.2 but it is a necessary and sufficient condition for all twice differentiable concave functions, i.e.

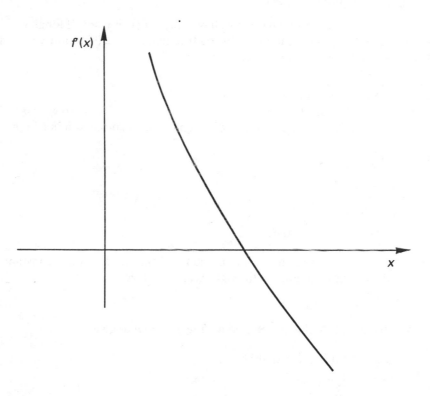

Figure 7.3

Theorem 7.3

A twice differentiable concave function of one variable is concave if and only if $f''(x) \leqslant 0$ for all x.

Let us show that if $f(x)$ is concave, then it must be true that $f''(x) \leqslant 0$. Consider any $y \geqslant x$. We know from (7.5) that the following two inequalities must be true:

$$f(x) \leqslant f(y) + f'(y)(x - y)$$

and

$$f(y) \leqslant f(x) + f'(x)(y - x)$$

Adding these together we obtain

$$f(x) + f(y) \leqslant f(x) + f(y) + [f'(x) - f'(y)](y - x)$$

or

$$[f'(x) - f'(y)](y - x) \geqslant 0$$

Since $(y - x) > 0$ if $y > x$ then we must have $f'(x) \geqslant f'(y)$ if $y > x$. If for all $y \geqslant x$ it is true that $f'(x) \geqslant f'(y)$ then it must be true that $f''(x) \leqslant 0$ for all x which is the property we needed to prove.

Proof of Sufficiency for Theorem 7.3

We now show that if $f''(x) \leqslant 0$ for all x, then f is concave. To do so we use the idea of integration as the inverse of differentiation, as discussed in Chapter 6.

Hence given

$$f''(x) \leqslant 0$$

we can argue that

$$\int_{x_0}^{x_0+h} f''(x)dx \leqslant \int_{x_0}^{x_0+h} 0 \, dx$$

But the indefinite integral of $f''(x)$ is $f'(x)$ and that of 0 is some constant. Hence the definite integral on the right is zero and we have

$$f'(x_0 + h) - f'(x_0) \leqslant 0$$

We now integrate this expression *with respect to h* to give

$$\int f'(x_0 + h)dh \leqslant \int f'(x_0)dh$$

or

$$f(x_0 + h) \leqslant f'(x_0)h + C$$

where C is some constant of integration. With $h = 0$ we can see that $C = f(x_0)$ and we obtain

$$f(x_0 + h) \leq f(x_0) + f'(x_0)h$$

Finally, putting $y = x_0 + h$ gives

$$f(y) \leq f(x_0) + f'(x_0)(y - x)$$

i.e. f is concave.

Example 7.1
Consider the function $f(x) = a + bx$ defined for all real x, where a and b are fixed real constants. Here $f'(x) = b$ and $f''(x) = 0$ and thus f is concave. Hence all linear (or affine) functions are concave. Note if $b \neq 0$ then f does not have a stationary point nor a maximum.

Example 7.2
$f(x) = ax^2 + bx + c$ defined for all x. Here $f'(x) = 2ax + b$ and $f''(x) = 2a$, hence if $a \leq 0$ then $f''(x) \leq 0$ for all x and f is concave, while if $a > 0$, then $f''(x) > 0$ for x and it is not concave. If $a < 0$ then f has a stationary point and a global maximum when $f'(x) = 0$, i.e. when $2ax + b = 0$ or $x = -b/2a$.

Example 7.3
$f(x) = x^3$, defined for all x. Here $f'(x) = 3x^2$ and $f''(x) = 6x$, which is positive (negative) as x is positive (negative) and thus f is not concave.

Example 7.4
$f(x) = -x^3 + 3x$ defined for all *positive* x. Here $f'(x) = -3x^2 + 3$ and $f''(x) = -6x$ and thus $f''(x) < 0$ for x in the domain of f, i.e. for all positive x, and f is concave. Note f has a stationary point and global maximum when $-3x^2 + 3 = 0$, i.e. when $x = +1$.

Example 7.5
$f(x) = x^\alpha$ defined for all positive x where $0 < \alpha < 1$. Here $f'(x) = \alpha x^{\alpha-1}$ and $f''(x) = \alpha(\alpha - 1)x^{\alpha-2}$. As $\alpha > 0$ and $\alpha - 1 < 0$ it follows that $f''(x) < 0$ for all $x > 0$, i.e. f is concave.

Example 7.6
$f(x) = \ln(x)$ defined for all positive x. Recall that $f'(x) = 1/x = x^{-1}$ and thus $f''(x) = -x^{-2}$ which is negative for all positive x and thus the natural logarithm function is concave. As $1/x \neq 0$ for all $x > 0$ there is no stationary nor maximum point.

2.5 Strict Concavity

We have already seen how the concept of concavity is useful to identify global maxima. Furthermore if we know that a function is strictly concave, then we can make even stronger statements when $f'(x) = 0$. We begin with the definition of strict concavity:

Definition 7.2: A function $f(x)$ is strictly concave if for all x and y, $x \neq y$, and every α, $0 < \alpha < 1$, we have

$$f[\alpha x + (1 - \alpha)y] > \alpha f(x) + (1 - \alpha)f(y)$$

The graphs drawn in Figures 7.1 and 7.2 are strictly concave functions. A linear function is a function that is concave but not strictly concave. Figure 7.4 is an example of a function that is not strictly concave but is concave and illustrates the attractiveness of strictly concave functions. The function is made up of a linear line between P and Q and the value of the function is k for all points between x and y. More importantly all these points are global maxima and it illustrates the point that if a function is concave but not strictly

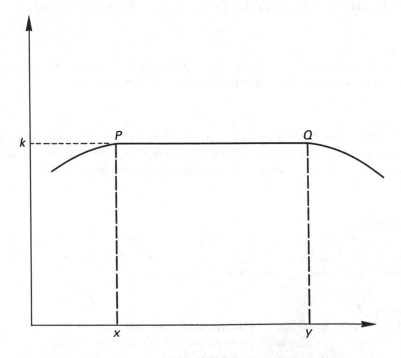

Figure 7.4

concave it may have many maxima. This feature cannot occur if the function is strictly concave:

Theorem 7.4
If $f(x)$ is strictly concave and has a global maximum at x^* then this maximum is unique.

To show that this is true we have to show that if x^* and y^* are both global maxima, then $x^* = y^*$. Suppose otherwise, i.e. x^* and y^* are both global maxima but $x^* \neq y^*$. Obviously it must be true that $f(x^*) \geq f(x)$ and $f(y^*) \geq f(x)$ for all x in the domain of $f(x)$. It follows that $f(x^*) \geq f(y^*)$ and $f(y^*) \geq f(x^*)$, hence $f(x^*) = f(y^*)$. Consider $z = \alpha x^* + (1 - \alpha)y^*$. Since $f(x)$ is strictly concave we know that for $0 < \alpha < 1$,

$$f(z) = f[\alpha x^* + (1 - \alpha)y^*] > \alpha f(x^*) + (1 - \alpha)f(y^*) \tag{7.10}$$

but since it must be true that $f(x^*) = f(y^*)$, (7.10) can be rewritten as

$$f(z) > \alpha f(x^*) + (1 - \alpha)f(x^*) = f(x^*)$$

However, this contradicts the fact that x^* is a global maximum, therefore the assumption that $y^* \neq x^*$ must be incorrect.

We will not discuss the issue of identifying strictly concave functions but will state the following property. If $f(x)$ is a twice differential function and $f''(x) < 0$ for all x then $f(x)$ is a strictly concave function.

Note that Examples 7.4, 7.5 and 7.6 are strictly concave functions.

3 Concave Functions of Many Variables

3.1 Definitions and Maximisation

All the properties and results shown in subsections 2.1, 2.2, 2.3 and 2.5 in the previous section carry over to many variables. In each of the arguments in these subsections the single variable can be changed to a vector and the arguments still follow exactly. The only exception comes in the identification of concave functions of many variables which we discuss in subsection 3.2 below. All the results of subsections 2.1, 2.2, 2.3 and 2.5 will be restated here for the general case. For the definition of a concave function of many variables we have:

Definition 7.3: A function f is concave if and only if for every pair **x**,**y** and every α between zero and one:

$$f[\alpha \mathbf{x} + (1 - \alpha)\mathbf{y}] \geq \alpha f(\mathbf{x}) + (1 - \alpha)f(\mathbf{y})$$

If $f(\mathbf{x})$ is differentiable then we have the alternative definition:

Definition 7.4: A differentiable function, $f(\mathbf{x})$, is concave if and only if for all $\mathbf{x},\mathbf{y}$ we have

$$f(\mathbf{y}) \leqslant f(\mathbf{x}) + f'(\mathbf{x})(\mathbf{y} - \mathbf{x}) = f(\mathbf{x}) + \sum_{i=1}^{n} f_i'(\mathbf{x})(y_i - x_i)$$

and

Theorem 7.5
Given a differentiable concave function, $f(\mathbf{x})$, a necessary and sufficient condition for $\mathbf{x}^*$ to be a global maximum of $f(\mathbf{x})$ is $f_i'(\mathbf{x}^*) = 0$ for all i, i.e. $\mathbf{x}^*$ is a stationary point of $f(\mathbf{x})$.

Finally we generalise Definition 7.2 and Theorem 7.4 to the case of many variables.

Definition 7.5: A function $f(\mathbf{x})$ is strictly concave if for all $\mathbf{x}$ and $\mathbf{y}$, $\mathbf{x} \neq \mathbf{y}$, and for all α between zero and one we have:

$$f[\alpha\mathbf{x} + (1 - \alpha)\mathbf{y}] > \alpha f(\mathbf{x}) + (1 - \alpha)f(\mathbf{y})$$

Theorem 7.6
If $f(\mathbf{x})$ is a strictly concave function and has a global maximum at $\mathbf{x}^*$ then this maximum is unique.

3.2 Identification of Concave Functions of Many Variables

The identification of concave functions of two variables is easier than with three or more variables which, in the general case, requires the use of the Hessian of the function. This is discussed in the Appendix, but in this subsection we restrict attention to functions of two variables and one of the most common functional forms of more variables.

To interpret Definition 7.3 in the two variable case we can think of $f(\mathbf{x})$ as a surface in three dimensions where the horizontal coordinates refer to x_1 and x_2 while the vertical coordinate indicates the value $f(x_1,x_2)$. Definition 7.3 tells us that if we take any two points on this surface and draw a straight line between them, the graph can never lie below any point on the line. Thus we should be able to say that as we move in a 'positive' direction the slope of the function cannot increase. This is a correct characterisation of a concave function but of course we have to be careful about the concept of a positive direction since we have two variables and not one. In the one variable case there is only one positive direction. In the two variable case there are an infinite number. As a result, the checking of concavity in the two variable case (and more variables) is rather technical and not immediately obvious. We require the second order derivatives to be negative in some sense and the exact form of this is left to the Appendix. Here we will state and use only the two variable case.

Theorem 7.7
A twice differentiable function is concave if and only if the following three conditions are satisfied for all $\mathbf{x}$:

   (i) $f_{11}(\mathbf{x}) \leq 0$
  (ii) $f_{22}(\mathbf{x}) \leq 0$
 (iii) $f_{11}(\mathbf{x}) f_{22}(\mathbf{x}) - f_{12}(\mathbf{x}) f_{21}(\mathbf{x}) \geq 0$

A sufficient condition for $f(\mathbf{x})$ to be strictly concave is that inequalities (i) to (iii) are strict for all $\mathbf{x}$.

Example 7.7
Let $y = f(x_1, x_2) = ax_1 + bx_2 + c$, defined for all x_1 and x_2, where a, b and c are constants. Is the function concave? Using Proposition 7.6 we see

$$f_1(\mathbf{x}) \quad = a$$
$$f_2(\mathbf{x}) \quad = b$$
$$f_{11}(\mathbf{x}) \quad = f_{22}(\mathbf{x}) = f_{12}(\mathbf{x}) = f_{21}(\mathbf{x}) = 0$$

and the conditions are satisfied. It is obvious from this example that all linear functions are concave.

Example 7.8
If $f(x_1, x_2) = ax_1^2 + bx_2^2 + 2cx_1x_2 + d$, for what values of a, b, c and d is f concave? We have

$$f_1(\mathbf{x}) \quad = 2ax_1 + 2cx_2$$
$$f_2(\mathbf{x}) \quad = 2bx_2 + 2cx_1$$
$$f_{11}(\mathbf{x}) = 2a \qquad f_{12}(\mathbf{x}) = 2c$$
$$f_{21}(\mathbf{x}) = 2c \qquad f_{22}(\mathbf{x}) = 2b$$

Proposition 7.6 shows that f is concave if and only if

$$a \leq 0$$
$$b \leq 0$$

and

$$ab - c^2 \geqslant 0$$

Example 7.9
If $f(x_1,x_2) = x_1^\alpha x_2^\beta$, defined for $x_1,x_2 > 0$, for what values of α and β is f concave?
    With this function we have

$$f_1(\mathbf{x}) = \alpha x_1^{\alpha-1} x_2^\beta$$

$$f_2(\mathbf{x}) = \beta x_1^\alpha x_2^{\beta-1}$$

$$f_{11} = \alpha(\alpha - 1)x_1^{\alpha-2} x_2^\beta$$

$$f_{22}(\mathbf{x}) = \beta(\beta - 1)x_1^\alpha x_2^\beta$$

and

$$f_{12}(\mathbf{x}) = f_{21}(\mathbf{x}) = \alpha\beta x_1^{\alpha-1} x_2^{\beta-1}$$

(i) and (ii) of Theorem 7.7 require

$$\alpha(\alpha - 1) \leqslant 0$$

$$\beta(\beta - 1) \leqslant 0$$

Considering first the condition $\alpha(\alpha - 1) \leqslant 0$ this implies that α and $\alpha - 1$ cannot both be positive nor can they both be negative. This suggests we must either have $\alpha \geqslant 0$ and $\alpha - 1 \leqslant 0$ or $\alpha \leqslant 0$ and $\alpha - 1 \geqslant 0$. However, the case of $\alpha \leqslant 0$ and $\alpha - 1 \geqslant 0$ is clearly impossible, so we must have $\alpha \geqslant 0$ and $\alpha - 1 \leqslant 0$, i.e. $0 \leqslant \alpha \leqslant 1$. A similar argument establishes $0 \leqslant \beta \leqslant 1$.
    (iii) of Theorem 7.7 requires

$$[\alpha(\alpha - 1)\beta(\beta - 1) - \alpha\beta\ \beta\alpha]x_1^{2\alpha-2} x_2^{2\beta-2}$$

to be non-negative. This will be non-negative if and only if

$$\alpha(\alpha - 1)\beta(\beta - 1) - \alpha\beta\ \beta\alpha \geqslant 0$$

i.e.

$$\alpha\beta(\alpha - 1)(\beta - 1) - (\alpha\beta)^2 \geqslant 0$$

or

$$\alpha\beta(\alpha\beta - \alpha - \beta + 1) - (\alpha\beta)^2 \geqslant 0$$

or

$$(\alpha\beta)^2 + \alpha\beta(-\alpha - \beta + 1) - (\alpha\beta)^2 \geqslant 0$$

or

$$\alpha\beta(-\alpha - \beta + 1) \geq 0$$

We already know that α and β must be non-negative if f is to be a concave function; therefore $\alpha\beta$ must be non-negative as well. Consequently either $\alpha = 0$ or $\beta = 0$ or $\alpha\beta(-\alpha - \beta + 1) \geq 0$ implies

$$-\alpha - \beta + 1 \geq 0$$

i.e.

$$\alpha + \beta \leq 1$$

To summarise: a function of the form $f(x_1^\alpha, x_2^\beta) = x_1 x_2$ is concave if and only if

(i) $\alpha \geq 0$
(ii) $\beta \geq 0$
(iii) $\alpha + \beta \leq 1$

This result generalises to the case of n variables, but we state only this fact here and will not verify it: A function of the form

$$f(x_1, x_2, \ldots, x_n) = x_1^{\alpha_1} x_2^{\alpha_2} x_3^{\alpha_3} \ldots x_n^{\alpha_n}$$

is concave if and only if

(i) $\alpha_i \geq 0$ for all $i = 1, \ldots, n$
(ii) $\sum_i \alpha_i \leq 1$

Although we will not consider the general n variable case in this subsection (see Appendix) there is one case that can be dealt with easily. This is worth dealing with separately since of all the types of concave functions of n variables one is likely to meet, this particular form is the most common. For example, when a consumer has a utility function defined over consumption levels in each of n periods it is usual to assume that this is the sum of n one variable functions, i.e.

$$u(x_1, x_2, x_3, \ldots, x_n) = u^1(x_1) + u^2(x_2) + u^3(x_3) + \ldots + u^n(x_n)$$

That is to say $u(\mathbf{x})$ is an additively separable function. We will state the result in the following Theorem.

Theorem 7.8
If a function $f(x_1, x_2, \ldots, x_n)$ can be written in the form:

$$f(\mathbf{x}) = g^1(x_1) + g^2(x_2) + \ldots + g^n(x_n)$$

where each $g^i(x_i)$ is a concave function then $f(\mathbf{x})$ is a concave function.

To show that $f(\mathbf{x})$ is concave we need to show (from Definition 7.3) that

$$f[\alpha\mathbf{x} + (1 - \alpha)\mathbf{y}] \geq \alpha f(\mathbf{x}) + (1 - \alpha)f(\mathbf{y})$$

for all $\mathbf{x}$ and $\mathbf{y}$ and all $0 \leq \alpha \leq 1$.
   Taking two vectors at random, $\mathbf{x}$ and $\mathbf{y}$, define a vector $\mathbf{z}$ with the property that each component z_i is given by

$$z_i = \alpha x_i + (1 - \alpha)y_i$$

The function of $f(\mathbf{x})$ evaluated at $\mathbf{z}$ gives

$$f(\mathbf{z}) = \sum_i g^i(z_i)$$

therefore

$$f(\mathbf{z}) = \sum_i g^i[\alpha x_i + (1 - \alpha)y_i]$$

and

$$f(\mathbf{z}) \geq \sum_i [\alpha g^i(x_i) + (1 - \alpha)g^i(y_i)]$$

The last inequality follows from the fact that each g^i is concave. The last inequality can be written as

$$f(\mathbf{z}) \geq \sum_i \alpha g^i(x_i) + \sum_i (1 - \alpha)g^i(y_i)$$

or

$$f(\mathbf{z}) \geq \alpha\sum_i g^i(x_i) + (1 - \alpha)\sum_i g^i(y_i)$$

This can be written as

$$f(\mathbf{z}) \geq \alpha f(\mathbf{x}) + (1 - \alpha)f(\mathbf{y})$$

thus f must be a concave function since the above inequality clearly holds for all $\mathbf{x}$ and $\mathbf{y}$ and for all $0 \leq \alpha \leq 1$.

Example 7.10
Is $f(x) = \sum_{i=1}^{n}\alpha_i \ln (x_i)$, $\alpha_i > 0$, $x_i > 0$, a concave function? Here the $g^i(x_i)$ = $\alpha_i \ln (x_i)$ and it is easy to show that $\alpha_i \ln (x_i)$ is concave using Theorem 7.3. Consequently Theorem 7.8 implies $f(\mathbf{x})$ is concave.

4   Convex Functions

There is an intimate relationship between concave and convex functions which will be obvious once we define a convex function.

Definition 7.6: $f(\mathbf{x})$ is convex if and only if for every pair $\mathbf{x},\mathbf{y}$ and every α between zero and one:

$$f[\alpha\mathbf{x} - (1 - \alpha)\mathbf{y}] \leqslant \alpha f(\mathbf{x}) + (1 - \alpha)f(\mathbf{y})$$

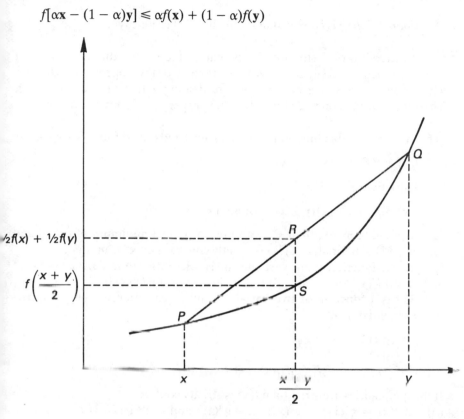

Figure 7.5

Figure 7.5 gives an example of a convex function of one variable. The point R has a horizontal coordinate $(y + x)/2$ and a vertical coordinate of $[f(y) + f(x)]/2$, i.e. it lies halfway between P and Q. The vertical coordinate of S is $f[(x + y)/2]$ and is no greater than the vertical coordinate of R, i.e.

$$f\left(\frac{y + x}{2}\right) < \frac{f(y)}{2} + \frac{f(x)}{2}$$

We have given the general definition of a convex function here, the one variable case being a special case of Definition 7.6. Comparing Definition 7.6 and Definition 7.3, the only difference between the two is the direction of the inequality, i.e. $f[\alpha x + (1 - \alpha)y]$ is less than or equal to $\alpha f(x) + (1 - \alpha)$ $f(y)$ if f is convex, and greater than or equal to this if $f(x)$ is concave. This relationship between concave and convex functions allows us to offer another useful definition of a convex function:

Definition 7.7: $f(x)$ is convex if and only if $-f(x)$ is concave.

The attraction of Definition 7.7 is that all the results that are given for concave functions apply to convex functions with the appropriate changes which have to be made because we are dealing with $f(x)$ and not $-f(x)$. Therefore we will conclude by stating the properties of convex functions:

(1)   A differentiable function $f(x)$ is convex if and only if for all x, y we have

$$f(y) \geq f(x) + f'(x)(y - x)$$

and is strictly convex if

$$f(y) > f(x) + f'(x)(y - x) \quad \text{for all} \quad x \neq y$$

(2)   If $f(x)$ is convex, then x^* is an interior global minimum of $f(x)$ if and only if $f_j(x^*) = 0$ for all j. If $f(x)$ is strictly convex then x^* is unique.
(3)   If f is a function of one variable and is twice differentiable, it is convex if and only if $f''(x) \geq 0$ for all x. It is strictly convex if $f''(x) > 0$.
(4)   If f is a function of two variables and twice differentiable then it is convex if and only if

(a) $f_{11}(x) \geq 0$
(b) $f_{22}(x) \geq 0$
(c) $f_{11}(x)f_{22}(x) - f_{12}(x)f_{21}(x) \geq 0$

If the inequalities are strict then $f(x)$ is strictly convex.
(5)   If $f(x) = g^1(x_1) + g^2(x_2) + \ldots + g^n(x_n)$ and each $g^i(x_i)$ is convex then $f(x)$ is convex. If each $g^i(x_i)$ is strictly convex then $f(x)$ is strictly convex.

Problem

7.1   Read the introduction to Chapter 14, Section 8, and show that a person is a risk lover if and only if his V–M utility function is strictly convex. Solution on p. 315.

Exercises

7.1   For each of the following functions use Theorems 7.1 and 7.2 to establish whether or not (i) it is concave and (ii) has a global maximum. In (a)–(e) the functions are defined over all real x.

(a) $f(x) = 3$ (i.e. f has a constant value of 3)
(b) $f(x) = 2x - 1$
(c) $f(x) = -3x + 2$
(d) $f(x) = -x^2 + 4x - 2$
(e) $f(x) = x^2$

Functions (f)–(i) are defined for all $x > 0$.

(f) $f(x) = x - 1/x$
(g) $f(x) = 2 \ln(x) - 3$
(h) $f(x) = \ln(x) - x$
(i) $f(x) = 3x^{1/3}$

7.2 Check whether each of the following functions is concave, and if it is concave indicate whether it has a global maximum or not.

(a) $f(x_1, x_2) = -x_1^2 - x_2^2$
(b) $f(x_1, x_2) = -x_1^2 + x_2^2$
(c) $f(x_1, x_2) = -3x_1^2 - x_2^2 + 3x_1x_2$
(d) $f(x_1, x_2) = -3x_1^2 - x_2^2 + 2x_1x_2 + 5x_1 - 6x_2 + 4$
(e) $f(x_1, x_2) = 4 \ln(x_1) + \ln(x_2)$
(f) $f(x_1, x_2) = x_1^{1/2} + x_2^{1/2}$
(g) $f(x_1, x_2) = \sqrt{(x_1)}\sqrt{(x_2)} = \sqrt{x_1 x_2}$
(h) $f(x_1, x_2) = x_1 x_2$
(i) $f(x_1, x_2) = \ln(x_1) + \sqrt{x_2}$
(j) $f(x_1, x_2, x_3) = \ln(x_1) - 2 \ln(x_2) + \ln(x_3)$
(k) $f(x_1, x_2, x_3) = x_1^{1/3} x_2^{1/6} x_3^{1/4}$

7.3 Show that
    (i) $f(x) = -\ln x > 0$, is convex;
    (ii) $f(x) = 1/x, x > 0$, is convex;
    (iii) $f(x) = x_1^{\beta_1} + x_2^{\beta_2} + \dots + x_n^{\beta_n}$, $x_i > 0$, $\beta_i \geq 1$, is convex.

7.4 Show that $f(x) = \sum_{i=1}^{n} \alpha_i x_i^{\beta_i}$, $x_i > 0$, $0 \leq \beta_i \leq 1$, $\alpha_i > 0$, is a concave function.

7.5 If $u(x) = \sum_{t=1}^{n} \delta^t u^t(x_t)$, show that $u(x)$ is strictly concave if each u^t is strictly concave and $\delta > 0$.

7.6 If $p = f(q)$ is a downward sloping demand curve with $f(q)$ concave, show that the marginal revenue curve must also be downward sloping.

7.7 Suppose a farmer has an inverse demand function $p = f(q)$ where $f'(q) < 0$ and sells q_1 in one period and q_2 in a second period, giving him total revenue of $q_1f(q_1) + q_2f(q_2)$. Suppose q_1 is greater than q_2. The government wishes to stabilise prices and requests him to sell $(q_1 + q_2)/2$ in each period. If storage of the commodity is costless, show that total revenue is greater if $f(q)$ is concave.

PART II

Constrained Optimisation

8

An Informal Introduction to Constrained Maximisation

1 Introduction

In previous chapters we have studied the maximisation of functions without a constraint. However, in economic analysis it is natural to consider the decision maker restricted in his choice of actions. In such cases he has to maximise (or minimise) the value of his objective function subject to constraints. The techniques required to analyse such a problem are based on the techniques used for unconstrained problems, in that we convert the constrained problem into an unconstrained one and then solve the latter. This chapter gives an informal introduction using two well known examples: firstly, the problem of a consumer maximising his utility subject to a budget constraint; and secondly, a firm minimising the cost of producing a given level of output. In the latter case the objective is to minimise costs and the constraint is that the firm must purchase sufficient inputs to produce the specified output given the relevant production function.

Both these problems have a standard diagrammatic representation which will be found in virtually all basic economic texts. The approach we follow is to outline this diagrammatic representation and to express it in mathematical terms. The direct statement of the diagrammatic properties can then be manipulated until we have an unconstrained problem with the same answer as the constrained one. Each step in the process has a simple economic interpretation which is helpful in seeing the relationships between the diagrammatic and mathematical approaches. The function whose unconstrained optimum gives the solution to the constrained problem is called the Lagrangian. Having introduced the Lagrangian for these two special cases, the chapter closes with an example where the Lagrangian is particularly simple and informative. At this point let us repeat that, unless it is stated otherwise, all functions in Chapter 8 to 12 are *assumed to be concave or convex*.

2   Maximisation of Utility Subject to a Budget Constraint

In order to represent the consumer's choice in diagrammatic terms we will restrict attention to two commodities. Let x_1 be the quantity of good 1 that is consumed, and x_2 the quantity of good 2. The commodities can be purchased for p_1 per unit and p_2 per unit respectively, i.e. the cost of x_1 is p_1x_1 and the cost of x_2 is p_2x_2. The constraint the consumer faces is that he can only consume quantities of the goods that he can afford. If his total income is m then his consumption must be restricted to those x_1 and x_2 which satisfy the following inequality:

$$p_1x_1 + p_2x_2 \leqslant m \tag{8.1}$$

Combinations of x_1 and x_2 that do not satisfy (8.1) are too expensive. The problem is to choose from all the combinations of x_1 and x_2 satisfying (8.1) that which gives the maximum satisfaction. Strictly speaking, the consumer is further constrained by the fact that it is not possible to consume negative quantities of goods. Such non-negativity constraints will be discussed in Chapter 13. The satisfaction the consumer obtains depends on his consumption of the goods and is represented by a utility function $u(x_1,x_2)$. The objective is to maximise utility subject to the budget constraint (8.1), i.e.

max $u(x_1,x_2)$

subject to $m - p_1x_1 - p_2x_2 \geqslant 0$

Note we have slightly rewritten the constraint to conform with a general style which will be employed throughout.

Figure 8.1 embodies the usual geometric analysis of the consumer's choice where the optimum is characterised by the tangency of indifference curves with budget lines. Let us re-run this argument and attempt to translate it into mathematical terms. The line PQ is the budget line in that it represents all those combinations of x_1 and x_2 whose cost $p_1x_1 + p_2x_2$ is equal to m. In particular, OP represents the maximum quantity of the second good the consumer can buy, namely m/p_2, while OQ represents the maximum quantity of the first good, namely m/p_1. We can note that the slope of the budget line is $-OP/OQ = -\dfrac{m}{p_2} \Big/ \dfrac{m}{p_1} = -\dfrac{p_1}{p_2}$. Included in the diagram are two indifference curves, the solid curve being tangential to the budget line at x^* and the broken curve illustrating non-tangency at $\hat{x}$. This last point cannot be the maximum because it is possible to move on to a higher indifference curve without leaving the budget line, i.e. by moving down to the right.

We have seen in Chapter 4 that the slope of indifference curves can be found from the consumer utility function $u(x_1,x_2)$. Thus if we write u_1 and

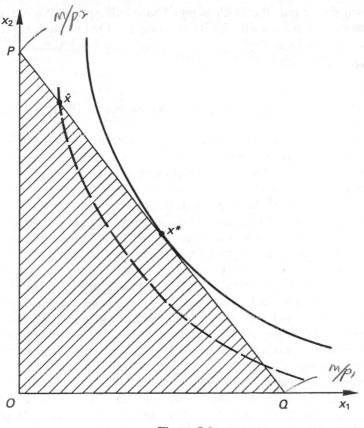

Figure 8.1

u_2 to represent the partial derivatives of the function u with respect to x_1 and x_2, we can interpret u_1 and u_2 as the marginal utilities of the two goods and identify the ratio u_1/u_2 with the marginal rate of substitution (MRS). As the slope of the indifference curve is minus MRS, it is equal to $-u_1/u_2$.

Now the tangency of the indifference curve at x^* can be expressed as saying the slopes of the budget line and indifference curve are equal, hence we have

$$-\frac{u_1^*}{u_2^*} = -\frac{p_1}{p_2}$$

or

$$\frac{u_1^*}{u_2^*} = \frac{p_1}{p_2} \qquad (8.2)$$

or less formally put, the MRS is equal to relative price. We can rewrite
(8.2) in various ways, each with its own interest. First we multiply through
by u_2 and divide by p_1 to give

$$\frac{u_1^*}{p_1} = \frac{u_2^*}{p_2} \tag{8.3}$$

It must be stressed that the partial derivatives in (8.2) and (8.3) are
evaluated at x_1^*, x_2^*.

Equation (8.3) has a very useful interpretation in terms of the marginal
utility of money. To see this, think of u_1^*/p_1 as u_1^* times $1/p_1$. $1/p_1$ tells us
the quantity of good 1 that can be bought with one unit of money (e.g. if $p_1 =$
½ we can buy 2 units ($1/½$), if $p_1 = 2$ we can only buy half a unit). u_1^* is
the marginal utility of the first good, therefore $u_1^*(1/p_1)$ is the product of
the quantity of good 1 that can be bought with one unit of money and the
level of utility the marginal unit produces, i.e. u_1^*/p_1 is the increase in
utility gained by spending one unit of money on the first good. Similarly
u_2^*/p_2 is the increase in utility gained by spending one unit of money on
the second good. Equation (8.3) tells us that these two marginal utilities of
money are equal to each other and thus there is no gain in transferring
expenditure from one good to the other since the gain in utility from more
consumption of the one good is exactly offset by the fall in consumption of
the other. If (8.3) was not valid then a small transfer of money from the good
offering the lower marginal utility of money to the one offering the higher
value would increase utility. Such gains could always be made until the ratios
were equal. u_1^*/p_1 is the marginal utility of a unit of money spent on good 1
and u_2^*/p_2 is the marginal utility of a unit of money spent on good 2.
Since these two must be equal we can refer unambiguously to *the* marginal
utility of money (i.e. we do not need to specify how it is spent). Referring to
the marginal utility of money as λ^*, (8.3) can be written as

$$\frac{u_1^*}{p_1} = \frac{u_2^*}{p_2} = \lambda^* \tag{8.4}$$

We can now write (8.4) as two separate equations

$$u_1^* = \lambda^* p_1 \tag{8.5}$$

and

$$u_2^* = \lambda^* p_2 \tag{8.6}$$

Again these two equations have a standard interpretation. Since λ^* is the
marginal utility of money, $\lambda^* p_1$ is the amount of utility foregone by buying
one extra unit of good 1, while u_1^* is the utility gained by consuming that
extra unit. (8.5) states that the marginal utility gained from the last unit of
good 1 consumed is equal to the amount of utility foregone by purchasing

that extra unit. (8.6) is the equivalent for good 2. (8.5) and (8.6) together imply (as did (8.3)) that there is no utility gain to be obtained from small changes in expenditure from one good to the other.

(8.5) and (8.6) are the most useful statements of the tangency condition for our purposes. However, these two equations do not contain all the information that is contained in Figure 8.1. (8.5) and (8.6) allow us to solve for those combinations of x_1 and x_2 which have the property that the slope of the indifference curve at x_1,x_2 is equal to the slope of the budget line. However, all the points along OB in Figure 8.2 have this property. To make sure we have the right point we need to add the fact that $p_1x_1^* + p_2x_2^* = m$.

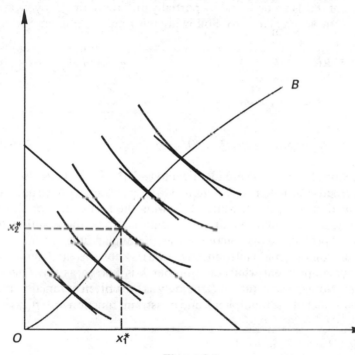

Figure 8.2

We can now summarise our diagrammatic characterisation of x_1^*,x_2^* in mathematical form:

$$u_1(x_1^*,x_2^*) = \lambda^*p_1 \qquad (8.7a)$$

$$u_2(x_1^*,x_2^*) = \lambda^*p_2 \qquad (8.7b)$$

$$m - p_1x_1^* - p_2x_2^* = 0 \qquad (8.7c)$$

Given these three equations we can (in principle) solve for the three unknowns (x_1^*,x_2^*,λ^*). Thus the three equations contain the information to determine the optimal consumption bundle and will give the same answer to that found by identifying the point of tangency in Figure 8.1.

The final step is to see how (8.7a) to (8.7c) relate to an unconstrained problem which gives the same answer as the constrained one. We know (8.7a) to (8.7c) contain the answer to the problem: maximise $u(x_1,x_2)$ subject to the constraint $m - p_1x_1 - p_2x_2 \geq 0$. Now notice the relationship between these three equations (8.7a)–(8.7c) and the following function of x_1,x_2 and λ:

$$L(x_1,x_2,\lambda) = u(x_1,x_2) + \lambda(m - p_1x_1 - p_2x_2) \tag{8.8}$$

The first order conditions for finding an unconstrained maximum or minimum of (8.8) can be found by partially differentiating L by x_1,x_2 and λ and setting these equal to zero. Following this route we obtain:

$$\frac{\partial L}{\partial x_1} = u_1^* - \lambda^* p_1 = 0 \tag{8.9}$$

$$\frac{\partial L}{\partial x_2} = u_2^* - \lambda^* p_2 = 0 \tag{8.10}$$

$$\frac{\partial L}{\partial \lambda} = m - p_1x_1^* - p_2x_2^* = 0 \tag{8.11}$$

But equations (8.9)–(8.11) are identical to (8.7a)–(8.7c). Thus although we are concerned with maximisation subject to a constraint, we have been able to find a function, $L(x_1,x_2,\lambda)$, which, following the first order conditions for unconstrained maximisation or minimisation, gives the solution to the constrained problem. This function is the Lagrangian function.

The function $L(x_1,x_2,\lambda)$ introduced in (8.8) is known as the *Lagrangian* for our consumer problem while the number λ is known as the *Lagrangian multiplier*. Note the structure of L, namely as the objective function $u(x_1,x_2)$ plus the product of the multiplier λ and constraint function $m - p_1x_1 - p_2x_2$.

Example 8.1
We suppose for this example that the consumer has a utility function of the form $u(x_1,x_2) = \ln x_1 + \ln x_2$. Thus the exact specification of the problem is

$$\max \quad \ln x_1 + \ln x_2$$

$$\text{subject to} \quad m - p_1x_1 - p_2x_2 \geq 0$$

Equation (8.8) in this case is

$$L(x_1,x_2,\lambda) = \ln x_1 + \ln x_2 + \lambda(m - p_1x_1 - p_2x_2)$$

Partially differentiating this Lagrangian with respect to x_1,x_2 and λ and setting equal to zero gives:

$$\frac{\partial L}{\partial x_1} = \frac{1}{x_1^*} - \lambda^* p_1 = 0 \tag{8.12}$$

$$\frac{\partial L}{\partial x_2} = \frac{1}{x_2^*} - \lambda^* p_2 = 0 \tag{8.13}$$

$$\frac{\partial L}{\partial \lambda} = m - p_1 x_1^* - p_2 x_2^* = 0 \tag{8.14}$$

Equations (8.12) and (8.13) can be combined by eliminating λ:

$$\frac{1/x_1^*}{1/x_2^*} = \frac{\lambda^* p_1}{\lambda^* p_2} = \frac{p_1}{p_2}$$

or

$$p_1 x_1^* = p_2 x_2^* \tag{8.15}$$

Even before we have calculated the optimal values of x_1, x_2 and λ, equation (8.15) contains some very interesting information. It tells us that for all levels of p_1 and p_2 the expenditure on the two commodities will always be the same. Replacing $p_2 x_2^*$ in equation (8.14) with $p_1 x_1^*$ gives

$$2 p_1 x_1^* = m$$

or

$$x_1^* = \frac{m}{2p_1} \tag{8.16}$$

A similar procedure gives

$$x_2^* = \frac{m}{2p_2} \tag{8.17}$$

In terms of our normal interest as economists, (8.16) and (8.17) constitute the main solution to our specific problem. These equations are usually referred to as the Marshallian demand functions and are the main focus of attention. They represent behavioural relationships between observed variables, i.e. the quantities demanded of each good, prices and income. One of the main themes of consumer theory is the analysis of the structure of these demand functions.

Besides equations (8.16) and (8.17), the complete statement of the solution requires solving for λ^*. Substituting for x_1^* into equation (8.12) from (8.16) gives

$$\lambda^* = \frac{2}{m}$$

3   Cost Minimisation Subject to an Output Constraint

The problem we consider in this section is of a firm which requires capital, k, and labour, l, to produce output, q. The production function, f, relates inputs to outputs, i.e. the function f tells us the maximum quantity of output that can be produced from given inputs,

$$q \leqslant f(k,l)$$

Labour is paid at a rate of w per unit and capital is purchased at r per unit. The objective of the firm is to minimise costs, i.e. minimise $wl + rk$. The constraint is that they must produce a given level of output, say $\bar{q}$, i.e. they must purchase sufficient quantities of k and l such that the inequality $\bar{q} \leqslant f(k,l)$ is satisfied. Thus the formal problem is

min $wl + rk$

subject to $f(k,l) - \bar{q} \geqslant 0$

The diagrammatic solution is given in Figure 8.3. For the given level of output required, $\bar{q}$, there will be many combinations of k and l that will just produce the given level of output $\bar{q}$. The line joining all these combinations

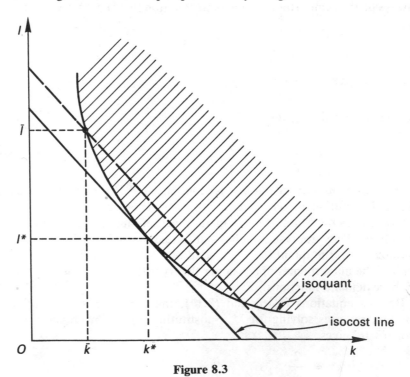

Figure 8.3

is called an isoquant (i.e. constant quantity of output). The isoquant for $\bar{q}$ is drawn in Figure 8.3 and any combination of k and l in the shaded region (including the boundary) will give an output greater than or equal to $\bar{q}$. This shaded area represents the feasible set. Associated with each combination of k and l will be a total cost $wl + rk$. Lines of equal cost (isocost lines) have identical shape to the consumer's budget line. For given w and r, the closer the line to the origin, the lower the cost. This is the equivalent of budget lines where, for given p_1 and p_2, the closer the budget line to the origin the lower the income level.

It is clear from Figure 8.3 that l^* and k^* are the optimum quantities of l and k. This is because any other point in the shaded region (e.g. $\bar{l}$ and $\bar{k}$) must have a higher cost associated with it and any isocost line lower than $rk^* + wl^*$ cannot intersect the shaded feasible set. Again the point l^*, k^* is a point of tangency, this time between the isoquant and the isocost line.

Following the approach of Section 2 we can see that the slope of the isocost line is $-r/w$. Similarly the slope of the isoquant is (minus) the marginal rate of technical substitution (the production function equivalent to the utility function's marginal rate of substitution). This is equal to (minus) the ratio of the marginal products, $-f_k/f_l$ (again the production function's equivalent to $-u_1/u_2$). Tangency requires these two slopes to be equal, i.e.

$$\frac{f_k^*}{f_l^*} = \frac{r}{w} \tag{8.18}$$

(directly equivalent to (8.2)). (8.18) can be written as

$$\frac{r}{f_k^*} = \frac{w}{f_l^*} = \lambda^* \tag{8.19}$$

giving

$$r = \lambda^* f_k^* \tag{8.20}$$

and

$$w = \lambda^* f_l^* \tag{8.21}$$

Again r/f_k^* and w/f_l^* can be separated to help our understanding of (8.19). f_l^* is the marginal product of labour and $1/f_l^*$ tells us how much labour is required to produce one extra unit of output (e.g. if $f_l^* = 3$, i.e. the marginal product of labour is 3 units, then we require 1/3 units of labour to produce one extra unit of output). If we multiply this by the cost of a unit of labour, w, we have the marginal cost of producing one extra unit of output using labour. Similarly r/f_k^* is the marginal cost of producing one extra unit of output by increasing capital. The tangency condition requires these to be equal, i.e. costs cannot be reduced if we reduce one of these inputs and increase the other by the amount required to keep output constant. Since it costs the same to bring about a small increase in output by increasing capital or labour it is meaningful to talk about *the* marginal cost of output, which is λ^*.

Again, as in Section 2, equations (8.20) and (8.21) imply we must have a tangency condition, but they do not guarantee that the point is x_1^*, x_2^*. We need to add another equation stating that we are on the boundary of the shaded region. This equation is

$$f(k^*, l^*) = \bar{q} \tag{8.22}$$

and (8.20)–(8.22) can be solved to give l^*, k^* and λ^*.

The problem we are considering in this section requires us to minimise costs subject to a constraint, but we have chosen to call the chapter 'an informal introduction to constrained maximisation'. This reflects a simple but important point which is that there is an essential equivalence between *maximisation* and *minimisation* problems. A minimisation problem can always be trivially converted to a maximisation problem and vice versa. For a particularly simple example, consider the function $f(x) = x^2$. This is minimised when $x = 0$ and is drawn in Figure 8.4a. To convert this to a maximisation problem we can maximise $-x^2$. This is drawn in Figure 8.4b and obviously the maximum point is $x = 0$. Thus simply by taking the negative of the objective function we have converted the minimisation problem to a maximisation one (i.e. the minimum of x^2 equals the maximum of $-x^2$). This process also works when we are minimising a function subject to a constraint. Consider the problem in this section and let us look at a point $\bar{l}, \bar{k}$ satisfying $f(k,l) \geq q$ where $\bar{l} \neq l^*$, $\bar{k} \neq k^*$ ($\bar{l}, \bar{k}$ in Figure 8.3 is such a point). Obviously $\bar{k}, \bar{l}$ do not minimise costs subject to the constraint, so it must be true that

$$w\bar{l} + r\bar{k} > wl^* + rk^* \tag{8.23}$$

or (multiplying both sides by minus one)

$$-w\bar{l} - r\bar{k} < -wl^* - rk^* \tag{8.24}$$

Hence if $wl^* + rk^*$ is less than any other $w\bar{l} + r\bar{k}$ satisfying the constraint, then $-wl^* - rk^*$ must be greater than any other $-w\bar{l} - r\bar{k}$ satisfying the constraint. So when a minimisation problem gives l^*, k^* as the solution, the maximisation of $-wl - rk$ must give l^*, k^* as the solution. We can establish in a similar fashion that any constrained minimisation problem can be converted into a maximisation problem by multiplying the objective function by minus one while leaving the constraint function(s) unchanged.

It is convenient to express minimisation problems as maximisation problems because then all our problems can be written in the same general way. Therefore we write the problem of this section as

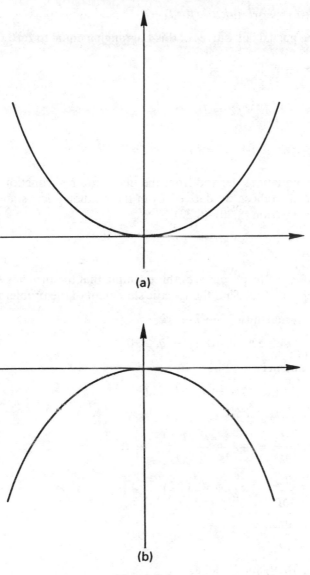

(a)

(b)

Figure 8.4

maximise $\quad -wl - rk$

subject to $\quad f(l,k) - \bar{q} \geqslant 0$

To construct the Lagrangian for this problem we form the function $L(l,k,\lambda)$ which is the sum of the objective function $-wl - rk$ and the product of a multiplier λ with the constraint function $f(k,l) - \bar{q}$, i.e.

$$L(l,k,\lambda) = -wl - rk + \lambda(f(k,l) - \bar{q}) \tag{8.25}$$

Setting the partial derivatives of this Lagrangian equal to zero yields:

$$\frac{\partial L}{\partial l} = -w + \lambda^* f_l^* = 0 \tag{8.26}$$

$$\frac{\partial L}{\partial k} = -r + \lambda^* f_k^* = 0 \tag{8.27}$$

$$\frac{\partial L}{\partial \lambda} = f(k^*,l^*) - \bar{q} = 0 \tag{8.28}$$

Again the equations derived from the unconstrained function, $L(x_1,x_2,\lambda)$, are identical to those we derived from the mathematical statement of the tangency condition (8.20)–(8.22).

Example 8.2
We suppose for the purposes of this example that the firm has a production function $q = l^{1/2}k^{1/2}$. Thus the specific statement of the problem is

$$\text{maximise} \quad -wl - rk$$

$$\text{subject to} \quad f(k,l) - \bar{q} \geqslant 0$$

The Lagrangian is

$$L(k,l,\lambda) = -wl - rk + \lambda(k^{1/2}l^{1/2} - \bar{q})$$

giving

$$\frac{\partial L}{\partial k} = -r + \frac{\lambda^*}{2}\left(\frac{l^*}{k^*}\right)^{1/2} = 0 \tag{8.29}$$

$$\frac{\partial L}{\partial l} = -w + \frac{\lambda^*}{2}\left(\frac{k^*}{l^*}\right)^{1/2} = 0 \tag{8.30}$$

$$\frac{\partial L}{\partial \lambda} = k^{*1/2}l^{*1/2} - \bar{q} = 0 \tag{8.31}$$

Rewriting (8.29) and (8.30) as

$$w = \frac{\lambda^*}{2}\left(\frac{k^*}{l^*}\right)^{1/2} \tag{8.32}$$

and

$$r = \frac{\lambda^*}{2}\left(\frac{l^*}{k^*}\right)^{1/2} \tag{8.33}$$

and dividing (8.32) by (8.33) gives

$$\frac{w}{r} = \frac{\left(\dfrac{k^*}{l^*}\right)^{1/2}}{\left(\dfrac{l^*}{k^*}\right)^{1/2}} = \frac{k^{*1/2}}{l^{*1/2}}\frac{k^{*1/2}}{l^{*1/2}} = \frac{k^*}{l^*} \tag{8.34}$$

Thus

$$k^* = \frac{w}{r} \, l^* \tag{8.35}$$

An interesting and special feature of this production function is that for any level of output the expenditure on capital, rk^*, is always exactly equal to the expenditure on wages, wl^*, irrespective of the wage rate, w, and cost of capital, r. Substituting for k^* from (8.35) into (8.31) gives

$$\bar{q} = \left(\frac{w}{r}\, l^*\right)^{1/2} l^{*1/2} = \left(\frac{w}{r}\right)^{1/2} l^*$$

i.e.

$$l^* = \bar{q}\left(\frac{r}{w}\right)^{1/2} \tag{8.36}$$

Since inputs are symmetric (or by substituting (8.36) into (8.31)):

$$k^* = \left(\frac{w}{r}\right)^{1/2} \bar{q}$$

To obtain λ^* we can substitute for l in (8.29) from (8.36) giving

$$\lambda^* = 2(wr)^{1/2}$$

λ^* is the marginal cost of production.

4   One Variable Constrained Maximisation

In the previous two sections we have taken two constrained maximisation problems which are probably familiar in a diagrammatic form, and we have stated the properties of the solutions in a mathematical form. The crucial point is that in both cases we have been able to find a function, the Lagrangian function, which has given the correct answer to the constrained maximisation problem when first order conditions for an unconstrained maximisation are applied to it. Obviously we would not have spent so much time introducing the Lagrangian function were it not for the fact that we can always find such a function. The next chapter shows why we can do this and the procedure we must follow to solve problems by this method. To form a bridge between the specific cases in this chapter and the general procedure of the following chapter, we will close with a discussion of constrained maximisation problems involving only one variable. Such problems are so simple we do not need to derive the Lagrangian to solve them. As a result the role of the Lagrangian can be clarified. Furthermore we can use examples to introduce the reader to the general results presented in the next chapter.

The general problem involving one variable and one constraint takes the form

$$\text{choose } x \text{ to maximise} \quad f(x) \tag{8.37}$$

$$\text{subject to} \quad g(x) \geqslant 0$$

where, as usual, f is the objective function and g is the constraint function. The associated Lagrangian is

$$L(x,\lambda) = f(x) + \lambda\, g(x) \tag{8.38}$$

i.e. objective function $+\ \lambda \times$ constraint function.

Example 8.3

(a) maximise $f(x) = -(x - 4)^2 + 36 = -x^2 + 8x + 22$

subject to $x \leqslant 2$ or $g(x) = 2 - x \geqslant 0$

Note the term $-(x - 4)^2$ in $f(x)$ has an unconstrained maximum value of zero when $x = 4$, so that the unconstrained maximum of $f(x)$ is 36 which occurs when $x = 4$. Furthermore, $f'(x) = -2x + 8$ and thus $f'(x) > 0$ for $x < 4$ and $f'(x) < 0$ for $x > 4$, i.e. $f(x)$ increases as x increases towards 4 after which it begins to decrease. The x-intercepts of the function are -2 and 10 respectively. The graph of $f(x)$ is drawn in Figure 8.5. We can see from the above discussion and from the figure that the constrained maximum of $f(x)$ subject to $x \leqslant 2$ will occur at $x = 2$, giving a maximum value of 32.

(b) maximise $f(x) = -(x - 4)^2 + 36$

subject to $x \leqslant 6$ or $g(x) = 6 - x \geqslant 0$

From our discussion of $f(x)$ above and Figure 8.5 we can see that in this case the constrained maximum of $f(x)$ subject to $x \leqslant 6$ is equal to the unconstrained maximum at $x = 4$. In this case we would say the constraint was *not binding* or that it was *slack*, in contrast to the *binding* or *tight* constraints we have considered so far.

(c) maximise $f(x) = -(x - 4)^2 + 36$

subject to $g(x) = 2(2 - x) \geqslant 0$

We can see that the constraint $2(2 - x) \geqslant 0$ is equivalent to the constraint

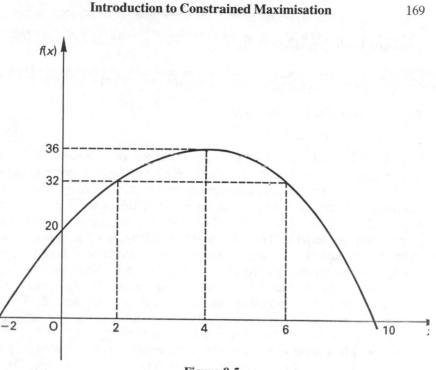

Figure 8.5

$2 - x \geqslant 0$ considered in (a) above. Hence the solution is identical. We use this example below to clarify a feature of Lagrangian multipliers.

(d)   maximise $f(x) = -(x - 4)^2 + 36$

   subject to $g(x) = -(2 - x)^2 \geqslant 0$

Here we have introduced a rather unusual constraint, namely $-(2 - x)^2 \geqslant 0$ which requires $(2 - x)^2 \leqslant 0$, but as $(2 - x)^2$ is the square of a number it cannot be negative; hence we must conclude that $(2 - x)^2 = 0$ and thus $x = 2$. In this case there is only one value of x which satisfies the constraint and hence that value must be the constrained maximum. Such cases rarely occur in economics and as they cause complications we shall exclude them (see our constraint qualification in the next chapter).

Consider now the use of the Lagrangian function to solve these problems. Recall that the basic aim in constructing the Lagrangian is to obtain a function $L(x,\lambda)$ whose unconstrained maximum with respect to the decision variable x is equal to the constrained maximum of the objective function $f(x)$ subject to $g(x) \geqslant 0$. Consider the Example 8.3(a) above which has a Lagrangian of the form

$$L(x,\lambda) = f(x) + \lambda(2 - x)$$

where

$$f(x) = -(x - 4)^2 + 36$$

We can rewrite this Lagrangian as

$$L(x,\lambda) = [f(x) + 2\lambda] - \lambda x \tag{8.39}$$

In Figure 8.6(a) we have drawn the graphs of the two elements of $L(x,\lambda)$ namely $f(x) + 2\lambda$ and λx, while in Figure 8.6(b) we have drawn a graph of $L(x,\lambda)$ reflecting the distance between the two graphs in Figure 8.6(a). The Lagrangian illustrated attains a maximum at $\hat{x}$, this occurring where the slope of $f(x) + 2\lambda$ equals the slope of λx. As these two slopes are $f'(\hat{x})$ and λ respectively, we require $f'(\hat{x}) = \lambda$. Clearly in this figure we have *not* chosen the correct value of λ to ensure that the unconstrained maximum of $L(x,\lambda)$ is the constrained maximum of $f(x)$ subject to $2 - x \geqslant 0$. What value of λ will do the trick? We know that the constrained maximum of $f(x)$ occurs at $x^* = 2$, yet the unconstrained maximum of $L(x,\lambda)$ occurs at $\hat{x}$ where $f'(\hat{x}) = \lambda$. Hence if we are to have $\hat{x} = x^* = 2$, then we require $\lambda = \lambda^* = f'(x^*)$. Yet $f'(x) = -2x + 8$, hence $\lambda^* = f'(2) = +4$.

Putting this a little more formally we can say that the unconstrained maximum $\hat{x}$ of the Lagrangian $L(x,\lambda) = f(x) + \lambda(2 - x)$ must be a stationary point of that Lagrangian; hence we will require

$$\left.\frac{\partial L}{\partial x}\right|_{x=\hat{x}} = f'(x) - \lambda = 0$$

i.e.

$$\lambda = f'(\hat{x})$$

If $\hat{x}$ is to be equal to the constrained maximum x^* of $f(x)$ subject to $2 - x \geqslant 0$ then we would require λ to be equal to

$$\lambda^* = f'(x^*) \tag{8.40}$$

Choosing this multiplier ensures that the Lagrangian $L(x,\lambda^*)$ has an unconstrained maximum at the optimal x^*. In Figure 8.6 we had a multiplier which was 'too low' and this led to the unconstrained maximum $\hat{x}$ of $L(x,\lambda)$ being greater than 2, i.e. the use of this λ would have led to the choice of an x which 'broke' the constraint $2 - x \geqslant 0$. Should we choose λ to be 'too large', i.e. greater than $\lambda^* = 4$, then we would have found $\hat{x}$ to be less than 2, and although such an $\hat{x}$ is feasible it would not be optimal. Thus we need to choose λ to be sufficiently large that $\hat{x}$ satisfies the constraint but sufficiently small to ensure that $\hat{x}$ is optimal.

While (8.40) gives us a relationship between the optimal value of x and the appropriate choice λ^* of the multiplier it does not in itself determine either

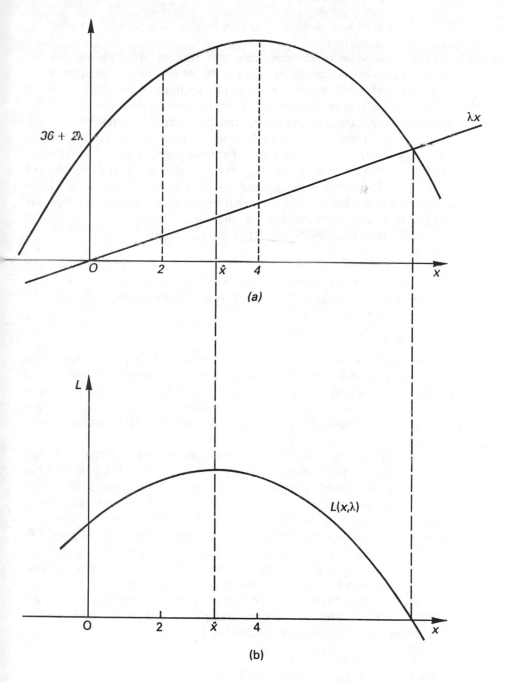

Figure 8.6

x^* or λ^*. Indeed use of the Lagrangian has introduced a new unknown, namely the multiplier λ^*.

In our discussion of the consumer and firm in previous sections we confidently asserted that the budget constraint and production constraint held with equality. It was this use of equalities in the constraints, together with the first order conditions on the Lagrangian that allowed us to solve for the decision variables and multiplier. In most economic examples with one constraint the constraint will be binding or tight in the sense that the constraint function will take a value of zero at the optimum. Nevertheless Example 8.3(b) above indicates that this is not necessarily true and we shall find it useful to develop our technique to allow for 'slack' constraints. This is particularly true when we turn to more than one constraint and in particular non-negative constraints discussed in Chapter 13.

Consider then Example 8.3(b) which has Lagrangian

$$L(x,\lambda) = f(x) + \lambda(6 - x)$$

which has a stationary point $\hat{x}$ where again $\lambda = f'(\hat{x})$. Yet we know the optimum is at $x^* = 4$ where $f'(x^*) = 0$, hence the appropriate choice of λ is $\lambda^* = 0$. Hence the appropriate Lagrangian is

$$L(x,\lambda^*) = f(x)$$

i.e. the Lagrangian is equal to the objective function. In a sense the constraint does not enter into the solution. This example illustrates a fundamental result which we develop in the next chapter, namely that at the optimum *either a constraint holds with equality or the associated multiplier is zero*. We can see that in either case we have sufficient information to solve out for all variables including the multiplier.

We can use Example 8.3(b) to illustrate another facet of the multiplier which we shall require for our technique to be complete. Consider what happens in this example if we attempt to force the constraint to hold with equality, i.e. we attempt to force $x^* = 6$. We find that our stationarity condition $\lambda^* = f'(x^*)$ implies $\lambda^* = -4$. We shall see that in solving a constrained maximisation problem with a constraint of the form $g(x) \geq 0$, i.e. the constraint function is required to be non-negative, then *the requisite Lagrangian multiplier λ^* must be non-negative*. Hence should we impose equality in the constraint and find that the implied multiplier is negative, as in Example 8.3(b), then we must conclude that the imposition was invalid and thus the constraint must be 'slack' and the multiplier must be zero.

Consider now Example 8.3(c) which has Lagrangian

$$L(x,\lambda^*) = f(x) - \lambda^* \, 2(2 - x)$$

which has a stationary point at x^* if

$$f'(x^*) - 2\lambda^* = 0$$

Imposing the constraint leads us to conclude

$$x^* = 2$$

hence

$$\lambda^* = \tfrac{1}{2} f'(x^*) = 2$$

As this $\lambda^* > 0$ we can conclude that imposing the constraint was valid and that the solution is $x^* = 2$. Not only does this illustrate the Lagrangian technique, it also illustrates that the value of the multiplier λ^* depends on the nature of the constraint function. In this example we have $\lambda^* = 2$ while in Example 8.3(a) we had $\lambda^* = 4$; although the constraints are 'effectively' the same, their precise functional expressions were different and this is reflected in the multiplier.

Finally let us consider Example 8.3(d) which has Lagrangian

$$L(x,\lambda) = f(x) - \lambda(2 - x)^2$$

which has a stationary point at $\hat{x}$ where

$$f'(\hat{x}) + 2\lambda(2 - \hat{x}) = 0$$

We know that the only feasible value of x is 2, hence this is the optimum. Putting $\hat{x} = 2$ in our stationarity condition we obtain

$$f'(2) + 0 = 0$$

but we know $f'(2) = 4$. That is to say the optimum $x^* = 2$ is not a stationary point of the Lagrangian whatever value λ takes. Thus, with such constraints, our Lagrangian method does not work. In the general discussion presented in the next chapter and Chapter 13 we shall exclude such troublesome cases by adopting the constraint qualification. Fortunately this qualification is invariably valid in economic problems.

Problem

8.1 Show that the utility functions $u(x_1,x_2) = x_1^{1/2}x_2^{1/2}$ and $v(x_1,x_2) = x_1^2 x_2^2$ represent the same preferences. Furthermore, confirm that the marginal rates of substitution associated with these two functions are equal. Hence find the (common) demand functions associated with these utility functions.

Solution on p. 280.

9

Lagrangian and Envelope Functions

1 Introduction

The previous chapter has shown that the Lagrangian function is a straightforward and natural structure in the context of constrained maximisation. We have also seen that all the constrained problems we wish to solve can be written in an identical form whether they are initially maximisation or minimisation problems. The purpose of this chapter is to discuss the Lagrangian approach to solving this general problem and to identify a procedure that can be followed in the general case. The problem is one of maximising a function $f(\mathbf{x})$ subject to a single constraint which can be written in a functional form. The function to be maximised, $f(\mathbf{x})$, is called the objective function. It is defined over $\mathbf{x}$, a vector of the relevant variables. The constraint is written as $g(\mathbf{x}) \geqslant 0$, where g is defined over the same variables. Thus the general statement of the problem which is considered in this chapter is:

The Basic Problem

  maximise $f(\mathbf{x})$ (9.1)

  subject to $g(\mathbf{x}) \geqslant 0$ (9.2)

Before proceeding to the solution of the general problem we show, by way of example, how the problems given in Chapter 8, Sections 2 and 3, are special cases of the general statement of the problem.

174

The problem in Chapter 8, Section 2, concerned maximisation of utility subject to a budget constraint. In this case the objective function $f(\mathbf{x})$ represents the utility function $u(x_1,x_2)$. The constraint $g(\mathbf{x}) \geq 0$ took the form of $m - p_1x_1 - p_2x_2 \geq 0$ in Section 2 of Chapter 8, i.e. $g(\mathbf{x}) = m - p_1x_1 - p_2x_2$, or in vector notation we have $g(x) = m - \mathbf{p}\,x$ where $\mathbf{p}$ is the vector of prices (p_1,p_2). In the problem of the firm given in Chapter 8, Section 3, the objective function was to minimise costs or, more helpfully, to maximise the negative value of costs. Thus $f(\mathbf{x}) = -wl - rk$ for that case and $g(\mathbf{x}) = f(k,l) - \bar{q}$, where $\mathbf{x} = (l,k)$.

2   The Lagrangian Theorem and its Use

We have already encountered the Lagrangian in the previous chapter and the definition of the Lagrangian for the basic problem is of similar form:

Definition 9.1: The Lagrangian function, $L(\mathbf{x},\lambda)$, associated with the basic problem in (9.1) and (9.2) is defined as:

$$L(\mathbf{x},\lambda) = f(\mathbf{x}) + \lambda g(\mathbf{x}) \tag{9.3}$$

where λ is the Lagrange multiplier.

Before we state the fundamental Lagrangian theorem of this chapter we offer the following definition which we shall require in that statement:

Definition 9.2: The constraint function $g(\mathbf{x})$ in (9.2) is said to satisfy the *constraint qualification* if there is at least one $\mathbf{x}$ such that $g(\mathbf{x}) > 0$.

By restricting attention to constraints satisfying this qualification we remove such troublesome and uninteresting examples as that in Example 8.3(d).

Lagrange Theorem
If $f(\mathbf{x})$ and $g(\mathbf{x})$ are concave functions and $g(\mathbf{x})$ satisfies the constraint qualification, the necessary and sufficient conditions for $\mathbf{x}^*$ to maximise $f(\mathbf{x})$ subject to $g(\mathbf{x}) \geq 0$ are that there exists a λ^* such that

  (i) $\mathbf{x}^*$ maximises $L(\mathbf{x},\lambda^*)$
  (ii) $\lambda^* \geq 0$
  (iii) $g(\mathbf{x}^*) \geq 0$
  (iv) $\lambda^* g(\mathbf{x}^*) = 0$

Before we attempt to prove this theorem let us consider how this result is used in practice. First we can note that as $f(\mathbf{x})$ and $g(\mathbf{x})$ are concave and $\lambda^* \geqslant 0$ it follows that the Lagrangian is concave in $\mathbf{x}$. Hence if f and g are differentiable, as we shall usually assume, then $\mathbf{x}^*$ maximises $L(\mathbf{x},\lambda^*)$ if and only if $\mathbf{x}^*$ is a stationary point of $L(\mathbf{x},\lambda^*)$. In this case then (i) can be replaced by

(i')　$\mathbf{x}^*$ is a stationary point of $L(\mathbf{x},\lambda^*)$, i.e.

$$\frac{\partial L}{\partial x_i}\Big|_{\mathbf{x}=\mathbf{x}^*} = 0$$

Next we note that (iv) implies that either $\lambda^* = 0$ or $g(\mathbf{x}^*) = 0$, and as in most economic examples the constraint will be binding, i.e. $g(\mathbf{x}^*) = 0$, we usually try to find a solution assuming this to be true. That is to say we solve the equations

$$\frac{\partial L}{\partial x_i}\Big|_{\mathbf{x}=\mathbf{x}^*} = 0 \qquad i = 1,\ldots,n$$

and

$$g(\mathbf{x}^*) = 0$$

for $\mathbf{x}^*$ and λ^*. We then check if the λ^* implied by these equations is non-negative; should the resulting λ^* be negative, we must conclude the constraint is 'slack', i.e. $g(\mathbf{x}^*) > 0$ and $\lambda^* = 0$.

In summary, the procedure is:

(1)　Identify the decision variables, $\mathbf{x}$, and the objective function, $f(\mathbf{x})$.

(2)　Write the constraint in the form of $g(\mathbf{x}) \geqslant 0$. Check there is at least one $\mathbf{x}$ such that $g(\mathbf{x}) > 0$.

(3)　Construct the Lagrangian:

$$L(\mathbf{x},\lambda) = f(\mathbf{x}) + \lambda g(\mathbf{x})$$

(4)　Differentiate $L(\mathbf{x},\lambda)$ with respect to each decision variable and set these partials equal to zero.

(5)　Set $g(\mathbf{x}) = 0$ and combine this equation with the equations obtained from (4) to solve for $\mathbf{x}^*$ and λ^*.

(6)　Check λ^* is non-negative. If the λ^* calculated in (5) is negative then we must reject the equation $g(\mathbf{x}^*) = 0$ and set $\lambda^* = 0$. Then solve the equations given by (4) for $\mathbf{x}^*$.

Example 9.1
Let us apply this procedure to the following familiar consumer problem:

maximise $u(x_1,x_2)$ ← *Obj. fn.*

subject to $p_1x_1 + p_2x_2 \leq m$

Here the decision variables are the quantity x_1,x_2 of the two goods consumed and the objective function is the utility function $u(x_1,x_2)$. The constraint can be written as $g(x_1,x_2) = m - p_1x_1 - p_2x_2 \geq 0$. Assuming $m > 0$ we can check that the constraint qualification holds, e.g. choose $x_1 = m/2p_1$ and $x_2 = 0$ for which $g(x_1,x_2) = \frac{1}{2}m > 0$. The Lagrangian is

$$L(x_1,x_2,\lambda^*) = u(x_1,x_2) + \lambda^*(m - p_1x_1 - p_2x_2)$$

which has partials

$$\frac{\partial L}{\partial x_1} = u_1'(x_1,x_2) - \lambda^*p_1$$

$$\frac{\partial L}{\partial x_2} = u_2'(x_1,x_2) - \lambda^*p_2$$

where the $u_i'(x_1,x_2)$ are the partials of the utility function and thus represent the marginal utilities of the two goods. The partials of L are zero at $x_i = x_i^*$ where

$$u_1'(x_1^*,x_2^*) = \lambda^*p_1 \tag{9.4}$$

$$u_2'(x_1^*,x_2^*) = \lambda^*p_2 \tag{9.5}$$

If we assume that the marginal utilities of the goods are both positive for all quantities consumed, we can immediately conclude from these last equations that λ^* cannot be zero. (Note we can also conclude that if either price is zero then we cannot have a maximum.) Thus from the fourth condition of the Lagrangian theorem we can conclude that $g(x_1^*,x_2^*) = 0$, i.e.

$$p_1x_1^* + p_2p_2^* = m \tag{9.6}$$

Equations (9.4) and (9.6) are the familiar results discussed in the previous chapter.

3   Interpreting the Lagrangian

The essential implication of the Lagrangian theorem is that concrete constrained maximisation problems can be solved by considering equivalent, albeit artificial, unconstrained maximisation problems. In this artificial problem the constraint of the original problem is in some sense absorbed into the objective function of the unconstrained problem. Let us see if we can construct an imaginary world where the Lagrangian might be a meaningful objective function. Imagine now a world where the decision maker can exchange units of his objective function for units of his constraint function. To clarify this notion, consider the case of the consumer who was able to exchange units of utility directly for money and let λ be the utility price of one unit of money. If the consumer has a budget m, faces money prices p_1, p_2 for the two consumption goods and chooses quantities x_1, x_2 such that $g = m - p_1 x_1 - p_2 x_2 \geq 0$, then he would obtain, in our imaginary world, utility $u(x_1, x_2)$ from consuming the goods *and* $\lambda g = \lambda(m - p_1 x_1 - p_2 x_2)$ by exchanging the surplus money g directly for utility. In this case his net utility could be $L(x_1, x_2, \lambda) = u(x_1, x_2) + \lambda(m - p_1 x_1 - p_2 x_2)$. Equally a choice of x_1, x_2 such that $g = m - p_1 x_1 - p_2 x_2 < 0$ would yield utility $u(x_1, x_2)$ from consumption of the goods but a *loss* of utility of $-\lambda g$ from the imaginary purchase of $-g$ units of money. Again the total utility would be $u(x_1, x_2) - (-\lambda g) = u(x_1, x_2) + \lambda g = u(x_1, x_2) + \lambda(m - p_1 x_1 - p_2 x_2) = L(x, \lambda)$. In either case we can interpret the Lagrangian as the net utility of choosing x_1, x_2 in our imaginary world. With this interpretation λ is the utility price of money.

More generally, translating a decision maker faced with our basic problem in (9.1) and (9.2) into our imaginary world, we can view λ as the exchange rate between units of the objective function $f(\mathbf{x})$ and units of the constraint function. Choice of an $\mathbf{x}$ such that $g(\mathbf{x}) > 0$ would allow the decision maker to 'sell' $g(\mathbf{x})$ units of the constraint for $\lambda g(\mathbf{x})$ units of the objective function, such that the net 'payoff' from $\mathbf{x}$ would be $f(\mathbf{x}) + \lambda g(\mathbf{x})$. Equally a choice of $\mathbf{x}$ such that $g(\mathbf{x}) < 0$ would involve the 'purchase' of $-g(\mathbf{x})$ units of the constraint at a 'cost' of $-\lambda g(\mathbf{x})$, hence the net payoff would again be the Lagrangian $f(\mathbf{x}) + \lambda g(\mathbf{x})$. Such interpretations of the Lagrangian have led to the use of the term *shadow price of constraints* when referring to Lagrangian multipliers. With this nomenclature and interpretation of the multipliers we can attempt to use our economic intuition to guide us in the correct choice of the multiplier. What shadow price will *just* induce the decision maker not to 'buy' any constraint units? We might suggest that the appropriate choice is to make λ equal to the marginal payoff of such a purchase.

Should the decision maker buy a marginal unit of the constraint it is as if he were buying a marginal relaxation of the constraint and thus possibly allowing him to increase the value of his objective function. Should the shadow price equal this marginal increase in his objective function due to a marginal relaxation of his constraint, then this would be just sufficient to stop the purchase of such a relaxation in our imaginary world. Rephrasing this in terms of the Lagrangian we can anticipate that the choice of a multiplier λ^* equal to the marginal payoff of a relaxation of the constraint will make the unconstrained maximum of the Lagrangian equal to the constrained maximum of the basic problem.

Interpreting the multiplier λ^* in this manner suggests that: (a) $\lambda^* \geq 0$ in that we expect a marginal relaxation of constraint *not* to reduce the potential payoff; and (b) if the constraint is 'slack' or not binding then a marginal relaxation will not increase the payoff, i.e. if $g(x^*) > 0$ then $\lambda^* = 0$, and, conversely (c) if $\lambda^* > 0$ then we would expect the constraint to be 'tight' or binding. In this way the conditions (ii) and (iv) in the Lagrangian theorem conform to our 'intuitive' interpretation of the multiplier.

4 The Envelope Function and the Lagrangian

In this section we aim to express the informal ideas of the previous section in a more formal manner. In our imaginary world the choice of x such that $g(x) < 0$ was seen as equivalent to buying a 'relaxation' of the constraint, the 'price' of these relaxations being the Lagrangian multiplier λ.

Given this interpretation of the Lagrange multiplier as the 'price' of relaxations of constraints, we need to ask what is the smallest 'price' at which the decision maker will choose *not* to relax his constraint? The answer should be intuitive: the maximum price he will pay for a marginal relaxation will be equal to the marginal increase in his objective function allowed by the relaxation. This is known as the *shadow price* of the constraint and the following discussion aims to develop this idea in a systematic manner. The vehicle for the development is the idea of envelope functions, which we shall introduce and analyse. As we shall see, the argument that the unconstrained maximisation of Lagrangians yields the solution to our original constrained problems is based on the fact that this envelope function is concave.

To proceed, let us define θ as the extent to which the constraint is relaxed. If the constraint is relaxed by θ units, then the decision maker faces the constraint $g(x) + \theta \geq 0$ instead of $g(x) \geq 0$. Put another way, the choice of x can be any x satisfying $g(x) \geq -\theta$ instead of being restricted to $g(x) \geq 0$. If θ is positive the constraint is being relaxed, but if θ is negative, then the constraint is tightened, since x is restricted to the region $g(x) \geq -\theta > 0$ instead of $g(x) \geq 0$.

We rephrase our question above in terms of θ. For which 'price' λ will the decision maker choose $\theta = 0$? To introduce envelope functions and their role in answering this question we reconsider the consumer example.

Example 9.2
We use the problem of Chapter 8, Section 2, where the consumer faced the constraint $m - p_1 x_1 - p_2 x_2 \geq 0$, or $p_1 x_1 + p_2 x_2 \leq m$. If the constraint is

relaxed by θ units then we have $m - p_1x_1 - p_2x_2 + \theta \geqslant 0$ or $p_1x_1 + p_2x_2 \leqslant m + \theta$. If θ is positive, this represents an increase in his budget and an expansion of the set of possible options. If θ is negative, this is a reduction in his budget and a reduction in the set of options.

What does the consumer gain if θ is positive? Obviously the maximum level of utility he can obtain facing a constraint $m - p_1x_1 - p_2x_2 + \theta \geqslant 0$ will be greater than that if he faced the constraint $m - p_1x_1 - p_2x_2 \geqslant 0$. However he also loses the amount $\theta\lambda$, this being the cost of relaxing his constraint by θ, the exact cost depending on the value of λ. To analyse which θ the decision maker would choose in this imaginary situation, we need to know the maximum utility the consumer can obtain for each θ. Let us denote this by $v(\theta)$. Thus $v(-1)$ is the maximum amount of utility the consumer can attain facing a constraint of $m - p_1x_1 - p_2x_2 - 1 \geqslant 0$ and $v(2)$ is the maximum amount of utility the consumer can attain facing a constraint of $m - p_1x_1 - p_2x_2 + 2 \geqslant 0$. In Figure 9.1 $v(-1)$ is the level of utility given by $\bar{x}_1$ and $\bar{x}_2$, i.e. $v(-1) = u(\bar{x}_1, \bar{x}_2)$ and similarly $v(2) = u(\hat{x}_1, \hat{x}_2)$. The line from the origin in Figure 9.1 goes through the combinations of x_1 and x_2 that are optimal for some constraint $m - p_1x_1 - p_2x_2 + \theta \geqslant 0$. Each x_1, x_2 on this line relates to a specific θ, and $v(\theta)$ is the level of utility at this point.

Figure 9.2 sketches $v(\theta)$ as a function of θ. The similarity between Figure 9.2 and the examples in Section 4 of Chapter 8 should be clear. We can now answer the question concerning the consumer's gains from a positive θ. We know he has to pay $\lambda\theta$ to relax his constraint by θ and $v(\theta)$ tells us how much utility he can get for a given θ. He will choose that θ which maximises his net payoff, namely $v(\theta)$ minus the cost of the relaxation $\lambda\theta$. This is the difference between the two curves in Figure 9.2 and the consumer will choose that $\hat{\theta}$ where the slope of the graph of v is equal to λ, i.e. where $v'(\theta) = \lambda$. The choice of θ depends on the specific λ and there will exist a λ^* which makes the consumer choose $\theta = 0$, namely λ^* equal to the slope of the graph of $v(\theta)$ when $\theta = 0$, i.e. $\lambda^* = v'(0)$.

Hence we can see that the 'price' $\lambda^* = v'(0)$ for a unit relaxation will be the smallest 'price' at which the consumer will choose not to buy a relaxation. Hence we can anticipate that $\lambda^* = v'(0)$ is the Lagrangian multiplier we require in the Lagrangian theorem. In the present context we can view the relaxation variable θ as a supplement to the consumer's budget and thus view $v(\theta)$ as the maximum utility available from the supplemented budget $m + \theta$, hence $v'(\theta)$ is the marginal utility of such budgetary supplements. In particular $v'(0)$ is the marginal utility of an initial supplement or in more traditional terms it is the marginal utility of money.

The use of the relaxation variable θ and the introduction of the function $v(\theta)$ can be extended to our general basic problem as in the following definition.

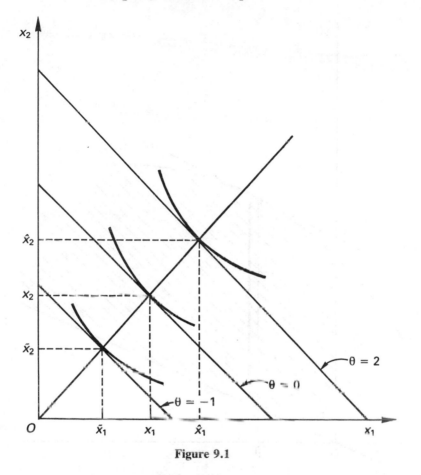

Figure 9.1

Definition 9.3: The envelope function, $v(\theta)$, associated with the problem: $\max f(\mathbf{x})$ subject to $g(\mathbf{x}) \geq 0$ is defined as follows:

$$v(\theta) = \text{maximum value of } f(\mathbf{x}) \text{ subject to the constraint } g(\mathbf{x}) + \theta \geq 0$$

This envelope function $v(\theta)$ will form the backbone of our proof of the Lagrangian theorem which we will present subsequently. But first we establish the concavity of $v(\theta)$, at least when $f(\mathbf{x})$ and $g(\mathbf{x})$ are concave.

5 The Concavity of the Envelope Function

In Figure 9.2 we drew the graph of the function $v(\theta)$, introduced in Example 9.2, on the assumption that $v(\theta)$ was concave. Although we did not stress it at the time this concavity of $v(\theta)$ is important for the argument

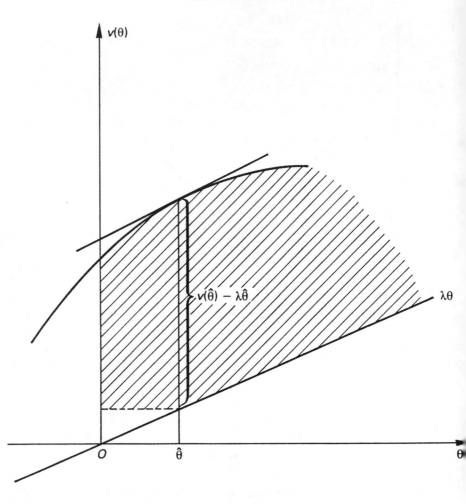

Figure 9.2

that $v(\theta) - \lambda\theta$ attains its maximum at that $\hat{\theta}$ where $v'(\hat{\theta}) = \lambda$. As our general argument is similar to that used in this example, we shall establish the validity of the following proposition.

If $f(\mathbf{x})$ and $g(\mathbf{x})$ are concave, then the envelope function $v(\theta)$ must also be concave.

To demonstrate the validity of this statement we proceed as follows.

Consider two values θ' and θ'' of θ and let $\hat{\theta}$ be a convex combination of them, i.e. $\hat{\theta} = \alpha\theta' + (1 - \alpha)\theta''$ where $0 \leq \alpha \leq 1$. We need to show that

$$v(\hat{\theta}) \geq \alpha v(\theta') + (1 - \alpha)v(\theta'') \qquad (9.7)$$

Now we know that $v(\theta')$ is the maximum value of $f(\mathbf{x})$ subject to $g(x) + \theta' \geq 0$; let this maximum occur at $\mathbf{x}'$ so that $v(\theta') = f(\mathbf{x}')$. Similarly we let $\mathbf{x}''$ be the maximum of $f(\mathbf{x})$ subject to $g(\mathbf{x}) + \theta'' \geq 0$, so that $v(\theta'') = f(\mathbf{x}'')$, and let $\hat{\mathbf{x}}$ be the maximum of $f(\mathbf{x})$ subject to $g(\mathbf{x}) + \hat{\theta} \geq 0$, so that $v(\hat{\theta}) = f(\hat{\mathbf{x}})$. Rewriting (9.7) we thus need to show that

$$f(\hat{\mathbf{x}}) \geq \alpha f(\mathbf{x}') + (1 - \alpha)f(\mathbf{x}'') \qquad (9.8)$$

Now consider $\mathbf{x}^* = \alpha\mathbf{x}' + (1 - \alpha)\mathbf{x}''$. The concavity of f implies

$$f(\mathbf{x}^*) \geq \alpha f(\mathbf{x}') + (1 - \alpha)f(\mathbf{x}'') \qquad (9.9)$$

and we show below that

$$f(\hat{\mathbf{x}}) \geq f(\mathbf{x}^*) \qquad (9.10)$$

We can see that (9.9) and (9.10) imply (9.8), which is the relation we wish to establish (since it is equivalent to (9.7)). Finally we now have to demonstrate that (9.10) holds. To do this, we show that $\mathbf{x}^*$ satisfies the constraint $g(\mathbf{x}) + \hat{\theta} \geq 0$, from which (9.10) follows, because $\hat{\mathbf{x}}$ gives the maximum value of $f(\mathbf{x})$ subject to $g(\mathbf{x}) + \hat{\theta} \geq 0$. To show $g(\mathbf{x}^*) + \hat{\theta} \geq 0$ we note that the concavity of g tells us that

$$g(\mathbf{x}^*) \geq \alpha g(\mathbf{x}') + (1 - \alpha)g(\mathbf{x}'')$$

and yet

$$g(\mathbf{x}^*) + \hat{\theta} = g(\mathbf{x}^*) + \alpha\theta' + (1 - \alpha)\theta''$$

and thus

$$g(\mathbf{x}^*) + \hat{\theta} \geq \alpha[g(\mathbf{x}') + \theta'] + (1 - \alpha)[g(\mathbf{x}'') + \theta''] \qquad (9.11)$$

Yet all terms of the RHS of (9.11) are non-negative, hence so is the LHS. This completes our demonstration.

Recalling our discussion of concavity in Chapter 7 we can note that if $v(\theta)$ is differentiable, then an alternative expression of our proposition is the following. For all θ and θ_0 we have

$$v(\theta) \leq v(\theta_0) + v'(\theta_0)(\theta - \theta_0) \qquad (9.12)$$

this being the formal expression of the fact that tangents to the graph of $vy(\theta)$ do not lie below that graph. In particular if $\theta_0 = 0$ then

$$v(\theta) \leq v(0) + v'(0)\theta \qquad (9.13)$$

If we set $\lambda^* = v'(0)$, (9.13) becomes

$$v(0) \geqslant v(\theta) - \lambda^*\theta \qquad (9.14)$$

To interpret inequality (9.14), let us consider an imaginary world where our decision maker can buy relaxations (or sell restrictions) on his constraint. Viewing $\lambda^* = v'(0)$ as the price of such relaxations, (9.14) says that if he chooses a zero relaxation i.e. $\theta = 0$, then the ensuing payoff $v(0)$ cannot be less than the net payoff $v(\theta) - \lambda^*\theta$ obtained by choosing any other relaxation. That is to say that the optimal relaxation in this imaginary world is the zero relaxation, i.e. the decision maker would choose $\theta = 0$, as long as the 'price' of relaxation is $\lambda^* = v'(0)$.

This should seem intuitive once it is recognised that $v'(0)$ is the marginal increase in the decision maker's objective function when allowed a marginal relaxation of his constraint. That is to say $v'(0)$ is the shadow price of his constraint and thus setting λ^* equal to this shadow price will deter any marginal relaxation of the constraint in our imaginary world.

To conclude this section, we can make a small technical note. We have assumed above that $v(\theta)$ is well defined for all θ around zero, this being implicit in our assuming $v'(0)$ exists. We can note that our assuming that the constraint function $g(\mathbf{x})$ satisfies the constraint qualification allows us to establish that $v(\theta)$ is indeed well defined for all sufficiently small θ.

6 The Proof of the Lagrangian Theorem

The aim of this section is to offer a proof of the Lagrangian Theorem presented in Section 2 of this chapter. The reader is thus asked to look back at the statement of the theorem. Note in particular that the theorem states that the four conditions (i) to (iv) are both necessary and sufficient. Hence in proving this theorem, we need to establish both the necessity and sufficiency of those conditions. It is the proof of necessity that proves to be the most complex, but as its proof is based on the envelope function introduced in the previous sections, we shall start with this proof of necessity.

Necessity

Our task is to show that if $\mathbf{x}^*$ maximises $f(\mathbf{x})$ subject to $g(\mathbf{x}) \geqslant 0$, where f and g are concave and g satisfies the constraint qualification, then there exists a λ^* such that

(i) $\mathbf{x}^*$ maximises $L(\mathbf{x},\lambda^*) = f(\mathbf{x}) + \lambda^*g(\mathbf{x})$
(ii) $\lambda^* \geqslant 0$

(iii) $g(\mathbf{x}^*) \geqslant 0$

(iv) $\lambda^* g(\mathbf{x}^*) = 0$

In effect our proof constructs a λ^* which satisfies these four conditions; indeed we shall argue that $\lambda^* = v'(0)$, where v is the envelope function, is the requisite number.

Condition (iii) can immediately be seen to be necessary, for if $\mathbf{x}^*$ is the constrained maximum of $f(\mathbf{x})$, then it must satisfy the constraint, i.e. we must have $g(\mathbf{x}^*) \geqslant 0$.

Consider then $\lambda^* = v'(0)$ where $v(\theta)$ is the envelope function introduced in the previous sections, so that λ^* is the marginal payoff of a relaxation of the constraint $g(\mathbf{x}) \geqslant 0$. As a relaxation of the constraint increases the set of possible choices of $\mathbf{x}$ such a relaxation cannot decrease the maximum value that $f(\mathbf{x})$ can attain. Hence the marginal payoff λ^* of a relaxation cannot be negative, i.e. our choice of $\lambda^* = v'(0)$ satisfies condition (ii).

Turning to condition (iv) we can note that it is equivalent to saying that at least one of λ^* or $g(\mathbf{x}^*)$ is equal to zero. We argue that either $g(\mathbf{x}^*) = 0$ or $\lambda^* = 0$. This follows from the fact that if $g(\mathbf{x}^*) \neq 0$ then $g(\mathbf{x}^*) > 0$, i.e. the constraint is slack or non-binding. Hence a marginal relaxation (or tightening) of this constraint will not alter the optimal value of $\mathbf{x}^*$. Indeed if the constraint is slack, then $\mathbf{x}^*$ must be a local maximum of $f(\mathbf{x})$, hence it must be a stationary point of $f(\mathbf{x})$, which in turn implies $\mathbf{x}^*$ is a global maximum of $f(\mathbf{x})$. Now 'small' changes in the constraint will leave $\mathbf{x}^*$ as a possible choice and thus $\mathbf{x}^*$ remains optimal. In this way we can argue that if $g(\mathbf{x}^*) > 0$ then the maximum value of $f(\mathbf{x})$ subject to $g(\mathbf{x}) + \theta \geqslant 0$ does *not* change from $f(\mathbf{x}^*)$ for small θ, hence for all small θ, $v(\theta) = f(\mathbf{x}^*)$ and $v'(0) = 0$. All in all $g(\mathbf{x}^*) > 0$ implies that the shadow price of the constraint $\lambda^* = v'(0)$ will be zero, and we have established λ^* satisfies condition (iv).

Finally we need to show that $\mathbf{x}^*$ is the unconstrained maximum of the Lagrangian $L(\mathbf{x}, \lambda^*) = f(\mathbf{x}) + \lambda^* g(\mathbf{x})$, i.e. we have to show that for all $\mathbf{x}$ we have

$$L(\mathbf{x}^*, \lambda^*) \geqslant L(\mathbf{x}, \lambda^*) \tag{9.15}$$

or

$$f(\mathbf{x}^*) + \lambda^* g(\mathbf{x}^*) \geqslant f(\mathbf{x}) + \lambda^* g(\mathbf{x}) \tag{9.16}$$

Yet we have already argued that $\lambda^* g(\mathbf{x}^*) = 0$; hence we need to show that for all $\mathbf{x}$ we have

$$f(\mathbf{x}^*) \geqslant f(\mathbf{x}) + \lambda^* g(\mathbf{x}) \tag{9.17}$$

The demonstration of (9.17) is based on the concavity of the envelope function. In particular it follows from (9.14) of the previous section, which stated that for all θ we have

$$v(0) \geqslant v(\theta) - \lambda^*\theta$$

Recalling the definition of $v(\theta)$ as the maximum value of $f(\mathbf{x})$ subject to $g(\mathbf{x}) + \theta \geqslant 0$ we can immediately confirm that

$$v(0) = f(\mathbf{x}^*) \tag{9.18}$$

Furthermore if we put $\theta = -g(\bar{\mathbf{x}})$ for any $\bar{\mathbf{x}}$ we see that the constraint $g(\mathbf{x}) + \theta \geqslant 0$ is equivalent to $g(\mathbf{x}) - g(\bar{\mathbf{x}}) \geqslant 0$ or $g(\mathbf{x}) \geqslant g(\bar{\mathbf{x}})$. Clearly $\bar{\mathbf{x}}$ itself satisfies this constraint and thus the maximum of $f(\mathbf{x})$ subject to this constraint cannot be less than $f(\bar{\mathbf{x}})$.

Hence

$$v[-g(\bar{\mathbf{x}})] \geqslant f(\bar{\mathbf{x}}) \tag{9.19}$$

We now replace $v(0)$ by $f(\mathbf{x}^*)$ and put $\theta = -g(\bar{\mathbf{x}})$ in (9.14) to obtain

$$f(\mathbf{x}^*) \geqslant v[-g(\bar{\mathbf{x}})] + \lambda^* g(\bar{\mathbf{x}})$$

and using (9.19) gives

$$f(\mathbf{x}^*) \geqslant f(\bar{\mathbf{x}}) + \lambda^* g(\bar{\mathbf{x}}) \tag{9.20}$$

But the choice of $\bar{\mathbf{x}}$ above was arbitrary and thus (9.20) is equivalent to (9.17), which in turn, we have argued, is equivalent to condition (i). All in all we have shown that (9.14) implies the validity of condition (i) of the Lagrangian Theorem when we choose $\lambda^* = v'(0)$.

This completes our proof of the necessity of the four conditions in the Lagrangian Theorem, in that we have shown that $\lambda^* = v'(0)$ satisfies these four conditions if $\mathbf{x}^*$ is the optimum choice of $\mathbf{x}$.

We stress at this juncture that although our proof is based on the envelope function it is *not* being suggested that one should construct this function to identify λ^*. Indeed we have seen in Section 2 that the use of the Lagrangian Theorem does not require the identification of λ^* with $v'(0)$. Rather this identification is useful only in our formal proof and in assisting our interpretation of Lagrangian multipliers.

Sufficiency

Here we argue that if $f(\mathbf{x})$ and $g(\mathbf{x})$ are concave, and there exists $\mathbf{x}^*$ and λ^* which satisfy the four conditions (i)–(iv) of the Lagrangian Theorem, then $\mathbf{x}^*$ maximises $f(\mathbf{x})$ subject to $g(\mathbf{x}) \geqslant 0$. We first note that condition (iii) $g(\mathbf{x}^*) \geqslant 0$ ensures that $\mathbf{x}^*$ is feasible; we need to show that for all $\mathbf{x}$ satisfying $g(\mathbf{x}) \geqslant 0$, we have

$$f(\mathbf{x}^*) \geqslant f(\mathbf{x}) \tag{9.21}$$

The obvious starting point to establish (9.21) is condition (i) which states that for all **x**

$$L(\mathbf{x}^*,\lambda^*) \geqslant L(\mathbf{x},\lambda^*)$$

or

$$f(\mathbf{x}^*) + \lambda^* g(\mathbf{x}^*) \geqslant f(\mathbf{x}) + \lambda^* g(\mathbf{x}) \qquad (9.22)$$

Now condition (iv) tells us $\lambda^* g(\mathbf{x}^*) = 0$; hence (9.22) becomes

$$f(\mathbf{x}^*) \geqslant f(\mathbf{x}) + \lambda^* g(\mathbf{x}) \qquad (9.23)$$

This holds for all **x**, but if we restrict ourselves to those **x** for which $g(\mathbf{x}) \geqslant 0$, then condition (ii) $\lambda^* \geqslant 0$ tells us $\lambda^* g(\mathbf{x}) \geqslant 0$; hence $f(\mathbf{x}) + \lambda^* g(\mathbf{x}) \geqslant f(\mathbf{x})$. Hence for all **x** satisfying $g(\mathbf{x}) \geqslant 0$ (9.23) becomes

$$f(\mathbf{x}^*) \geqslant f(\mathbf{x})$$

i.e. it reduces to (9.21). This completes the proof of the sufficiency of the four conditions.

Problems

9.1 If $u(\mathbf{x})$ is a utility function defined over n goods of the form

$$u(\mathbf{x}) = x_1^{\alpha_1} x_2^{\alpha_2} \ldots x_n^{\alpha_n}$$

where $\sum_{i=1}^{n} \alpha_i = \alpha_1 + \alpha_2 + \ldots + \alpha_n < 1$, what is the proportion of income that the associated consumer will spend on each good?
Solution on p. 281.

9.2 Consider the utility function

$$u(x_1,x_2) = (x_1^\rho + x_2^\rho)/\rho$$

where $\rho \neq 0$ and $\rho < 1$. Find the associated demand functions and show that the two goods are gross substitutes if and only if $0 < \rho < 1$. Recall good 1 is a gross substitute for good 2 if the demand for good 1 increases as the price of good 2 increases.
Solution on p. 282.

9.3 A consumer, in allocating an initial asset holding m over $T + 1$ periods, faces the following budget constraint:

$$\sum_{t=0}^{T} \frac{p_t C_t}{(1 + r)^t} \leqslant m$$

where p_t is the price of consumption and C_t is the level of consumption in period t, while r is the rate of interest that can be earned on assets. The consumer's utility function takes the form

$$V(\mathbf{c}) = \sum_{t=0}^{T} \frac{u(c_t)}{(1 + \rho)^t} = u(c_0) + \frac{u(c_1)}{1 + \rho} + \ldots + \frac{|u(c_T)}{(1 + \rho)^T}$$

where $u(c_t)$ is strictly concave and ρ is the rate of subjective discount. Show that consumption will be constant, i.e. $c_t = c_{t+1}$ for all $t = 0,\ldots,T - 1$, if and only if $\dfrac{P_t}{P_{t+1}} = \dfrac{1 + \rho}{1 + r}$.

(*Hint*: recall that the derivative function of strictly concave function is strictly monotonically decreasing and thus is one-to-one and has an inverse function.)

Solution on page p. 297.

9.4   Consider the following problem: choose c_t to

$$\text{maximise} \quad \int_0^T u(c_t)e^{-\rho t}dt$$

$$\text{subject to} \quad \int_0^T c_t e^{-rt}dt \leq \frac{y}{r}(1 - e^{-rT})$$

While such problems are, strictly speaking, beyond the scope of this text we can argue that we should form the Lagrangian:

$$L = \int_0^T u(c_t)e^{-\rho t}dt + \lambda[W - \int_0^T c_t e^{-rt}dt]$$

$$= \int_0^T [u(c_t)e^{-\rho t} - \lambda c_t e^{-rt}]dt + \lambda W$$

where

$$W = \frac{y}{r}[1 - e^{-rt}]$$

and λ is a *constant* Lagrangian multiplier. We now argue that the Lagrangian is maximised by choosing each c_t to maximise the last integrand, namely:

$$u(c_t)e^{-\rho t} - \lambda c_t e^{-rt}$$

If $u(c_t) = \ln(c_t)$ write down the first order condition for c_t and c_0. By dividing these two conditions, eliminate λ and find an expression for c_t in terms of c_0. Now put this expression for c_t into the budget constraint

$$\int_0^T c_t e^{-rt}dt = W$$

and thus find c_0 and then c_t.

Solution on p. 299.

9.5 Consider a firm choosing its level of inputs according to the following non-profit-maximising criteria:

(i) Choose inputs k,l to maximise revenue subject to a lower bound on profits, i.e. choose k,l to maximise $pf(k,l)$ subject to $pf(k,l) - wl - rk \geqslant \tau$.

(ii) Choose k,l to maximise employment l subject to a lower bound on profits, i.e. maximise l subject to $pf(k,l) - wl - rk \geqslant \tau$.

Show that the firm using objective (i) will still minimise costs in that the marginal rate of technical substitution MRTS $= \dfrac{f_l}{f_k}$ will be equal to the ratio $\dfrac{w}{r}$. Furthermore show that the firm using objective (ii) will have MRTS smaller than this relative price. Hence, insofar as MRTS is an increasing function of the capital–labour ratio, we can conclude the firm in (ii) will have a lower capital–labour ratio.
Solution on p. 355.

9.6 A consumer has a maximum of T hours to allocate between leisure L and work l. If the real wage rate is w and there is a tax rate t on earned income, then the consumption available to the consumer is

$$c = (1 - t)wl$$

If the consumer has utility function

$$u(c,L) = (c^{1-\rho} + L^{1-\rho})/(1 - \rho)$$

where $0 < \rho < 1$, find the optimal level of labour supply l. Note $L = T - l$. Show that this labour supply will decrease as the tax rate t increases.
Solution on page p. 306.

9.7 Consider a situation where there are n identical consumers with the utility function used in problem 9.6 above. Each pays the same tax rate t as in 9.6, but now each receives an equal share of government expenditure (= total tax revenue). Hence in this case the consumer consumption will be given by

$$c = (1 - t)wl + g$$

where g is the consumer's share of government expenditure. Find an expression for the optimal supply of labour l. Note that $\dfrac{\partial g}{\partial l} = \dfrac{wt}{n}$.
Show that an increase in t still reduces labour supply.
Solution on p. 307.

10

The Indirect Utility Function

1 Introduction

The steps outlined in the second section of the last chapter give solutions to Problems 9.1 to 9.3 without difficulty. However, the main drawback of the Lagrangian approach is that this simplicity is far from the general rule. Indeed for most utility and production functions we cannot derive specific functions describing the behaviour of consumer or firm. Fortunately there is another procedure which we can adopt that avoids these problems, in that it allows us to side-step the Lagrangian conditions and is thus frequently used in both theoretical and applied economics, the procedure is based on the notions of duality. The Lagrangian approach uses the information about the consumer or firm contained in utility and production functions. In contrast the dual, or indirect, approach uses information about the firm or consumer contained in different, but closely related, functions. These are called optimal value functions. An optimal value function is a functional relationship between exogenous variables and the optimal level of the objective function given those exogenous variables. For example, a function that relates the optimal level of utility a consumer can obtain to his budget and the prices of goods is an example of an optimal value function. This function is known as the indirect utility function, and in this chapter we shall concentrate on this function and use it to introduce the basic ideas of duality. In particular we shall introduce a result known as Roy's Identity which tells us how we can construct a consumer's demand function given his indirect utility function. The prospect being that we can *start* our analysis of the consumer by considering this indirect utility function rather than the usual

190

(direct) utility function. As we shall see, once understood this alternative route is generally much simpler. Indeed the construction of demand functions from the indirect utility functions involves the relatively straightforward process of differentiation — we do not have to solve any equations.

2 The Indirect Utility Function

We begin our discussion with the optimal value function briefly mentioned in Section 1, i.e. the optimal level of utility a consumer can achieve as a function of the price of goods and his income. This is referred to as the indirect utility function to distinguish it from the utility function defined over consumption, which is frequently referred to as the direct utility function. The terminology is almost self-explanatory, since the indirect utility function gives the level of utility (not as a direct function of commodities consumed, but only indirectly) as a function of the prices and income which themselves determine the commodities consumed. Formally we have:

Definition 10.1: The indirect utility function, $v(\mathbf{p},m)$ is defined by $v(\mathbf{p},m) =$ maximum value of $u(\mathbf{x})$ subject to the constraint $m - \mathbf{px} \geqslant 0$.

Before discussing the properties of the indirect utility function we show how it is derived from the direct utility function, $u(\mathbf{x})$. For the case where there are only two goods and income, m, is held constant, this can be done diagrammatically. The direct indifference curves are drawn in Figure 10.1(a). These have the familiar property that the further the indifference curve lies from the origin, the higher the level of utility. The indirect indifference curves drawn in Figure 10.1(b) are less familiar. The first point to notice is that the figure is drawn for a fixed level of income, m. Each indifference curve represents all the combinations of p_1 and p_2 that allow the consumer to achieve the same level of utility when he maximises $u(x_1,x_2)$ subject to $m - p_1x_1 - p_2x_2 \geqslant 0$. Therefore each indifference curve represents a different level of utility, as in Figure 10.1(a). However, there is one major difference between 10.1(a) and 10.1(b). In Figure 10.1(b) the consumer is *better* off, the closer the indifference curve is to the origin, i.e. indifference curve 1 is associated with higher utility than indifference curve 2. Why is this so? Let us compare prices $\hat{p}_1$, $\hat{p}_2$ with $\bar{p}_1$, $\bar{p}_2$, both of which are given in Figure 10.1(b). Now $\bar{p}_1$ is less than $\hat{p}_1$ and $\bar{p}_2$ is less than $\hat{p}_2$. Given the same income, the consumer must be able to purchase more of both goods with prices $\bar{p}_1,\bar{p}_2$ than with $\hat{p}_1,\hat{p}_2$ and must be better off as a result.

The question we now wish to consider is, how do we construct Figure 10.1(b) from 10.1(a)? Figure 10.2 shows how this can be done. The north-east quadrant gives the conventional direct indifference curves.

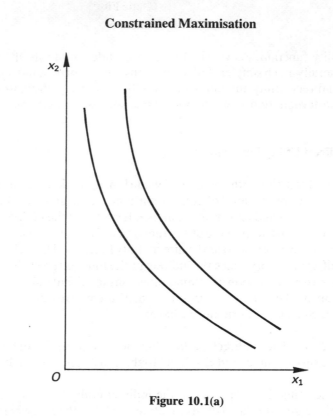

Figure 10.1(a)

Consider a point such as $\bar{x}$ in this quadrant and draw the tangent to the indifference curve at $\bar{x}$. An obvious but important point is that this tangent is the budget line for which $\bar{x}$ is the optimal choice. We now need to find the prices that generate this price line with income m. In Figure 10.2, $\hat{x}_1$ and $\hat{x}_2$ indicate the points where this budget line cuts the x_1 and x_2 axes. We can interpret $\hat{x}_1$ in the same way as in Chapter 8, Section 2, i.e. $\hat{x}_1$ is the maximum quantity of good 1 that can be purchased given income m. Obviously this occurs when none of good 2 is purchased, i.e. $\hat{x}_1 = m/p_1$ or $p_1 = m/\hat{x}_1$. Thus, given m and $\hat{x}_1$, we can find p_1. In Figure 10.2 this is done in the south-east quadrant of the figure. This quadrant has x_1 and p_1 as its axes and the line drawn gives all the points, i.e. all the combinations of p_1 and x_1, with the property that $p_1x_1 = m$. Given $\bar{x}_1$ we can find the p_1 associated with it. This is $\bar{p}_1$. An identical process for $\bar{x}_2$ using the north-west quadrant gives $\bar{p}_2$. Now consider this point, $\bar{p}$, in the south-west quadrant of Figure 10.2. This point has the property that given income m and prices $\bar{p}$ the maximum utility the consumer can achieve is $u(\bar{x})$, since with $\bar{p}$ and m the consumer is restricted to the budget line drawn in the north-east quadrant of Figure 10.2.

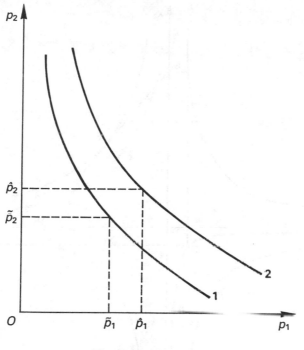

Figure 10.1(b)

This gives the first step in our construction of Figure 10.1(b). If we now choose a point like $\bar{x}$ on the same direct indifference curve, we obtain a point like $\bar{p}$ By doing this for every point on indifference curve 1 in the north-east quadrant we obtain an indifference curve 1 in the south-west quadrant. The level of utility associated with each of these points is identical. If we choose a point on another direct indifference curve, say $\bar{\bar{x}}$, we obtain a point $\bar{\bar{p}}$ and again we can derive the indirect indifference curve through $\bar{\bar{p}}$ from the direct indifference curve through $\bar{\bar{x}}$. By doing this for every point in the north-east quadrant we can construct Figure 10.1(b) from 10.1(a).

Figure 10.2 can be read the other way round, as follows. If we start at the point $\bar{p}$ we can obtain $\hat{x}_1,\hat{x}_2$, and interpret these as being the maximum quantities of the two goods which can be purchased from income m when prices are $\bar{p}_1$ and $\bar{p}_2$. Hence the line between $\hat{x}_1$ and $\hat{x}_2$ is the budget line associated with prices $\bar{p}_1,\bar{p}_2$. If we now find the indifference curve tangential to this budget line, we will identify the consumer's demand $\bar{x}_1,\bar{x}_2$ associated with prices $\bar{p}_1,\bar{p}_2$. The direct utility $u(\bar{x}_1,\bar{x}_2)$ yielded by those quantities, i.e. the utility associated with the indifference

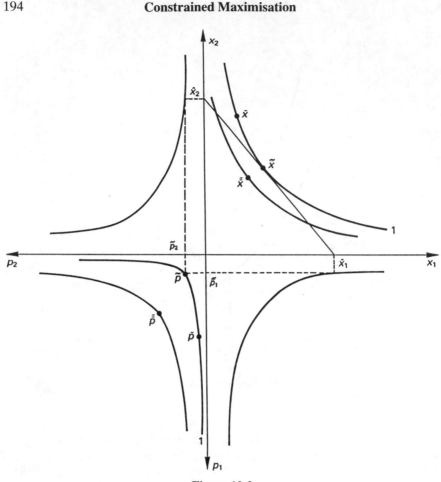

Figure 10.2

curve through $\tilde{x}$, will be the indirect utility $v(\bar{p}_1,\bar{p}_2,m)$ associated with prices $\bar{p}_1,\bar{p}_2$ and income m. Thus if we write

$$\tilde{x}_1 = x_1(\bar{p}_1,\bar{p}_2,m) \tag{10.1}$$

$$\tilde{x}_2 = x_2(\bar{p}_1,\bar{p}_2,m) \tag{10.2}$$

where the functions on the right-hand sides are the consumer's demand functions, we can assert

$$v(\bar{p}_1,\bar{p}_2,m) = u[x_1(\bar{p}_1,\bar{p}_2,m), \quad x_2(\bar{p}_1,\bar{p}_2,m)]$$

which states that the value of the indirect utility function at $\bar{p}_1,\bar{p}_2,m$ is equal to the direct utility function evaluated at the demands associated with those prices and income. Hence to construct v from u we first construct the demand functions and substitute them into u. In the case when there are many goods we can represent the vector of demand functions as $x(p,m) =$ $[x_1(p,m), x_2(p,m),...,x_n(p,m)]$ and define the indirect utility function in the following way:

Definition 10.2: Given direct utility function $u(x)$ the indirect utility function is

$$v(p,m) = u[x(p,m)]$$

where $x(p,m)$ is the vector of demand functions.

Given the above definition of the indirect utility function we can now derive the indirect utility function from the direct utility function, using the Lagrangian procedure outlined in the previous chapter.

Example 10.1

Let us derive the indirect utility function from the direct utility function $u(x_1,x_2) = \ln x_1 + \ln x_2$. We have already derived the demand functions from this direct utility function in Example 8.1. These were

$$x_1 = \frac{m}{2p_1}$$

$$x_2 = \frac{m}{2p_2}$$

Therefore:

$$v(p_1,p_2,m) = u[x_1(p_1,p_2,m), x_2(p_1,p_2,m)]$$

$$= \ln \frac{m}{2p_1} + \ln \frac{m}{2p_2}$$

$$= \ln\left(\frac{m}{2p_1} \frac{m}{2p_2} \right)$$

therefore

$$v(p_1,p_2,m) = \ln\left(\frac{m^2}{4p_1p_2} \right)$$

3 Characteristic Properties of Indirect Utility Functions

Comparing the above example with the introduction to this chapter, you may feel there is a contradiction in our discussion. We claimed in the introduction it was easier to derive equations describing the behaviour of consumers or producers from optimal value functions than from the direct utility or production functions. For the special case in this section, the claim is that it is easier to derive demand functions from the indirect rather than the direct utility function. This is important because it is not always easy to derive explicit demand functions from the direct utility function. However, in Example 10.1, to derive the indirect utility function we have had to derive the demand functions using the Lagrange procedure. Since this was the very problem we were hoping to side-step, we appear to have a major contradiction.

Unfortunately this cannot be fully answered until Chapter 12. However, until this question is answered one can be forgiven for questioning the relevance of optimal value functions. Therefore we will briefly consider this issue here in the context of direct utility functions. Besides motivating our discussion of the indirect utility function, it also explains why we will need to analyse the specific properties of indirect utility functions.

In the above discussion we have been at pains to derive the indirect from the direct utility function. This has served two roles, in that it allows us to illustrate the concept of an indirect utility function and to stress that its properties can be derived from the direct utility function. The fundamental theoretical building block is the direct utility function. Nevertheless, as we shall see in the next chapter, once we have an indirect utility function we can very easily identify the consumer's demand functions. We can thus ask ourselves the following question. Can we write down an indirect utility function without having to construct it from a direct function? For if we can, then the construction and analysis of demand functions can be simplified. What we would like to be able to do is to check whether a given function of prices and income is an indirect utility function, or equivalently whether it possesses those properties which characterise indirect utility functions.

This question of characterising indirect functions raises some subtle problems. Below we shall list various properties of indirect utility functions, these properties being derived from the above definitions. It is *necessary* that all indirect utility functions exhibit these properties. If a function is to be a potential indirect utility function, it must possess these properties. To complete our enquiry we must ask ourselves whether these properties are *sufficient* to guarantee that the function is an indirect utility function. It is this question of sufficiency that is relatively complex, and we shall not attempt to give a complete answer in this text. (Some attempt is made, however, in Section 6.) At present let us just indicate that the answer is positive. That is to say, if we write down a function satisfying the properties of $v(\mathbf{p}, m)$ listed below, then we can assert that it is a legitimate indirect utility function, *there being no necessity of our deriving it from* a direct function.

At the end of the day, this allows us to start our analysis of the consumer with indirect rather than direct utility functions, which, given the simplicity of deriving demand functions and the useful properties of indirect functions, is often a major advantage.

Similar remarks are valid for the expenditure, cost and profit functions discussed in the next chapter.

It is clear from the above discussion that we will need to establish the basic properties of indirect utility functions and we now turn to this problem.

Properties of the Indirect Utility Function[1]

(1)   If $\mathbf{p}' \geqslant \mathbf{p}$ then $v(\mathbf{p}',m) \leqslant v(\mathbf{p},m)$

(2)   If $m' \geqslant m$ then $v(\mathbf{p},m') \geqslant v(\mathbf{p},m)$

(3) $v(\mathbf{p},m) = v(\alpha\mathbf{p},\alpha m)$ for all $\alpha > 0$, i.e. $v(\mathbf{p},m)$ is homogeneous of degree zero in prices and income

(4)   If $v(\mathbf{p},m) = v(\mathbf{p}',m)$ then[2] $v[\alpha\mathbf{p} + (1 - \alpha)\mathbf{p}',m] \leqslant v(\mathbf{p},m) = v(\mathbf{p}',m), 0 \leqslant \alpha \leqslant 1$

quasi convex.

An increase in prices with income constant reduces the set of options available and consequently cannot lead to an increase in utility. A decrease in income with prices constant has the same effect. Properties (1) and (2) follow immediately from this fact. Property (3) is also straightforward, since if all prices and income are increased by the same proportion, then the budget constraint cannot be affected, i.e. if $\mathbf{p}\,\hat{\mathbf{x}} = m$ then $\alpha\mathbf{p}\,\hat{\mathbf{x}} = \alpha m$ for all $\alpha > 0$. If the budget constraint is not affected, then the maximum level of utility, given prices $\mathbf{p}$ and income m, must be the same as that with prices $\alpha\mathbf{p}$ and income αm.

The only property that is not immediately obvious is Property (4). We have automatically assumed this in Figure 10.1(b). Having derived such a figure from Figure 10.1(a) (using Figure 10.2) we know this property is true in the 2-good case, but what is the intuition behind this? Figure 10.3 shows the budget sets for prices p_1', p_2' and p_1,p_2, given income m in both cases. The budget constraint for prices $\alpha p_1' + (1 - \alpha)p_1, \alpha p_2' + (1 - \alpha)p_2$ is also drawn. Because all three budget lines cross in the same place the maximum utility, given the budget constraint $[\alpha p_1' + (1 - \alpha)p_1]x_1 + [\alpha p_2' + (1 - \alpha)p_2]x_2 = m$ must also be a feasible level of utility, given one of the two sets of prices p_1', p_2' or p_1, p_2. For example, if $\hat{\mathbf{x}}$ maximises utility given the budget constraint $[\alpha p_1' + (1 - \alpha)p_1]x_1 + [\alpha p_2' + (1 - \alpha)p_2]x_2 \leqslant m$,

---

[1] As we pointed out in Chapter 3, we restrict attention to differentiable functions. Therefore we only consider $v(\mathbf{p},m)$ which are differentiable in prices and income. It is possible to show that whenever $u(x)$ is twice differentiable, then $v(\mathbf{p},m)$ is also differentiable.

[2] In the terminology of Chapter 13, $v(\mathbf{p},m)$ is quasi-convex.

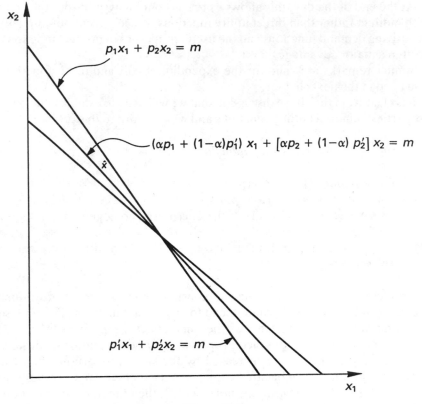

x_2

$p_1 x_1 + p_2 x_2 = m$

$(\alpha p_1 + (1-\alpha)p_1') \, x_1 + [\alpha p_2 + (1-\alpha) \, p_2'] \, x_2 = m$

$\hat{x}$

$p_1' x_1 + p_2' x_2 = m$

x_1

Figure 10.3

then the maximum utility given budget constraint $p_1 x_1 + p_2 x_2 \leq m$ must be at least as great as that given $\hat{x}$, since $\hat{x}$ is contained in the latter budget constraint. This argument easily generalises to the case of more than two commodities.

To see this, suppose we have prices **p** and **p**' and income m such that $v(\mathbf{p}',m) = v(\mathbf{p},m)$. Suppose for a given α, $\hat{x}$ is the level of consumption that gives maximum utility subject to the constraint

$$[\alpha \mathbf{p}' + (1-\alpha)\mathbf{p}]\hat{x} \leq m \qquad (10.3)$$

We can rewrite the above constraint as

$$\alpha \mathbf{p}' \hat{x} + (1-\alpha)\mathbf{p} \, \hat{x} \leq \alpha m + (1-\alpha)m \qquad (10.4)$$

We know $\hat{x}$ satisfies (10.3) therefore it also satisfies (10.4). If $\alpha \mathbf{p}' \hat{x} \leq \alpha m$, then $\hat{x}$ would also be a feasible consumption level given prices $\mathbf{p}'$, therefore $v(\mathbf{p}',m)$ must be greater than or equal to $v(\alpha \mathbf{p}' + (1-\alpha)\mathbf{p},m)$. But if $\alpha \mathbf{p}' \hat{x} > \alpha m$, then (10.4) tells us that $(1-\alpha)\mathbf{p} \, \hat{x} < (1-\alpha)m$. Thus $\hat{x}$ is a feasible consumption level given prices $\mathbf{p}$, so it must be true that $v(\mathbf{p},m) \geqslant v(\alpha\mathbf{p}' + (1 - \alpha)\mathbf{p},m)$. So again Property (4) must still hold. Therefore whether $\alpha\mathbf{p}'\hat{\mathbf{x}} \leqslant \alpha m$ or $\alpha\mathbf{p}'\hat{\mathbf{x}} > \alpha m$, Property (4) will be true. This was shown to hold for any given α and obviously will be true for all $0 \leqslant \alpha \leqslant 1$.

4 Roy's Identity

Our assertion is that, given a consumer's indirect utility function $v(\mathbf{p},m)$, we can construct his demand functions; indeed, we assert this is a relatively simple process. To demonstrate the validity of this assertion consider Figure 10.4 where we have drawn the standard diagram characterising a consumer's demands by the tangency of an indifference curve and his budget line. In the discussion that follows we shall hold the money income or budget m fixed. In

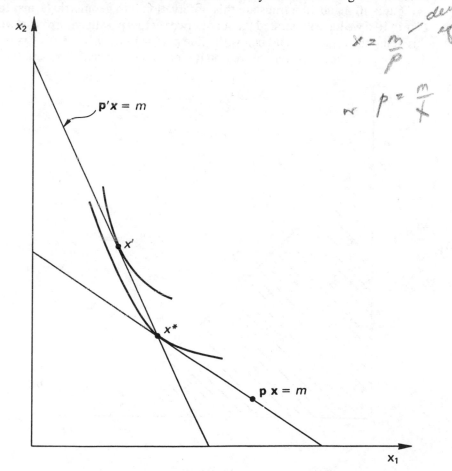

Figure 10.4

Figure 10.4 the vector $\mathbf{x}^*$ maximises utility subject to the budget constraint $\mathbf{px} \leqslant m$ i.e. $\mathbf{x}^*$ is the consumer's demand vector. We have also drawn an additional budget line associated with a different vector $\mathbf{p}'$ of prices such that $\mathbf{x}^*$ also lies on this second budget line. For this second set of prices $\mathbf{x}^*$ is *not* utility maximising, indeed this occurs at $\mathbf{x}'$ which yields a utility no less than $\mathbf{x}^*$, i.e. $u(\mathbf{x}') \geqslant u(\mathbf{x}^*)$. Thus Figure 10.4 illustrates the fact if $\mathbf{x}^*$ maximises utility at prices $\mathbf{p}$, then for any price vector $\mathbf{p}'$ satisfying $\mathbf{p}'\mathbf{x}^* \leqslant m$ the consumer can attain a utility level no lower than that at $\mathbf{x}^*$. Yet the utility of $\mathbf{x}^*$ is the indirect utility of $\mathbf{p}$, i.e. $u(\mathbf{x}^*) = v(\mathbf{p},m)$, while the utility of $\mathbf{x}'$ is equal to the indirect utility of $\mathbf{p}'$, i.e. $u(\mathbf{x}') = v(\mathbf{p}',m)$. Hence we have $v(\mathbf{p}^*,m) \leqslant v(\mathbf{p}',m)$, this being true for all $\mathbf{p}'$ satisfying $\mathbf{p}'\mathbf{x}^* \leqslant m$. But this tells us that if $\mathbf{x}^*$ is the demand vector at prices $\mathbf{p}$, then $\mathbf{p}$ minimises $v(\mathbf{p}',m)$ subject to $\mathbf{p}'\mathbf{x}^* \leqslant m$.

Figures 10.4 and 10.5 translate this observation into geometric terms. In Figure 10.5 we have illustrated the set of price vectors $\mathbf{p}'$ satisfying $\mathbf{p}'\mathbf{x}^* \leqslant m$, this being the region on and below the line $\mathbf{p}'\mathbf{x}^* = m$ i.e. $p_1'x_1^* + p_2'x_2^* = m$. Thus for any price vector in this region it is possible to purchase $\mathbf{x}^*$ and thus

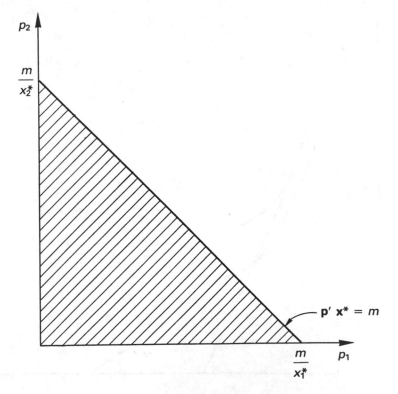

Figure 10.5

the utility available at these prices cannot be less than that offered by $\mathbf{x}^*$. The end points of the line $\mathbf{p'x}^* = m$ meet the axes at m/x_1^* and m/x_2^*, these being the maximum prices of goods 1 and 2 at which it would be possible to purchase $\mathbf{x}^*$. Hence the slope of this 'indirect' or 'dual' budget line is minus the ratio of m/x_2^* and m/x_1^* i.e. $-x_1^*/x_2^*$. We have argued that if $\mathbf{x}^*$ is the consumer's vector of demands at prices $\mathbf{p}$, then $\mathbf{p}$ minimises the indirect utility $v(\mathbf{p'},m)$ subject to the constraint $\mathbf{p'x}^* = m$. Recalling that indirect indifference curves lying higher in our diagram correspond to *lower* indirect utility, we can see that the minimisation of $v(\mathbf{p'},m)$ subject to $\mathbf{p'x}^* \leqslant m$ corresponds to the point of tangency between indirect indifference curves and the indirect budget line illustrated in Figure 10.6.

This observation immediately gives a geometric means of constructing consumer demands from indirect indifference curves. For any given price vector $\mathbf{p}$, we draw the indirect indifference passing through it as in Figure 10.6. Next we draw the tangent to this curve at $\mathbf{p}$ and identify the prices p_1^*

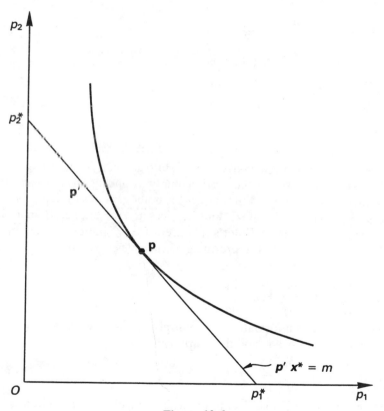

Figure 10.6

and p_2^* at which this tangent meets the price axes. We can then find $\mathbf{x}^*$, the demand vector, from the fact that $x_1^* = m/p_1^*$ and $x_2^* = m/p_2^*$.

To convert this geometric process into an algebraic one, we note that the slope of an indirect indifference curve is equal to minus the ratio of the partials of the indirect utility function. The *analogy* with 'ordinary' indifference curves is complete — we simply have to replace quantities by prices. Hence the slope of the indirect indifference curve through $\mathbf{p}$ is $-\dfrac{\partial v}{\partial p_1} \Big/ \dfrac{\partial v}{\partial p_2}$. But the indirect budget line has a slope equal to $-x_1^*/x_2^*$, hence we have

$$+\frac{x_1^*}{x_2^*} = +\frac{\partial v/\partial p_1}{\partial v/\partial p_2} \tag{10.5}$$

This is Roy's Identity in its relative form, for it tells us that the ratio of the consumer's demands is equal to the ratio of the partials of its indirect utility function. Multiplying through by $\partial v/\partial p_2$ and dividing by x_1^* allows us to rewrite (10.5) as

$$\frac{\partial v/\partial p_1}{x_1^*} = \frac{\partial v/\partial p_2}{x_2^*} = -\lambda^*, \quad \text{say.} \tag{10.6}$$

Alternatively we can write (10.6) as

$$\frac{\partial v}{\partial p_1} = -\lambda^* x_1^*$$
$$\frac{\partial v}{\partial p_2} = -\lambda^* x_2^* \tag{10.7}$$

We need to identify λ^* to convert (10.7) into a means of identifying $\mathbf{x}^*$. To do this we make use of the homogeneity property of indirect utility functions. Recall we argued that $v(\mathbf{p}, m)$ is homogeneous of degree zero in prices $\mathbf{p}$ and money m, i.e. if we double prices and the budget, then utility is unchanged. Appealing to Euler's Theorem (see Chapter 5) we can thus conclude that the sum of the products of variables and partials is equal to zero, i.e.

$$p_1 \frac{\partial v}{\partial p_1} + p_2 \frac{\partial v}{\partial p_2} + m \frac{\partial v}{\partial m} = 0 \tag{10.8}$$

To make use of this information we multiply the two equations in (10.7) by p_1 and p_2 respectively and add them up to give us:

$$p_1 \frac{\partial v}{\partial p_1} + p_2 \frac{\partial v}{\partial p_2} = -\lambda^* (p_1 x_1^* + p_2 x_2^*) \tag{10.9}$$

But $\mathbf{x}^*$ maximises utility subject to the usual budget constraint, hence

$$p_1 x_1^* + p_2 x_2^* = m \tag{10.10}$$

Substituting (10.10) into the right-hand side of (10.9) we see that the sum of the first two terms on the left-hand side of (10.8) is $-\lambda^* m$; hence

$$\lambda^* = \frac{\partial v}{\partial m} \qquad (10.11)$$

That is to say the common ratio in (10.6) is equal to $\partial v/\partial m$, the marginal utility of money and (10.7) can be written as

$$x_1^* = -\frac{\partial v/\partial p_1}{\partial v/\partial m}$$

$$x_2^* = -\frac{\partial v/\partial p_2}{\partial v/\partial m} \qquad (10.12)$$

This is Roy's Identity for the 2-good case. It tells us we can find the consumer's demand functions directly from its indirect utility function simply by differentiating the latter with respect to prices and money.

5 Optimal Value Functions and Lagrangians

In this section we lay the foundations to the envelope theorem of Chapter 12 by clarifying the relationship between optimal value functions and Lagrangians. To illustrate this relationship and the envelope theorem we continue with our discussion of the consumer indirect utility function and Roy's Identity.

Let x^* be the consumer's vector of demands at prices p and budget m, so that x^* maximises $u(x)$ subject to $m - p\,x \geq 0$. By the definition of the indirect utility function we have

$$v(p,m) = u(x^*) \qquad (10.13)$$

Furthermore if $L(x, \lambda^*; p,m) = u(x) + \lambda^*(m - px)$ is the Lagrangian of the utility maximisation problem we have

$$u(x^*) = L(x^*, \lambda^*; p,m) \qquad (10.14)$$

this following from the fact that

$$\lambda^*(m - p\,x^*) = 0 \qquad (10.15)$$

That is to say that at the optimum either the constraint holds with equality or the shadow price of the constraint is zero. We can recall that x^* is an unconstrained maximum of the Lagrangian hence

$$L(x^*, \lambda^*; p,m) \geq L(x, \lambda^*; p,m) \qquad (10.16)$$

this being true for all x. Combining (10.13), (10.14) and (10.16) gives us the following inequality

$$v(\mathbf{p},m) \geqslant L(\mathbf{x},\lambda^*;\mathbf{p},m) \tag{10.17}$$

or equivalently

$$v(\mathbf{p},m) \geqslant u(\mathbf{x}) + \lambda^*(m - \mathbf{p}\,\mathbf{x}) \tag{10.18}$$

It is to be stressed that this last inequality is true for all $\mathbf{p}$, m and $\mathbf{x}$, provided λ^* is the shadow price associated with the budget constrained determined by $\mathbf{p}$ and m. Note as these parameters $\mathbf{p},m$ vary, so will λ^*, i.e. λ^* is a function of $\mathbf{p}$ and m. Let us consider a particular combination $\hat{\mathbf{p}}$, $\hat{m}$ of prices and budget and let $\hat{\mathbf{x}}$ be the vector of demands at these prices and budget. We can obtain the following two inequalities from (10.18).

$$v(\hat{\mathbf{p}},m) \geqslant u(\hat{\mathbf{x}}) + \hat{\lambda}_1(m - \hat{\mathbf{p}}\,\hat{\mathbf{x}}) \tag{10.19}$$

and

$$v(\mathbf{p},\hat{m}) \geqslant u(\hat{\mathbf{x}}) + \hat{\lambda}_2(\hat{m} - \mathbf{p}\,\hat{\mathbf{x}}) \tag{10.20}$$

where $\hat{\lambda}_1$ is a function of $\hat{\mathbf{p}}$ and m, while $\hat{\lambda}_2$ is a function of $\mathbf{p}$ and m. Now Figure 10.7 illustrates the inequality in (10.19), where we have drawn the graph of $v(\hat{\mathbf{p}},m)$, seen as a function of m, and the graph of the Lagrangian $L(\hat{\mathbf{x}},\hat{\lambda};\hat{\mathbf{p}},m)$, also seen as a function of m. (10.19) tells us that the former graph lies on or above the latter. Yet, as indicated, the graphs will meet when $m = \hat{m}$ because $\hat{\mathbf{x}}$ is optimal at $(\hat{\mathbf{p}},\hat{m})$; it now follows that the graphs are tangential at $\hat{m}$. But this means the partial derivative of v with respect to m equals the partial derivative of L with respect to m when $m = \hat{m}$, i.e.

$$\frac{\partial v}{\partial m} = \frac{\partial L}{\partial m} \quad \text{when } m = \hat{m} \tag{10.21}$$

Yet

$$\frac{\partial L}{\partial m} = \frac{\partial}{\partial m}[u(\hat{\mathbf{x}}) + \hat{\lambda}(m - \hat{\mathbf{p}}\,\hat{\mathbf{x}})]$$

$$= \hat{\lambda} + \frac{\partial\hat{\lambda}}{m}(m - \hat{\mathbf{p}}\,\hat{\mathbf{x}})$$

and in general we will have $\hat{m} - \hat{\mathbf{p}}\hat{\mathbf{x}} = 0$, or if not, then $\partial\hat{\lambda}/\partial m = 0$ at $m = \hat{m}$.[3] Hence we finally obtain

$$\frac{\partial v}{\partial m} = \hat{\lambda} \quad \text{at } m = \hat{m} \tag{10.22}$$

---

[3] That is to say if the budget constraint were slack, i.e. the consumer attained a 'bliss' point within the budget set, then not only will the shadow price λ of the constraint be zero, it will remain zero for small changes in the budget. Hence $\partial\lambda/\partial m = 0$.

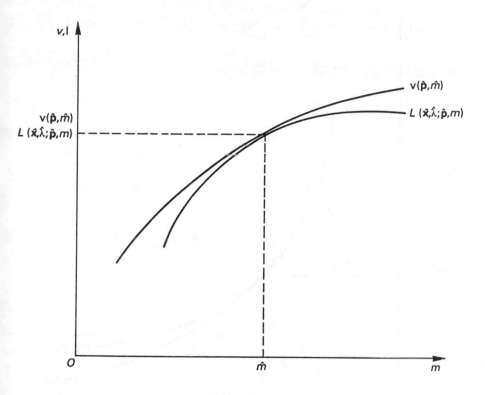

Figure 10.7

That is to say the Lagrangian multiplier is equal to the marginal utility of money.

A similar argument for prices based on (10.20), see Figure 10.8, leads to the conclusion

$$\frac{\partial v}{\partial p_i} = \frac{\partial L}{\partial p_i} \quad \text{at } p = \hat{p}$$

or

$$\frac{\partial v}{\partial p_i} = \frac{\partial}{\partial p_i} [u(\hat{x}) + \hat{\lambda}(\hat{m} - \mathbf{p}\,\hat{x})]$$

therefore

$$\frac{\partial v}{\partial p_i} = -\hat{\lambda}\hat{x}_i \qquad (10.23)$$

Combining (10.23) with (10.22) yields Roy's Identity

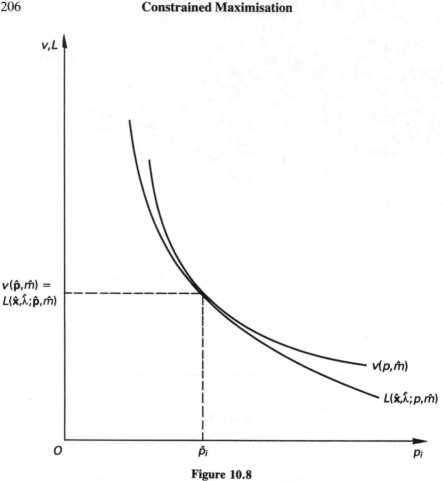

Figure 10.8

Here all other prices fixed at their $\hat{p}$ values

$$\hat{x}_i = -\frac{\partial v^l/\partial p_i}{\partial v/\partial m} \tag{10.24}$$

Reconsider Figures 10.7 and 10.8, and imagine $\hat{m}$ and p_i are allowed to move to and fro. For each $\hat{m}$ we obtain a new graph in Figure 10.7 for the Lagrangian while the graph of v remains unchanged, similarly for prices $\hat{p}_i$ in Figure 10.8. In this way we can consider the indirect utility function being the envelope of all the Lagrangians, in that its graph envelops all their graphs. It is this sort of geometric view that gives the general theorem its name.

In Chapter 12 we shall give a statement and proof of a general 'envelope theorem' and show that this is a useful means of deriving all those standard duality theorems of which Roy's Identity is but one.

Example 10.2
In Example 8.1 we derived the demand functions for the utility function
$u(x_1,x_2) = lnx_1 + lnx_2$ and thus obtained the indirect utility function

$$v(p,m) = \ln \left(\frac{m^2}{4p_1p_2} \right) = \ln(m^2) - \ln(4p_1p_2)$$

$$= 2\ln(m) - \ln p_1 - \ln p_2 - \ln 4$$

Hence

$$\frac{\partial v}{\partial m} = \frac{2}{m} , \quad \frac{\partial v}{\partial p_1} = -\frac{1}{p_1} \quad \text{and} \quad \frac{\partial v}{\partial p_2} = -\frac{1}{p_2}$$

and using Roy's Identity

$$x_1^* = -\frac{-1/p_1}{2/m} = \frac{m}{2p_1}$$

and

$$x_2^* = -\frac{-1/p_2}{2/m} = \frac{m}{2p_2}$$

6   The Duality of Indirect and Direct Utility Functions

We have seen how to derive the indirect utility function from the direct utility function. In this section we will show how to reverse this process and derive the direct from the indirect utility functions. The simplest diagrammatic representation is given in Figure 10.9. This figure reproduces Figure 10.2; thus the south-west quadrant contains the indirect indifference curve and we wish to derive the associated direct indifference curve in the north-east quadrant. Consider a point **p** in the south-west quadrant. From the previous discussion of this figure we know that the budget line associated with this point is that labelled 1 in the north-east quadrant. Now somewhere along this budget line the indifference curve we require is tangential to this budget constraint. The question is where? Let us draw in the north-east quadrant the budget lines associated with two points, **p′** and **p″**, one each side of **p** in the south-west quadrant. These budget constraints are 2 and 3 in Figure 10.9. The area A gives the region of budget constraint 1 that lies outside of budget constraints 2 and 3. Now the indifference curve that is tangential to 1 must also be tangential to 2 and 3, since all three budget constraints give the same maximum utility. A moment's reflection shows that the indifference curve must be tangential to 1 in the region A. since if it were not, the maximum level

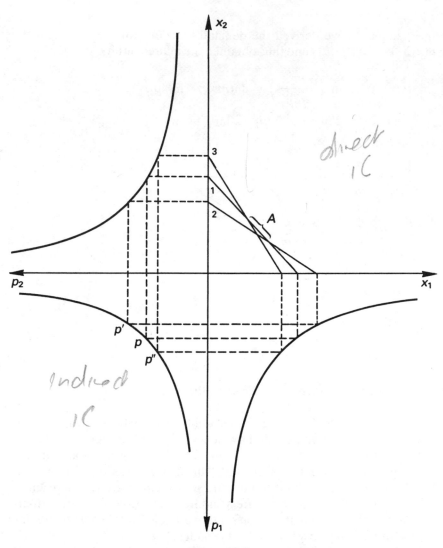

Figure 10.9

of utility associated with one of the other constraints, 2 or 3, must be higher. Once we know that the indifference curve must be tangential in the region A, we can pick two other points closer to **p** and follow the same reasoning. As we do this the region A contracts to a single point. This point must be on the direct indifference curve we require. We can repeat this process for each point on the indirect indifference curve and obtain the direct indifference curve in the north-east quadrant. The north-east quadrant of Figure 10.9 is reproduced in Figure 10.10 and the budget constraints are drawn for a large number of points

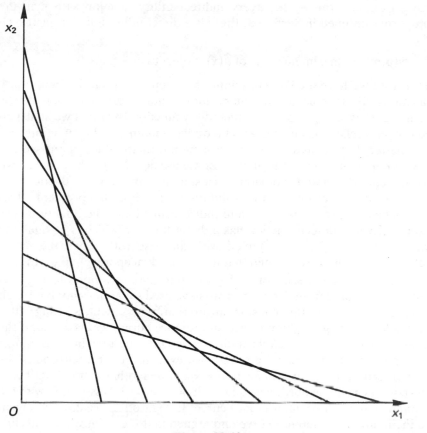

Figure 10.10

on the indirect indifference curve. For each budget constraint the indifference curve must be tangential to a point in the section of the budget constraint which lies outside all the other budget constraints. It is clear from Figure 10.10 that if we draw the budget constraint for each point on the indirect indifference curve, then the outer boundary of all these budget constraints represents the direct indifference curve we are seeking.

At this point we have established diagrammatically the crucial point that we hinted at in Section 2, in our discussion following Example 10.1. In Section 2 we have shown that, given a direct utility function, we can derive an indirect utility function associated with it. Furthermore in Section 3 we have outlined the properties that all indirect utility functions derived in this way must satisfy. Figure 10.9 shows that the reverse is true. Taking any indirect utility function which can be represented in the south-west quadrant of Figure 10.9, we can derive a direct utility function associated with it. Stating this in more general terms — for every indirect utility function satisfying the properties outlined in Section 3, there is a direct utility function $u(\mathbf{x})$ such that

$$v(\mathbf{p},m) \ = \ \text{maximum value of } u(\mathbf{x}) \text{ subject to } m - \mathbf{px} \geqslant 0$$

Therefore we have a complete duality between direct and indirect utility functions. If we pick a particular indirect utility function then this is equivalent to picking a specific direct utility function. Whether we analyse a consumer's behaviour starting with his direct or indirect utility function does not matter. Both contain exactly the same information, given one we can always derive the other. Which function we use depends on the problem we wish to consider, and it is obviously sensible to start with the function that takes us most quickly to the solution of the specific problem. This equivalence between the direct and indirect function is the duality theory proper. Every indirect function has a direct function which is its dual and vice versa. It is this fact coupled with the ease with which the major relationships can be established that makes the dual approach so useful.

Returning to our discussion of Figure 10.9, the derivation of the direct indifference curve from the indirect we have used so far does not lend itself to generalisation. We thus consider an alternative argument. Starting with a particular point, $\mathbf{p}$, in the indirect indifference curve, we have found the equivalent point on the direct indifference curve by drawing the budget constraints for points very close to $\mathbf{p}$. However, from our discussion of the indirect indifference curve in Section 4, we have another method of finding the point x_1,x_2 in the north-east quadrant of Figure 10.9 associated with the point $\mathbf{p}$ on the indirect indifference curve. In Figure 10.6 we drew a tangent to the indirect indifference curve and argued that the point where this line cuts the p_1 axis is $p_1^* = m/x_1^*$, where x_1^* is the consumption of good 1 that maximises utility given prices p_1,p_2 and income m. A similar argument holds for the point where this line cuts the p_2 axis. The north-west and south-east quadrants of Figure 10.9 transfer p_i to x_i^*. Therefore we can also find the x_1^*,x_2^* which maximise $u(x_1,x_2)$ subject to $p_1x_1 + p_2x_2 = m$ as in Figure 10.11. Given the point $\mathbf{p}$ in the south-west quadrant the tangent identifies $p_1^* = m/x_1^*$ and $p_2^* = m/x_2^*$. We transfer x_1^* to the north-east quadrant via the south-east quadrant and x_2^* via the north-west quadrant. The level of utility associated with the direct indifference curve passing through the point x_1^*,x_2^* is the same as the level of utility associated with the indirect indifference curve passing through $\mathbf{p}$. By repeating this process for each point on the indirect indifference curve, we obtain the direct indifference curve shown in the north-east quadrant of Figure 10.11. Finally we generate a formal procedure based on Figure 10.5 where we argued that the relationship between p_1,p_2,x_1^*,x_2^* and any other prices p_1',p_2' satisfying the equation

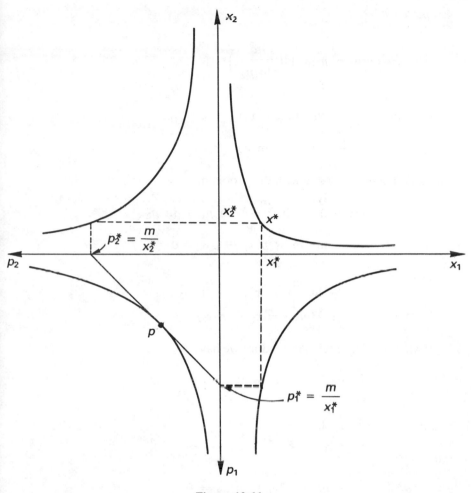

Figure 10.11

$$p_1'x_1^* + p_2'x_2^* = m$$

was that

$$v(p_1',p_2',m) \geqslant v(p_1,p_2,m) \tag{10.25}$$

(10.25) tells us how to derive the direct indifference curve from the indirect. Take any x_1',x_2' and minimise $v(p_1,p_2,m)$ subject to the constraint $p_1x_1' + p_2x_2' = m$. We can then solve for p_1,p_2 as functions of x_1',x_2' and m and substitute back into $v(p_1,p_2,m)$. Although this procedure is not always easy it will, in principle, derive $u(\mathbf{x})$ from $v(\mathbf{p},m)$.

Example 10.3
Consider

$$v(p_1,p_2,m) = \ln\left(\frac{m^2}{4p_1p_2}\right)$$

Writing the indirect utility function as

$$\ln \frac{m^2}{4} - \ln p_1 - \ln p_2$$

the Lagrangian associated with the problem:

$$\text{maximise} \quad - \ln \frac{m^2}{4} + \ln p_1 + \ln p_2$$

$$\text{subject to} \quad m - p_1x_1 - p_2x_2 = 0$$

is

$$L = - \ln \frac{m^2}{4} + \ln p_1 + \ln p_2$$
$$+ \lambda(m - p_1x_1 - p_2x_2)$$

Following the Lagrangian procedure we have

$$\frac{\partial L}{\partial p_1} = \frac{1}{p_1^*} - \lambda^*x_1 = 0$$

$$\frac{\partial L}{\partial p_2} = \frac{1}{p_2^*} - \lambda^*x_2 = 0$$

$$\frac{\partial L}{\partial \lambda} = m - p_1^*x_1 - p_2^*x_2 = 0$$

(remember we are solving for the p_1,p_2 that solve the problem for given x_1,x_2). Solving the first order conditions we have

$$\frac{1}{\lambda} = p_1^*x_1 = p_2^*x_2 = \frac{m}{2}$$

giving

$$p_1^* = \frac{m}{2x_1} \quad \text{and} \quad p_2^* = \frac{m}{2x_2}$$

Substituting these into $v(\mathbf{p},m)$ we have

$$u(\mathbf{x}) = v(p_1^*,p_2^*,m) = \ln \frac{m^2}{4} - \ln \frac{m}{2x_1} - \ln \frac{m}{2x_2}$$

$$= \ln \frac{m^2}{4} - \ln \frac{m^2}{4} + \ln x_1 + \ln x_2$$

$$= \ln x_1 + \ln x_2$$

Problems

10.1 Find the indirect utility function $v(p_1,p_2,m)$ associated with the utility function $u(x_1,x_2) = x_1^\alpha x_2^\beta$.
Solution on p. 284.

10.2 Find the direct utility function $u(x_1,x_2)$ associated with the indirect function $v(p_1,p_2,m) = \dfrac{m^{\alpha+\beta}}{p_1^\alpha p_2^\beta}$
Solution on p. 285.

10.3 Derive the Marshallian demand functions if the indirect utility function has the following forms:

(a) $v(\mathbf{p},m) = \dfrac{m^\sigma}{p_1^{\alpha_1} p_2^{\alpha_2} \cdots p_n^{\alpha_n}}$

where $\sigma = \alpha_1 + \alpha_2 + \ldots + \alpha_n$

(b) $v(p_1,p_2,m) = m(p_1^{-\sigma} + p_2^{-\sigma})^{1/\sigma}$

where now $\sigma = \dfrac{\rho}{1-\rho}$

Solution on p. 287.

10.4 Given a (Marshallian) demand function $x_i(\mathbf{p},m)$ for a good, the associated income elasticity of demand is

$$\eta = \frac{m}{x_i} \frac{\partial x_i}{\partial m}$$

If a consumer's indirect utility function takes the form

$$v(\mathbf{p},m) = m\phi(\mathbf{p})$$

show the consumer's demand for each good has a unit income elasticity.
Solution on p. 294.

10.5 Consider a set of consumers and let $x_i^h(\mathbf{p},m^h)$ be the h'th consumer's (Marshallian) demand for the i'th good, where m^h is that consumer's income. The aggregate demand of the set of consumers is simply the sum of their individual demands and thus takes the form

$$x_i(\mathbf{p},\mathbf{m}) = \sum_h x_i^h(\mathbf{p},m^h)$$

where $\mathbf{m}$ is the vector of incomes. The problem of *aggregation* in consumer theory is to find conditions where the aggregate demand can be treated as if it were the demands of an individual who receives the aggregate income $m = \sum_h m^h$. Consider the situation where the h'th consumer's indirect utility function takes the form

$$v^h(\mathbf{p},m^h) = \alpha(\mathbf{p})m^h + \beta^h(\mathbf{p})$$

Note $\alpha(\mathbf{p})$ does *not* depend on h. Show that the aggregate demand can be viewed as being generated by the indirect utility function

$$v(\mathbf{p},m) = \alpha(\mathbf{p})m + \beta(\mathbf{p})$$

where $\beta(\mathbf{p}) = \sum_h \beta^h(\mathbf{p})$
Solution on p. 294.

10.6 Derive the (Marshallian) demand functions associated with the indirect utility function

$$v(p_1,p_2,m) = \frac{m - \alpha p_1 - \beta p_2}{p_1^\gamma p_2^\delta}$$

where $\delta = 1 - \gamma$ and α,β,γ are all positive. Interpret these demand functions by viewing α,β as 'survival' or 'necessary' quantities of the two goods.
Solution on p. 295.

11

Expenditure, Cost and Profit Functions

1 Introduction

In the previous chapter we offered an extended discussion of the indirect utility function and suggested that the indirect and direct utility functions are dual to each other. The use of the term 'dual' is left rather vague in economics, and the best definition we can offer is the following. Two functions are dual to each other if we can in principle construct one from the other, or, a little more loosely, if they contain the same information. The reader will not be surprised to hear that there are duality relations other than that between direct and indirect utility functions. Our aim in this chapter is to discuss some of the most common examples of such duality.

2 Expenditure Functions

Apart from the indirect utility function, a second optimal value function that is frequently used in consumer theory is the expenditure function. The expenditure function tells us the minimum level of expenditure a consumer needs to obtain a given level of utility for a given set of commodity prices. Figure 11.1 shows the minimum level of expenditure necessary to attain utility level $\bar{u}$, given prices p_1 and p_2. The minimum level of expenditure in this case is $p_1 x_1^* + p_2 x_2^*$. Call this m^*, where x_1^* and x_2^* are the optimum levels of consumption, given prices p_1 and p_2, and this level of expenditure. The shaded region in Figure 11.1 shows all the feasible combinations of x_1 and x_2 that will give $u(x_1,x_2) \geq \bar{u}$. Any lower level of expenditure than

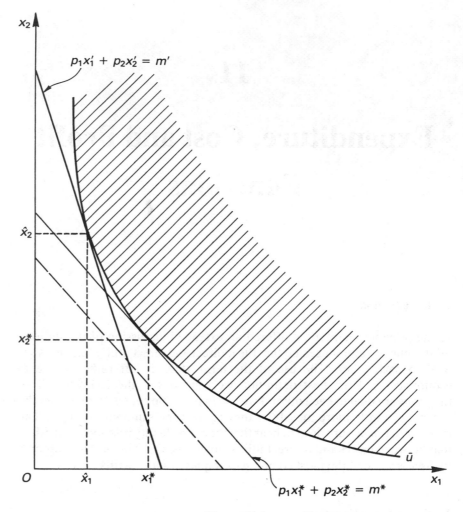

Figure 11.1

$p_1 x_1^* + p_2 x_2^*$, e.g. the broken line, will not enable the consumer to attain utility level $\bar{u}$. If the prices had been different, e.g. p_1', p_2', then we would require (in general) a different level of expenditure to achieve utility level $\bar{u}$. In this case, from Figure 11.1, we would require $p_1' \hat{x}_1 + p_2' \hat{x}_2$ (call this level of expenditure m'). Putting this in functional form, let us write $e(p_1, p_2, \bar{u})$ for the minimum level of expenditure needed to obtain utility level $\bar{u}$, given prices p_1 and p_2. Then Figure 11.1 shows that

$$m^* = e(p_1, p_2, \bar{u})$$

and

$$m' = e(p_1',p_2',\bar{u})$$

Generally we have:

Definition 11.1: The expenditure function, $e(\mathbf{p},u)$, is defined by $e(\mathbf{p},u)$ = minimum level of $\mathbf{p}\,\mathbf{x}$ satisfying the constraint $u(\mathbf{x}) \geq \bar{u}$.

We can see immediately from Figure 11.1 how to derive the expenditure function from the direct utility function. Given utility level $\bar{u}$ and prices p_1 and p_2, we need to find x_1^* and x_2^*, the minimum expenditure level being simply $p_1x_1^* + p_2x_2^*$. For the case of many commodities we follow a similar approach. Firstly we solve the problem

$$\text{maximise} -\mathbf{p}\,\mathbf{x}\,\text{subject to}\,u(\mathbf{x}) \geq u \tag{11.1}$$

This will give a solution in the form of optimal consumption levels as functions of $\mathbf{p}$ and u. Thus we obtain n functions: $x_1 = x_1(\mathbf{p},u)$, $x_2 = x_2(\mathbf{p},u)$, ..., $x_n = x_n(\mathbf{p},u)$. These can be written in vector notation:

$$\mathbf{x} = \mathbf{x}(\mathbf{p},u) \tag{11.2}$$

It is helpful at this point to compare (11.2) with (10.1) and (10.2). We have described (10.1) and (10.2) as demand functions. They gave the optimal consumptions levels of x_1 and x_2 as functions of prices and income. These are the conventional demand functions we use in economics. If we wish to determine the change in demand for a good, given a particular change in price, we usually assume income is held constant. However (11.2) can also be interpreted as demand functions. These give the demand for commodities as functions of prices and a given level of utility. Thus as prices change and quantities adjust, it is the level of *utility* that is being held constant and *not* the level of income. Such demand functions are called Hicksian demand functions. Conventional demand functions, those given in (10.1) and (10.2), are frequently called Marshallian demand functions. The term demand function without any qualification will refer to Marshallian demand functions. We can now give an alternative definition of the expenditure function.

Definition 11.2: The expenditure function is

$$e(\mathbf{p},u) = \mathbf{p}\,\mathbf{x}(\mathbf{p},u)$$

where $\mathbf{x}(\mathbf{p},u)$ is the vector of Hicksian demand functions.

Example 11.1
Consider the direct utility function

$$u(\mathbf{x}) = x_1^{1/2}x_2^{1/2}$$

(11.1) can now be written:

maximise $-p_1x_1 - p_2x_2$ subject to $x_1^{1/2}x_2^{1/2} - \bar{u} \geq 0$

The Lagrangian is:

$$L = -p_1x_1 - p_2x_2 + \lambda(x_1^{1/2}x_2^{1/2} - \bar{u})$$

giving

$$\frac{\partial L}{\partial x_1} = -p_1 + \frac{\lambda^*}{2}\ x_1^{*-1/2}x_2^{*-1/2} = 0 \tag{11.3}$$

$$\frac{\partial L}{\partial x_2} = -p_2 + \frac{\lambda^*}{2}\ x_1^{*1/2}x_2^{*-1/2} = 0 \tag{11.4}$$

$$\frac{\partial L}{\partial \lambda} = x_1^{*1/2}x_2^{*1/2} - \bar{u} = 0 \tag{11.5}$$

Taking p_1 to the right-hand side of (11.3) and p_2 to the right-hand side of (11.4) and dividing the former by the latter gives

$$\frac{x_1^{*-1/2}x_2^{*1/2}}{x_1^{*1/2}x_2^{*-1/2}} = \frac{p_1}{p_2}$$

or

$$\frac{x_2^*}{x_1^*} = \frac{p_1}{p_2} \tag{11.6}$$

Taking $\bar{u}$ to the right-hand side of (11.5) and squaring both sides gives

$$x_1^*x_2^* = \bar{u}^2 \tag{11.7}$$

Substituting for x_2^* in (11.7) from (11.6) we obtain

$$\frac{p_1}{p_2}\cdot x_1^{*2} = \bar{u}^2$$

hence

$$x_1^* = \left(\frac{p_2}{p_1}\right)^{1/2}\bar{u}$$

similarly

$$x_2^* = \left(\frac{p_1}{p_2}\right)^{1/2}\bar{u}$$

therefore we have

$$e(\mathbf{p},\bar{u}) = p_1x_1^* + p_2x_2^* = p_1\left(\frac{p_2}{p_1}\right)^{1/2}\bar{u} + p_2\left(\frac{p_1}{p_2}\right)^{1/2}\bar{u}$$

thus the expenditure function is

$$e(\mathbf{p},u) = 2p_1^{1/2}p_2^{1/2}\bar{u}$$

Having seen how the expenditure function and the indirect utility function are derived from the direct utility function, there must obviously be some relation between them. To see this relationship look at Figure 11.2 which shows the indifference curve for a specified level of utility, $\bar{u}$, and a budget line $\mathbf{px} = \bar{m}$; $\bar{u}$ and $\bar{m}$ are picked in such a way that the budget constraint is tangential to the indifference curve at $\mathbf{x}^*$. Clearly $\mathbf{x}^*$ maximises utility subject to the constraint $\mathbf{px} \leqslant \bar{m}$. Put another way, this tells us that $\bar{u}$ is the maximum utility given the budget constraint $\mathbf{px} \leqslant \bar{m}$, i.e. $v(p,\bar{m}) = \bar{u}$. It is also obvious from the figure that the minimum expenditure necessary to achieve utility $\bar{u}$, given prices $\mathbf{p}$, is $\bar{m}$, i.e. $e(\mathbf{p},\bar{u}) = \bar{m}$. Since both these relationships between $\bar{u}$ and $\bar{m}$ must be true, we have the following relation between expenditure functions and indirect utility function:

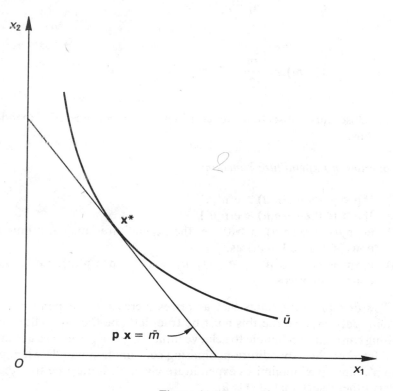

Figure 11.2

Definition 11.3:

$$e(\mathbf{p},\bar{u}) = \bar{m} \text{ if and only if } v(\mathbf{p},\bar{m}) = \bar{u}. \tag{11.8}$$

This shows us how we can derive the indirect utility function from the expenditure function. Given $e(\mathbf{p},u) = m$ we rewrite this, in terms of u, as a function of $\mathbf{p}$ and m, i.e. $u = v(\mathbf{p},m)$.

Example 11.2
To derive the indirect utility function when

$$e(\mathbf{p},u) = 2p_1^{1/2}p_2^{1/2}u$$

write

$$m = 2p_1^{1/2}p_2^{1/2}u$$

giving

$$u = \frac{m}{2}\, p_1^{-1/2}p_2^{-1/2}$$

i.e.

$$v(\mathbf{p},m) = \frac{m}{2}\, p_1^{-1/2}p_2^{-1/2}$$

To close this subsection we consider the properties of expenditure functions.

Properties of Expenditure Functions

(1)   If $\mathbf{p} \geqslant \mathbf{p}'$ then $e(\mathbf{p},u) \geqslant e(\mathbf{p}',u)$.
(2)   If $u \geqslant u'$ then $e(\mathbf{p},u) \geqslant e(\mathbf{p},u')$.
(3) $e(\alpha\mathbf{p},u) = \alpha e(\mathbf{p},u)$, $\alpha > 0$, i.e. the expenditure function is homogeneous of degree 1 in prices.
(4) $e[\alpha\mathbf{p} + (1 - \alpha)\mathbf{p}',u] \geqslant \alpha e(\mathbf{p},u) + (1 - \alpha)e(\mathbf{p}',u)$, i.e. $e(\mathbf{p},u)$ is concave in prices.

The first property states that as prices increase the expenditure level cannot decrease. To see this must be true, let $\hat{x}$ be the expenditure-minimising consumption bundle to achieve utility $\bar{u}$, given prices p as in 1 above, and let $\mathbf{x}'$ be the expenditure-minimising consumption bundle when prices are $\mathbf{p}'$. Since $\mathbf{p}'\mathbf{x}'$ minimises expenditure given $\mathbf{p}'$, it must be true that for every other $\mathbf{x}$ such that $u(\mathbf{x}) \geqslant \bar{u}$:

$$\mathbf{p}'\mathbf{x} \geqslant e(\mathbf{p}',\bar{u}) \tag{11.9}$$

But since $\mathbf{p} \geqslant \mathbf{p}'$ it must be true that $\mathbf{p}\,\hat{\mathbf{x}} \geqslant \mathbf{p}'\hat{\mathbf{x}}$; therefore we must have

$$e(\mathbf{p},\bar{u}) = \mathbf{p}\,\hat{\mathbf{x}} \geqslant \mathbf{p}'\hat{\mathbf{x}} \geqslant e(\mathbf{p}',\bar{u})$$

as required.

The second property is straightforward. In Figure 11.3, if $\bar{m} = e(\mathbf{p},\bar{u})$, then given prices $\mathbf{p}$, the shaded area and the constraint represent the only points where $\mathbf{p}\,\mathbf{x} \leqslant \bar{m}$. If we wish to attain a higher level of utility, e.g. $\hat{u}$, then this can only be possible by increasing expenditure.

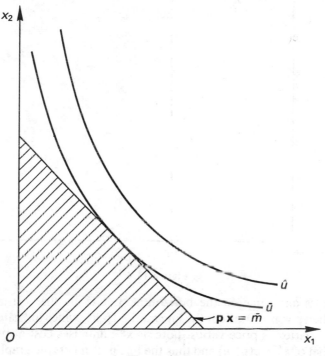

Figure 11.3

To see that the expenditure function must be homogeneous of degree 1 in prices, multiply both sides of (11.9) by λ, i.e.

$$\lambda\mathbf{p}'\mathbf{x} \geqslant \lambda e(\mathbf{p}',\bar{u}) = \lambda(\mathbf{p}'\mathbf{x}') \qquad (11.10)$$

(11.10) tells us that if prices are $\lambda\mathbf{p}'$, then for all $\mathbf{x} \neq \mathbf{x}'$ satisfying $u(\mathbf{x}) \geqslant \bar{u}$, expenditure is greater than $\lambda e(\mathbf{p}',\bar{u})$. Therefore $\lambda e(\mathbf{p}',\bar{u})$ is the minimised expenditure given $\lambda\mathbf{p}'$, i.e. $\lambda e(\mathbf{p}',\bar{u})$ must be equal to $e(\lambda\mathbf{p}',\bar{u})$.

The fourth property is the most useful and probably the least obvious. To get some intuition of why this property holds let us change one price, p_1, while holding the others constant. Figure 11.4 shows expenditure on the

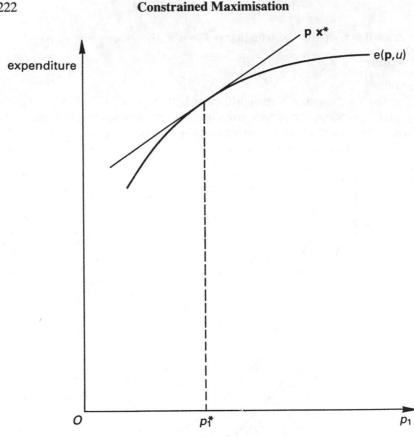

Figure 11.4

vertical axis and price on the horizontal. Let x^* be the cost-minimising
choice when $p = p^*$. Consider the line marked $p\ x^*$, which indicates how the
cost of x^* varies as price varies, note as x^* minimises cost at prices p^* it
follows that $p^*x^* = e(p^*,u)$ and thus the line $p\ x^*$ meets the graph of $e(p,u)$
when $p = p^*$. Since we can always attain the desired level of utility from
consuming x^*, then for any other $p_1 \neq p_1^*$ it must be true that the minimum
expenditure necessary to achieve the desired level of utility must be less than
or equal to $p\ x^*$, i.e.

$$e(p,u) \leqslant p\ x^*$$

Hence the graph of $e(p,u)$ must lie below (or to be more exact cannot lie
above) the line $p\ x^*$, but as this touches the graph when $p = p^*$ it follows that
it is the tangent to that graph. Hence $e(p,u)$ is concave because its graph
does not lie above its tangents, see Chapter 7. This argument generalises
straightforwardly to all prices as follows.

Let x minimise expenditure when prices are $\alpha p + (1 - \alpha)p'$, i.e.

$$e[\alpha p + (1 - \alpha)p',u] = [\alpha p + (1 - \alpha)p']x \qquad (11.11)$$

Following the argument we used for p_1, if prices are p', then the minimum expenditure to achieve the required utility cannot be greater than $p'x$, i.e.

$$e(p',u) \leq p'x \qquad (11.12)$$

Similarly it must be true that

$$e(p,u) \leq p \, x \qquad (11.13)$$

If we multiply (11.12) by $(1 - \alpha)$ and (11.13) by α and add together, we obtain

$$\alpha e(p,u) + (1 - \alpha)e(p',u) \leq \alpha p \, x + (1 - \alpha)(p'x)$$

Substituting for the right-hand side from (11.11) gives

$$\alpha e(p,u) + (1 - \alpha)(p',u) \leq e[\alpha p + (1 - \alpha)p',u]$$

as required.

Producha Toory

3 The Cost Function

3.1 Unrestricted Cost Functions

The first optimal value function we wish to consider for the firm is the cost function. The cost function tells us the minimum cost of achieving a given level of output for a given set of input prices. If we consider a firm using capital and labour as inputs and paying w per unit for the latter and r per unit for the former we have:

Definition 11.4: The cost function, $c(y,w,r)$, is defined: $c(y,w,r) =$ minimum level of $wl + rk$ satisfying the constraint $f(k,l) \geq y$, f being the production function.

At this point it is worth comparing the definition above with the definition of the expenditure function. Apart from notational differences they are identical. Indeed it is not uncommon to see the expenditure function called the 'consumer's cost function'. All the figures and arguments used in the previous subsection apply directly to the cost function. All that is required is to relabel the variables. Utility (u) becomes output (y), x becomes l and k, and p becomes the input prices r and k. There is no point in reproducing the whole line of argument from Section 2. We will quickly outline the main statements for the cost function but will avoid any further discussion.

To derive the cost function from the production function, $y = f(k,l)$, we first solve the problem

$$\text{maximise} -wl - rk \text{ subject to } f(k,l) \geqslant y \tag{11.14}$$

This will give functions

$$k = k(y,w,r) \tag{11.15}$$

and

$$l = l(y,w,r) \tag{11.16}$$

(11.15) and (11.16) give the demand for inputs as functions of the target level of output and prices. These are not the conventional input demand functions since they are not the input levels that maximise profit given w,r and output price. They are input demand functions that are conditional on the stated level of output and are referred to as the conditional input (or factor) demand functions. The difference between a firm's input demand functions and the conditional demand functions is very similar to the difference between the Marshallian and Hicksian demand functions. However, the analogy is not complete, since the input demand functions of a firm are derived from profit maximisation with a production constraint, while the Marshallian demand functions are derived from utility maximisation subject to a budget constraint. Given (11.15) and (11.16), we can define the cost function in the following way:

Definition 11.5: The cost function is

$$c(y,w,r) = wl(y,w,r) + rk(y,w,r)$$

where $l(y,w,r)$ and $k(y,w,r)$ are the conditional input demand functions.

Example 11.3
Let us derive the cost function from the production function $y = f(k,l) = k^{1/2}l^{1/2}$. We have already solved the problem

$$\text{maximise} -wl - rk \text{ subject to } (kl)^{1/2} \geqslant y$$

in Example 8.2. This gave conditional input demand of

$$l = y\left(\frac{r}{w}\right)^{1/2}$$

$$k = y\left(\frac{w}{r}\right)^{1/2}$$

Using the above definition we have

$$c(y,w,r) = yw\left(\frac{r}{w}\right)^{1/2} + yr\left(\frac{w}{r}\right)^{1/2}$$

$$= 2y(wr)^{1/2}$$

3.2 Restricted Cost Functions

Although we have not stated it specifically, we have been assuming that both k and l are variable when we have derived the cost function. This corresponds to the long-run time period in economics (i.e. when all factors of production are variable). However, we are often interested in shorter periods when one of the inputs is fixed. Almost always we assume that capital is fixed and labour is flexible in the short run. As a result the cost function we need to consider will be different to the one we have analysed. In the short run we are only interested in the cost of producing a certain level of output when capital is restricted to a specific level. This cost function is referred to as the restricted cost function.

Definition 11.6: The restricted cost function $c(y,w,r,\bar{k})$ is defined

$c(y,w,r,\bar{k}) = $ minimum $wl + rk$ subject to $f(l,k) \geq y$ and $k = \bar{k}$.

As an example we derive the restricted cost function for the case of Example 11.3.

Example 11.4
If $y = k^{1/2}l^{1/2}$ then

$$l = \frac{y^2}{k}$$

thus

$$c(y,w,r,k) = wl + rk$$

$$= w\frac{y^2}{k} + rk$$

Figure 11.5 shows the relationship between $c(y,w,r)$ and $c(y,w,r,\hat{k})$. If $y = 0$ then $c(y,w,r) = 0$, since if no output is produced no inputs are required. However, $c(y,w,r,\hat{k}) = r\hat{k}$ since in the short run the firm is restricted to $k = \hat{k}$ and even if output is zero, costs must be $r\hat{k}$. The difference between the two cost functions will decline as y rises until $y = \hat{y}$. $\hat{y}$ is the level of output such that the firm maximising

$$pf(k,l) - wl - rk$$

with no restrictions on l and k would actually choose $k = \hat{k}$. At this point the fact that the firm is restricted to $k = \hat{k}$ is irrelevant, since $\hat{k}$ happens to be the optimal level of capital required. However, once y is increased beyond

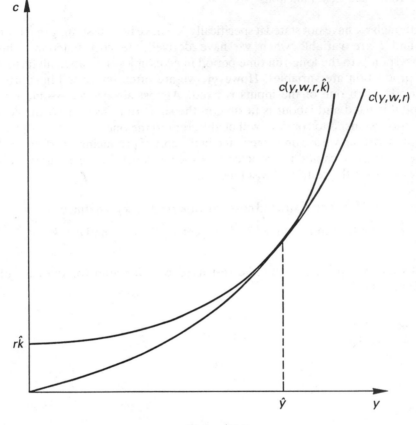

Figure 11.5

this stage, then optimality would require $k > \hat{k}$. Since the firm in the short run is restricted to use less k and more l than they would wish, the cost of producing any level of $y > \hat{y}$ will be greater than in the long run, i.e.

$$c(y,w,r,\bar{k}) > c(y,w,r) \quad \text{if} \quad y > \hat{y}$$

This figure also shows how we can derive the cost function from the restricted cost function. If we minimise $c(y,w,r,k)$ with respect to k, i.e.

$$c_k(y,w,r,k) = 0$$

we obtain

$$k = z(y,w,r)$$

This function tells us for any y,w and r the k that minimises costs. In the example used for Figure 11.5 we would have

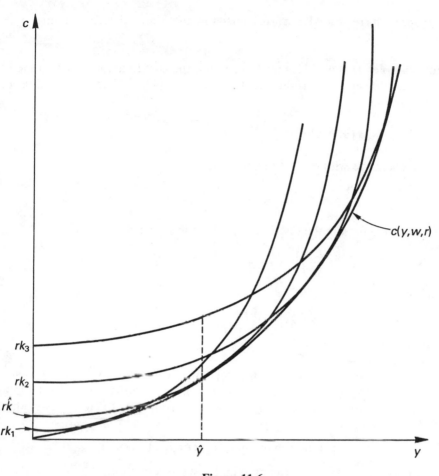

Figure 11.6

$$\hat{k} = z(\hat{y},w,r)$$

To see this look at Figure 11.6 which gives the cost function $c(y,w,r)$ and four restricted cost functions for four levels of k, $k_1 < \hat{k} < k_2 < k_3$. For each k we can read off the cost of producing $\hat{y}$ if k is restricted to the specific level. It is clear from Figure 11.6 that $k = \hat{k}$ minimises $c(\hat{y},w,r,k)$. At $y = \hat{y}$ we have the following relationship:

$$c(\hat{y},w,r,\hat{k}) = c(\hat{y},w,r)$$

or, replacing $\hat{k}$ with $z(\hat{y},w,r)$:

$$c[\hat{y},w,r,z(\hat{y},w,r)] = c(\hat{y},w,r)$$

Thus once we have found the k that minimises $c(y,w,r,k)$, we can substitute for this in the restricted cost function to find the (unrestricted) cost function.

Example 11.5
In Examples 11.3 and 11.4 we have found the cost function and restricted cost function for the production function $y = (kl)^{1/2}$. The restricted cost function was

$$c(y,w,r,k) = w \frac{y^2}{k} + rk$$

Minimising this with respect to k we find

$$\frac{wy^2}{k^2} = r \quad \text{or} \quad k = \left(\frac{w}{r} \right)^{1/2} y$$

Substituting for k in the restricted cost function we have

$$wy^2 \left(\frac{r}{w} \right)^{1/2} \frac{1}{y} + r \left(\frac{w}{r} \right)^{1/2} y$$

therefore

$$c(y,w,r) = 2y(wr)^{1/2}$$

(as given in Example 10.4).

   Having defined costs as a function y it is very easy to find how costs increase as we increase y. Thus partially differentiating the cost function with respect to y gives the marginal cost of production. Thus we have the following relationships:

$c_y(y,w,r)$ = long-run marginal cost of production

$c_y(y,w,r,k)$ = short-run marginal cost of production

   Finally we can move directly to the properties of the cost functions since the justification for these has already been given in Section 2.

3.3 Properties of Cost Functions

Properties of the Cost Function
(1)   If $w \geq w'$ and $r \geq r'$, then $c(y,w,r) \geq c(y,w',r')$.
(2)   If $y \geq y'$, then $c(y,w,r) \geq c(y',w,r)$.
(3) $c(y,\alpha w,\alpha r) = \alpha c(y,w,r)$, $\alpha > 0$, i.e. the cost function is homogeneous of degree 1 in input prices.
(4) $c[y,\alpha w + (1 - \alpha)w', \alpha r + (1 - \alpha)r'] \geq \alpha c(y,w,r) + (1 - \alpha) c(y,w',r')$, i.e. $c(y,w,r)$ is concave in prices.

The properties of the restricted cost function are mostly similar but are worth stating separately.

Properties of the Restricted Cost Function
(1) If $w' \geq w$ and $r' \geq r$, then $c(y,w',r',k) \geq c(y,w,r,k)$.
(2) If $y' \geq y$, then $c(y',w,r,k) \geq c(y,w,r,k)$.
(3) $c(y,\alpha w,\alpha r,k) = \alpha c(y,w,r,k)$, $\alpha > 0$.
(4) $c[y,\alpha w + (1 - \alpha)w',\ \alpha r + (1 - \alpha)r',k] = \alpha c(y,w,r,k) + (1 - \alpha)$
     $c(y,w',r',k)$, $0 \leq \alpha \leq 1$.
(5) $c[y,w,r,\alpha k + (1 - \alpha)k'] \leq \alpha c(y,w,r,k) + (1 - \alpha)c(y,w,r,k')$, $0 \leq \alpha$
     ≤ 1, i.e. the restricted cost function is convex in k.

Properties (1), (2) and (3) are identical to the (unrestricted) cost function properties. Property (4) is now an equality rather than inequality, because with only two factors of production there is no room for manoeuvre. If k is fixed at $\hat{k}$, then the l that minimises costs subject to $f(l,\hat{k}) \geq y$ will be the same l, say $\hat{l}$, regardless of prices. Therefore, since

$$\alpha(w\hat{l} + r\hat{k}) + (1 - \alpha)(w'\hat{l} + r'\hat{k}) = [\alpha w + (1 - \alpha)w']\hat{l}$$
$$+ [\alpha r + (1 - \alpha)r']\hat{k}$$

we have Property (4). We ought to add a word of warning at this point. This subsection and the following one assume two inputs. In contrast when discussing the indirect utility function and the expenditure function we assumed many commodities. There is nothing to stop us deriving a cost function for a production function for many inputs. All the results and properties of this subsection carry over to this case with the exception of this fourth property. If we have more than two inputs and one of these is fixed, then the equivalent Property (4) for the restricted cost function would be that the restricted cost function is concave in input prices.

Property (5) is perhaps less obvious, but is clear if we derive the restricted cost function from the production function. The south-west quadrant of Figure 11.7 gives the isoquant associated with the level of production y. If the level of k is fixed at k_3, and w and r are such that they give constant cost lines as shown in the diagram then the minimum cost, call this c_3, is given by the line through the isoquant at $k = k_3$. This line cuts the l axis at l_3. Thus l_3 is how much labour could be bought with the money needed to produce output y when $k = k_3$, i.e. $l_3 = c_3/w$ (the argument here is similar to that used elsewhere for consumers). Knowing l_3 and w we can find c_3. The north-west quadrant of Figure 11.7 does this. It is drawn for $w = 2$, thus the relationship between c_3 and l_3 is that $l_3 = c_3/2$. The south-east quadrant of the diagram simply reflects k from one axis to the other. Thus for $k = k_3$ we have the value $c(y,w,r,k_3)$ in the north-east quadrant. Repeating this for

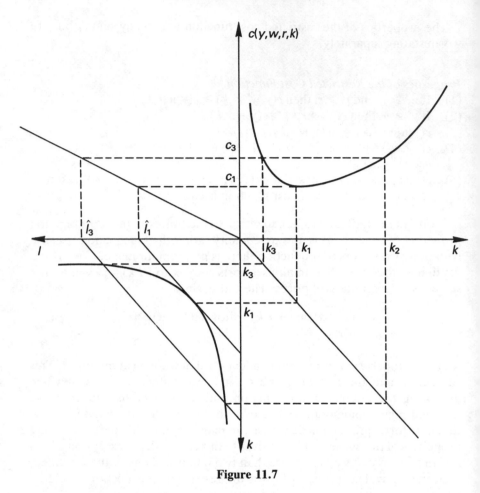

Figure 11.7

$k = k_2$ also gives the same cost level. Obviously $k = k_1$ gives the minimum cost level. Repeating the process for all k gives $c(y,w,r,k)$. The convexity of $c(y,w,r,k)$ in k comes from the shape of the isoquant. Figure 11.8 gives the same argument in a slightly different form. To produce output level y with $k = k'$ we need $l = l'$, and with $k = \hat{k}$ we need $l = \hat{l}$. If $k = \alpha\hat{k} + (1 - \alpha)k'$ then we would need costs of $\alpha c(y,w,r,\hat{k}) + (1 - \alpha)c(y,w,r,k')$ if we required $l = \alpha\hat{l} + (1 - \alpha)l'$ to produce output y. But with $k = \alpha\hat{k} + (1 - \alpha)k'$ we require only $l^* < \alpha\hat{l} + (1 - \alpha)l'$ labour, thus the cost of producing y with $k = \alpha\hat{k} + (1 - \alpha)k'$ must be less than $\alpha c(y,w,r,\hat{k}) + (1 - \alpha)c(y,w,r,k')$.

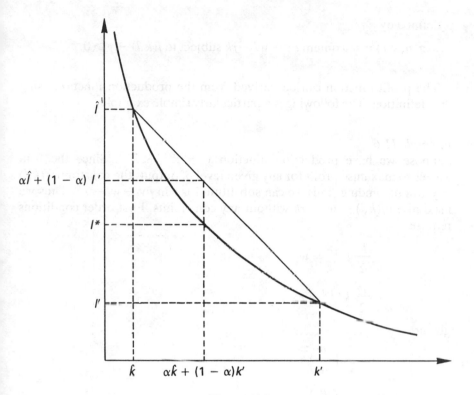

Figure 11.8

4 The Profit Function

The final optimal value function we wish to discuss is the profit function. This function relates the maximum level of profits to output prices and input prices. The exact statement of the profit function depends on the structure of the firm and the time period we are considering. In the long run (when both inputs are variable) we shall consider a profit function for a perfectly competitive firm and for a monopolist. In the short run (when one of the inputs is fixed) we shall consider a 'restricted' profit function for a competitive firm. We will spend most of our time discussing the profit function for a perfectly competitive firm purchasing capital and labour at r and w respectively and selling its output at p per unit.

4.1 Unrestricted Profit Functions

Definition 11.7: The profit function of a perfectly competitive firm $\pi(p,w,r)$

is defined by

$$\pi(p,w,r) = \text{maximum } py - wl - rk \text{ subject to } f(k,l) - y \geq 0$$

The profit function can be derived from the production function using this definition. The following is a particularly simple example.

Example 11.6
Suppose we have production function $y = l^{1/2} + k^{1/2}$. Since the firm wishes to maximise profit for any given level of output, the constraint $f(k,l) = y$ will be binding; thus we can substitute for y in $py - wl - rk$. Thus we maximise $pf(k,l) - wl - rk$ without any constraints. First order conditions require

$$\frac{p}{2} l^{-1/2} = w$$

$$\frac{p}{2} k^{-1/2} = r$$

giving

$$l = \left(\frac{p}{2w}\right)^2$$

$$k = \left(\frac{p}{2r}\right)^2$$

i.e.

$$\pi(p,w,r) = p\left(\frac{p}{2w} + \frac{p}{2r}\right) - w\left(\frac{p}{2w}\right)^2 - r\left(\frac{p}{2r}\right)^2$$

$$= \frac{p^2}{4}\left(\frac{1}{w} + \frac{1}{r}\right)$$

In order to derive the profit function in this example we substituted for y with $f(k,l)$. However, there is another method of deriving the profit function. Instead of replacing y with terms in k and l we could have left the revenue part of $py - wl - rk$ as a function of y (i.e. left py) and rewritten the cost part of $py - wl - rk$ as a function of y. This function, relating the optimal level of $-wl - rk$ to output, is the cost function, which we have already discussed. Thus instead of writing $pf(k,l) - wl - rk$ and maximising with respect to k and l, we could have written $py - c(y,w,r)$. If we maximise $py - c(y,w,r)$ with respect to y does this give us the same output and profit as maximising $pf(k,l) - wl - rk$? The answer must be yes.

Suppose this were not true, i.e. by maximising $pf(k,l) - wl - rk$ we use inputs $\bar{l}$ and $\hat{k}$ and produce output $\hat{y}$, but by maximising $py - c(y,w,r)$ we produce output $y^* \neq \hat{y}$. Suppose $\bar{l}$, $\hat{k}$ do not minimise costs subject to $f(k,l) \geq \hat{y}$. Then there exists $\bar{l},\bar{k}$ such that $f(\bar{k},\bar{l}) = \hat{y}$ and $r\bar{k} + wl <$ $r\hat{k} + w\hat{l}$. But then $\hat{k},\hat{l}$ cannot have maximised $pf(k,l) - wl - rk$ since

$$p\hat{y} - w\bar{l} - r\bar{k} > p\hat{y} - w\hat{l} - r\hat{k}$$

Therefore if $\hat{l}$ and $\hat{k}$ maximise profit, then $w\hat{l} + r\hat{k} = c(\hat{y},w,r)$. Thus we can write $pf(\hat{k},l) - w\hat{l} - r\hat{k}$ as $p\hat{y} - c(\hat{y},w,r)$. But since y^* was chosen to maximise $py - c(y,w,r)$ it must follow that $y^* = \hat{y}$. Thus maximising $pf(k,l) - wl - rk$ with respect to k and l gives the same output and profit as maximising $py - c(y,w,r)$ with respect to y. Therefore we have the following definition of the profit function:

Definition 11.8: The profit function $\pi(p,w,r)$ is defined by

$$\pi(p,w,r) = \text{maximum } py - c(y,w,r)$$

The above definition shows that if we know the cost function then we can derive the profit function directly from the cost function. Figure 11.9 shows this relationship diagrammatically. Start with $c(y,w',r')$ in Figure 11.9(a). If output price is p^1, then for given y the revenue of the firm is p^1y and the costs $c(y,w',r')$. The point where the difference between these two curves is maximised gives profit π^1. In Figure 11.9(a) we have drawn in a vertical line at the point $y = 1$. The point where p^1y cuts this line is $p^1y = p^1$. Thus we carry this point over to Figure 11.9(b) and plot the level of profit π^1 in the horizontal axis of Figure 11.9(b). Repeating this process with output price set at p^2, we obtain π^2 as the maximum profit. Doing this for each p we obtain $\pi(p,w',r')$ from $c(y,w',r')$. Choosing different input prices, $(\hat{w},\hat{r})$, we obtain $\pi(p,\hat{w},\hat{r})$ from $c(y,\hat{w},\hat{r})$.

To derive $\pi(p,w,r)$ from $c(y,w,r)$ we maximise $py - c(y,w,r)$ obtaining

$$p = c_y(y,w,r) \tag{11.17}$$

We know from Section 4 that $c_y(y,w,r)$ is the marginal cost of production, thus (11.17) is the familiar condition that marginal revenue equals marginal cost which, for a perfectly competitive firm, implies price equals marginal cost. We can then solve (11.17) for y as a function of p and substitute this into $py - c(y,w,r)$.

Example 11.7

Suppose the cost function is of the form $c(y,w,r) = y^\alpha \phi(w,r)$. Profit is

$$\pi = py - y^\alpha \phi(w,r), \alpha > 1 \tag{11.18}$$

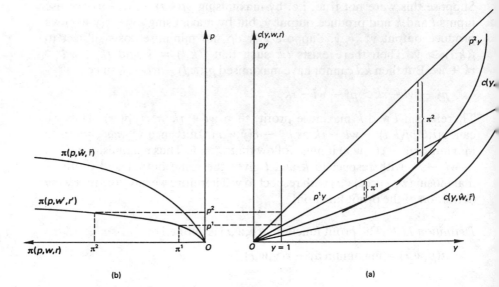

Figure 11.9

thus

$$\frac{\partial \pi}{\partial y} = p - \alpha y^{\alpha - 1}\phi(w,r) = 0$$

i.e.

$$y = \left[\frac{p}{\alpha\phi(w,r)}\right]^{\frac{1}{\alpha - 1}}$$

Substituting into (11.18) we have

$$\pi(p,w,r) = p\left[\frac{p}{\alpha\phi(w,r)}\right]^{\frac{1}{\alpha - 1}} - \left[\frac{p}{\alpha\phi(w,r)}\right]^{\frac{1}{\alpha - 1}}\phi(w,r)$$

$$= \left[\frac{p^{\alpha}}{\alpha\phi(w,r)}\right]^{\frac{1}{\alpha - 1}}\left(1 - \frac{1}{\alpha}\right)$$

We can now turn to the properties of the profit function for a perfectly competitive firm.

Properties of a Profit Function of a Perfectly Competitive firm:

(1) If $p' \geq p$, then $\pi(p',w,r) \geq \pi(p,w,r)$.

(2) If $w' \geq w, r' \geq r$ then $\pi(p,w',r') \leq \pi(p,w,r)$.

(3) $\pi(\alpha p, \alpha w, \alpha r) = \alpha \pi(p,w,r)$, $\alpha > 0$, i.e. the profit function is homogeneous of degree 1 in output price and input prices.

(4) $\pi[\alpha p + (1 - \alpha)p', w, r] \leq \alpha \pi(p,w,r) + (1 - \alpha)\pi(p',w,r)$, $0 \leq \alpha \leq 1$, i.e. the profit function is convex in output price.

(5) $\pi[p, \alpha w + (1 - \alpha)w', \alpha r + (1 - \alpha)r'] \leq \alpha \pi(p,w,r) + (1 - \alpha)$ $\pi(p,w',r')$, $0 \leq \alpha \leq 1$, i.e. the profit function is convex in input prices.

Properties (1) and (2) are obvious. Property (3) follows from Property (3) of the cost function, i.e.

$$c(y, \alpha w, \alpha r) = \alpha c(y,w,r)$$

This implies

$$\alpha p y - c(y, \alpha w, \alpha r) = \alpha[py - c(y,w,r)]$$

Thus maximum profits with prices $\alpha p, \alpha w, \alpha r$ are α of maximum profits given prices p, w, r.

We can show Property (4) using an argument similar to that employed for Property (4) of the expenditure function. Figure 11.10 shows the maximum level of profit, $\hat{\pi}$, with price $\hat{p}$ for a given set of input prices. If p increases above $\hat{p}$, then if the firm did not change output, profits would increase as shown by the line $p\hat{y} - c(\hat{y},w,r)$. However, for any price other than $\hat{p}$, say $\bar{p}$, the firm may do better if they change the output level. Therefore $\pi(p,w,r)$ can never lie below the tangent at $\hat{p}$. This must be true for all tangents to $\pi(p,w,r)$, therefore $\pi(p,w,r)$ must be convex in p.

This type of geometric explanation can also be used for a special case of Property (5) when only one input price is changed, e.g. w. If p and r remain constant, then as w increases to $\hat{w}$ from $\bar{w}$ the firm could retain the same levels of l and k, say $\bar{l}$ and $\bar{k}$. Thus profits would fall along the line $p\bar{y} - w\bar{l} - r\bar{k}$ which is tangential to $\pi(p,w,r)$ at $\pi(p,\bar{w},r)$. But at $\hat{w}$ there may be a better choice of inputs than $\bar{l}$ and $\bar{k}$, giving a higher maximum profit than $p\bar{y} - w\bar{l} - r\bar{k}$. This is drawn in Figure 11.11. Again since all tangents must lie below $\pi(p,w,r)$ then $\pi(p,w,r)$ must be convex in w.

To see that Property (5) holds in the general case, let y be optimal production given p, w, and r, y' be optimal given p, w' and r', and y^* be optimal given p, $\alpha w + (1 - \alpha)w'$ and $\alpha r + (1 - \alpha)r'$. If Property (5) were *not* true, we would have the following inequality:

$$\pi[p, \alpha w + (1 - \alpha)w', \alpha r + (1 - \alpha)r']$$
$$> \alpha \pi(p,w,r) + (1 - \alpha)\pi(p,w',r') \qquad (11.19)$$

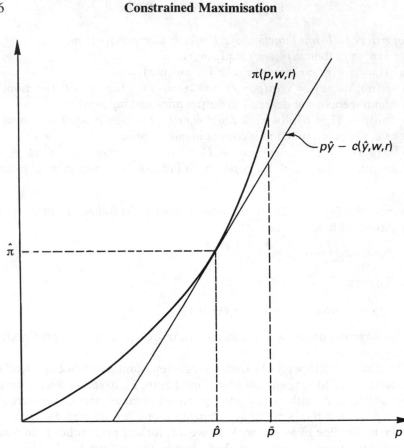

Figure 11.10

for at least one profit function and set of input prices. (11.19) can be written:

$$py^* - c[y^*, \alpha w + (1 - \alpha)w', \alpha r + (1 - \alpha)r'] > \alpha[py - c(y,w,r)]$$
$$+ (1 - \alpha)[py' - c(y',w',r')]$$

Since y and y' were optimal given the relevant prices it must also be true that:

$$py^* - c[y^*, \alpha w + (1 - \alpha)w', \alpha r + (1 - \alpha)r'] > \alpha[py^* - c(y^*,w,r)]$$
$$+ (1 - \alpha)[py^* - c(y^*,w',r')]$$

or (since $\alpha py^* + (1 - \alpha)py^* = py^*$):

$$c[y^*, \alpha w + (1 - \alpha)w', \alpha r + (1 - \alpha)r'] < \alpha c(y^*,w,r)$$
$$+ (1 - \alpha)c(y^*,w',r') \qquad (11.20)$$

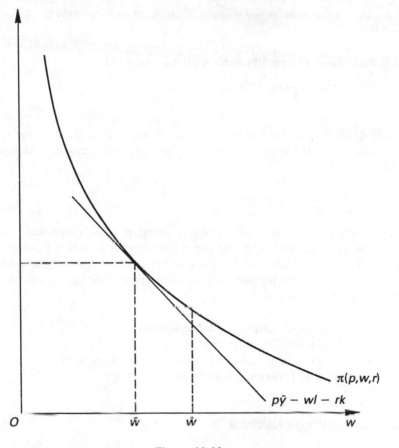

Figure 11.11

However, (11.20) completely contradicts Property (4) of a cost function. Therefore our initial inequality in (11.19) must be wrong. Since (11.19) is wrong, the only alternative is:

$$\pi[p,\alpha w \ + \ (1 \ - \ \alpha)w',\alpha r \ + \ (1 \ - \ \alpha)r'] \ \leqslant \ \alpha\pi(p,w,r)$$
$$+ \ (1-\alpha)\pi(p,w',r')$$

which is Property (5), as required.

Let us now turn our attention to a monopolist. Unlike a perfectly competitive firm, the monopolist faces a price for his output which depends on the quantity he sells. His profit can be written

$$p(y)y - c(y,w,r)$$

and maximised with respect to y. Since p depends on y, it cannot be an argument in the monopolist's profit function, which can only be defined on w and r.

Definition 11.9: The profit function for a monopoly is:

$$\pi(w,r) = \max_{y} p(y)y - c(y,w,r)$$

The profit function can then be derived in a similar method to that for the perfectly competitive profit function. The only difference is that the first order condition:

$$p(y) + y\frac{dp}{dy} = c_y(y,w,r)$$

is no longer the simple price equals marginal cost condition. Clearly Properties (1), (3) and (4) of the profit function for a perfectly competitive firm have no equivalent here but the other two properties must be the same. A quick glance at the justification for these shows that they do not depend on the fact that p is fixed.

Properties of a Profit Function of a Monopolist:
(1) If $w' \geqslant w$ and $r' \geqslant r$, then $\pi(w',r') \leqslant \pi(w,r)$.
(2) $\pi[\alpha w + (1 - \alpha)w', \alpha r + (1 - \alpha)r'] \leqslant \alpha\pi(w,r) + (1 - \alpha)\pi(w',r')$,
     i.e. the profit function is convex in input prices.

4.2 Restricted Profit Functions

Finally we come to the restricted profit function. This is defined:

Definition 11.10: The restricted profit function for a competitive firm is:

$$\pi(p,w,r,k) = \max_{y} py - c(y,w,r,k)$$

where $c(y,w,r,k)$ is the restricted cost function.

The method of derivation from $c(y,w,r,k)$ is the same as before except that the necessary first order condition

$$p = c_y(y,w,r,k)$$

states that price must be equal to short-run marginal cost. Figure 11.12 shows the profit function and two restricted profit functions for different p (when $k = \bar{k}$ and $\hat{k}$, $\hat{k} > \bar{k}$, for the restricted profit function). The diagram is similar to that of the restricted and unrestricted cost function in

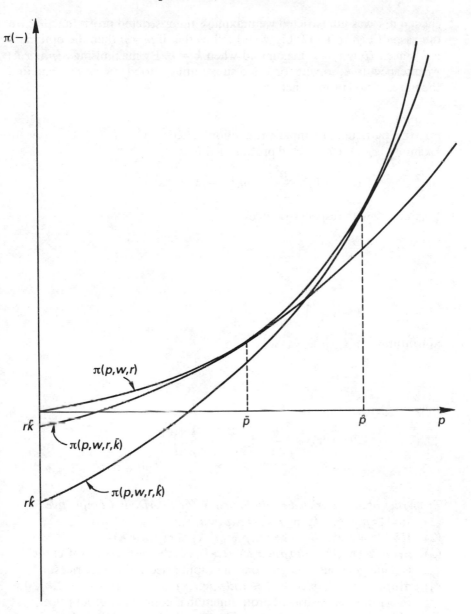

Figure 11.12

Figure 11.6. However, when (for given p, w and r) the restricted level of k is different from that chosen when k is not restricted, the restricted profit function lies below the unrestricted profit function. For the cost function the opposite was obviously true. Thus, for any p, to find the k that would be chosen if k was unrestricted we maximise the restricted profit function. In the case of Figure 11.12 this would tell us that if $p = \bar{p}$ then the optimal k is $\bar{k}$ since $\pi(\bar{p},w,r,k)$ is maximised when $k = \bar{k}$. By maximising $\pi(p,w,r,k)$ with respect to k, solving for k and substituting into $\pi(p,w,r,k)$ we can find the unrestricted profit function.

Example 11.8
For the particularly simple production function $y = l^{1/2} + k^{1/2}$ used in Example 11.7, the restricted profit function is

$$(p,w,r,k) = \frac{p^2}{4w} + pk^{1/2} - rk$$

Maximising with respect to k gives

$$\frac{p}{2} k^{-1/2} = r$$

or

$$k = \left(\frac{p}{2r}\right)^2$$

Substituting into $\pi(p,w,r,k)$ we obtain

$$\frac{p^2}{4w} + \frac{p^2}{4r}$$

thus

$$\pi(p,w,r) = \frac{p^2}{4}\left(\frac{1}{w} + \frac{1}{r}\right)$$

as in Example 10.7.

Properties of the Restricted Profit Function for a Perfectly Competitive Firm:
(1) If $p' \geqslant p$, then $\pi(p',w,r,k) \geqslant \pi(p,w,r,k)$.
(2) If $w' \geqslant w$ and $r' \geqslant r$, then $\pi(p,w',r',k) \leqslant \pi(p,w,r,k)$.
(3) $\pi(\alpha p,\alpha w,\alpha r,k) = \alpha\pi(p,w,r,k)$, $\alpha > 0$, i.e. the restricted profit function is homogeneous of degree one in output price and input prices.
(4) $\pi[\alpha p + (1 - \alpha)p',w,r,k] \leqslant \alpha\pi(p,w,r,k) + (1 - \alpha)\pi(p,w',r',k)$, $0 \leqslant \alpha \leqslant 1$, i.e. the restricted profit function is convex in output price.
(5) $\pi[p,\alpha w + (1 - \alpha)w',\alpha r + (1 - \alpha)r'],k] \leqslant \alpha\pi(p,w,r,k) + (1 - \alpha)\pi(p,w',r',k)$, $0 \leqslant \alpha \leqslant 1$, i.e. the restricted profit function is convex in input prices.
(6) If the production function is strictly concave, then $\pi[p,w,r,\alpha k + (1 - \alpha)k'] > \alpha\pi(p,w,r,k) + (1 - \alpha)\pi(p,w,r,k')$ for $0 < \alpha < 1$, i.e. the restricted profit function is strictly concave in k.

Properties (1)–(5) all follow immediately from the arguments used for the unrestricted profit function. The only point to notice is that in Property (5) if $w = w'$, then we must have an equality. This is true because when k is fixed, the component of cost rk is a fixed cost. If r changes but w does not, then this is a fixed cost change and will not affect the optimal choice of l, thus $\pi[p,w,\alpha r + (1 - \alpha)r',k] = \alpha\pi(p,w,r,k) + (1 - \alpha)\pi(p,w,r',k)$.

Property (6) is the only new property, but this one is important since (implicitly) we have already used this fact when maximising $\pi(p,w,r,k)$ with respect to k. We should add at this point that all the properties of profit functions we have analysed must be true *if* a profit function exists. If one does not exist, then we have no need to evaluate properties. This is crucial in the context of deriving a profit function from a restricted profit function, since it is quite possible to have a cost function such that a restricted profit function exists for every possible k but an unrestricted profit function does not exist. This is explored in Chapter 15. If an unrestricted profit function does not exist, then there is no solution to the problem: $\max_k \pi(p,w,r,k)$.

Given k' and k, let l' and l be the amounts of labour that maximise restricted profits. Suppose now that with capital fixed at $\alpha k + (1 - \alpha)k'$, we set labour at the level $\alpha l + (1 - \alpha)l'$, since the production function is strictly concave:

$$f[\alpha l + (1 - \alpha)l', \alpha k + (1 - \alpha)k'] > \alpha f(l,k) + (1 - \alpha)f(l',k') \qquad (11.21)$$

Let us write the above inequality as:

$$y^* > \alpha y + (1 - \alpha)y'$$

Profit with labour $\alpha l + (1 - \alpha)l'$ and capital $\alpha k + (1 - \alpha)k'$ is

$$py^* - w[\alpha l + (1 - \alpha)l'] - r[\alpha k + (1 - \alpha)k]$$

with l and k is

$$py - wl - rk$$

and with l' and k' is

$$py' - wl' - rk'$$

Now

$$w[\alpha l + (1 - \alpha)l'] + r[\alpha k + (1 - \alpha)k'] = \alpha wl + \alpha rk + (1 - \alpha)wl'$$
$$+ (1 - \alpha)rk$$

thus the result holds if

$$py^* > \alpha py + (1-\alpha)py' \tag{11.22}.$$

(11.22) must be true given (11.21), thus Property (6) must be true.

For the restricted profit function of a monopolist similar properties to Properties (2), (5) and (6) hold. However, for Property (6) we need to limit further the cases for concavity to hold. It is sometimes helpful to think of the monopolist's profit function in the following way. The monopolist has a revenue function $p(y)y$ or $p[f(k,l)]f(k,l)$. Let us write this as $R(k,l)$ and assume it is a strictly concave function. Profits are

$$R(k,l) - wl - rk$$

which can be thought of as a special case of a perfect competitor's profit where output price is set at 1 and the production function is $R = R(k,l)$ instead of $y = f(k,l)$. Here we can think of revenue, R, as output instead of money. Thus the cost function of a competitive firm with $f(k,l) = R(k,l)$ is a type of cost function for this monopolist: it is the minimum cost of the inputs required to attain revenue R. We can then treat R as an output having price unity, and maximise

$$R - c(R,w,r)$$

This is identical to maximising

$$py - c(y,w,r)$$

for a competitive firm with $f(k,l) = R(k,l)$ and $p = 1$. Thus the profit function for the firm with $f(k,l) = R(k,l)$, evaluated when $p = 1$ is the profit function for the monopolist with revenue function $R(k,l)$, i.e.

$$\pi(p,w,r) = \pi(w,r) \text{ if } p = 1$$

This equivalence will also hold for restricted profit functions. Thus all properties concerning w,r and k that hold for perfectly competitive firms with strictly concave production functions must also hold for all monopolies with strictly concave revenue functions. Consequently if the revenue function is strictly concave, then the restricted profit function for a monopolist must be strictly concave in k. In this case we can derive the unrestricted profit function for the monopolist from the restricted profit function by maximising with respect to k and substituting for k, as we have already done for the perfectly competitive firm.

Problems

11.1   Derive the expenditure function associated with the utility function $u(x_1,x_2) = (x_1^\rho + x_2^\rho)^{1/\rho}$ where $\rho < 1$.
        Solution on p. 284.

11.2 Find the expenditure function of the indirect utility function

$$v(\mathbf{p},m) = \left(\frac{\alpha}{p_1}\right)^\alpha \left(\frac{\beta}{p_2}\right)^\beta \left(\frac{m}{\alpha+\beta}\right)^{\alpha+\beta}$$

Solution on p. 284.

11.3 What is the indirect utility function if the expenditure function is

$$e(\mathbf{p},u) = u(p_1^{-\sigma} + p_2^{-\sigma})^{-1/\sigma}?$$

Solution on p. 285.

11.4 Construct a firm's cost function $c(y,w,r)$ if its production function is

$$y = l^\alpha k^\beta$$

Solution on p. 325.

11.5 Reconstruct the production function from the cost function

$$c(y,w,r) = y^\gamma(a_1 w + a_2 r)$$

Solution on p. 329.

11.6 Given a production function $f(k,l)$ we define the short-run or restricted cost function $c^s(y,w,r,k)$ as the minimum cost of producing output y, given the capital stock k is fixed, and the prices w,r of labour and capital services respectively. Find the short-run cost function if $f(k,l) = l^\alpha k^\beta$. Now find the output at which the average short-run cost is minimised.
Solution on p. 330.

11.7 Given that the (long-run) cost function $c(y,w,r)$ is the minimum value of the function $k \to c^s(y,w,r,k)$, where c^s is the short-run cost function, find $c(y,w,r)$ if

$$c^s(y,w,r,k) = \frac{wy}{k} + rk$$

Solution on p. 333.

11.8 Viewing both the short-run STC and long-run LTC costs as functions of output, show that the short-run marginal cost SMC equals the long-run marginal cost LMC at that level of output at which STC = LTC.
Solution on p. 331.

11.9 Given the (long-run) cost function

$$c(y,w,r) = 2y^2(w r)^{1/2}$$

find the associated profit function $\pi(p,w,r)$.
Solution on p. 339.

11.10 Given the (long-run) cost function $c(y,w,r) = y^\gamma\phi(w,r)$ for some
function $\phi(w,r)$ and $\gamma < 1$, show that there is no profit function in the
sense that there is no profit-maximising profit.
Solution on p. 337.

11.11 Given production function $y = l^{1/2}k^\beta$, find the short-run and
long-run profit functions given $\beta < \frac{1}{2}$.
Solution on p. 339.

11.12 For a monopolist the profit function $\pi(w,r)$ is a function of input
prices only (assuming as usual that the input markets are
competitive). Thus $\pi(w,r)$ tells us the maximum profits the
monopolist can attain given the input prices. Find $\pi(w,r)$ when the
monopolist's cost function is

$$c(y,w,r) = y\phi(w,r)$$

and demand price is

$$p(y) = y^\varepsilon$$

where $-1 < \varepsilon < 0$
Solution on p. 348.

12

The Envelope Theorem

1 Introduction

In Chapter 10, Section 5, we considered the relationship between a consumer's indirect utility function and the Lagrangian of the utility maximisation problem. We argued that the partial derivatives of the indirect utility function were equal to the partial derivatives of the Lagrangian with respect to prices **p** and budget m, where we hold the decision values and Lagrangian multiplier constant at their optimal values. Using this argument we were able to present an alternative derivation of Roy's Identity. In this chapter we present a general theorem relating the derivatives of optimal value functions to those of associated Lagrangians. The argument parallels completely that given in Chapter 10, Section 5, and the reader may wish to refer back to that section before reading this chapter. Having established the general Envelope Theorem we apply it to expenditure, cost and profit functions and hence derive the famous Shephard and Hotelling Lemmas.

2 The Envelope Theorem

Our aim in this chapter is to state and justify the general envelope theorem illustrated in Chapter 10, Section 5. Hence we consider the general constrained maximisation problem

maximise $f(\mathbf{x},\boldsymbol{\psi})$ subject to $g(\mathbf{x},\boldsymbol{\psi}) \geqslant 0$

Here the decision variables are denoted by **x** while the parameters of the decision problem are denoted by ψ. For example, in the case of the consumer ψ would include both the prices and the budget while the objective function $f(\mathbf{x},\psi)$ would be equal to the utility function and the constraint function $g(\mathbf{x},\psi)$ be equal to the budget excess $m - \mathbf{p}\ \mathbf{x}$. In this case the parameter affects only the constraint function, but in other cases, e.g. cost minimisation, this will not be true.

Definition 12.1: The optimal value function $V(\psi)$ associated with the above maximisation problem is defined by

$$V(\psi) = \text{maximum value of } f(\mathbf{x},\psi) \text{ subject to } g(\mathbf{x},\psi) \geq 0$$

We also recall that the Lagrangian associated with this problem is given by

$$L(x,\lambda;\psi) = f(\mathbf{x},\psi) + \lambda g(x,\psi) \tag{12.1}$$

We also know that $\mathbf{x}^*$ is the solution to the problem if and only if there is a λ^* satisfying the following three conditions:

(i) $\lambda^* \geq 0$
(ii) $\lambda^* g(\mathbf{x}^*,\psi) = 0$ $\qquad\qquad\qquad\qquad$ (12.2)
(iii) $\mathbf{x}^*$ maximises $L(\mathbf{x},\lambda^*;\psi)$

It follows from (12.2)(ii) that

$$V(\psi) = f(\mathbf{x}^*,\psi) = L(\mathbf{x}^*,\lambda^*;\psi) \tag{12.3}$$

and from (12.2)(iii) that

$$L(\mathbf{x}^*,\lambda^*;\psi) \geq f(\mathbf{x},\psi) + \lambda^* g(\mathbf{x},\psi) \tag{12.4}$$

From (12.3) and (12.4) we obtain

$$V(\psi) \geq f(\mathbf{x},\psi) + \lambda^* g(\mathbf{x},\psi) \tag{12.5}$$

By analogy with Chapter 10, Section 5, we consider a particular vector $\hat{\psi}$ of parameters and let $\hat{\mathbf{x}}$ be the maximum of $f(\mathbf{x},\hat{\psi})$ subject to $g(\mathbf{x},\hat{\psi}) \geq 0$. Hence (12.5) becomes

$$V(\psi) \geq f(\hat{\mathbf{x}},\psi) + \overset{*}{\lambda} g(\hat{\mathbf{x}},\psi) \tag{12.6}$$

with the inequality becoming equality at $\psi = \hat{\psi}$. As in the consumer example we can conclude that the derivative of V at $\hat{\psi}$ is equal to the derivative of $L(\hat{\mathbf{x}},\hat{\lambda};\psi) = f(\hat{\mathbf{x}},\psi) + \lambda^* g(\hat{\mathbf{x}},\psi)$. Hence for each ψ_i we obtain

$$\frac{\partial V}{\partial \psi_i} = \frac{\partial L}{\partial \psi_i}\bigg|_{\mathbf{x}=\hat{\mathbf{x}}\text{ constant}} \tag{12.7}$$

Note we have indicated here that when we differentiate the Lagrangian we keep x constant, then we substitute in $\hat{x}$ for x.

The one complication that arises here is that the multiplier λ^* also depends upon the parameters ψ, thus when we differentiate the Lagrangian we obtain a term of the form $\partial\lambda^*/\partial\psi_i\, g(x^*,\psi)$. Yet we know that either $g(x^*,\psi) = 0$ or $g(x^*,\psi) > 0$ and $\lambda^* = 0$; in the latter case small changes in ψ will leave the shadow price λ^* equal to zero, hence we will have $\partial\lambda^*/\partial\psi_i = 0$. In either case $\partial\lambda^*/\partial\psi_i g(x^*,\psi) = 0$. This means we might as well treat λ^* as constant here, giving us

The Envelope Theorem
The partial derivatives $\partial V/\partial\psi_i$ of the optimal value function are equal to the partial derivatives with respect to ψ_i of the associated Lagrangian, where the decision variables and shadow price are held constant at their optimal values i.e.

$$\frac{\partial V}{\partial\psi_i} = \frac{\partial L}{\partial\psi_i}\bigg|_{x=\hat{x}\text{ and }\lambda=\hat{\lambda}\text{ constant}} \tag{12.8}$$

or

$$\frac{\partial V}{\partial\psi_i} = \frac{\partial f}{\partial\psi_i}\bigg|_{x=\hat{x}\text{ constant}} + \hat{\lambda}\frac{\partial g}{\partial\psi_i}\bigg|_{x=\hat{x}\text{ constant}} \tag{12.9}$$

Here $\hat{\lambda}$ is the multiplier associated with $\psi = \hat{\psi}$

3 Applications to Consumer Behaviour

3.1 The Indirect Utility Function and Roy's Identity

Let us reconsider Roy's Identity using the Envelope Theorem. Here the optimisation problem is

maximise $u(x)$ subject to $m - \mathbf{p}\,x \geqslant 0$

so that the decision variables are x and the parameters are m and $\mathbf{p}$. The optimal value function is the indirect utility function $v(\mathbf{p},m)$ and the Lagrangian is

$$L(x,\lambda;\mathbf{p},m) = u(x) + \lambda(m - \mathbf{p}\,x)$$

The Envelope Theorem tells us that to find the partial derivatives of v, we differentiate L with respect to prices $\mathbf{p}$ and budget m while leaving x and λ fixed, then we substitute in the optimal values x^* and λ^* of the decision variables and multiplier.

Here we have

$$\frac{\partial L}{\partial m}\bigg|_{x,\lambda \text{ constant}} = \lambda$$

and

$$\frac{\partial L}{\partial p_i}\bigg|_{x,\lambda \text{ constant}} = -\lambda x_i$$

hence

$$\frac{\partial V}{\partial m} = \lambda^*$$

and

$$\frac{\partial V}{\partial p_i} = -\lambda^* x_i^*$$

which again yield Roy's Identity

$$x_i^* = -\frac{\partial V/\partial p_i}{\partial V/\partial m}$$

Note the optimal $\mathbf{x}^*$ is the vector of Marshallian demands.

3.2 The Expenditure Function and Shephard Lemma

Recall that the consumer's expenditure function $e(\mathbf{p},u)$ tells us the minimum cost of attaining the level of utility u given prices are $\mathbf{p}$. Hence the optimisation problem is

maximise $-\mathbf{p}\,\mathbf{x}$ subject to $u(\mathbf{x}) - u \geqslant 0$

Note the optimal value function here is $-e(\mathbf{p},u)$.

The associated Lagrangian is thus

$$L = -\mathbf{p}\,\mathbf{x} + \lambda[u(x) - u]$$

and thus

$$\frac{\partial L}{\partial u}\bigg|_{x,\lambda \text{ constant}} = -\lambda$$

and

$$\frac{\partial L}{\partial p_i}\bigg|_{x,\lambda \text{ constant}} = -x_i$$

The Envelope Theorem now tells us that

$$-\frac{\partial e}{\partial u} = -\lambda^*$$

$$-\frac{\partial e}{\partial p_i} = -x_i^*$$

In particular we obtain Shephard's Lemma (for the consumer)

$$x_i^* = \frac{\partial e}{\partial p_i}$$

the x_i^* being the Hicksian (or compensated) demands.

Example 12.1

If the consumer has expenditure function $e(\mathbf{p},u) = 2p_1^{1/2}p_2^{1/2}u$, then the Hicksian demands are

$$x_1^* = \frac{\partial e}{\partial p_1} = \left(\frac{p_2}{p_1}\right)^{1/2} u$$

and

$$x_2^* = \frac{\partial e}{\partial p_2} = \left(\frac{p_1}{p_2}\right)^{1/2} u$$

4 Applications to the Firm

4.1 The Cost Function and Shephard's Lemma

Recall $c(y,r,w)$ is the minimum cost of producing output y when r and w are the prices of capital and labour. The optimisation problem is

  maximise $- rk - wl$ subject to $f(k,l) - y \geqslant 0$

which has optimal value function equal to $-c(y,r,w)$.
The Lagrangian is

$$L = -rk - wl + \lambda[f(k,l) - y]$$

so that

$$\left.\frac{\partial L}{\partial y}\right|_{k,l,\lambda \text{ constant}} = -\lambda$$

and

$$\left.\frac{\partial L}{\partial r}\right|_{k,l,\lambda \text{ constant}} = -k$$

$$\frac{\partial L}{\partial w}\bigg|_{k,l,\lambda \text{ constant}} = -l$$

hence

$$k^* = \frac{\partial c}{\partial r} \qquad \text{Shephard's Lemma}$$

$$l^* = \frac{\partial c}{\partial w}$$

$$\lambda^* = \frac{\partial c}{\partial y} \qquad \text{(marginal cost)}$$

Example 12.2
In the case of cost function

$$c(y,w,r) = y(wa_1 + ra_2)$$

the a_1's being positive, we obtain input demands given by

$$l^* = a_1 y$$
$$k^* = a_2 y$$

namely the constant proportion demands.

4.2 Profit Function and Hotelling's Lemma

In this case $\pi(p,w,r)$ is the maximum profits obtainable when the price of output is p and those of capital and labour are r and w respectively.
    Hence we have the Lagrangian

$$L = py - rk - wl + \lambda[f(k,l) - y]$$

such that holding y, k, l and λ constant we obtain

$$\frac{\partial L}{\partial p} = y \qquad \frac{\partial L}{\partial r} = -k \qquad \frac{\partial L}{\partial w} = -l$$

Hence we obtain Hotelling's Lemma, namely

$$\frac{\partial \pi}{\partial p} = y^* \qquad \frac{\partial \pi}{\partial r} = -k^* \qquad \frac{\partial \pi}{\partial w} = -l^*$$

these being the optimal levels of outputs and inputs respectively.

Example 12.3
With profit function

$$\pi = \frac{p^2}{8(rw)^{1/2}}$$

we obtain optimal output

$$y^* = \frac{\partial \pi}{\partial p} = \frac{p}{4(rw)^{1/2}}$$

and respective inputs

$$k^* = \frac{\partial \pi}{\partial r} = \frac{p^2}{16(r^3 w)^{1/2}}$$

and

$$l^* = \frac{p^2}{16(rw^3)^{1/2}}$$

In the case of the restricted profit function $(p,w,r,\bar{k})$ where the firm is restricted to use $\bar{k}$ units of capital, we have a Lagrangian

$$L = py - wl = r\bar{k} + [f(l,\bar{k}) - y]$$

so that keeping y and l constant – note $\bar{k}$ is now a parameter, we obtain

$$\frac{\partial L}{\partial p} = y \quad \frac{\partial L}{\partial w} = -l \quad \frac{\partial L}{\partial r} = -\bar{k} \quad \frac{\partial L}{\partial k} = -r + \frac{\partial f}{\partial k}$$

and thus the optimal output and labour input are given by

$$y^* = \frac{\partial \pi}{\partial p}, \quad l^* = -\frac{\partial \pi}{\partial w}$$

Finally in this section we can consider the profit function of a monopolist $\pi(r,w)$ giving the maximum profits attainable when input prices are r and w. The optimisation problem is

maximise $p(y)y - rk - wl$ subject to $f(k,l) - y \geq 0$

the decision variables being y,k and l and $p(y)$ being the demand price function. This has Lagrangian

$$L = p(y)y - rk - wl + \lambda[f(k,l) - y]$$

and thus holding y, k, l and λ constant, we obtain

$$\frac{\partial L}{\partial r} = -k \quad \frac{\partial L}{\partial w} = -l$$

so that the optimal inputs are given by

$$k^* = -\frac{\partial \pi}{r} \quad \text{and} \quad l^* = -\frac{\partial \pi}{\partial w}$$

Problems

12.1   If a consumer's expenditure function is given implicitly as

$$\ln[e(\mathbf{p},u)] = a + \alpha\ln(p_1) + (1 - \alpha)\ln(p_2) + \tfrac{1}{2}\gamma[\ln(p_1)]^2$$

$$+ \tfrac{1}{2}\gamma[\ln(p_2)]^2 - \gamma\ln(p_1)\ln(p_2) + u\beta\left(\frac{p_1}{p_2}\right)^{\delta}$$

find the proportion of expenditure directed to the Hicksian demand for each commodity.
Solution on p. 295.

12.2   Given a consumer's expenditure function is

$$e(\mathbf{p},u) = 2(p_1 p_2 u)^{1/2}$$

find the associated indirect utility function, Hicksian and Marshallian demand functions. By substituting the above expression for $e(\mathbf{p},u)$ in place of m in your expression for the Marshallian demands $x_i^m(\mathbf{p},m)$ confirm that

$$x_i^m[\mathbf{p},e(\mathbf{p},u)] = x_i^H(\mathbf{p},u)$$

Here x_i^H indicates the Hicksian demand.
Solution on p. 288.

12.3   Show that Hicksian demand curves cannot be upward sloping.
Solution on p. 289.

12.4   Using Young's Theorem, see the Appendix, show that

$$\frac{\partial x_i^H}{\partial p_j} = \frac{\partial x_j^H}{\partial p_i}$$

where x_i^H is a consumer's Hicksian demand for the i'th good.
Solution on p. 289.

12.5   We know that the Hicksian and Marshallian demands are related as follows

$$x_i^H(\mathbf{p},u) = x_i^m[\mathbf{p},e(\mathbf{p},u)]$$

Differentiate both sides of this equation with respect to p_i. Note p_i enters the right-hand side in two ways and thus you will have to differentiate it 'totally' and use the chain rule. Now let $u = v(\mathbf{p},m)$ and conclude

$$\frac{\partial x_i^m}{\partial p_i} = \frac{\partial x_i^H}{\partial p_i} - \frac{\partial x_m^i}{\partial m} x_i^m$$

This is known as the Slutsky equation and the two terms on the right-hand side are called the substitution and income effects respectively.

Solution on p. 290.

12.6 Repeat Problem 12.5 by differentiating by p_j and concluding

$$\frac{\partial x_i^m}{\partial p_j} = \frac{\partial x_i^H}{\partial p_j} - \frac{\partial x_i^m}{\partial m} x_j^m$$

Solution on p. 291.

12.7 Use the Slutsky equation of Problem 12.5 to show that Giffen goods must be inferior. Recall that a good is a Giffen good if its demand increases as its price increases, while it is inferior if its demand decreases as income increases.

Solution on p. 291.

12.8 Using the Slutsky equation of Problem 12.6 show that $\partial x_i^m/\partial p_j = \partial x_j^m/\partial p_i$ if and only if the income elasticities of the (Marshallian) demands are equal for good i and j.

Solution on p. 291.

12.9 Decompose $\partial x_1^m/\partial p_1$ and $\partial x_1^m/\partial p_2$ in the manner of the above Slutsky equations, given the indirect utility function

$$v(\mathbf{p},m) = \frac{m^2}{4p_1p_2}$$

Solution on p. 292.

12.10 A consumer pays prices $\hat{\mathbf{p}}$ for its consumption goods where $\hat{p}_1$ includes a unit tax, i.e. $\hat{p}_1 = p_1 + t_1$ where p_1 is the producer's price and t_1 is a tax. Furthermore the consumer pays a tax T from income so that its disposable income is $m-T$. Hence the consumer's (Marshallian) demand for the first good will be $x_1^M(\hat{\mathbf{p}},m-T)$, and the total tax (TT) raised by the government will be

$$\text{TT} = T + t_1 x_1^M$$

If t and T are to be simultaneously changed so as to leave total tax TT constant, then we can view T as an implicit function of t_1. Show that the derivative of this implicit function is given by

$$\frac{\partial T}{\partial t_1} = \frac{x_1^M + t_1 \partial x_1^M / \partial p_1}{1 - t_1 \partial x_1^M / \partial m}$$

The utility obtained by the consumer will be $v(\hat{p}, m-T)$. Show that a rise in t_1, with T moving to keep TT constant, will reduce the consumer's utility.

Solution on p. 308.

12.11 Consider a monopolist selling its produce to a single consumer in such a way that the consumer has to pay a two-part tariff. That is to say the consumer has to pay a fixed tariff γ before he can purchase any quantity of the output and then he pays a price p_0 for each unit consumed. Given that the consumer can attain a level of utility $\bar{u}$ without purchasing any of the firm's produce, the firm will aim to maximise profits

$$\pi = p_0 y + \gamma - c(y, w, r)$$

subject to

$$v(p_0, \mathbf{p}, m - \gamma) \geqslant \bar{u}$$

Here y will be the quantity demanded by the consumer assuming it has paid the initial tariff γ. By re-expressing the constraint as

$$m - \gamma - e(p_0, \mathbf{p}, \bar{u}) \geqslant 0$$

show that the firm will choose γ and p_0 such that

$$\gamma = m - e(p_0, \mathbf{p}, \bar{u})$$

and thus $v(p_0, \mathbf{p}, m - \gamma) = \bar{u}$, and

$$p_0 = \frac{\partial c}{\partial y}$$

Solution on p. 349.

12.12 Given a change in prices from $\mathbf{p}^0$ to $\mathbf{p}^1$ the equivalent variation EV is defined implicitly by the equation

$$v(\mathbf{p}^0, m - \text{EV}) = v(\mathbf{p}^1, m)$$

where v is a consumer's indirect utility function. Equally the compensating variation CV is implicitly defined by

$$v(\mathbf{p}^1, m + \text{CV}) = v(\mathbf{p}^0, m)$$

Show that

$$m - \text{EV} = e(\mathbf{p}^0, u^1)$$

and thus

$$EV = c(\mathbf{p}^1, u^1) - e(\mathbf{p}^0, u^1)$$

where $u^1 = v(\mathbf{p}^1, m)$ and e is the consumer's expenditure function. Similarly conclude

$$CV = e(\mathbf{p}^1, u^0) - e(\mathbf{p}^0, u^0)$$

where $u^0 = v(\mathbf{p}^0, m)$

Hence conclude

$$EV = \int_{p_i^0}^{p_i^1} \frac{\partial e}{\partial p_i}(\mathbf{p}, u^1) dp_i = \int_{p_i^0}^{p_i^1} x_i^{H}(\mathbf{p}, u^1) dp_i$$

and

$$CV = \int_{p_i^0}^{p_i^1} \frac{\partial e}{\partial p_i}(\mathbf{p}, u^0) dp_i = \int_{p_i^0}^{p_i^1} x_i^{H}(\mathbf{p}, u^0) dp_i$$

Solution on p. 309.

12.13 Consider approximating EV and CV by replacing the Hicksian by Marshallian demands in the last expressions for EV and CV in Problem 12.12. Under what circumstances would this 'approximation' be exactly right?
Solution on p. 310.

12.14 Given a firm's profit function is

$$\pi(p,w,r) = \frac{p^2}{4}\left(\frac{1}{w} + \frac{1}{r}\right)$$

find the firm's supply and input demand functions.
Solution on p. 342.

12.15 Given a firm's short run or restricted profit function

$$\pi(p,w,r,k) = \frac{p^2}{4w} + pk^{1/2} - rk$$

find the short-run supply and demand functions.
Solution on p. 342.

12.16 A firm's cost function takes the form

$$c(y,w,r) = \phi(y)[\alpha w + \beta r + 2\gamma(wr)^{1/2}],$$

for some $\phi(y)$. Find the firm's demands for inputs conditional on the output y.
Solution on p. 336.

12.17 Show that a competitive firm's supply curve cannot be downward sloping.
Solution on p. 341.

12.18   Show that a competitive firm's (unconditional) input demand curves cannot be upward sloping.
Solution on p. 341.

12.19   Show that a competitive firm's input demands conditional on output cannot be upward sloping.
Solution on p. 335.

12.20   A union is attempting to set the wage w for its members employed in a competitive industry with aggregate profit function $\pi(p,w,r)$, where the price of output p is considered fixed, i.e. independent of w. The union has L members and each member can earn a wage $\bar{w}$ outside the industry. Hence the union aims to maximise
$$wl + (L - l)\bar{w}$$

where l is the number employed in the industry. What would be the first order condition for the optimal w?
Solution on p. 364.

12.21   Reconsider Problem 12.20 when the union can fix a two-part tariff, i.e. it charges each firm a fixed charge C and a wage w for each unit of labour employed.
Solution on p. 367.

12.22   When discussing wage bargaining it is important to distinguish between situations where the firm can sign binding contracts with the union from the situation where contracts can be renegotiated. In particular we must distinguish between binding wage bargains made before a firm invests in its capital and the renegotiated bargain made after a firm has committed its capital. Consider then a union with the same objective as that in Problem 12.20. Find the ensuing wage and employment when the wage is made under the following conditions:

(a)   The firm has fixed capital stock k and faces a restricted or short-run profit function of the form

$$\pi(p,w,r,k) - Ap^{\alpha}w^{\varepsilon}k^{\delta} - rk$$

(b)   The firm can obtain a binding contract before investing in capital, and thus its demand for labour and capital will be given by Hotelling's Lemma applied to the long-run profit function associated with the short-run function in (a) above.
Solution on p. 365.

12.23   A firm is the sole employer of a union's members and the union has objective function

$$u(w)l^* + u(\bar{w})(L - l^*)$$

where l^* is the number employed by the firm and $\bar{w}$ is the wage members can be assured to obtain elsewhere. The firm maximises its profit subject to the constraint that the union's objective function has value no less than $\bar{u}$. Discuss the ensuing employment and wage rate if the function $u(w)$ is (a) linear and (b) strictly concave.

Solution on p. 368.

13

Extensions to the Theory of Optimisation

1 Introduction

Up to this juncture we have restricted our discussion of global and constrained optimisation problems to those involving concave or convex functions. The first task of this chapter is to extend our discussion to a broader class of functions; in particular we shall introduce the concept of indirectly concave functions, and show that the previously established results carry over to indirectly concave functions. In particular, we shall establish the necessity and sufficiency of stationarity for the maximisation of an indirectly concave function. Furthermore, the Lagrangian Theorem of Chapter 9 can be restated for this extended class of functions. It is usual for economic theorists to use an even broader class of functions, namely the class of quasi-concave functions. While we shall offer a definition of quasi-concavity and show that concave and indirectly concave functions are quasi-concave, we shall not attempt to extend our Lagrangian to this class of functions. This is not a major restriction on our results because in practice most quasi-concave functions are indirectly concave.

The second extension offered in this chapter is a restatement of the Lagrangian Theorem in the case where there is more than one constraint. Furthermore, we shall use this extension to establish the famous Kuhn–Tucker conditions when the decision variables are constrained to be non-negative.

2 Monotonic Transformations and Indirect Concavity

2.1 Monotonic Transformations

The reader is already familiar with the argument that a consumer's utility function is defined only up to a monotonic transformation (see Problem 8.1). To facilitate the discussion of this point we state the following definition.

Definition 13.1: A differentiable function $h(r)$ of a real variable is said to be (strictly) monotonically increasing if its derivative is positive everywhere i.e. $h'(r) > 0$ for all r in the domain of h.

A monotonic transformation of a function $f(x)$ is a composite function of the form $h[f(x)]$ where h is a (strictly) monotonically increasing function. Thus we say $F(x)$ is a monotonic transformation of $f(x)$ if there is a monotonically increasing function $h(r)$ such that $F(x) = h[f(x)]$.

Figure 13.1 illustrates our definition of a monotonically increasing function furthermore this diagram illustrates the following proposition.

Theorem 13.1
If h is a differentiable monotonically increasing function and if $r > s$ then $h(r) > h(s)$.

To see the validity of this theorem we note that

$$h(r) - h(s) = \int_s^r h'(x)dx$$

this being greater than zero because $h'(x)$ is positive for all values of x between s and r. Figure 13.2 illustrates this argument in that it contains a graph of $h'(r)$ together with the area under that graph bounded by r and s. As the graph lies above the abscissa for all r, we can conclude that the shaded area is indeed positive.

Theorem 13.2
If $h(r)$ is monotonically increasing, then it has an inverse function h^{-1} such that $h^{-1}[h(r)] = r$ for all r in the domain of h. Furthermore h^{-1} is monotonically increasing. Hence $r > s$ if and only if $h(r) > h(s)$.

Figure 13.3 illustrates the argument that a monotonically increasing function h has an inverse h^{-1}; in that diagram we simply 'read' the graph of h 'backwards', i.e. we start from values on the ordinate and use the graph to trace the value of h^{-1} on the abscissa. The diagram clearly

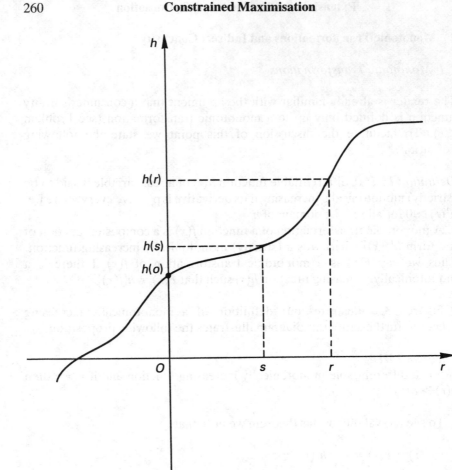

Figure 13.1

demonstrates that if $s = h(r)$ then $h^{-1}(s) = r$, so that $h^{-1}[h(r)]$ $= r$ for all r as asserted. To demonstrate that h^{-1} is also monotonically increasing, we have to establish that the derivative of h^{-1} is positive. If we apply the chain rule of differentiation to the left-hand side of the equation $h^{-1}[h(r)] = r$, we obtain

$$\frac{dh^{-1}}{ds} \frac{dh}{dr} = 1$$

hence

$$\frac{dh^{-1}}{ds} = 1 \bigg/ \frac{dh}{dr}$$

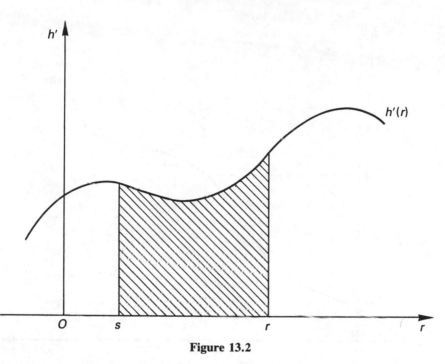

Figure 13.2

Hence the derivative of the inverse function is the reciprocal of the derivative of the original function. As this latter derivative is positive, so too is the former, i.e. $dh/dr > 0$ implies $(dh^{-1})/ds > 0$ as asserted in the theorem.

Finally we note that if $h(r) > h(s)$ then, by the monotonicity of h^{-1}, we have $h^{-1}[h(r)] > h^{-1}[h(s)]$, i.e. $r > s$.

Returning to our consumer with utility function $u(\mathbf{x})$ we can now argue that if $v(\mathbf{x})$ is a monotonic transformation of $u(\mathbf{x})$, then it represents the same preferences as $u(\mathbf{x})$. To say a consumer with utility function $u(\mathbf{x})$ prefers $\mathbf{x}'$ to $\mathbf{x}''$ means that $u(\mathbf{x}') > u(\mathbf{x}'')$. Yet if $v(\mathbf{x}) = h[u(\mathbf{x})]$, where h is monotonic, then $v(\mathbf{x}') > v(\mathbf{x}'')$ if and only if $u(\mathbf{x}') > u(\mathbf{x}'')$; hence $v(\mathbf{x}') > v(\mathbf{x}'')$ if and only if the consumer prefers $\mathbf{x}'$ to $\mathbf{x}''$. Insofar as we are concerned with the preferences of the consumer, we can conclude that the specific structure of the consumer's utility function is not important in that we can monotonically transform it in any way we like.

2.2 Indirect Concavity

The immediate implication of allowing monotonic transformations of utility functions is that we can no longer restrict ourselves to concave functions

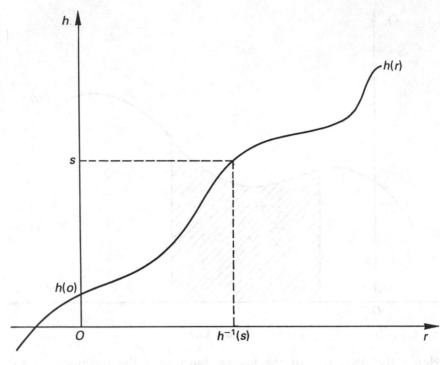

Figure 13.3

because a monotonic transform of a concave function is not necessarily concave. A simple illustration of this fact is the following example of a function in one variable. Let $f(x) = x$ and $h(r) = e^r$ then $F(x) = h[f(x)] = e^x$, and while f is concave, F is not. In general then we would not wish to restrict utility functions to being concave. Indeed it is often an irritation to restrict them so; for example, the utility function $u(x_1x_2) = x_1x_2$ is not concave although it is a much simpler function to use in examples than the equivalent concave $v(x_1,x_2) = \sqrt{(x_1x_2)}$. We are thus led to the following broader class of functions.

Definition 13.2: A function $f(x)$ is indirectly concave if it is a monotonic transformation of a concave function.

We note that this class of function is closed with respect to monotonic transformations, that is to say, a monotonic transformation of an indirectly concave function is indirectly concave. If $f(\mathbf{x}) = h_1[g(\mathbf{x})]$ where g is concave, and $F(\mathbf{x}) = h_2[f(\mathbf{x})]$, h_1 and h_2 both being monotonic, then defining $h(r) = h_2[h_1(r)]$ we can confirm that

$$\frac{dh}{dr} = \frac{dh_2}{ds}\frac{dh_1}{dr} > 0 \text{ and conclude } F(\mathbf{x}) = h[g(\mathbf{x})] \text{ is indirectly concave}$$

Having extended the concept of concavity, we need to consider whether our results on the identification of optima can be extended to include this broader class of functions. The following proposition goes part way to giving a positive answer to this question.

Theorem 13.3
(a)   If $F(\mathbf{x})$ is a monotonic transformation of $f(\mathbf{x})$ then:
   (i) $\mathbf{x}^*$ is a stationary point of F if and only if it is a stationary point of f.
   (ii) $\mathbf{x}^*$ is the maximum of F in a set S if and only if it is the maximum of f in S.
(b)   If $F(\mathbf{x})$ is indirectly concave, then $\mathbf{x}^*$ is a global maximum of F if and only if it is a stationary point of F.

The first half of this theorem is quite general in the sense that it makes no reference to concavity and it effectively states that stationarity and optimality are invariant to monotonic transformations of the objection function. If h is the monotonic transformation so that $F(\mathbf{x}) = h[f(\mathbf{x})]$, then the chain rule of differentiation tells us that the ith partial derivative of F is

$$F_i'(\mathbf{x}) = h'(r)f_i'(\mathbf{x})$$

where $r = f(\mathbf{x})$. As $h'(r) \neq 0$ for all r we can conclude that $F_i'(\mathbf{x}) = 0$ if and only if $f_i'(\mathbf{x}) = 0$; hence $\mathbf{x}^*$ is a stationary point of F if and only if it is a stationary point of f. Furthermore to say $\mathbf{x}^*$ maximises $F(\mathbf{x})$ in the set S is equivalent to saying $h[f(\mathbf{x}^*)] \geqslant h[f(\mathbf{x})]$ for all $\mathbf{x}$ in S, but by the monotonicity of h this last condition is equivalent to $f(\mathbf{x}^*) \geqslant f(\mathbf{x})$ for all $\mathbf{x}$ in S, which in turn says $\mathbf{x}^*$ is the maximum of f in S.

To establish part (b) of the theorem is now straightforward. Using (a)(ii) we know $\mathbf{x}^*$ is a global maximum of F if and only if it is a global maximum of f. But now we know f is concave, hence $\mathbf{x}^*$ is a global maximum of f if and only if $\mathbf{x}^*$ is a stationary point of f. Combining these two statements with (a)(i) allows us to conclude the validity of (b).

Two features of this theorem are worthy of emphasis. First (a)(ii) tells us that if we are searching for the maximum of a function we can consider a monotonic transformation of the function without changing the maximum, though clearly we will change the maximum *value*. For example, if we require the maximum of the function $f(x) = e^{-x^2}$ then we could consider $F(x) = \ln[f(x)] = -x^2$. As the maximum of $F(x) = -x^2$ occurs at $x = 0$, we can deduce that $x = 0$ is also the maximum of $f(x)$ and hence its maximum value is $f(0) = e^{-0} = 1$. The second point to be stressed is that for indirectly concave functions, stationarity is necessary and sufficient for a maximum. Our example above, $f(x) = e^{-x^2}$, is a monotonic transformation, $h(r) = e^r$, of a concave function $g(x) = -x^2$, hence it is indirectly concave. Hence its maximum is given by $f'(x) = -2xe^{-x^2} = 0$ which occurs at $x = 0$.

2.3 Lagrangians and Indirect Concavity

In this section we extend the Lagrangian Theorem of Chapter 9 to the case where the objective and constraining functions are indirectly concave.

Theorem 13.4
If $f(\mathbf{x})$ and $g(\mathbf{x})$ are indirectly concave functions of n variables, then necessary and sufficient conditions for $\mathbf{x}^*$ to be the maximum of $f(\mathbf{x})$ subject to $g(\mathbf{x}) \geq 0$ are as follows. There exist a λ^* such that:

  (i) $\lambda^* \geq 0$
  (ii) $g(\mathbf{x}^*) \geq 0$
  (iii) $\lambda^* g(\mathbf{x}^*) = 0$
  (iv) $\mathbf{x}^*$ is a stationary point of the Lagrangian

$$L = f(\mathbf{x}) + \lambda^* g(\mathbf{x})$$

  i.e. $f_i'(\mathbf{x}^*) + \lambda^* g_i'(\mathbf{x}^*) = 0$ for all i

To establish this result we proceed 'indirectly', i.e. we first convert the problem into the equivalent concave problem. Let $f(\mathbf{x}) = h_1[F(\mathbf{x})]$ and $g(\mathbf{x}) = h_2[G(\mathbf{x})]$ where h_1, h_2 are monotonically increasing and F, G are concave. Note first that $g(\mathbf{x}) \geq 0$ is equivalent to $h_2[G(\mathbf{x})] \geq 0$ or $G(\mathbf{x}) \geq h_2^{-1}(0)$, hence the constraint $g(\mathbf{x}) \geq 0$ is equivalent to the constraint $G(\mathbf{x}) - r \geq 0$ where $r = h_2^{-1}(0)$. Hence the maximum of $f(\mathbf{x})$ subject to $g(\mathbf{x}) \geq 0$ is equal to the maximum of $F(\mathbf{x})$ subject to $G(\mathbf{x}) - r \geq 0$. Yet we know from our discussion in Chapter 9 that necessary and sufficient conditions for $\mathbf{x}^*$ to be the maximum of the concave function $F(\mathbf{x})$ subject to the concave constraint $G(\mathbf{x}) - r \geq 0$ are as follows. There exists a μ^* such that:

  (a) $\mu^* \geq 0$
  (b) $G(\mathbf{x}^*) - r \geq 0$
  (c) $\mu^*[G(\mathbf{x}^*) - r] = 0$
  (d) $\mathbf{x}^*$ is a stationary point of

$$L = F(\mathbf{x}) + \mu^*[G(\mathbf{x}) - r]$$

i.e. $f_i'(\mathbf{x}^*) + \mu^* G_i'(\mathbf{x}^*) = 0$ for all i

We now show that these four conditions are equivalent to the four conditions of the theorem. Let us concentrate on the fourth condition of stationarity for the moment. The chain rule of differentiation tells us that

$$f_i'(\mathbf{x}^*) = h_1'(r_1) F_i'(\mathbf{x}^*)$$

and

$$g_i'(\mathbf{x}^*) = h_2'(r_2) G_i'(\mathbf{x}^*)$$

where $r_1 = F(\mathbf{x}^*)$ and $r_2 = G(\mathbf{x}^*)$. If we now let $\alpha = h_1'(r_1) > 0$ and $\beta = h_1'(r_2) > 0$, we can proceed as follows. Take the fourth condition (d) and multiply through by α to give

$$\alpha F_i'(\mathbf{x}^*) + \alpha \mu^* G_i'(\mathbf{x}^*) = 0$$

Now the first term is $f_i'(\mathbf{x}^*)$, while the second can be written as

$$\frac{\alpha \mu^*}{\beta} \beta G_i'(\mathbf{x}^*) = \lambda^* g_i'(\mathbf{x}^*) \text{ where}$$

$\lambda^* = \alpha \mu^*/\beta$. Hence we obtain

$$f_i'(\mathbf{x}^*) + \lambda^* g_i'(\mathbf{x}^*) = 0$$

i.e. condition (iv) of the theorem is equivalent to (d) above with $\lambda^* = \alpha \mu^*/\beta$. Now let us proceed through the other three conditions. Condition (a) $\mu^* \geq 0$ can now be seen as equivalent to (i) $\lambda^* = \alpha/\beta \, \mu^* \geq 0$ as $\alpha/\beta > 0$. Condition (b) $G(\mathbf{x}^*) - r \geq 0$ we already know to be equivalent to (ii) $g(\mathbf{x}^*) \geq 0$. Condition (c) can be restated as

$$\mu^* = 0 \text{ if } G(\mathbf{x}^*) - r > 0$$

$$G(\mathbf{x}^*) - r = 0 \text{ if } \mu^* > 0$$

these being equivalent to

$$\lambda^* = 0 \text{ if } g(\mathbf{x}^*) > 0$$

$$g(\mathbf{x}^*) = 0 \text{ if } \lambda^* > 0$$

i.e. (c) is equivalent to (iii).
Therefore, the conditions (a)—(d) are equivalent to (i)—(iv) where $\lambda^* = \alpha/\beta \, \mu^*$ and we can conclude that (i)—(iv) are necessary and sufficient for the optimality of $\mathbf{x}^*$.

We can note that strictly speaking Theorem 13.4 should contain a constraint qualification, namely, that there exists at least one $\mathbf{x}$ for which $g(\mathbf{x}) > 0$.

Example 13.1

Consider the utility function $u(x_1,x_2) = x_1x_2$. To see that u is indirectly concave for positive x_i we note that $u(x_1,x_2) = h[v(x_1,x_2)]$ where $v(x_1,x_2) = x_1^{1/2}x_2^{1/2} = \sqrt{(x_1x_2)}$ and $h(r) = r^2$. We know v is concave for positive x_i and $h'(r) = 2r > 0$ for $r > 0$, hence u is a monotonic transformation of a concave function, i.e. it is indirectly concave for positive x_i.

Applying Theorem 13.4 to the following problem:

$$\text{maximise } u(x_1,x_2) \text{ subject to } m - p_1x_1 - p_2x_2 \geqslant 0$$

we can proceed as before.

We first try a solution with $\lambda^* > 0$ so that

$$p_1x_1^* + p_2x_2^* = m \tag{13.1}$$

The stationarity conditions are then given differentiating the Lagrangian

$$L = x_1x_2 + \lambda^*(m - p_1x_1 - p_2x_2)$$

which yields

$$\frac{\partial L}{\partial x_1} = x_2^* - \lambda^*p_1 = 0 \tag{13.2}$$

$$\frac{\partial L}{\partial x_2} = x_1^* - \lambda^*p_2 = 0 \tag{13.3}$$

From (13.2) and (13.3) we obtain

$$\frac{x_2^*}{x_1^*} = \frac{p_1}{p_2}$$

or

$$p_1x_1^* = p_2x_2^* \tag{13.4}$$

Combining (13.4) and (13.1) yields

$$x_1^* = \frac{m}{2p_1} \quad x_2^* = \frac{m}{2p_2} \tag{13.5}$$

and hence

$$\lambda^* = \frac{m}{2p_1p_2} > 0$$

Having confirmed λ^* is positive we can conclude (13.5) gives the required maximum.

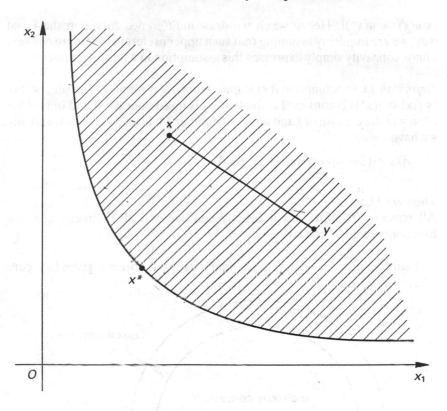

Figure 13.4

3 Quasi-Concavity

Traditionally, economic theories have not concentrated on indirect concavity; rather a more general idea has predominated in the literature, namely, that of quasi-concavity. To introduce this idea we again stay with consumer theory where this concept is most commonly used. In Figure 13.4 we have drawn the usual sort of indifference curve passing through a point $\mathbf{x}^*$. The feature of this familiar diagram which we wish to stress is the shape of the area lying above and on that indifference curve. As illustrated, if we consider any two points $\mathbf{x}$, $\mathbf{y}$ lying on or above the indifference curve, then the straight line between these two points will also lie above or on that indifference curve. If a set of points contains the straight line between any pair of its elements we say that set is *convex*. If we represent the preferences of the consumer by a utility function $u(\mathbf{x})$, then the area above or on the indifference curve represents the following *upper preferences set* $s(\mathbf{x}^*) =$

[x:u(**x**) $\geqslant$ u(**x***)]. Hence when we draw indifference curves in the usual way, we are implicitly assuming that such upper preferences sets are convex. Quasi-concavity simply expresses this assumption in a formal manner.

Definition 13.3: A function f(**x**) is *quasi-concave* if for all **x*** the set s(**x***) = [x:f(**x**) $\geqslant$ f(**x***)] is convex. Equivalently f is quasi-concave if and only if for all **x**, **y** in the domain of f and any real number λ lying between zero and one we have

$$f[\lambda \mathbf{x} + (1 - \lambda)\mathbf{y}] \geqslant \min [f(\mathbf{x}), f(\mathbf{y})]$$

Theorem 13.5
All concave functions are indirectly concave and all indirectly concave functions are quasi-concave.

A simple suggestive diagram summarising this theorem is given in Figure 13.5.

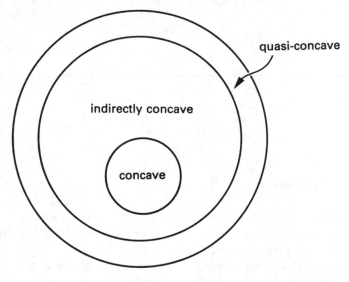

Figure 13.5

Thus the set of concave functions is contained in the set of indirectly concave functions which in turn is contained in the set of quasi-concave functions. In this way we see that the concept of quasi-concavity is more general than indirect concavity which in turn is more general than concavity.

Confirmation of the first statement in Theorem 13.5 is immediately obtained by noting that any concave function can be considered as a monotonic transformation of itself, for the identity function $h(r) = r$ is monotonically increasing. To establish the statement of the proposition we let $F(x) = h[f(x)]$ be an indirectly concave function, i.e. h is monotonic and f is concave. Consider two points x, y and let $z = \lambda x + (1 - \lambda)y$ where $0 \leqslant \lambda \leqslant 1$. We show that $F(z) \geqslant \min[F(x), F(y)]$ which establishes that F is quasi-concave. As f is concave we can conclude that $f(z) \geqslant \lambda f(x) + (1 - \lambda)f(y) \geqslant \min[f(x), f(y)]$ this last inequality following from the fact that both $f(x)$ and $f(y)$ are no less than $\min[f(x), f(y)]$, and the fact that λ and $1 - \lambda$ are both non-negative. In this way we see that any concave function is quasi-concave. Next we note that quasi-concavity is invariant to monotonic transformations, i.e. if $f(x)$ is quasi-concave and $F(x) = h[f(x)]$ is a monotonic transformation of f, then F is quasi-concave. With x, y and z as before we know

$$f(z) \geqslant \min[f(x), f(y)]$$

hence

$$F(z) = h[f(z)] \geqslant h\{\min[f(x), f(y)]\}$$

Yet this last term is equal to $\min\{h[f(x)], h[f(y)]\}$ hence

$$F(z) \geqslant \min[F(x), F(y)]$$

Although quasi-concavity is the more general concept and is used widely in economic theory, it can be shown that any quasi-concave utility function can be approximated by an indirectly concave utility function to any degree of approximation required. Indeed it is likely that in most applications the implicit or explicit assumptions will imply that a quasi-concave function is indirectly concave. Hence in effect the class of indirectly concave functions is adequate for most of our theory and hence we shall not pursue quasi-concavity further.

4 Lagrangians with Several Constraints and the Kuhn–Tucker Conditions

4.1 Several Constraints

Up to now we have concerned ourselves with optimisation problems involving only one constraint, while it is not uncommon to face problems where there are two or more constraints. For example, a correct statement of the consumer's choice between n consumption goods would take the form

maximise $\quad u(x)$

subject to $\quad m - px \geqslant 0$

and $\quad x_i \geqslant 0 \quad i = 1, \dots, n$

That is to say we should constrain the quantities x_i consumed to be non-negative as the consumption of a negative quantity is meaningless. In this case we would have a total of $n + 1$ constraints, rather than the one budget constraint. In most situations our ignoring the non-negativity constraint is not serious in that the solution so obtained involves positive quantities. Nevertheless, we can construct examples where the non-negativity constraint is important.

Example 13.2
Consider a consumer between consumption c and leisure l, where the choice of a quantity l of leisure is equivalent to the choice of working $h = T - l$ hours. If the consumer has an endowment of 'real' wealth A, then the budget constraint takes the form

$$c \leqslant A + wh = A + w(T - l)$$

where w is the 'real' wage rate. The non-negativity constraints faced by the consumer here as $c \geqslant 0$, $l \geqslant 0$ and $h \geqslant 0$ or $T - l \geqslant 0$. Let us assume the consumer's utility function is

$$u(c,l) = cl = c(T - h)$$

then if we proceed by ignoring the non-negativity constraints we would write down the Lagrangian

$$L = c(T - h) + (A + wh - c)$$

Looking for a solution with $\lambda^* > 0$ we require

$$c^* = wh^* + A \tag{13.6}$$

and

$$\frac{\partial L}{\partial c} = T - h^* - \lambda^* = 0 \tag{13.7}$$

$$\frac{\partial L}{\partial h} = -c^* + {}^*w = 0 \tag{13.8}$$

(13.7) and (13.8) imply

$$c^* = w(T - h^*) \tag{13.9}$$

hence (13.6) and (13.9) imply

$$w(T - h^*) = wh^* + A$$

or

$$h^* = \frac{wT - A}{2w} \tag{13.10}$$

and

$$c^* = \frac{wT + A}{2} \tag{13.11}$$

From (13.10) we can see that ignoring the non-negative constraint on h is legitimate as long as $A \leq wT$, but should $A > wT$ then this procedure would be incorrect.

The analysis of optimisation problems with non-negativity constraints is often associated with the Kuhn–Tucker conditions which we discuss in the next section. In this section we offer a general form of the Lagrangian Theorem to cover several constraints from which the Kuhn–Tucker conditions can be derived.

Theorem 13.6
Let $f(\mathbf{x})$ and $g_j(\mathbf{x})$ $j = 1,...,m$ be $m + 1$ indirectly concave functions. Necessary and sufficient conditions for $\mathbf{x}^*$ to be the maximum of $f(\mathbf{x})$ subject to $g_j(\mathbf{x}) \geq 0$ $j = 1,...,m$ are as follows. There exist λ_j^* $j = 1,...,m$ such that:

  (i) $\lambda_j^* \geq 0$ $j = 1,...,m$
  (ii) $g_j(\mathbf{x}^*) \geq 0$ $j = 1,...,m$
  (iii) $\lambda_j^* g_j(\mathbf{x}^*) = 0$ $j = 1,...,m$
  (iv) $\mathbf{x}^*$ is a stationary point of the Lagrangian

$$L = f(\mathbf{x}) + \lambda_1^* g_1(\mathbf{x}) + ... + \lambda_m^* g_m(\mathbf{x})$$

$$= f(\mathbf{x}) + \sum_{j=1}^{m} \lambda_j^* g_j(\mathbf{x})$$

The origin and interpretation of the Lagrangian multipliers λ_j^* is identical here as in the single constraint case. Thus we can view λ_j^* as the shadow price of the jth constraint or as the maximum 'amount' the decision maker would 'pay' for a marginal relaxation of the jth constraint. As before, we form the Lagrangian by adding the products of the multipliers and the associated constraints to the objective function. We then differentiate this Lagrangian with respect to the decision variables, i.e. the x_i's and set these derivatives equal to zero. The main complication is the manipulation of the complementary slackness conditions in (iii), i.e. in deciding whether to try $\lambda_j^* = 0$ or $g_j^*(\mathbf{x}^*) = 0$. The mechanical procedure here is simply to try all possible combinations, this being fruitful in preliminary exercises. Fortunately, in most situations our more informal understanding of the problem will guide us to the most likely combination of 'tight' and 'slack' constraints. Clearly this requires some practice in that it is as much an 'art' as a mechanical exercise.

Before discussing the formal background to the theorem we can note that, as before, we need to qualify the theorem by saying that we are assuming that the *constraint qualification* is satisfied, i.e. there is at least one **x** such that $g_j(\mathbf{x}) > 0$ for all $j = 1,\ldots,m$.

We will not attempt to offer a formal proof of the theorem—rather we simply outline its nature. The reader may care to re-read Chapter 9 interpreting $g(\mathbf{x})$, θ and λ as m-vectors whose jth components are $g_j(\mathbf{x})$, θ_j and λ_j respectively. Here θ_j is a measure of the degree of relaxation of the jth constraint so that the jth relaxed constraint is $g_j(\mathbf{x}) + \theta_j \geq 0$. The envelope function $v(\theta)$ is now a function of the m variables θ_j, and tells us the maximum payoff if the constraints are relaxed by the amount θ. If f and the g_j's $j = 1,\ldots,m$ are concave then $v(\theta)$ is also concave. From this property we deduce the Lagrangian Theorem as in Chapter 9. Note $\lambda g(\mathbf{x})$ is now to be read as the dot product between the vectors λ and $g(\mathbf{x})$, i.e. $\sum_{j=1}^{m}\lambda_j g_j(\mathbf{x})$ $= \lambda_1 g_1(\mathbf{x}) + \ldots + \lambda_m g_m(\mathbf{x})$. The only complication we might mention is that our implicit assumption that $v(\theta)$ is differentiable may be difficult to sustain when there are several constraints. As we mentioned in Chapter 9 this differentiability is not essential to the argument and the result goes through as stated.

In this way we can see the Lagrangian Theorem extends to several concave constraints, and the extension to indirectly concave functions closely follows that in subsection 2.3 of this chapter.

Taking the theorem as valid, let us look at it in practice by reconsidering our labour supply example above.

Example 13.3

$$\text{maximise} \quad c(T - h)$$

$$\text{subject to} \quad A + wh - c \geq 0$$

$$\text{and} \quad c \geq 0, h \geq 0, T - h \geq 0$$

We have then four constraints and all functions are indirectly concave. Indeed, all the constraint functions are linear and thus concave. We assume T and $A \geq 0$ and thus $c = 0$, $h = 0$ satisfy the constraints, i.e. the constraint qualification is satisfied. We form the Lagrangian

$$L = c(T - h) + \lambda(A + wh - c) + \mu_1 c + \mu_2 h + \mu_3(T - h)$$

and differentiate with respect to c and h to yield:

$$\frac{\partial L}{\partial c} = T - h^* - \lambda^* + \mu_1^* = 0 \tag{13.12}$$

$$\frac{\partial L}{\partial h} = -c + \lambda^* w + \mu_2^* - \mu_3^* = 0 \tag{13.13}$$

If we anticipate that the wealth A is not large, we might expect the consumer to work, and generally we would expect positive consumption and positive leisure consumption. In this we would look for $c^* > 0$, $h^* > 0$ and $T - h^* > 0$ so that $\mu_i^* = 0$, $i = 1,2,3$, and equations (13.12) and (13.13) become

$$T - h^* = \lambda^* \tag{13.14}$$

$$c^* = \lambda w \tag{13.15}$$

Furthermore we might expect the budget constraint to hold with equality hence

$$A + wh^* - c^* = 0 \tag{13.16}$$

(13.14), (13.15) and (13.16) as before give us

$$h^* = \frac{wT - A}{2w} \tag{13.17}$$

$$c^* = \frac{wT + A}{2} \tag{13.18}$$

Again this is fine as long as $A \leqslant wT$. Should we wish to consider the 'wealthy' case $A > wT$, then we try the case where $\mu_2^* \neq 0$ and $h^* = 0$. The budget constraint then gives $c^* = A$, (1) will give $\lambda^* = T > 0$ and (2) gives $\mu_2^* = c^* - \lambda^* w = A - wT$ which will be positive if $A > wT$.

4.2 The Kuhn–Tucker Conditions

In many economic decisions agents face non-negativity constraints on their decision variables as well as the more economic constraints such as budget limitations or technical productivity constraints. The Kuhn–Tucker conditions offer an alternative method of tackling such problems, although these are equivalent to the conditions coming from the Lagrangian Theorem in the previous section. Indeed, we shall derive them from that result.

Theorem 13.7 (Kuhn–Tucker)
Consider an optimisation problem of the form maximise $f(\mathbf{x})$ subject to $g(\mathbf{x}) \geqslant 0$ and to the non-negativity constraints $x_i \geqslant 0$ $i = 1,\dots,n$. If f and g are indirectly concave, then necessary and sufficient conditions for $\mathbf{x}^*$ to be a solution of this optimisation problem are as follows. There exists a λ^* such that:

(i) $\lambda^* \geqslant 0$
(ii) $g(\mathbf{x}^*) \geqslant 0$
(iii) $\lambda^* g(\mathbf{x}^*) = 0$

(iv) If $l = f(\mathbf{x}) + \lambda^* g(\mathbf{x})$ then

$$\frac{\partial l}{\partial x_i} = f_i'(\mathbf{x}^*) + \lambda^* g_i'(\mathbf{x}) \leqslant 0 \quad i = 1,\ldots,n$$

(v) $x_i^* \geqslant 0 \quad i = 1,\ldots,n$

(vi) $x_i^* \dfrac{\partial l^*}{\partial x_i} = 0 \quad i = 1,\ldots,n$

We have stated the result for one supplementary constraint, though it is valid should there be several constraints over and above the non-negativity constraints when (i) to (iii) hold for each of these constraints. The main novelty in the conditions is the replacement of stationarity of the Lagrangian by the condition that its derivative be non-positive, although we do have the complementary slackness condition (vi) which tells us that either x_i^* is zero or the derivative of the Lagrangian with respect to x_i^* is zero. As usual we need a constraint qualification, namely that there is an $\mathbf{x}$ such that $x_i > 0$ for i and $g(\mathbf{x}) > 0$.

To derive this theorem from that in the previous section we introduce an extended Lagrangian

$$L = f(\mathbf{x}) + \lambda g(\mathbf{x}) + \mu_1 x_1 + \ldots + \mu_n x_n$$

and apply Theorem 13.6 to obtain the following conditions:

(a) $\lambda^* \geqslant 0, \mu_i^* \geqslant 0 \quad i = 1,\ldots,n$
(b) $g(\mathbf{x}^*) \geqslant 0, x_i^* \geqslant 0 \quad i = 1,\ldots,n$
(c) $\lambda^* g(\mathbf{x}^*) = 0, \mu_i^* x_i^* = 0 \quad i = 1,\ldots n$

(d) $\dfrac{\partial L^*}{\partial x_i} = f_i'(\mathbf{x}^*) + \lambda^* g_i'(\mathbf{x}) + \mu_i^* = 0 \quad i = 1,\ldots n$

As $\mu_i^* \geqslant 0$ (d) is equivalent to

$$\frac{\partial L^*}{\partial x_i} = f_i'(\mathbf{x}^*) + \lambda^* g_i'(\mathbf{x}) = -\mu_i^* \leqslant 0$$

While $\mu_i^* x_i^* = 0$ tells us $-\mu_i^* x_i^* = 0$ and thus $x_i^* \dfrac{\partial L^*}{\partial x_i} = 0, i = 1,\ldots n.$ All the remaining conditions (i), (ii), (iii) and (v) are explicit in (a), (b) or (c).

Problems

13.1 A consumer, in allocating an initial asset holding m over $T + 1$ periods, faces the following budget constraint

$$\sum_{t=0}^{T} \frac{p_t c_t}{(1 + r)^t} \leqslant m$$

where p_t is the price of consumption and c_t is the level of consumption in period t, while r is the rate of interest or discount on assets. The consumer utility function takes the form

$$u(c_0, c_1, \ldots, c_T) = c_0 c_1 \ldots c_T$$

Confirm that this is indirectly concave and find the optimal consumption levels. (*Hint*: note that the partial derivative of u with respect to c_i is $u(\mathbf{c})/c_i$.)
Solution on p. 296.

13.2 Consider a consumer facing a two-period allocation of wealth where the wealth is made of the present value of current m_0 and future m_1 incomes. The budget constraint now takes the form

$$p_0 c_0 + \frac{p_1 c_1}{1 + r} \leq m_0 + \frac{m_1}{1 + r}$$

Find the optimal choices of c_0, c_1 if the consumer's utility function is

$$u(c_0, c_1) = c_0 c_1$$

Solution on p. 297.

13.3 Consider the marginal propensity to consume $\partial c_0/\partial m_0$ in the solution to Problem 13.2 when (a) m_1 does not vary as m_0 varies, (b) when m_1 is expected to move proportionally, so that $m_1 = \delta m_0$, say. Solution on p. 298.

13.4 Consider the following extension of Problem 13.2. A consumer receives incomes m_t over $T + 1$ periods, $t = 0, \ldots, T$, which have net present value NPV given by

$$\text{NPV} = \sum_{t=0}^{T} \frac{m_t}{(1 + r)^t}$$

where r is the rate of discount. If the consumer's utility function is $u(c_0, \ldots, c_T) = c_0 c_1 \ldots c_T$ show that the consumptions are

$$c_t = \frac{W}{(T + 1)(1 + r)^t p_t}$$

and thus conclude that if T is large a 'windfall' increase in W will not greatly affect consumption in any one period. Solution on p. 298.

13.5 Find a consumer's expenditure function if its utility function is $u(x_1, x_2) = x_1 x_2$.
Solution on p. 283.

13.6 Consider a consumer that not only faces a budget constraint but also a leisure time constraint. Thus we can consider the consumption of a unit quantity of each good as requiring a certain leisure time. In the case of two goods let t_1, t_2 be such consumption times and let T be the total leisure time available so that the consumer faces the constraint

$$t_1 x_1 + t_2 x_2 \leqslant T$$

where x_1 and x_2 are as usual the quantities of the two goods consumed. Find the optimal quantities and the shadow prices of the two constraints when the consumer's utility function is $u(x_1, x_2) = x_1 x_2$, $t_1 = t_2 = 1$, $T = 10$, and the prices of goods are $p_1 = 1$, $p_2 = 2$ and budget is $M = 12$. If the government can tax the consumer and use the revenue to increase T, would the consumer benefit by such a transfer?

Solution on p. 303.

13.7 A pure public good is such that everyone obtains positive utility from its existence however it is provided or whoever pays for its production. Consider a two-consumer, two-good world where the second good is a pure public good, so that each consumer's utility function takes the form $u^i(x_1^i, x_2^1 + x_2^2)$ $i = 1,2$, where x_j^i is the amount of the j'th good purchased by the i'th consumer. Confirm that if the consumers choose their purchases separately, the marginal rate of substitution will equal the relative prices of the goods as usual. Compare this situation to one where the two consumers coordinate their choices so as to generate an efficient outcome. A situation is (Pareto) efficient if it is *not* possible to make one consumer better off without making the other consumer worse off. Hence in an efficient outcome each consumer's utility must be at a maximum subject to the constraint that the other consumer's utility is not reduced. Hence to characterise an efficient outcome we can solve the following problem:

maximise $\quad u^1(x_1^1, x_2)$

subject to $\quad p_1(x_1^1 + x_1^2) + p_2 x_2 \leqslant m^1 + m^2$

and $\quad u^2(x_1^2, x_2) \geqslant \bar{u}$

Here x_2 is the total amount of the public good purchased by the two consumers, while the first constraint is the joint budget constraint with m^i being the i'th consumer's income. Show that in an efficient outcome the *sum* of the two consumer's marginal rates of substitution will equal the relative price of the public good.

Solution on p. 312.

PART III

Solutions to Problems:
The Theory of the
Consumer and Firm

Part III contains solutions to the problems set in the two previous parts. The start of each solution is indicated by the bold number on the left of the page, and the end of the solution is indicated by the ■ on the right. Part III serves the secondary purpose of converting the student's solutions into a systematic analysis of the behaviour of consumer and firm. For this reason the solutions are not presented in the order of the questions in the two previous parts and are embodied in an economic commentary. To obtain the maximum benefit from this part of the book, students are advised to tackle the problems in the order given in Parts I and II before systematically tackling Part III.

14

Consumer Theory

1 The Consumption Decision

The object of consumer theory is to characterise a consumer's pattern of consumption and to predict how this will change as external parameters change, notably prices and income. The critical assumption is that the consumer has a preference ordering over all feasible combinations of commodities and always consumes the most preferred bundle amongst those available. We further assume that the consumer's preferences can be represented by a monotonically increasing, indirectly concave utility function (see Chapter 13). Writing $u(\mathbf{x})$ for this utility function we say $u(\mathbf{x}^1) > u(\mathbf{x}^0)$ if and only if the consumer prefers $\mathbf{x}^1$ to $\mathbf{x}^0$. In this way the consumer's problem becomes a constrained maximisation problem, namely to choose $\mathbf{x}$ to maximise $u(\mathbf{x})$ subject to the budget constraint $\mathbf{px} \leqslant m$ where $\mathbf{p}$ is the price vector and m is the consumer's budget.

4.1 Consider the following two utility functions defined over two commodities, $u(x_1,x_2) = x_1^{1/2}x_2^{1/2}$ and $v(x_1,x_2) = x_1^2 x_2^2$. The marginal utility of the first good will be given by

$$\frac{\partial u}{\partial x_1} = \frac{1}{2} x_1^{-1/2}x_2^{1/2} \tag{14.1}$$

and

$$\frac{\partial v}{\partial x_1} = 2 \, x_1 x_2^2 \tag{14.2}$$

respectively. We can see that the first of these is inversely related to x_1 and the second directly related to x_1. Indeed we have

279

$$\frac{\partial^2 u}{\partial x_1^2} = - \frac{1}{4} x_1^{-3/2} x_2^{1/2} < 0$$

and

$$\frac{\partial^2 v}{\partial x_1^2} = 2x_2^2 > 0$$

indicating that the utility function u exhibits diminishing marginal utility while v exhibits increasing marginal utility.   ∎

We can note that $v(x_1,x_2) = [u(x_1,x_2)]^4$ or $v(x_1,x_2) = \phi(u(x_1,x_2))$ where $\phi(r) = r^4$. As $\phi'(r) = 4r^3 > 0$ for $r > 0$ we can say that v is a monotonic transformation of u. Furthermore we know u is concave (see Chapter 7 Section 3) hence v is indirectly concave (see Chapter 13).

8.1   Despite their different functional forms both u and v represent the same preferences. This follows from the fact that $u(\mathbf{x}^1) > u(\mathbf{x}^0)$ if and only if $\phi[u(\mathbf{x}^1)] > \phi[u(\mathbf{x}^0)]$, i.e. if and only if $v(\mathbf{x}^1) > v(\mathbf{x}^0)$. Hence the consumer associated with utility function u will prefer $\mathbf{x}^1$ to $\mathbf{x}^0$ if and only if the consumer associated with v prefers $\mathbf{x}^1$ to $\mathbf{x}^0$. It follows that the indifference curves of u are identical to those of v and in particular the marginal rate of substitution for the two functions are equal. To confirm this we can note that

$$\frac{\partial u}{\partial x_2} = \frac{1}{2} x_1^{1/2} x_2^{-1/2} \tag{14.3}$$

and

$$\frac{\partial v}{\partial x_2} = 2 \; x_1^2 x_2 \tag{14.4}$$

Combining (14.1) and (14.3) we find the marginal rate of substitution for u is

$$\frac{\partial u}{\partial x_1} \bigg/ \frac{\partial u}{\partial x_2} = \frac{x_2}{x_1}$$

and that for v is

$$\frac{\partial v}{\partial x_1} \bigg/ \frac{\partial v}{\partial x_2} = \frac{x_2}{x_1}$$

Hence the marginal condition for the consumer optimum is given by the same equation, namely

$$\frac{x_2^*}{x_1^*} = \frac{p_1}{p_2} \tag{14.5}$$

Combining this with the budget constraint

$$p_1x_1^* + p_2x_2^* = m \tag{14.6}$$

gives

$$x_1^* = \frac{m}{2p_1} \text{ and } x_2^* = \frac{m}{2p_2} \tag{14.7}$$

∎

The standard method of solving constrained maximisation problems is to appeal to the Lagrangian Theorem (see Chapters 9 and 13). For the consumer problem this usually involves our forming the Lagrangian

$$L = u(\mathbf{x}) + \lambda(m - \mathbf{px})$$

9.1 If we consider the case where

$$u(\mathbf{x}) = x_1^{\alpha_1} x_2^{\alpha_2} \ldots \ldots x_n^{\alpha_n}$$

where $\alpha_i > 0$, $i = 1,\ldots,n$ and $\sum_{i=1}^{n} \alpha_i \leq 1$, then, as this function is concave, we can use the Lagrangian Theorem of Chapter 9 with Lagrangian

$$L = x_1^{\alpha_1} x_2^{\alpha_2} \ldots \ldots x_n^{\alpha_n} + \lambda(m - p_1x_1 - p_2x_2 - \ldots - p_nx_n)$$

Before proceeding to the conditions for a maximum we note that for $i = 1,\ldots,n$

$$\frac{\partial u}{\partial x_i} = \alpha_i x_1^{\alpha_1} x_2^{\alpha_2} \ldots x_i^{\alpha_i - 1} \ldots x_n^{\alpha_n}$$

$$= \frac{\alpha_i u(\mathbf{x})}{x_i}$$

hence

$$\frac{\partial L}{\partial x_i} = \frac{\alpha_i u(\mathbf{x})}{x_i} - \lambda p_i \tag{14.8}$$

The conditions for an optimum are thus

$$\text{for } i = 1,\ldots,n \quad \frac{\alpha_i u(\mathbf{x}^*)}{x_i^*} = \lambda p_i \tag{14.9}$$

and

$$\lambda(m - \mathbf{px}^*) = 0 \tag{14.10}$$

As usual we try for a solution where $\lambda > 0$ and equality in the budget constraint, so that

$$m = \mathbf{px}^* \tag{14.11}$$

(14.9) tells us that $p_i x_i^* = \alpha_i \dfrac{u(\mathbf{x}^*)}{\lambda}$ and

$$\mathbf{px}^* = \left(\sum_{i=1}^{n} \alpha_i\right) \frac{u(\mathbf{x}^*)}{\lambda} \tag{14.12}$$

(14.11) and (14.12) imply $\dfrac{u(\mathbf{x}^*)}{\lambda} = \dfrac{m}{\Sigma \alpha_i}$ which together with (14.9) gives

$$x_i^* = \frac{\alpha_i}{\Sigma \alpha_i} \frac{m}{p_i} \tag{14.13}$$

These imply

$$\lambda = \frac{\Sigma \alpha_i u(\mathbf{x}^*)}{m} > 0$$

Hence the proportion of income $p_i x_i/m$ spent on the ith good is $\alpha_i/\Sigma\alpha_i$ and is independent of prices. ∎

If the quantity consumed x_i^* of the ith good increases as the price p_j of the jth good increases, where $j \neq i$, we say the ith good is a *gross substitute* for the jth good. While if x_i^* decreases as p_j increases, we say the ith good is a *gross complement* for the jth good.

9.2 In the case where

$$u(x_1,x_2) = \frac{x_1^\rho + x_2^\rho}{\rho} \quad \rho \neq 0 \text{ and } \rho < 1$$

as u is concave (see Theorem 7.8), we can use the Lagrangian method to confirm that the optimal quantities are

$$x_1^* = \frac{m}{(p_1^{1-\gamma} + p_2^{1-\gamma})p_1^\gamma}$$

$$x_2^* = \frac{m}{(p_1^{1-\gamma} + p_2^{1-\gamma})p_2^\gamma}$$

where

$$\gamma = \frac{1}{1 - \rho}$$

Differentiating these expressions respectively with respect to p_2 and p_1 we obtain

$$\frac{\partial x_1}{\partial p_2} = \frac{-(1 - \gamma)m}{(p_1^{1-\gamma} + p_2^{1-\gamma})^2 p_1^\gamma p_2^\gamma}$$

and

$$\frac{\partial x_2}{\partial p_1} = \frac{-(1 - \gamma)m}{(p_1^{1-\gamma} + p_2^{1-\gamma})^2 p_1^\gamma p_2^\gamma}$$

hence

$$\frac{\partial x_1}{\partial p_2} = \frac{x_2}{p_1} > 0 \text{ if and only if } 1 - \gamma < 0$$

which is true if and only if $0 < \rho < 1$. That is to say, x_1 and x_2 are gross substitutes for each other if and only if $0 < \rho < 1$. They will be gross complements otherwise. ∎

2   Indirect Utility, Expenditure and Demand Functions

2.1 Indirect Utility and Expenditure Functions

Because of Roy's Identity and Shephard's Lemma (see Chapters 10 and 12) it is often more useful to describe consumer preferences in terms of their indirect utility or expenditure functions. The indirect utility function $v(\mathbf{p},m)$ is defined as the maximum utility level attainable given income m and prices $\mathbf{p}$, while expenditure function $e(\mathbf{p},u)$ gives the minimum expenditure necessary to attain utility level u given commodity prices $\mathbf{p}$. The relation between these two functions can be summarised as follows:

$$e(\mathbf{p}, v(\mathbf{p},m)) = m \tag{14.14}$$

$$v(\mathbf{p}, e(\mathbf{p},u)) = u \tag{14.15}$$

We can view (14.14) as an equation which determines $v(\mathbf{p},m)$ given $e(\mathbf{p},u)$, while (14.15) determines $e(\mathbf{p},u)$ given $v(\mathbf{p},m)$.

13.5   If the utility function of a consumer is $u(x_1,x_2) = x_1x_2$ then we can construct the expenditure function from the solution to the following problem (see Chapter 11).

minimise $p_1x_1 + p_2x_2$

subject to $x_1x_2 \geqslant u$

Forming the Lagrangian

$$L = -p_1x_1 - p_2x_2 + \lambda(x_1x_2 - u)$$

and looking for a solution with $\lambda > 0$ we obtain the following conditions:

$$\frac{\partial L}{\partial x_1} = -p_1 + \lambda x_2^* = 0$$

$$\frac{\partial L}{\partial x_2} = -p_2 + \lambda x_1^* = 0$$

and

$$x_1^* x_2^* = u$$

hence

$$x_2^* = \frac{p_1}{\lambda}, x_1^* = \frac{p_2}{\lambda} \text{ and } \frac{p_1 p_2}{\lambda^2} = u$$

in which case

$$\frac{1}{\lambda} = \left(\frac{u}{p_1 p_2}\right)^{1/2} > 0 \text{ and}$$

$$x_1^* = \left(u \frac{p_2}{p_1}\right)^{1/2}, x_2^* = \left(u \frac{p_1}{p_2}\right)^{1/2}$$

It follows that

$$e(\mathbf{p},u) = p_1 x_1^* + p_2 x_2^* = 2(p_2 p_1 u)^{1/2}$$ ■

The indirectly utility function associated with this expenditure function can be found by applying (14.14) which, in this case, implies

$$(p_1 p_2 v(\mathbf{p},m))^{1/2} = m$$

hence

$$v(\mathbf{p},m) = \frac{m^2}{p_1 p_2}$$

(handwritten: $m = 2(p_2 p_1 u)^{\frac{1}{2}}$; $m = 2(p_2^{\frac{1}{2}} 2 p_1^{\frac{1}{2}} u^{\frac{1}{2}})$; $2u^{\frac{1}{2}} = \frac{m}{2p_1^{\frac{1}{2}} 2 p_2^{\frac{1}{2}}}$; $u^{\frac{1}{2}} = \frac{m}{p_1^{\frac{1}{2}} p_2^{\frac{1}{2}}}$; $v^{\frac{1}{2}} = \frac{m^2}{p_1 p_2}$)

10.1   Similarly if the utility function is

$$u(x_1,x_2) = x_1^\alpha x_2^\beta$$

then   ■

$$v(\mathbf{p},m) = \left(\frac{\alpha}{p_1}\right)^\alpha \left(\frac{\beta}{p_2}\right)^\beta \left(\frac{m}{\alpha+\beta}\right)^{\alpha+\beta}$$

(handwritten: $\left(\frac{\alpha}{p_1}\right)^\alpha \left(\frac{\beta}{p_2}\right)^\beta \left(\frac{m}{\alpha+\beta}\right)^{\alpha+\beta} = U$)

and

11.2

$$e(\mathbf{p},u) = (\alpha + \beta)\left[u\left(\frac{p_1}{\alpha}\right)^\alpha \left(\frac{p_2}{\beta}\right)^\beta\right]^{\frac{1}{\alpha+\beta}}$$ ■

(handwritten: $\left(\frac{m}{\alpha+\beta}\right)^{\alpha+\beta} = \frac{U}{\left(\frac{\alpha}{p_1}\right)^\alpha \left(\frac{\beta}{p_2}\right)^\beta}$; $\left(\frac{M}{\alpha+\beta}\right)^{\alpha+\beta} = U\left(\frac{p_1}{\alpha}\right)^\alpha \left(\frac{p_2}{\beta}\right)^\beta$)

11.1   And again if

$$u(x_1,x_2) = (x_1^\rho + x_2^\rho)^{1/\rho}, \quad \rho < 1$$

then   ■

(handwritten: $M = \alpha + \beta \left[U\left(\frac{p_1}{\alpha}\right)^\alpha \left(\frac{p_2}{\beta}\right)^\beta\right]^{\frac{1}{\alpha+\beta}}$)

$$e(\mathbf{p},u) = u(p_1^{-\sigma} + p_2^{-\sigma})^{-1/\sigma}$$

where

$$\sigma = \frac{\rho}{1 - \rho}$$

and

11.3

$$v(\mathbf{p},m) = m(p_1^{-\sigma} + p_2^{-\sigma})^{1/\sigma}$$ ∎

Given an expenditure or indirect utility we can, in principle, obtain the (direct) utility function from the following fact (see Chapter 10):

$$u(\mathbf{x}) = \text{minimum over } \mathbf{p} \text{ of } v(\mathbf{p},m) \text{ subject to the constraint } \mathbf{px} = m$$

10.2 For example if

$$e(\mathbf{p},u) = (p_1^\alpha p_2^\beta u)^{\frac{1}{\alpha + \beta}}$$

then

$$v(\mathbf{p},m) = m^{\alpha+\beta} p_1^{-\alpha} p_2^{-\beta}$$

To find $u(\mathbf{x})$ we form the Lagrangian

$$L = -m^{\alpha+\beta} p_1^{-\alpha} p_2^{-\beta} + \lambda(m - p_1 x_1 - p_2 x_2)$$

and looking for a solution with $\lambda > 0$ we obtain the following conditions:

$$\frac{\partial L}{\partial p_1} = \alpha m^{\alpha+\beta} p_1^{-\alpha-1} p_2^{-\beta} - \lambda x_1 = 0$$

$$\frac{\partial L}{\partial p_2} = \beta m^{\alpha+\beta} p_1^{-\alpha} p_2^{-\beta-1} - \lambda x_2 = 0$$

and

$$p_1 x_1 + p_2 x_2 = m$$

The first two equations imply

$$p_2 x_2 = \frac{\beta}{\alpha} p_1 x_1$$

which together with the third equation imply

$$p_1 = \frac{\alpha m}{(\alpha + \beta)x_1}, p_2 = \frac{\beta m}{(\alpha + \beta)x_2}$$

Substituting these expressions for **p** into $v(\mathbf{p},m)$ gives us

$$u(\mathbf{x}) = Ax_1^\alpha x_2^\beta$$

where

$$A = \frac{(\alpha + \beta)^{\alpha+\beta}}{\alpha^\alpha \beta^\beta} \qquad\qquad \blacksquare$$

Figures 14.1(a) and (b) illustrate a problem with the above procedure for deriving (direct) utility from indirect utility functions. Hence we have drawn indifference curves for two (direct) utility functions and in the case of Figure 14.1(a) the indifference curve is not convex above, i.e. the associated utility function is not quasi-concave. Despite their difference both the illustrated utility functions will have the same indirect utility function. Any attempt to reconstruct the utility function from the indirect will lead to the quasi-concave function associated with Figure 14.1(b). In this respect the direct utility function may contain more information than the indirect. Nevertheless the indirect function contains all the economically relevant information about

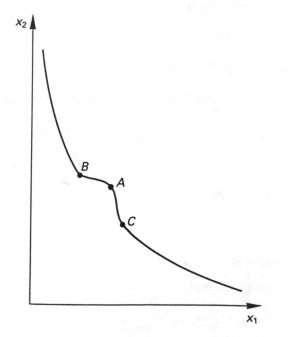

Figure 14.1 (a)

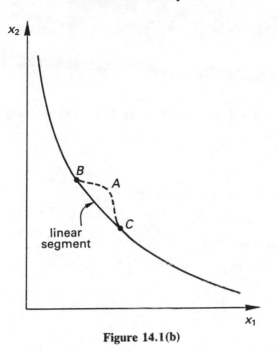

x_2

B

A

linear
segment

C

x_1

Figure 14.1(b)

the consumer's preferences, for combinations such as A in Figure 14.1(a)
would never be chosen.

2.2 Demand Functions and their Properties

As indicated above, the derivation of demand function from indirect utility
or expenditure functions is relatively straightforward when compared to the
process of solving the utility maximisation problem. For example, we can
use Roy's Identity (see Chapters 10 and 12) to construct the (Marshallian)
demand functions directly from indirect utility functions, for the Identity
says the demand functions $x_i(\mathbf{p},m)$ are given by

$$x_i(\mathbf{p},m) = \frac{-\partial v/\partial p_i}{\partial v/\partial m}$$

10.3 For example the indirect utility function associated with

$$u(\mathbf{x}) = x_1^{\alpha_1}x_2^{\alpha_2}...x_n^{\alpha_n}$$

is

$$v(\mathbf{p},m) = m^\sigma p_1^{-\alpha_1} p_2^{-\alpha_2} \ldots p_n^{-\alpha_n}$$

where

$$\sigma = \sum_{i=1}^{n} \alpha_i$$

Roy's Identity thus tells us that the demand functions associated with these preferences are

$$x_i(\mathbf{p},m) = \frac{-\partial v/\partial p_i}{\partial v/\partial m} = \frac{\alpha_i m}{\sigma p_i}$$

Or again, given direct utility function

$$u(x_1,x_2) = (x_1^p + x_2^p)^{1/p}$$

we have indirect function

$$v(p_1,p_2,m) = m(p_1^{-\sigma} + p_2^{-\sigma})^{1/\sigma}$$

where

$$\sigma = \frac{\rho}{1 - \rho}$$

Hence

$$x_1(p_1,p_2,m) = m(p_1^{-\sigma} + p_2^{-\sigma})^{-1} p_1^{-\sigma-1}$$

and

$$x_2(p_1,p_2,m) = m(p_1^{-\sigma} + p_2^{-\sigma})^{-1} p_2^{-\sigma-1}$$
■

If we start with the expenditure function $e(\mathbf{p},u)$ Shephard's Lemma (see Chapters 11, 12) tells us that the Hicksian demand functions $x_i(\mathbf{p},u)$ are given by

$$x_i(\mathbf{p},u) = \frac{\partial e}{\partial p_i}$$

12.2   Furthermore we can assert that the Marshallian demand functions $x^M(\mathbf{p},m)$ can be derived from the Hicksian $x^H(\mathbf{p},u)$ and vice versa because

$$x^M(\mathbf{p},m) = x^H[\mathbf{p},v(\mathbf{p},m)]$$

and

$$x^H(\mathbf{p},u) = x^M[\mathbf{p},e(\mathbf{p},u)]$$

For example if

$$e(\mathbf{p},u) = 2(p_1p_2u)^{1/2} \;\gtrsim\; m$$

then

$$U^{1/2} \;\gtrsim\; \frac{m}{2(p_1p_2)^{1/2}}$$

$$v(\mathbf{p},m) = \frac{m^2}{4p_1p_2}$$

and

$$U = \frac{m^2}{4p_1p_2}$$

$$x_1^H = \frac{\partial e}{\partial p_1} = \left(u\,\frac{p_2}{p_1}\right)^{1/2}$$

$$x_2^H = \frac{\partial e}{\partial p_2} = u\left(\frac{p_1}{p_2}\right)^{1/2}$$

while finally

$$x_1^M = \frac{-\partial v/\partial p_1}{\partial v/\partial m} = \frac{m}{2p_1}$$

$$x_2^M = \frac{-\partial v/\partial p_2}{\partial v/\partial m} = \frac{m}{2p_2}$$

To confirm the relationships between $\mathbf{x}^M$ and $\mathbf{x}^H$ we can substitute $v(\mathbf{p},m)$ for u in x_1^H to give

$$x_1^H[\mathbf{p},v(\mathbf{p},m)] = \left(\frac{m^2}{4p_1p_2}\,\frac{p_2}{p_1}\right)^{1/2} = \frac{m}{2p_1} = x_1^M$$

and we can substitute $e(\mathbf{p},u)$ into x_1^M to obtain

$$x_1^M[\mathbf{p},e(\mathbf{p},u)] = 2\left(\frac{p_1p_2u}{2p_1}\right)^{1/2} = \left(\frac{p_2}{p_1}u\right)^{1/2} = x_1^H \qquad \blacksquare$$

12.3 The slope of the Hicksian demand curve is given by

$$\frac{\partial x_i(\mathbf{p},u)}{\partial p_i} = \frac{\partial^2 e(\mathbf{p},u)}{\partial p_i^2} \leq 0 \tag{14.16}$$

The inequality arises from the fact that $e(\mathbf{p},u)$ is concave in prices (see Chapter 11) and thus the second derivative with respect to a single price is non-positive (see Chapter 7). Hence Hicksian demand curves cannot be upward sloping. $\blacksquare$

12.4 Changes in Hicksian demands due to changes in prices, so that utility is held constant, are usually referred to as (net) substitution effects. In particular (14.16) is known as the own price (net) substitution effect while

$$\frac{\partial x_i(\mathbf{p},u)}{\partial p_j} = \frac{\partial^2 e(\mathbf{p},u)}{\partial p_j \partial p_i} \qquad i \neq j$$

is the cross (net) substitution effect. If this cross effect is positive we say the ith good is a (net) *substitute* for the jth good, while if it is negative we say it is a (net) *complement*. Compare this with the notions of gross substitutes and complements discussed in the previous section. Young's Theorem (see the Appendix) tells us that the cross second order partials of a continuously differentiable function are equal, for example

$$\frac{\partial^2 e}{\partial p_j \partial p_i} = \frac{\partial^2 e}{\partial p_i \partial p_j}$$

Hence

$$\frac{\partial x_i(\mathbf{p},u)}{\partial p_j} = \frac{\partial x_j(\mathbf{p},u)}{\partial p_i} \qquad \blacksquare$$

12.5   It is useful to distinguish between the substitution and income effects of a price change on (Marshallian) demands. The formal expression of this decomposition is the Slutsky equation. To derive this equation we again use the following relationship:

$$x_i^H(\mathbf{p},u) = x_i^M[\mathbf{p},e(\mathbf{p},u)]$$

Differentiating both sides of this equation with respect to p_i yields

$$\frac{\partial x_i^H(\mathbf{p},u)}{\partial p_i} = \frac{\partial x_i^M [\mathbf{p},e(\mathbf{p},u)]}{\partial p_i} + \frac{\partial x_i^M}{\partial m}\frac{\partial e(\mathbf{p},u)}{\partial p_i}$$

We now use the fact that $\dfrac{\partial e}{\partial p_i} = x_i^H$, then substitute $u = v(\mathbf{p},m)$ and rearrange to obtain

$$\frac{\partial x_i^M}{\partial p_i} = \frac{\partial x_i^H}{\partial p_i} - \frac{\partial x_i^M}{\partial m} x_i^M \qquad (14.17)$$

where x_i^M, $\dfrac{\partial x_i^M}{\partial p_i}$ and $\dfrac{\partial x_i^M}{\partial m}$ are evaluated at $(\mathbf{p},m)$ while $\dfrac{\partial x_i^H}{\partial p_i}$ is evaluated at

$(\mathbf{p},v(\mathbf{p},m))$. (14.17) is the the Slutsky equation giving the decomposition of the gross effect of a change in the ith price on the ith good. The first term on the right-hand side $\partial x_i^H/\partial p_i$ is the (net) substitution effect, this being the effect if income was simultaneously changed so as to leave utility unchanged. The second term $-\dfrac{\partial x_i^M}{\partial m} x_i^M$ is the income effect. This is the

product of the effect $\partial x_i^M/\partial m$ on the demand for good i when income rises and $-x_i^M$ which determines the fall in income equivalent in purchasing power terms to the rise in price. $\blacksquare$

12.7 If $\dfrac{\partial x_i^M}{\partial m} > 0$

then the ith is said to be a normal good while if $\partial x_i^M / \partial m < 0$ then it is an inferior good. Figure 14.2(a) shows the Hicksian and Marshallian demand curves for an inferior good and Figure 14.2(b) those for a normal good.

The fact that Hicksian demand curves cannot slope upwards is not sufficient to guarantee that Marshallian demand curves cannot slope upwards. If the ith good is inferior so that $\partial x_i^M / \partial m < 0$ and x_i^M is 'large' then, although $\partial x_i^H / \partial p_i \leqslant 0$, it is possible that overall $\partial x_i^M / \partial p_i > 0$. Such goods are called Giffen goods and are no more than a theoretical curiosity. If the good in question is a normal good it cannot be a Giffen good. It is clear from (14.17) that a Giffen good must be an inferior good but an inferior good need not be a Giffen good. ∎

12.6 By similar techniques we can obtain

$$\frac{\partial x_i^M}{\partial p_j} = \frac{\partial x_i^H}{\partial p_j} - \frac{\partial x_i^M}{\partial m} x_j^M \qquad (14.18)$$

where

x_j^M, $\dfrac{\partial x_i^M}{\partial p_j}\bigg|$ and $\dfrac{\partial x_i^M}{\partial m}$ are evaluated at $(\mathbf{p}, m)$

and $\dfrac{\partial x_i^H}{\partial p_j}$ is evaluated at $[\mathbf{p}, v(\mathbf{p}, m)]$ ∎

12.8 Inspecting (14.18) we can investigate when the net effect of a rise in the jth price on the demand for the ith good is equal to the net effect of a rise in the price of the ith good on the demand for the jth good, i.e. when

$$\frac{\partial x_i^M}{\partial p_i} = \frac{\partial x_j^M}{\partial p_i}$$

From (14.18) we can conclude that this equality is true if and only if

$$\frac{\partial x_i^M}{\partial m} x_j^M = \frac{\partial x_j^M}{\partial m} x_i^M$$

or

$$\frac{m}{x_i^M} \frac{\partial x_i^M}{\partial m} = \frac{m}{x_j^M} \frac{\partial x_j^M}{m}\bigg|$$

i.e. the two income elasticities are identical. ∎

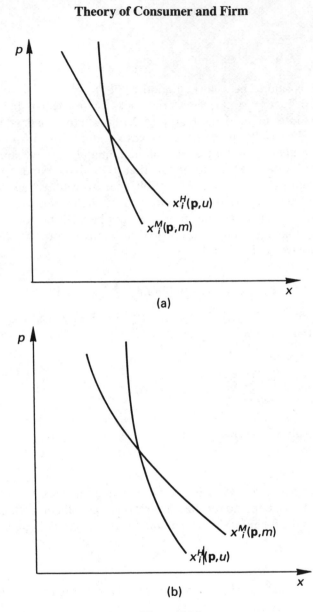

Figure 14.2

12.9 To illustrate the Slutsky decomposition, consider the case where

$$v(\mathbf{p},m) \; = \; \frac{m^2}{4p_1p_2}$$

and

$$e(\mathbf{p},u) = 2(p_1 p_2 u)^{1/2}$$

so that

$$x_i^H = \frac{\partial e}{\partial p_1} = \left(u \frac{p_2}{p_1}\right)^{1/2}$$

and

$$\frac{\partial x_1^H}{\partial p_1} = -\frac{1}{2}(up_2)^{1/2}p_1^{-3/2} \tag{14.19}$$

Furthermore

$$x_1^M = -\frac{\partial v/\partial p_1}{\partial v/\partial m} = \frac{m}{2p_1}$$

so that

$$\frac{\partial x_1^M}{\partial p_1} = -\frac{m}{2p_1^2} \tag{14.20}$$

If we evaluate (14.19) at $u = v(\mathbf{p},m) = \dfrac{m^2}{4p_1 p_2}$ we obtain the substitution effect $\dfrac{\partial x_1^H}{\partial p_1} = -\dfrac{m}{4p_1^2}$, while the income effect is $-\dfrac{\partial x_1^M}{\partial m}x_1^m = -\dfrac{1}{2p_1}\cdot\dfrac{m}{2p_1} = -\dfrac{m}{4p_1^2}$ We can thus confirm that the sum of substitution and income effect is equal to $\partial x_1^M/\partial p_1$ as stated in the Slutsky equation. In this case the two effects are equal. Similarly we obtain

$$\frac{\partial x_i^M}{\partial p_2} = \frac{m}{4p_1 p_2} - \frac{m}{4p_1 p_2} = 0$$

so that the two effects exactly offset each other. ∎

3 Aggregation and the Structure of the Indirect Utility Function

The theory described so far has been in terms of a single consumer, but often we are interested in analysing the behaviour of a large number of consumers, e.g. the aggregate behaviour of the economy. A difficulty arises here because aggregate demand is likely to depend upon the distribution of income and we cannot proceed as if the aggregate demand can be derived from the maximisation of an 'aggregate' utility function subject to an aggregate budget constraint.

We say that the individual consumer demands can be aggregated if the aggregate demands, i.e. the sum of the individual demands, can be treated as if they were generated by the maximisation of an aggregate utility function subject to an aggregate budget constraint. An aggregate utility function is one whose arguments are the aggregate demands of the consumers. Thus if x^h is the demand of the hth consumer the aggregate demand would be $x = \sum_h x^h$, the sum being over all consumers. Equally the aggregate budget constraint would state that the value of the aggregate demands must not exceed the aggregate income, the latter being the sum of the individual incomes.

10.4   If the indirect utility function is of the form

$$v(\mathbf{p},m) = m\phi(\mathbf{p})$$

then the (Marshallian) demand functions are of the form

$$x_i(\mathbf{p},m) = - \frac{m}{\phi(\mathbf{p})} \frac{\partial\phi}{\partial p_i}$$

for which the income elasticity $\dfrac{m}{x_i} \dfrac{\partial x_i}{\partial m}$ is equal to one for all prices and income.　■

If $v^h(\mathbf{p},m^h)$ is the indirect utility of the hth consumer and m^h is the corresponding income, then a sufficient condition for the aggregation of demands is, in fact:

$$v^h(\mathbf{p},m^h) = m^h\phi(\mathbf{p})$$

for each h. In this case all consumers have unit income elasticity and the proportion of income going on any good is the same for all consumers. Hence any redistribution of income will not affect the structure of demand.

10.5   Although sufficient this structure is not necessary, indeed a necessary and sufficient condition for the aggregation of demands is that the indirect utility functions have the Gorman polar form, namely

$$v^h(\mathbf{p},m^h) = \alpha(\mathbf{p})m^h + \beta^h(\mathbf{p})$$

where α and β^h are such as to ensure v^h is an indirect utility function.

The demands associated with these preferences are

$$x_i^h(\mathbf{p},m^h) = a_i(\mathbf{p})m^h + b_i^h(\mathbf{p})$$

where

$$a_i(\mathbf{p}) = - \frac{1}{\alpha} \frac{\partial\alpha}{\partial p_i} \quad \text{and} \quad b_i^h = - \frac{1}{\alpha} \frac{\partial\beta^h}{\partial p_i}$$

Note $\alpha(\mathbf{p})$ and $a_i(\mathbf{p})$ are independent of h, i.e. they are the same for all consumers, hence again any transfer of income between consumers will not alter the aggregate pattern of demand. Indeed the aggregate demand will be given by

$$x_i(\mathbf{p},m) = \sum_h x_i^h = a_i(\mathbf{p})m + b_i(\mathbf{p})$$

where

$$m = \sum_h m^h \quad \text{and} \quad b_i(\mathbf{p}) = \sum_h b_i^h(\mathbf{p})$$

An indirect utility function which would generate this demand function is

$$v(\mathbf{p},m) = \alpha(\mathbf{p})m + \beta(\mathbf{p})$$

where

$$\beta(\mathbf{p}) = \sum_h \beta^h(\mathbf{p}) \qquad \blacksquare$$

10.6 A well known special case of this class of functions is

$$V(p_1,p_2,m) = \frac{m - \alpha p_1 - \beta p_2}{p_1^\gamma \, p_2^{1-\gamma}}$$

where α, β and γ are positive constants. We assume that $\alpha p_1 + \beta p_2 \leq m$. The demand functions generated by these preferences are

$$x_1(\mathbf{p},m) = \alpha + \frac{\gamma}{p_1}(m - \alpha p_1 - \beta p_2) \tag{14.21}$$

and

$$x_2(\mathbf{p},m) = \beta + \frac{(1-\gamma)}{p_2}(m - \alpha p_1 - \beta p_2) \tag{14.22}$$

We can interpret α and β as 'survival' or 'necessary' quantities of the two goods, so that we can say the consumer allocates a proportion γ of 'excess income' $(m - \alpha p_1 - \beta p_2)$ to the first good and the remaining $(1 - \gamma)$ to the second good. The demand functions in (14.21) and (14.22) constitute the linear expenditure system for two goods. $\qquad \blacksquare$

12.1 Another special case is given by the expenditure function defined implicitly by

$$\ln[e(p_1,p_2,u)] = a + \alpha \ln(p_1) + (1 - \alpha)\ln(p_2)$$

$$+ \frac{1}{2}(\gamma \ln p_1)^2 + \frac{1}{2}\gamma(\ln p_2)^2 - \gamma \ln(p_1)\ln(p_2)$$

$$+ u\beta\left(\frac{p_1}{p_2}\right)^\delta$$

Differentiating with respect to p_1 gives

$$\frac{1}{e}\frac{\partial e}{\partial p_1} = \frac{\alpha}{p_1} + \frac{\gamma}{p_1}\ln(p_1) - \frac{\gamma}{p_1}\ln(p_2) + \frac{u\beta\delta}{p_1}\left(\frac{p_1}{p_1}\right)^\delta$$

Hence the proportion W_1 of expenditure directed to the Hicksian demand for the first good is given by

$$W_1 = \frac{p_1}{e}\frac{\partial e}{\partial p_1} = \alpha + \gamma\ln\left(\frac{p_1}{p_2}\right) + u\beta\delta\left(\frac{p_1}{p_2}\right)^\delta$$

Similarly the proportion of expenditure going to the Hicksian demand for the second good is

$$W_2 = \alpha + \gamma\ln\left(\frac{p_2}{p_1}\right) + u\beta\delta\left(\frac{p_2}{p_1}\right)^\delta$$

This system of demands is the two-good case of the Almost Ideal Demand System (AIDS).

4 Intertemporal Consumption

The analysis of the previous sections can be applied to a consumer choosing a stream of consumptions over a number of different time periods as long as we correctly interpret the prices. Nevertheless it is useful to make the intertemporal structure of a consumer's decision explicit.

4.1 Discrete Time Model

The first task is to specify the budget constraint faced by a consumer planning consumption over a number of periods. Consider then a consumer choosing a pattern of consumption c_t over the $T+1$ periods $t = 0,1,2,...,T$. Here we can think of c_t as the quantity of single consumption goods consumed in period t. If the price of the good in period t is known to be p_t then the present value of c_t, i.e. the equivalent value in period $t = 0$, will be $\frac{p_t}{(1+r)^t}c_t$, where r is the rate of interest (assumed constant). Hence if the consumer has a current budget of m he faces the constraint that the sum of the present values of his stream of consumption cannot exceed m, i.e.

$$p_0c_0 + \frac{p_1c_1}{(1+r)} + \frac{p_2c_2}{(1+r)^2} + ...+ \frac{p_Tc_T}{(1+r)^T} \leq m$$

13.1 If the consumer has a utility function of the form

$$u(c_0,...,c_T) = c_0c_1c_2...c_T$$

then the optimal stream c_t will satisfy

$$p_t c_t = \frac{p_{t-1} c_{t-1}}{(1+r)} \qquad t = 0,\ldots,T-1$$

That is to say the present values of the expenditures in each period will be equal to each other. Hence if the price is constant so that $p_t = p_{t+1}$, and the rate of interest r is positive, then the quantity consumed increases with time. Indeed we have as a solution

$$c_t = \frac{m(1+r)^t}{(T+1)p_t}$$

■

In this example the consumer considers consumption in each period as equivalent. It is usual to assume consumers discount future consumptions, i.e. consider future consumptions as yielding a smaller utility.

9.3 For example we have an additively separable utility function of the form

discrete.

$$V(c_0,\ldots,c_T) = u(c_0) + \frac{u(c_1)}{(1+\rho)} + \ldots + \frac{u(c_T)}{(1+\rho)^T}$$

where ρ is the subjective rate of discount or time preference. With the above budget constraint the consumer's optimal consumption stream will satisfy

$$\frac{\partial u(c_t)/\partial c_t}{\partial u(c_{t+1})/\partial c_{t+1}} = \frac{p_t(1+r)}{p_{t+1}(1+\rho)}$$

Assuming u is strictly concave, so that its derivative is monotonically decreasing, then $c_t = c_{t+1}$ if and only if $\dfrac{\partial u(c_t)}{\partial c_t} = \dfrac{\partial u(c_{t+1})}{\partial c_{t+1}}$, i.e. if and only if $\dfrac{p_t}{p_{t+1}} = \dfrac{1+\rho}{1+r}$ Should prices be equal then $c_t = c_{t+1}$ if and only if the rate of time preference equals the rate of interest. ■

13.2 Our next step is to introduce the possibility of the consumer receiving a stream of income over the planning period. Thus in the two-period case we can imagine the consumer has incomes m_0 and m_1 in the current and future periods. Hence the present value of his income will be m_0 + $m_1/(1+r)$ and the budget constraint will be *two period*

$$p_0 c_0 + \frac{p_1 c_1}{1+r} \leq m_0 + \frac{m_1}{1+r}$$

If $u(c_0,c_1) = c_0 c_1$ is the consumer's utility function, then the optimal consumptions will be

$$c_0 = \frac{m_0 + m_1/(1+r)}{2p_0} \quad, c_1 = \frac{m_0(1+r) + m_1}{2p_1}$$

and

$$\frac{\partial c_0}{\partial m_0} = \frac{1}{2p_0}$$ ∎

13.3 Here we have treated m_1 as if the consumer knows its value in the current period, but often it will be uncertain and the consumer will have to form expectations of what value it will take. Should an increase in current income lead the *expected* future income to rise, then we can now see that the *marginal propensity to consume* $\partial c_0/\partial m_0$ will be higher. For example if we consider the case where the expected value of m_1 is given by $m_1 = \delta m_0$ then the above consumption pattern would become

$$c_0 = \frac{m_0(1+\varepsilon)}{2p_0} \quad, c_1 = \frac{m_0(1+r+\delta)}{2p_1}$$

where $\varepsilon = \left(\frac{\delta}{1+r}\right)$ Hence $\frac{\partial c_0}{\partial m_0} = \frac{1+\varepsilon}{2p_0}$ and the marginal propensity to consume has increased by a factor of ε. ∎

13.4 Consider the general T period case of the above example where m_t is the (expected) income in period t, so that the consumer's net present value is $W = \sum_{t=0}^{T} \left(\frac{m_t}{(1+r)^t}\right)$ and the budget constraint is $\sum_{t=0}^{T} p_t c_t \leq W$. If the preferences are given by $u(c_0...c_T) = c_0 c_1...c_T$ then the present value of expenditures in the $T+1$ periods will be equal and

$$c_t = \frac{W(1+r)^t}{(T+1)p_t}, t = 0,...,T$$

In particular $c_0 = W/[(T+1)p_0]$. Hence if the consumer receives a 'windfall' increase in current income which does not induce a revision of expected future incomes, there will be a minimal impact on current consumption if T is large. ∎

4.2 Continuous Time

3.7 Should we wish to model consumption as a continuous process, then we need to clarify the nature of discounting and the compounding of interest in continuous time. If r is the annual rate of interest and interest is compounded once a year, then an investment of P will be worth $P(1+r)$ at the end of the year. However if interest is calculated each half-year, then the

principal will increase to a value of $P(1 + r/2)^2$ at the end of the year.
Likewise if interest is paid n times a year, then the end of year value
will be $P\left(1 + \dfrac{r}{n}\right)^n$ and after t years the value will be $P\left(1 + \dfrac{r}{n}\right)^{nt}$.
We can view continuous compounding as the limit of this process as n
approaches infinity, hence at the end of t years with continuous compound-
ing the value y would be given by $y = \lim_{n\to\infty} P\left(1 + \dfrac{r}{n}\right)^{nt} = P$
$\lim_{n\to\infty}\left(1 + \dfrac{r}{n}\right)^{nt}$.

Let $y_n = P\left(1 + \dfrac{r}{n}\right)^{nt}$, then $\ln(y_n) = \ln P + nt \ln\left(1 + \dfrac{r}{n}\right)$

Now it can be shown (see Appendix) that if x is less than one in absolute size
then

$$\ln(1 + x) = x - \frac{x^2}{2} + \frac{x^3}{3} - \frac{x^4}{4} + \dots$$

hence for large n we have

$$\ln\left(1 + \frac{r}{n}\right) = \frac{r}{n} - \frac{r^2}{2n^2} + \frac{r^3}{3n^3} - \dots$$

and thus

$$\ln y_n = \ln P + rt - \frac{r_t^2}{2n} + \frac{r^3 t}{3n^2} - \dots$$

Now as n approaches infinity, all the terms on the right-hand side except the
first two go to zero; hence we have

$$\ln y = \lim_{n\to\infty} \ln y_n = \ln P + rt$$

and

$$y = Pe^{rt} \qquad\blacksquare$$

6.4 If the consumer receives a constant income flow y every instant over
the period from $t = 0$ to $t = T$, then the present value of this income stream
would be equal to

$$\int_0^T ye^{-rt}dt$$

$$= \left[\frac{-ye^{-rt}}{r}\right]_0^T = \frac{y}{r}(1 - e^{-rT}) \qquad\blacksquare$$

9.4 Viewing a flow of consumption c_t as generating a flow of instantaneous
utility $u(c_t)$ which is then discounted at rate ρ, we can view the consumer
problem as

maximise $\int_0^T u(c_t)e^{-\rho t}\,dt$

subject to $\int_0^T p_t c_t e^{-rt}\,dt \leq \dfrac{y}{r}[1 - e^{-rT}]$

Strictly speaking such problems fall outside the scope of this text. Essentially the problem is that the consumer is now choosing an infinite number of variables c_t as t runs continuously from zero to T and the methods developed in this text are not necessarily applicable. Nevertheless this particular case can be tackled as follows. We first construct the Lagrangian

$$L = \int_0^T u(c_t)^{-\rho t}\,dt + \lambda\left[\frac{y}{r}(1 - e^{-rT}) - \int_0^T p_t c_t e^{-rt}\,dt\right]$$

$$= \int_0^T [u(c_t)e^{-\rho t} - \lambda p_t c_t e^{-rt}]\,dt + \lambda\frac{y}{r}[1 - e^{-rT}]$$

We now argue that to maximise L we need to maximise the integrand $u(c_t)e^{-\rho t} - \lambda p_t c_t e^{-rt}$ for each t. The crucial factor that allows us to make this argument is that changes in the integrand at one time t do not change the value of the integrand at any other time. Hence we are able independently to maximise the integrand at each instant. The rest of the task is straightforward. The stationarity condition for the maximum of the integrand is

$$\frac{\partial u(c_t)e^{-\rho t}}{\partial c_t} - \lambda p_t e^{-rt} = 0$$

i.e.

$$\frac{\partial u(c_t)}{\partial c_t} = \lambda p_t e^{(\rho - r)t}$$

It follows that the marginal rate of substitution between c_t and c_0 will be given by

MRS $= \dfrac{\partial u(c_t)/\partial c_t}{\partial u(c_0)/\partial c_0} = \dfrac{p_t}{p_0}e^{(\rho - r)t}$

If $u(c_t) = \ln c_t$ then we have

$$p_t c_t = p_0 c_0 e^{(r - \rho)t}$$

Substituting this into the budget constraint gives

$$\int_0^T p_0 c_0 e^{-\rho t}\,dt = \frac{y}{r}(1 - e^{-rT})$$

or

$$\frac{p_0 c_0}{\rho} (1 - e^{-\rho T}) = \frac{y}{r} (1 - e^{-rT})$$

or

$$c_0 = \frac{\rho y}{r p_0} \frac{1 - e^{-rT}}{1 - e^{-\rho T}}$$

finally

$$c_t = \frac{\rho}{r} \frac{y}{p_t} \frac{1 - e^{-rt}}{1 - e^{-\rho T}} e^{(r-\rho)t} \qquad \blacksquare$$

4.3 Time Inconsistency

5.8 A problem that can arise in intertemporal decision making is the inconsistency of plans made at different times. This is best illustrated with a simple example. Consider then a consumer with a three-period horizon. In period $t = 0$ he has a utility function of the form

$$v_0(c_0, c_1) = u(c_0) + u(c_1)$$

where, as before, c_0, c_1 are the levels of consumption in periods $t = 0, 1$ respectively. Note that the consumer has completely discounted consumption in the period $t = 2$, though he has given equal weight to those in periods $t = 0, 1$. The consumer has an initial 'real' income of m_0 which he can spend on c_0 or save (without earning interest) for future consumption. He will *not* plan to save any of his income for consumption in period $t = 2$ given his preferences at $t = 0$, and thus he will plan to consume all his savings in period $t = 1$. Let s_0 be his planned proportion of income to be saved at $t = 0$, so that his utility will be

$$u[(1 - s_0)m_0] + u(s_0 m_0)$$

hence the optimal savings ratio will satisfy

$$m_0 \frac{\partial u\{(1 - s_0)m_0\}}{\partial c} = m_0 \frac{\partial u(s_0 m_0)}{\partial c}$$

Cancelling the m_0, and assuming as usual u is strictly concave so that $\frac{\partial u}{\partial c}$ is monotonically decreasing, we can conclude

$$(1 - s_0)m_0 = s_0 m_0$$

hence

$$s_0 = \frac{1}{2}$$ ∎

That is to say the consumer plans to divide his initial income equally between the first two periods and not to leave any for the third period. But consider the consumer in period $t = 1$ and let us assume his preferences at this date are

$$v_1(c_1, c_2) = u(c_1) + u(c_2)$$

Again he discounts any consumption occurring more than one period ahead. The important point is that he no longer discounts consumption in period $t = 2$. Given he now has income $m_1 = s_0 m_0$ and we let s_1 be the proportion of income he plans to save in the second period, then we can readily check that he will plan to have $s_1 = 1/2$. Thus when he reaches period $t = 1$ he will consume $(1 - s_1)s_0 m_0 = \frac{1}{4} m_0$ and not $s_0 m_0 = \frac{1}{2} m_0$ as he originally planned in period $t = 0$, i.e. his plan made in period $t = 0$ is intertemporally inconsistent. It should be stressed that this inconsistency does not arise from a change in the environment of the consumer, rather it arises from the structure of the consumer's preferences. In particular it arises from the uneven way he discounts future consumption; his marginal rate of substitution between consumption in period $t = 1$ and $t = 2$ is different when viewed from period $t = 0$ to that viewed from period $t = 1$.

Clearly the consumer will (generally) not choose to consume half his income at $t = 0$ because he will realise that at $t = 1$ he will not consume all of his income. Anticipating that at period $t = 1$ he will save a proportion s_1 of his income, at $t = 0$ he will wish to maximise:

$$u([1 - s_0]m_0) + u([1 - s_1]s_0 m_0)$$

so that the optimal s_0 will satisfy

$$m_0 \frac{\partial u([1 - s_0]m_0)}{\partial c} = (1 - s_1)m_0 \frac{\partial u([1 - s_1]s_0 m_0)}{\partial c}$$

Cancelling the m_0 we can see that ratio of the marginal utility at $t = 0$ to that at $t = 1$ will be $1 - s_1 < 1$ and thus the marginal utility will be lower in period $t = 0$. As u is strictly concave this will imply greater consumption at $t = 0$, i.e.

$$(1 - s_0)m_0 > (1 - s_1)s_0 m_0$$

hence

$$s_0 < \frac{1}{2 - s_1}$$

Yet this does *not* tell us whether s_0 will be less or greater than 1/2, i.e. it is not clear that the consumer will save more or less if he anticipates his saving in period $t = 1$. By explicitly anticipating the correct level of savings in period $t = 1$, the consumer achieves a consumption plan that is time consistent; the plan initiated at $t = 0$ is not rejected later. However, the marginal utility in period $t = 0$, $u'(c_0)$ is lower than in period $t = 1$, $u'(c_1)$, and a consumption plan which slightly reduced consumption in period $t = 0$ and increased consumption in period $t = 1$ would increase utility at period $t = 0$, $v_0(c_1,c_2)$, and at period $t = 1$, $v_1(c_1,c_2)$. Therefore it is possible to find another plan which allows more utility at every period than the time consistent plan. However, unless some method is found of binding the consumer to follow this plan at period $t = 1$, he will reject it at period $t = 1$, i.e. the superior plan is time inconsistent.

4.4 Allocation of Time

Consumption is not an instantaneous process, rather it takes varied amounts of time to consume different goods. Hence the consumer has the problem of allocating his time within any given period. This allocation includes the work–leisure trade-off which we discuss in the next section and the allocation of that leisure time between the consumption of different commodities. It is stressed that this is not a minor issue in that significant government decisions, such as the construction of motorways and airports, implicitly involve the evaluation of the marginal value of time.

13.6   Consider then a consumer who faces two constraints, namely the usual budget constraint, and the constraint that the total time allocated to the consumption of goods is bounded above. In the two-good case we can let p_1, p_2 be their prices, and m the income, so that the budget constraint is

$$p_0 x_1 + p_2 x_2 \leqslant m$$

With t_1, t_2 being the amount of time required to consume one unit of the two goods respectively, and T the maximum amount of time available, the time constraint will be

$$t_1 x_1 + t_2 x_2 \leqslant T$$

With utility function $u(x_1, x_2)$ the Lagrangian for the consumer problem is now

$$L = u(x_1, x_2) + \lambda(m - p_1 x_1 - p_2 x_2) + \rho(T - t_1 x_1 - t_2 x_2)$$

Here we can view ρ as the marginal utility of time, it being the shadow price of the time constraint. Our first order conditions are

$$\frac{\partial L}{\partial x_1} = \frac{\partial u}{\partial x_1} - \lambda p_1 - \rho t_1 = 0$$

$$\frac{\partial L}{\partial x_2} = \frac{\partial u}{\partial x_2} - \lambda p_2 - \rho t_2 = 0$$

λ and $(m - p_1 x_1 - p_2 x_2) \geqslant 0$, their product being zero

ρ and $(T - t_1 x_1 - t_2 x_2) \geqslant 0$, their product being zero

There are four possibilities here, namely

(i) $\lambda = 0$ and $\rho = 0$
(ii) $\lambda > 0$ and $\rho = 0$
(iii) $\lambda = 0$ and $\rho > 0$
(iv) $\lambda > 0$ and $\rho > 0$

The first case is of little interest, indeed it is impossible if marginal utilities are positive, and we shall ignore it. The remaining three cases correspond respectively to the diagrams (a), (b), (c) in Figure 14.3. For example if $u = x_1 x_2$. $p_1 = 1, p_2 = 2, t_1 = t_2 = 1, m = 12$ and $T = 10$, our conditions are

$$x_2 = \lambda + \rho$$

$$x_1 = 2\lambda + \rho$$

λ and $(12 - x_1 - 2x_2) \geqslant 0$, their product being zero

ρ and $(10 - x_1 - x_2) \geqslant 0$, their product being zero

Should we try case (iii) with $\rho > 0$ and $\lambda = 0$, then we require $x_1 x_2$ and ρ to satisfy

$$x_2 = \rho$$

$$x_1 = \rho$$

$$10 = x_1 - x_2 = 0$$

These equations imply $x_1 = x_2 = \rho = 5$. But these values of x_1, x_2 do *not* satisfy the budget constraint, hence this cannot be the solution. If we try case (iv) $\rho > 0$ and $\lambda > 0$, then x_1, x_2 would be given by

$$12 - x_1 - 2x_2 = 0$$

$$10 - x_1 - x_2 = 0$$

i.e. $x_1 = 8, x_2 = 2$, in which case

$$2 = \lambda + \rho$$

$$8 = 2\lambda + \rho$$

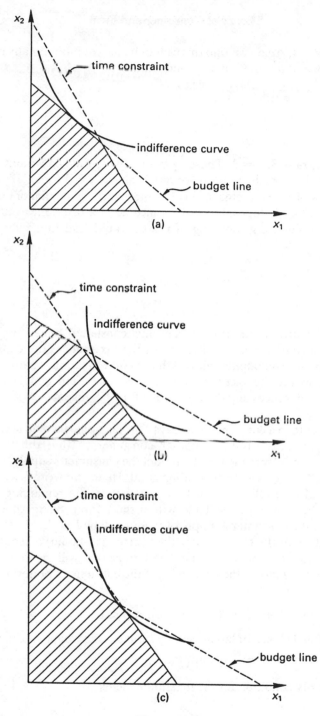

(a)

(b)

(c)

Figure 14.3

i.e. $\lambda = 6, \rho = -4$. Again we find this cannot be the solution. Finally if we try case (ii) $\lambda > 0$ and $\rho = 0$, then x_1, x_2 and λ satisfy

$$x_2 = \lambda$$

$$x_1 = 2\lambda$$

$$12 - x_1 = 2x_2 = 0$$

hence $x_1 = 6, x_2 = 3, \lambda = 3$. These x_1, x_2 satisfy the time constraint and we can conclude they are the required optimal values.

In this example the marginal utility of time is zero, while that of income is positive; hence any proposal to reduce income, via taxation, to pay for a time-saving project, e.g. building of roads, would lead to a reduction of utility.   ■

5   Taxation

The most important question concerning consumer behaviour in the presence of income tax is whether or not the tax reduces the consumer's supply of labour. The popular view is that income taxation is a disincentive to work. However the incentive effect is complex and depends on the structure of preferences and the use made of the tax revenue.

9.6   Consider then a consumer who pays a proportional income tax, this tax revenue being transferred to another consumer so that the tax payer receives no benefit from the tax. To model the consumer's supply of labour we introduce leisure as a utility yielding good. Hence we write L to indicate the amount of time allocated for leisure activities, the remaining $T - L$, where T is the total time available within the period, being allocated to work. Hence the consumer's supply of labour will be $l = T - L$. If w is the real wage rate and t the tax rate, then the net (or take-home) real pay for the supplied labour will be $(1 - t)wl$, and thus this will be the level of consumption available to the consumer. If the consumer's preferences take the form

$$u(c,L) = (c^{1-\rho} + L^{1-\rho})/(1 - \rho)   \qquad 0 < \rho < 1$$

then the optimal choice of labour supply l will be that which maximises

$$\{[(1 - t)wl]^{1-\rho} + (T - l)^{1-\rho}\}/(1 - \rho)$$

The stationarity condition for the maximum yields

$$l = \frac{T}{1 + [(1 - t)w]^{\sigma}}$$

where

$$\sigma = 1 - \frac{1}{\rho} < 0$$

hence

$$\frac{\partial l}{\partial t} < 0$$

That is to say income tax is a disincentive to work. Note if $\rho > 1$ then income tax is an incentive to work. ∎

9.7 The above case assumes all taxation is used for redistributive purposes, whereas frequently taxation is used to buy commodities which the consumer would have bought directly. Suppose we have n identical consumers facing the same tax rate, and that the total tax revenue is distributed evenly between the consumers. As all consumers are identical and treated identically they will make identical choices. Let us thus consider a typical consumer supplying l units of labour. With wage rate w and tax rate t, he will consume directly $(1 - t)wl$ and indirectly, i.e. via government expenditure, a quantity g, this being $1/n$ times total tax revenue. Note that for each consumer a unit increase in labour supply will increase g by tw/n, i.e. $\partial g/\partial l = tw/n$. The optimal labour supply is thus that which maximises $u(c,L)$ where $L = T - l$ and now $c = (1 - t)wl + g$. The first order condition will thus require

$$\left[(1 - t)w + \frac{tw}{n} \right] \frac{\partial u}{\partial c} = \frac{\partial u}{\partial L}$$

If $u(c,L) = (c^{1-\rho} + L^{1-\rho})/(1 - \rho)$ as before, this condition becomes

$$\left[(1 - t)w + \frac{tw}{n} \right] \left[(1 - t)wl + g \right]^{-\rho} = (T - l)^{-\rho}$$

or

$$\left[(1 - t)w + \frac{tw}{n} \right]^{-\frac{1}{\rho}} \left[(1 - t)wl + g \right] = T - l$$

As all consumers will choose the same labour supply, then total tax revenue will be $ntwl$ and thus $g = twl$ and we obtain

$$\left[(1 - t)w + \frac{tw}{n} \right]^{-\frac{1}{\rho}} = T - l$$

or

$$l = T - \left\{ \left[1 - t \left(1 - \frac{1}{n} \right) \right] w \right\}^{-\frac{1}{\rho}}$$

hence

$$\frac{\partial l}{\partial t} = -\frac{1}{\rho}\left(1-\frac{1}{n}\right)w\left\{\left[1-t\left(1-\frac{1}{n}\right)\right]w\right\}^{-\frac{1}{\rho}-1} < 0$$

and

$$\frac{\partial l}{\partial n} = -\frac{1}{\rho}\,tw\,\frac{1}{n^2}\left\{\left[1-t\left(1-\frac{1}{n}\right)\right]w\right\}^{-\frac{1}{\rho}-1} < 0$$

regardless of the value of ρ. That is to say in this case higher taxes are a disincentive to effort, and that for any given tax rate the larger the population the lower the individual labour supply.   ∎

Turning to indirect taxes we can provide a simple discussion of the notion that income taxes are generally preferable to indirect taxes if we abstract from incentive to work effects. The argument is that the government can switch from indirect to direct tax and make a consumer better off without reducing the total tax revenue.

12.10   Suppose the consumer purchases n commodities at prices $\hat{\mathbf{p}}$, where for example the first price $\hat{p}_1$ is equal to the sum of the producer's price p_1 and a unit tax t_1, i.e. $\hat{p}_1 = p_1 + t_1$. If the government also raises income tax T from the consumer's original budget of m, then the consumer's (Marshallian) demand for the first good will be $x_1^M(\hat{\mathbf{p}}, m - T)$. Hence the tax revenue from the first good would be $t_1 x_1^M(\hat{\mathbf{p}}, m - T)$ and total tax revenue would be $T + t_1 x_1^M(\hat{\mathbf{p}}, m - T)$. We first ask what the relationship needs to be between t_1 and T to keep this total tax revenue constant. If we view T as a function of t_1, differentiate total revenue by t_1 and put this derivative to zero we obtain

$$\frac{\partial T}{\partial t_1} + x_1^M + t_1\frac{\partial x_1^M}{\partial \hat{p}} - t_1\frac{\partial x_1^M}{\partial m}\frac{\partial T}{\partial t_t} = 0$$

where x_1^M and its partials are evaluated at $(\hat{\mathbf{p}}, m - T)$. Hence

$$\frac{\partial T}{\partial t_1} = -\frac{x_1^M + t_1\partial x_1^M/\partial \hat{p}_1}{1 - t_1\partial x_1^M/\partial m}$$

Now the maximum level of utility the consumer can attain in this tax regime is given by $v(\hat{\mathbf{p}}, m - T)$ where v is his indirect utility function. Hence the marginal change in utility induced by a change in t_1, with T being adjusted to keep total tax constant, is

$$\frac{\partial v}{\partial t_1} = \frac{\partial v}{\partial \hat{p}_1} - \frac{\partial v}{\partial m}\frac{\partial T}{\partial t_1} = -\left(x_1^M + \frac{\partial T}{\partial t_1}\right)\frac{\partial v}{\partial m}$$

Here we have used Roy's Identity. Now

$$x_1^M + \frac{\partial T}{\partial t_1} = - \frac{t_1(\partial x_1^M/\partial \hat{p}_1 + x_1^M \partial x_1^M/\partial m)}{1 - t_1 \partial x_1^M/\partial m}$$

The term in parenthesis is equal to the substitution effect $\partial x_1^H/\partial \hat{p}_1$ evaluated at $[\hat{p}, v(\hat{p},m - T)]$ — see the discussion of Slutsky's decomposition in subsection 2.2 of this chapter. Hence

$$\frac{\partial v}{\partial t_1} = + \frac{t_1 \partial x_1^H/\partial \hat{p}_1}{1 - t_1 \partial x_1^M/\partial m} \frac{\partial v}{\partial m}$$

We know that $\frac{\partial v}{\partial m} \geqslant 0$. $\frac{\partial x_1^H}{\partial \hat{p}_1} \leqslant 0$ and thus $\frac{\partial v}{\partial t_1}$ has effectively the same sign as $t_1 \frac{\partial x^M}{\partial m} - 1$.

Hence the shift to direct from indirect tax, i.e. a reduction in t_1, will be desirable if $t_1 \frac{\partial x^M}{\partial m} < 1$. This inequality tells us that the rise in indirect tax due to a marginal decrease in income tax — which would increase disposable income — is less than one. In general it will be satisfied and it will always hold for 'sufficiently small' t_1. ∎

6 Consumer Surplus

12.12 In evaluating policies it is often useful to attach a monetary value to the effects of a price change on a consumer. There are two common ways of doing this. We can ask what reduction in income with prices remaining at the old level would be equivalent to the proposed price changes. This change in income is known as the *equivalent variation* (EV). Alternatively we can ask what increase in income would 'compensate' for the price change, i.e. what change in income at the new prices would return the consumer to the old level of utility. This measure is known as the *compensating variation* (CV). The indirect utility and expenditure functions are the ideal vehicles to discuss these ideas. Let $v(\mathbf{p}_1 m)$ be as usual the indirect utility function, and let $\mathbf{p}^0$ and $\mathbf{p}^1$ be the old and new price vectors respectively. The EV is thus defined by

$$v(\mathbf{p}^0,m - \mathrm{EV}) = v(\mathbf{p}^1,m)$$

m being the consumer's income. In contrast the CV is defined by

$$v(\mathbf{p}^1,m + \mathrm{CV}) = v(\mathbf{p}^0,m)$$

If now $e(\mathbf{p},u)$ is the consumer's expenditure function and we write $u^0 = v(\mathbf{p}^0,m)$ and $u^1 = v(\mathbf{p}^1,m)$ then we have

$$v(\mathbf{p}^0,m - \mathrm{EV}) = u^1$$

and

$$v(\mathbf{p}^1,m + \mathrm{CV}) = u^0$$

Hence $e[\mathbf{p}^0, v(\mathbf{p}^0, m - EV)] = e(\mathbf{p}^0, u^1)$, but the left-hand side of this equation is $m - EV$ and thus

$$m - EV = e(\mathbf{p}^0, u^1)$$

and

$$EV = m - e(\mathbf{p}^0, u^1)$$
$$= e(\mathbf{p}^1, u^1) - e(\mathbf{p}^0, u^1)$$

Similarly we have

$$e[\mathbf{p}^1, v(\mathbf{p}^1, m + CV)] = e(\mathbf{p}^1, u^0)$$

and thus

$$m + CV = e(\mathbf{p}^1, u^0)$$

and

$$CV = e(\mathbf{p}^1, u^0) - m$$
$$= e(\mathbf{p}^1, u^0) - e(\mathbf{p}^0, u^0)$$

If we consider a change in one price, say the ith price from p_i^0 to p_i^1, then we can consider these expressions for EV and CV as the values of definite integrals. Hence

$$EV = \int_{p_i^0}^{p_i^1} \frac{\partial e(\mathbf{p}, u^1)}{\partial p_i} dp_i = \int_{p_i^0}^{p_i^1} x_i^H(\mathbf{p}, u^1) dp_i$$

The first equality arises from the fact that the indefinite integral of $\dfrac{\partial e}{\partial p_i}$ is $e + c$, where c is a 'constant', i.e. c is independent of p_i. The second equality follows from Shephard's Lemma.

Similarly we have

$$CV = \int_{p_i^0}^{p_i^1} \frac{\partial e(\mathbf{p}, u^0)}{\partial p_i} dp_i$$
$$= \int_{p_i^0}^{p_i^1} x_i^H(\mathbf{p}, u^0) dp_i \qquad\blacksquare$$

Either of these equations offers monetary measures of the change in the consumer utility due to the change in the price. The difference lies in the fact that the equivalent variation EV uses the level of utility *after* the price change as a basis, while the compensating variation CV uses the utility level *before* the price change.

12.13   The difficulty in practice with these two expressions is that they involve the unobservable Hicksian demands. It is common to use approximations to these expressions, replacing the Hicksian by the Marshallian demand functions. We thus obtain

Marshallian approximation

to $$EV = \int_{p_i^0}^{p_i^1} x_i^M(\mathbf{p},m)dp_i$$

Marshallian approximation

to $$CV = \int_{p_i^0}^{p_i^1} x_i^M(\mathbf{p},m)dp_i$$

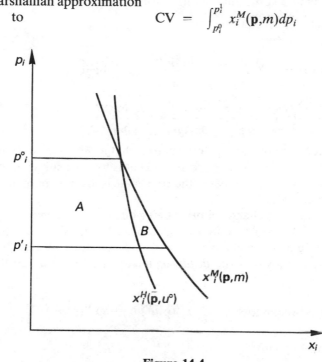

Figure 14.4

Note these two expressions are now equal to each other. Figure 14.4 shows the relationship between the true and approximate CV. In drawing the Marshallian demand curve we have assumed the good to be a normal good. Note well that the diagram is drawn with the *independent variable* price measured along the vertical axis, as is usual when drawing supply and demand curves. (The historical reason for this fact is that Marshall treated quantities as the independent variables and viewed the demand curve as giving the demand price.) Hence the areas in the diagram associated with the expressions for the true and approximate CV are the areas between the vertical axis and the respective demand curve. Thus the area marked A corresponds to the true CV, while $A + B$ represent the approximate CV.

To investigate the possibility that the approximate CV equals the true value we note from the Slutsky decomposition that

$$\frac{\partial x_i^H(\mathbf{p},u^0)}{\partial p_i} - \frac{\partial x_i^M(\mathbf{p},m)}{\partial p_i} = x_i \frac{\partial x_i^M(\mathbf{p},m)}{\partial m}$$

If the right-hand side of this equation is zero, then we can conclude that the Hicksian and Marshallian demands move together, i.e. they are equal to each other. Now a sufficient condition for the expression to be zero is that the derivative $\dfrac{\partial x_i^M(\mathbf{p},m)}{\partial m} = 0$.

Yet as $x_i^M(\mathbf{p},m) = -\dfrac{\partial v(\mathbf{p},m)}{\partial p_i} \bigg/ \dfrac{\partial v(\mathbf{p},m)}{\partial m}$ we obtain

$$\frac{\partial x_i^M}{\partial m} = -\left(\frac{\partial v}{\partial m} \frac{\partial^2 v}{\partial m \partial p_i} - \frac{\partial v}{\partial p_i} \frac{\partial^2 v}{\partial m^2} \right) \bigg/ \left(\frac{\partial v}{\partial m} \right)^2$$

A sufficient condition for this to be zero is that $\partial v/\partial m$ be a constant so that the two second order partials are zero. That is to say a sufficient condition for the approximate CV to equal the true value is that the marginal utility of money be constant. ∎

If we consider the change in price being due to a unit commodity tax, we can compare the loss of utility as measured by the CV, say, to the tax revenue raised by the commodity tax. The difference between the CV and the revenue is known as the *deadweight loss* or *excess burden* of the tax. Hence we have

$$\text{true deadweight loss} = \int_{p_i^0}^{p_i^1} x_i^H(\mathbf{p},u^0)dp_i - t_i x_i^M(\mathbf{p}^1,m)$$

and

$$\text{approximate deadweight loss} = \int_{p_i^0}^{p_i^1} x_i^M(\mathbf{p},m)dp_i - t_i x_i^M(\mathbf{p}^1,m)$$

where $p_i^1 = p_i^0 + t_i$ and t_i is the unit tax rate. These two measures are illustrated by areas $A + B$ and A respectively in Figure 14.5. While the error in the use of the approximation to measure CV may be small as suggested in Figure 14.4, this will not necessarily be the case when we use the approximate deadweight loss again as suggested in Figure 14.5.

7   Public Provision of Goods

13.7   A *pure public good* is one with the property that everyone obtains positive utility from its existence however it is provided or whoever pays for its production. While few goods will enter into such a tight description we

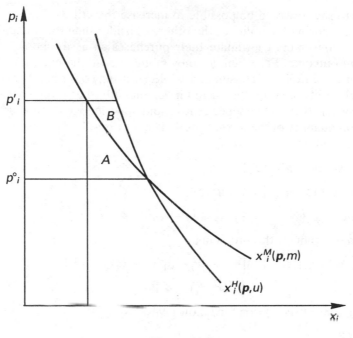

Figure 14.5

may attempt to view national defence or street cleaning as approximating this conception. Unless individual consumers coordinate their expenditure, i.e. via a government agency, it is likely that such public goods will be undersupplied, the danger being that individuals may 'free ride' on the provision of the good by other consumers. As an illustration, consider a 2-consumer, 2-good world where the second good is a pure public good.

The first consumer chooses x_1^1, x_2^1 to maximise $u^1(x_1^1, x_2^1 + x_2^2)$ subject to his budget constraint $p_1 x_1^1 + p_2 x_2^1 \leq m^1$. The second consumer chooses x_1^2, x_2^2 to maximise $u^2(x_1^2, x_2^1 + x_2^2)$ subject to his budget constraint $p_1 x_1^2 + p_2 x_2^2 \leq m^2$. Acting independently they will choose the quantities of the two goods such that their individual marginal rates of substitution are equal to the relative price, i.e.

$$\text{MRS}^1 = \frac{\partial u^1 / \partial x_1^1}{\partial u^1 / \partial x_2^1} = \frac{p_1}{p_2}$$

and

$$\text{MRS}^2 = \frac{\partial u^2 / \partial x_1^2}{\partial u^2 / \partial x_2^2} = \frac{p_1}{p_2}$$

We shall see that such independent decisions would be Pareto inefficient;

that is to say, it would be possible to increase the utility of one consumer without reducing the utility of the other. Consider then the possibility that the two consumers coordinate their purchases so as to choose a Pareto efficient outcome. For example, they might choose the quantities so as to maximise the utility of consumer 1 while ensuring consumer 2 gets at least as much utility as when they acted independently. Let $\bar{u}^2$ be consumer 2's utility when they act independently, and now let $x_2 = x_1^2 + x_2^2$ be the common quantity of the second good. The maximisation problem is now as follows. Choose x_1^1, x_1^2, x_2 to

maximise $u^1(x_1^1, x_2)$

subject to $u^2(x_1^2, x_2) \geq \bar{u}^2$

and $p_1(x_1^1 + x_1^2) + p_2 x_2 \leq m^1 + m^2$

The Lagrangian for this problem is

$$L = u^1(x_1^1, x_2) + \lambda[m^1 + m^2 - p_1(x_1^1 + x_1^2) - p_2 x_2]$$
$$+ \rho[u^2(x_1^2, x_2) - \bar{u}^2]$$

The stationarity condition for L now gives

$$\frac{\partial u^1}{\partial x_1^1} = \lambda p_1$$

$$\rho \frac{\partial u^2}{\partial x_1^2} = \lambda p_1$$

and

$$\frac{\partial u^1}{\partial x_2} + \rho \frac{\partial u^2}{\partial x_2} = \lambda p_2$$

If we divide the third equation by λp_1 we obtain

$$\frac{1}{\lambda p_1} \frac{\partial u^1}{\partial x_2} + \frac{\rho}{\lambda p_1} \frac{\partial u^2}{\partial x_2} = \frac{p_2}{p_1}$$

Using the first equation we can replace the $1/\lambda p_1$ by the reciprocal of $\partial u^1/\partial x_1^1$, and using the second equation we can replace $\dfrac{\rho}{\lambda p_1}$ by the reciprocal of $\partial u^2/\partial x_1^2$. We then obtain

$$\text{MRS}^1 + \text{MRS}^2 = \frac{p_2}{p_1}$$

i.e. the *sum* of the marginal rates of substitution will be equal to the relative price. This is in contrast to the case where the consumers acted independently where the individual MRS were both equal to the relative price. It follows that the independent choices could not generate this efficient outcome. We can note that this argument remains valid for any feasible choice of $\bar{u}^2$; hence we can conclude the independent choices are not efficient. ∎

8 Uncertainty

7.1 Suppose an individual is faced with the choice between risky alternative actions, i.e. actions whose outcome is uncertain. For example, an action such as the purchase of a lottery may lead to his having a net income of x with probability p, or income y with probability $(1 - p)$. How is a rational individual to choose between such risky alternatives? There is an important theorem known as the Expected Utility Theorem which can be summarised as follows. Under 'reasonable' assumptions a rational individual choosing between acts with uncertain outcomes will have a utility function defined over the set of outcomes such that the best act is that which maximises the individual's expected utility. This utility function is known as the von Neumann Morgenstern or simply V–M utility function in honour of those authors who proved the result in their seminal work on *The Theory of Games and Economic Behaviour*. To illustrate the theorem we can consider the consumer choosing between lotteries such as the one described above. Insofar as we measure the outcome by the net income the consumer has after the lottery, then our theorem says a rational consumer will have a utility function defined over income, $u(m)$ say, and the best lottery will be that which maximises the expected value of $u(m)$. In the case where the consumer obtains income x with probability p and y with probability $(1 - p)$, then the associated expected utility will be $pu(x) + (1 - p)u(y)$, this being the utility he would obtain on average if he played the lottery an indefinite number of times. We can note that the theorem also tells us that the V–M utility function is unique up to a linear transformation. Hence if we have a V–M utility function $u(x)$, then the function $v(x) = \alpha u(x) + \beta$ where $\alpha > 0, \beta$ are constants, will also represent the same preferences, but we *cannot* use arbitrary monotonic transformations.

A 'fair bet' is a lottery such that the expected profit from playing it is zero. Hence if we obtain a net gain of g with probability p and a net loss of $-c$ with probability $1 - p$, then we have a fair bet if $pg - (1 - p)c = 0$. If a consumer has initial income w, then playing such a fair bet would give him $w + g$ with probability p and $w - c$ with probability $1 - p$. The expected utility of playing the fair bet is thus

$$pu(w + g) + (1 - p)u(w - c)$$

where u is the consumer's V–M utility function.

A person is said to be *risk averse* if and only if he always prefers not to play a fair bet, *risk neutral* if and only if he is indifferent to playing or not playing a fair bet and *risk loving* if and only if he always prefers to play a fair bet. Hence our consumer above is risk averse if and only if

$$pu(w + g) + (1 - p)u(w - c) \leqslant u(w)$$

for all w, p, g and c satisfying $pg - (1 - p)c = 0, 0 \leqslant p \leqslant 1$.

If we write $x = w + g$ and $y = w - c$, so that $w = px + (1 - p)y$, then this condition is equivalent to

$$pu(x) + (1 - p)u(y) \leqslant u[px + (1 - p)y]$$

for all x, y and $0 \leqslant p \leqslant 1$. But this simply states that u is concave. That is to say, an individual is risk averse if and only if his V–M utility function is concave. Equally we can argue that he is risk loving if and only if his V–M utility function is convex.   ∎

3.5 Taking this further we might hope to have a measure of the risk aversion of an individual. Recalling that we are thinking of the outcome of the acts being measured by a single variable, usually thought of as money, we can offer two measures of risk aversion. The *absolute measure of risk aversion* is given by

$$\rho^A(x) = - \frac{u''(x)}{u'(x)}$$

i.e. minus the ratio of the second to the first order derivative of the V–M utility function. The *relative measure of risk aversion* is given by

$$\rho^R(x) = - \frac{u''(x)x}{u'(x)}$$

This last measure can be viewed as the elasticity of marginal utility with respect to x.

As an example consider the V–M function

$$u(x) = \frac{\alpha + \beta x^{1-\rho}}{1 - \rho}$$

which gives

$$\rho^A(x) = \frac{\rho}{x}$$

while

$$\rho^R(x) = x\rho^A(x) = \rho$$ ∎

Hence this utility function exhibits constant relative risk aversion. Indeed if we treat $\rho^R(x) = \rho$, where ρ is constant, as a differential equation in $u(x)$ we can show that all constant relative risk averse V–M functions take the form $a + bx^{1-\rho}$ for constants a, b.

6.2 In some circumstances the uncertainty is only present on one side of a transaction, and this can generate difficulties. For example, a seller may know the quality of the good or service he is supplying, while the buyer does not know the quality. Now it may pay the supplier of a high quality good to attempt to 'signal' to the buyer his good's quality. An interesting example of this idea is the interpretation of educational achievement as signals of the quality of a person's productive capacity. Let us measure the level of academic achievement by a variable y, and let n denote a measure of an individual's innate capacity (both for productive and academic work). Let us assume the cost to the individual of achieving a level y is given by y/n. If the employer offers a wage structure related to y of the form $w(y)$, then an individual of type n will choose to maximise $w(y) - y/n$, the marginal condition for the optimum being

$$\frac{dw}{dy} = \frac{1}{n}$$

If we view n as being the individual's (marginal) productivity and the firm sets $w(y)$ to satisfy

$$\frac{dw}{dy} = \frac{1}{w}$$

we can see that we will have $w = n$. Hence with wage structure satisfying

$$w \frac{dw}{dy} = 1$$

or

$$\frac{1}{2} w^2 = y + k$$

or

$$w = [2(y + k)]^{1/2}$$

for some constant k, the firm will pay individuals their marginal product even though he is unable to observe their individual productivity! The level of educational achievement acts as a perfect signal of the individual's productivity level. ∎

If $w = 0$ when $y = 0$, so that we require $k = 0$, then the wage schedule will be

$$w = (2y)^{1/2}$$

Given this wage schedule, an individual of type n will choose to attain a level y of academic achievement given by

$$(2y)^{-1/2} = n^{-1}$$

i.e.

$$y = \frac{n^2}{2}$$

and thus obtains wage

$$w = n$$

as noted above. Hence the net return to his education will be

$$w - \frac{y}{n} = \frac{n}{2}$$

15

Costs and the Competitive Firm

1 Production Functions

1.1 Introduction

The basic description of the technology of a firm is the production set which contains all the feasible combinations of inputs and outputs. However, although the production set is a complete description of the technology of the firm, it is more useful in economics to summarise this information in other forms, one of the most common being the production function which maps from inputs onto the maximum feasible level of output, e.g.

$$y = f(k,l) \tag{15.1}$$

where y is output, k is capital employed and l is labour employed. It is customary to distinguish between the long-run and the short-run production function. In the long run all factors are variable, and the short run is defined as the period when one of the factors of production is fixed (usually capital). Thus (15.1) is a long-run function and the associated family of partial functions with k fixed is the set of short-run production functions.

1.2 Average and Marginal Productivities

Let us consider the short-run production function with the capital employed $\bar{k}$ fixed. The average productivity function AP_l for labour is then defined by the ratio of total output $f(\bar{k},l)$ and the labour input l, i.e.

319

$$AP_l = \frac{f(\bar{k},l)}{l}$$

In contrast the marginal productivity function MP_l for labour is the change in output for a 'marginal' change in the labour input, i.e.

$$MP_l = \frac{\partial f(\bar{k},l)}{\partial l}$$

5.2 We can readily confirm that a necessary condition for a maximum of the average productivity function AP_l, seen as a function of labour input l with capital $\bar{k}$ fixed, is that the average equals the marginal productivity. This condition is in fact the stationarity condition for such a maximum, as can be seen by differentiating AP_l with respect to l, and setting this derivative equal to zero.

$$\frac{\partial AP_l}{\partial l} = \frac{\partial}{\partial l}\left(\frac{f(\bar{k},l)}{l}\right) = \frac{l\frac{\partial f(\bar{k},l)}{\partial l} - f(\bar{k},l)}{l^2}$$

This last equality comes from the quotient rule of differentiation. This derivative will thus be zero when

$$l\frac{\partial f}{\partial l}(\bar{k},l) = f(\bar{k},l)$$

or

$$MP_l = \frac{\partial f}{\partial l}(\bar{k},l) = \frac{f(\bar{k},l)}{l} = AP_l$$

Figure 15.1 illustrates this result. ∎

4.2 In the case of the generalised Cobb–Douglas production, namely

$$y = Al^\alpha k^\beta$$

where A,α,β are positive constants, we can see that

$$AP_l = \frac{Al^\alpha \bar{k}^\beta}{l} = Al^{\alpha-1}\bar{k}^\beta$$

hence

$$\frac{\partial AP_l}{\partial l} = (\alpha - 1)Al^{\alpha-2}\bar{k}^\beta \tag{15.2}$$

and thus if $\alpha < 1$, then this derivative is negative and we can conclude average productivity of labour falls as the labour input increases.

In this case MP_l is a constant proportion of AP_l, for we have

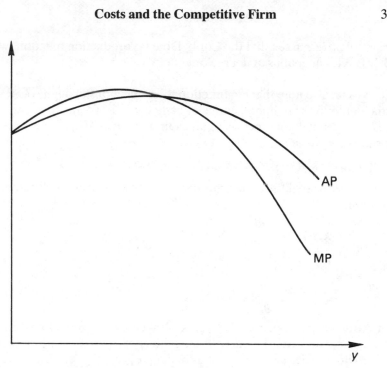

Figure 15.1

$$\text{MP}_l = \alpha A l^{\alpha-1} k^\beta = \alpha \text{AP}_l \qquad \blacksquare$$

Hence we cannot have $\text{AP}_l = \text{MP}_l$, unless $\alpha = 1$. Indeed if $\alpha < 1$ then $\text{MP}_l < \text{AP}_l$ for all labour inputs l. It follows that AP_l does not have a stationary point in that we cannot have $\partial \text{AP}_l/\partial l = 0$ — this being clear from the above expression (15.2) for $\partial \text{AP}_l/\partial l$.

Normally a reference to the Cobb–Douglas production function implicitly requires the α,β to add up to 1, i.e. $\alpha + \beta = 1$. It is in this sense that we have above the generalised form in that we did not require $\alpha + \beta = 1$.

We can note that the generalised Cobb–Douglas production function is homogenous of degree $\alpha + \beta$. For if

$$y = f(k,l) = A l^\alpha k^\beta$$

then

$$
\begin{aligned}
f(\lambda k, \lambda l) &= A(\lambda l)^\alpha (\lambda k)^\beta \\
&= A\lambda^\alpha l^\alpha \lambda^\beta k^\beta \\
&= \lambda^{\alpha+\beta} A l^\alpha k^\beta \\
&= \lambda^{\alpha+\beta} f(k,l)
\end{aligned}
$$

In particular we can see that the Cobb–Douglas production function, with $\alpha + \beta = 1$, is homogenous of degree one.

4.3　We can also note that if a function is homogenous of degree k, then its partial derivatives are homogenous of degree $k - 1$. To illustrate this result we use our production function as an example. Given $f(k,l)$ is homogenous of degree k we have

$$f(\lambda k,\lambda l) = \lambda^k f(k,l)$$

for all $\lambda > 0$. If we differentiate both sides of this equation with respect to l we obtain

$$\lambda \frac{\partial f}{\partial l} (\lambda k,\lambda l) = \lambda^k \frac{\partial f}{\partial l} (k,l)$$

hence

$$\frac{\partial f}{\partial l} (\lambda k,\lambda l) = \lambda^{k-1} \frac{\partial f}{\partial l} (k,l)$$

In particular we can see that the Cobb–Douglas production function, indeed any production function homogenous of degree one, has marginal productivities which are homogenous of degree zero. ∎

More specifically in the Cobb–Douglas case we have

$$MP_l = \alpha A l^{\alpha-1} k^\beta$$

yet as $\alpha + \beta = 1$ we have $\alpha - 1 = -\beta$, thus

$$MP_l = \alpha A \left(\frac{k}{l} \right)^\beta$$

Similarly

$$MP_k = \beta A \left(\frac{l}{k} \right)^\alpha$$

It is useful to stress the relationship between the degree of homogeneity and returns to scale. If a production function is homogenous of degree one, such as the Cobb–Douglas case, then a doubling of all inputs doubles the output. That is to say, the function exhibits constant returns to scale. Equally if the production function is homogenous of degree k then a doubling of inputs will increase output by more (less) than a factor of two if $k > 1$ $(k < 1)$. That is to say if $k > 1$ then the function exhibits increasing returns to scale and if $k < 1$ decreasing returns to scale.

1.3 Elasticity of Substitution

As we have seen repeatedly in the text we can represent a production function with two inputs diagrammatically, using isoquants. The marginal rate of technical substitution $MRTS_{lk}$ is defined as minus the slope of the isoquant (see Chapter 8). More formally we have

$$MRTS_{lk} = \frac{f_k}{f_l}$$

where f_l, f_k are the partial derivatives of the production function f with respect to l and k, these being evaluated at (k,l).

We now introduce the *elasticity of substitution* σ which is defined as follows:

$$\sigma = \frac{\text{percentage change in } l/k}{\text{percentage change in } MRTS_{lk}}$$

$$= \frac{MRTS_{lk}}{(l/k)} \frac{\partial(l/k)}{\partial(MRTS_{lk})} \tag{15.3}$$

The rationale of this measure comes from recalling that a cost-minimising firm will set the $MRTS_{lk}$ equal to the ratio of the input prices, hence σ implicitly measures the elasticity of the input ratio l/k with respect to the relative price of inputs.

We can note that in finding σ for a given production function we usually find $\partial(MRTS_{lk})/\partial(l/k)$ and then use the reciprocal of this derivative to give the value of $\partial(l/k)/\partial(MRTS_{lk})$ in (15.3). We can also note that for any homogenous production function $f(k,l)$ we can always write $MRTS_{lk}$ as a function of (l/k).

4.4 In the case of the generalised Cobb–Douglas production function we have

$$MRTS_{lk} = \frac{f_k}{f_l} = \frac{\beta l}{\alpha k}$$

hence

$$\frac{\partial(MRTS_{lk})}{\partial(l/k)} = \frac{\beta}{\alpha}$$

and thus

$$\sigma = \frac{(\beta l/\alpha k)}{(l/k)} \frac{\alpha}{\beta} = 1$$

That is to say all Cobb–Douglas production functions have a unit elasticity of substitution. Hence for such functions a doubling of the relative price of labour will lead to a doubling of the capital–labour ratio.

This feature of Cobb–Douglas functions is often considered too restrictive and this had led to the search for alternative structures. The CES (constant elasticity of substitution) production function takes the form

$$y = f(k,l) = \gamma[\alpha l^\rho + (1 - \alpha)k^\rho]^{1/\rho} \tag{15.4}$$

where $\gamma > 0$, $0 < \alpha < 1$ and $\rho < 1$. If we write $z = \alpha l^\rho + (1 - \alpha)k^\rho$ so that $f(k,l) = \gamma z^{1/\rho}$ we have the following

$$f_k = \frac{1}{\rho} \gamma z^{1/\rho - 1} \frac{\partial z}{\partial k}, f_l = \frac{1}{\rho} \gamma z^{1/\rho - 1} \frac{\partial z}{\partial l}$$

hence

$$\frac{f_k}{f_l} = \frac{\partial z/\partial k}{\partial z/\partial l} = \frac{(1 - \alpha)\rho k^{\rho-1}}{\alpha \rho l^{\rho-1}} = \frac{1 - \alpha}{\alpha}\left(\frac{k}{l}\right)^{\rho-1}$$

or

$$\mathrm{MRTS}_{lk} = \frac{f_k}{f_l} = \frac{1 - \alpha}{\alpha}\left(\frac{l}{k}\right)^{1-\rho}$$

It follows that

$$\frac{\partial(\mathrm{MRTS}_{lk})}{\partial(l/k)} = \frac{1 - \alpha}{\alpha}(1 - \rho)\left(\frac{l}{k}\right)^{-\rho}$$

and

$$\sigma = \frac{\mathrm{MRTS}_{lk}}{(l/k)} \frac{\alpha}{1 - \alpha} \frac{1}{1 - \rho}\left(\frac{l}{k}\right)^\rho$$

$$= \frac{1 - \alpha}{\alpha}\left(\frac{l}{k}\right)^{-\rho} \frac{\alpha}{1 - \alpha} \frac{1}{1 - \rho}\left(\frac{l}{k}\right)^\rho$$

i.e.

$$\sigma = \frac{1}{1 - \rho}$$

Thus with a CES production function we have, as the name suggests, a constant elasticity of substitution equal to $1/(1 - \rho)$. Hence a doubling of the relative price of labour will lead to more (less) than a doubling of the capital–labour ratio if $\rho > 0$ ($\rho < 0$).

Although it is not obvious, the Cobb–Douglas is a special case of the CES production function, namely when $\rho = 0$. Furthermore, we can assert that as ρ approaches minus infinity, the CES converges onto the Leontief production function. In this limiting case the elasticity of substitution is zero, and the marginal rate of substitution MRTS_{lk} is zero if $l < k$ and infinite if $l > k$, as in Figure 15.2. Note also as ρ approaches 1, the CES function approaches a linear form and thus the isoquants approach straight lines as illustrated in Figure 15.3.

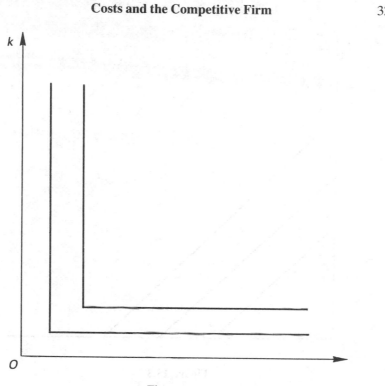

Figure 15.2

1.4 Long-Run Cost Functions

The long-run (or unrestricted) cost function $c(y,w,r)$ is defined as the minimum cost of producing output y, given input prices w and r, when both the capital and labour are flexible.

11.4 For example, if the production function takes the form $f(k,l) = l^\alpha k^\beta$, then the cost minimisation problem can be written as follows:

maximise $-wl - rk$ subject to $l^\alpha k^\beta \geqslant y$

This has Lagrangian

$$L = -wl - rk + \lambda(l^\alpha k^\beta - y)$$

and the first order conditions are

$$\frac{\partial L}{\partial l} = -w + \lambda(\alpha l^{\alpha-1} k^\beta) = 0$$

$$\frac{\partial L}{\partial k} = -r + \lambda(\beta l^\alpha k^{\beta-1}) = 0$$

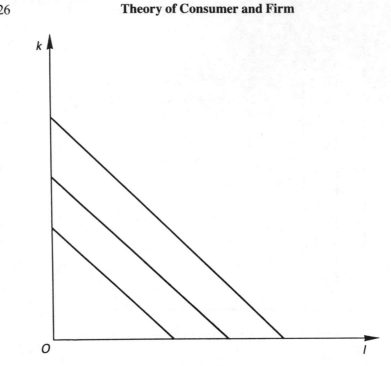

Figure 15.3

and

$$\lambda(l^\alpha k^\beta - y) = 0$$

Looking for a solution with $\lambda > 0$ we will have

$$l^\alpha k^\beta = y \qquad (15.5)$$

Taking w and r to the right-hand side of the first two equations, and then dividing the first by the second gives

$$\frac{\alpha k}{\beta l} = \frac{w}{r}$$

Using this expression to substitute for k in (15.5) implies

$$l^\alpha \left(\frac{\beta}{\alpha} \frac{w}{r} l \right)^\beta = y$$

or

$$l = y^\gamma \left(\frac{\alpha}{\beta} \frac{r}{w} \right)^{\beta\gamma} \qquad (15.6)$$

where $\gamma = \dfrac{1}{\alpha + \beta}$, from which we obtain

$$k = y^{\gamma}\left(\frac{\beta}{\alpha}\frac{w}{r}\right)^{\alpha\gamma} \tag{15.7}$$

Note $\alpha\gamma + \beta\gamma = 1$. Multiplying (15.6) by w and (15.7) by r and adding gives us the cost function, which after some tidying up can be written as

$$c(y,w,r) = \frac{y^{\gamma}}{\gamma}\left(\frac{w}{\alpha}\right)^{\alpha\gamma}\left(\frac{r}{\beta}\right)^{\beta\gamma}$$

$$= \frac{1}{\gamma}\left[y\left(\frac{w}{\alpha}\right)^{\alpha}\left(\frac{r}{\beta}\right)^{\beta}\right]^{\gamma} \qquad\blacksquare$$

3.4 An alternative way of writing this cost function is

$$c(y,r,w) = y^{\gamma}\phi(w,r) \tag{15.8}$$

where

$$\phi(w,r) = \frac{1}{\gamma}\left[\left(\frac{w}{\alpha}\right)^{\alpha}\left(\frac{r}{\beta}\right)^{\beta}\right]^{\gamma}$$

can be interpreted as the unit cost of production. Indeed the cost function associated with any homogenous production function can be written in the form of (15.8) with $\phi(w,r)$ being the minimum cost of producing unit output and $\gamma = 1/k$ where k is the degree of homogeneity.

If we have a cost function of the form (15.8) then the average cost function takes the following form:

$$AC = \frac{c(y,w,r)}{y} = y^{\gamma-1}\phi(w,r)$$

which is a constant, rising or falling function of output as $\gamma = 1, \gamma > 1$ or $\gamma < 1$ respectively. If $\gamma = 1/k$, k being the degree of homogeneity of the production function, is equal to one then $k = 1$ and thus the production function exhibits constant returns to scale and generates a constant average cost function. If $\gamma = 1/k > 1$ (< 1) then $k < 1$ (> 1) and the production function exhibits decreasing (increasing) returns to scale and generates a rising (falling) average cost function. $\blacksquare$

We can see that homogenous production functions, such as the Cobb–Douglas and CES, do not generate the familiar U-shaped, i.e. falling then rising, average cost curves that we tend to meet in introductory discussions of the firm. It is possible to generate production functions which generate such U-shaped (long-run) average cost curves. Indeed the class of *homothetic* production functions will generate almost all possible cost curves. A production function is homothetic if it is a monotonic transformation (see Chapter 13) of a homogenous production. In this case we can write the cost function in the form

$$c(y,w,r) = h(y)\phi(w,r)$$

where $h(y)$ is a monotonic function of output.

5.3 We can confirm that average cost AC is rising or falling as marginal cost MC is greater or less than AC respectively. In particular a necessary condition for AC to be at a minimum is that $AC = MC$. To see this we note that

$$AC = \frac{c(y,w,r)}{y}$$

hence

$$\frac{\partial AC}{\partial y} = \frac{y\frac{\partial c}{\partial y} - c}{y^2}$$

by the quotient rule of differentiation. Hence the sign of $\frac{\partial AC}{\partial y}$ is equal to the sign of $\frac{\partial c}{\partial y} - \frac{c}{y} = MC - AC$. That is to say AC is rising if $MC > AC$, falling if $MC < AC$ and stationary if $MC = AC$. (See Figure 15.4.) ∎

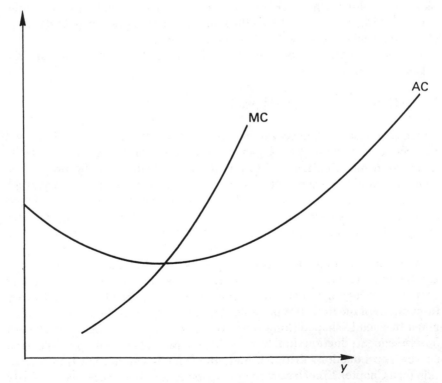

Figure 15.4

11.5 Production and long-run cost functions can be viewed as being dual to each other in that under certain circumstances the cost function is an alternative way of summarising the production possibilities. Thus not only can we construct the cost from the production function, but we can reverse this process and construct the production function from the cost function (see Chapter 12).

For example if we have cost function

$$c(y,w,r) = y^\gamma(a_1w + a_2r)$$

then the maximum quantity $f(k,l)$ that can be produced from inputs (k,l) is given as follows:

$f(k,l)$ = the maximum y such that $wl + rk \geqslant c(y,w,r)$
for all $w,k > 0$

= the maximum y such that $wl + rk \geqslant y^\gamma(a_1w + a_2r)$ for all $w,k > 0$

= the maximum y such that $y \leqslant \left(\dfrac{wl + rk}{a_1w + a_2r}\right)^{1/\gamma}$ for all $w,k > 0$

To find this maximum y we need to find the minimum value of the expression on the right-hand side. As the power function with power $1/\gamma$ is monotonic, which is readily confirmed from the derivative, the minimum of this expression is the minimum of $(wl + rk)/(a_1w + a_2r)$. To find the minimum of this term we divide the numerator and denominator by r and with $t = w/r$ we obtain $g(t) = (lt + k)/(a_1t + a_2)^2$. To seek for a minimum of this function we find the derivative with respect to t, namely $g'(t) - (a_2l - a_1k)/(a_1t + a_2)^2$. If $a_2l = a_1k$, i.e. $l/a_1 = k/a_2$, then the derivative $g'(t)$ is zero everywhere, indeed our expression $g(t)$ has the constant value $l/a_1 = k/a_2$. Hence in this case we require $y \leqslant (l/a_1)^{1/\gamma} = (k/a_2)^{1/\gamma}$. Consider now the case where $a_2l > a_1k$, i.e. $l/a_1 > k/a_2$ so that $g'(t)$ is positive everywhere. We can conclude that the minimum value of $g(t)$ occurs when $t = 0$; note $t \geqslant 0$ and thus $t = 0$ is the smallest possible value of t. Hence in this case we require $y < (k/a_2)^{1/\gamma}$. If $a_2l < a_1k$, i.e. $l/a_1 < k/a_2$, then $g'(t)$ is negative everywhere, and thus to find the minimum value of $g(t)$ we must let t approach infinity. In this case we require $y \leqslant (l/a_1)^{1/\gamma}$. All this can be summarised by saying

$$y \leqslant \min[(l/a_1)^{1/\gamma}, (k/a_2)^{1/\gamma}]$$

Hence the required production function is

$$f(k,l) = \min[(l/a_1)^{1/\gamma}, (k/a_2)^{1/\gamma}]$$

i.e. the Leontief production function. ∎

If the production function is not quasi-concave (see Chapter 13) then it is not possible to reproduce the production from the cost function exactly —

see our discussion of the similar situation with the utility function presented in the last chapter.

1.5 Short-Run Cost Functions

Short-run (or restricted) cost functions arise when we consider one or more of the inputs to be restricted to their current values and thus the firm is not free to choose their value. The most interesting example of such a restricted input is capital. In this discussion we shall remain with the simple two-input — labour and capital — analysis, and thus in treating capital as fixed, we find that the cost minimisation problems are relatively trivial. Nevertheless we can draw out the relationship between short- and long-run cost functions. We shall thus denote the short-run cost function by $c^s(y,w,r,k)$, this being the minimum cost of producing output y when the prices of input are w,r and capital is fixed at the level k.

11.6   If the production function is the Cobb–Douglas function

$$y = l^\alpha k^\beta$$

Treating k as fixed we can view this expression as telling us the amount of labour required to produce y, namely

$$l^s = \left(\frac{y}{k^\beta}\right)^{1/\alpha} \qquad\qquad (15.9)$$

Hence the restricted cost function will be

$$c^s(y,w,r,k) = w\left(\frac{y}{k^\beta}\right)^{1/\alpha} + rk \qquad\qquad (15.10)$$

We can rewrite this expression as

$$\text{STC} = \text{SVC} + \text{SFC}$$

where

$$\text{STC} = c^s(y,w,r,k) = \text{short-run total cost}$$

$$\text{SVC} = w\left(\frac{y}{k^\beta}\right)^{1/\alpha} = \text{short-run variable cost}$$

$$\text{SFC} = rk = \text{short-run fixed cost}$$

From the previous section we know that the associated long-run total cost function will be given by

$$\text{LTC} = y^\gamma \phi(w,r)$$

where

$$\gamma = \frac{1}{\alpha + \beta} \text{ and } \phi(w,r) = \frac{1}{\gamma}\left[\left(\frac{w}{\alpha}\right)^{\alpha}\left(\frac{r}{\beta}\right)^{\beta}\right]^{\gamma}$$

Let us compare the long- and short-run average cost functions.

$$\text{SATC} = \frac{\text{STC}}{y} = \frac{w}{k^{\alpha/\beta}} y^{\frac{1}{\alpha}-1} + \frac{rk}{y}$$

which has a derivative equal to

$$\frac{\partial \text{SATC}}{\partial y} = \frac{w}{k^{\alpha/\beta}}\left(\frac{1}{\alpha} - 1\right)y^{\frac{1}{\alpha}-2} - \frac{rk}{y^2}$$

and if $0 < \alpha < 1$ this is zero when

$$y = \left(\frac{rk^{\frac{\alpha}{\beta}+1}}{w\left(\frac{1}{\alpha}-1\right)}\right)^{\alpha}$$

Furthermore the derivative is negative (positive) for y smaller (larger) than this last value. Hence the SATC curve is U-shaped. ∎

We have already seen that the long-run average cost curve is either falling, constant or rising as γ is less, equal to or greater than one. We might anticipate that the short-run fixed capital stock is the optimal level of capital for some level of output and thus that the short- and long-run cost functions coincide at least for this level of output. Furthermore we might anticipate that the short-run cost is never less than the long-run cost for any output because, in the long run, capital can be changed to its optimal level.

Indeed with l^s being as above in (15.9) the optimal short-run level of labour, we have
11.8

$$\text{STC} = c^s(y,w,r,k) = wl^s + rk \geq c(y,w,r) = \text{LTC}$$

for all y. The inequality follows from the fact that $c(y,w,r)$ is the minimum value of $wl + rk$ for all k,l satisfying $f(k,l) \geq y$. Hence the STC curve will lie above or on the LTC curve. It follows that

$$\text{SATC} = \frac{\text{STC}}{y} \geq \frac{\text{LTC}}{y} = \text{LAC}$$

for all $y \geq 0$, hence the short-run average total cost SATC curve will lie above or on the long-run cost LAC curve.

Furthermore we can argue that in general the optimal level of capital will be zero for zero output, and will increase continuously to infinity as output goes off to infinity. Hence, given w and r, there will be some level of output

$y(k)$ for which k is the optimal level of capital stock, and that at this output short- and long-run total costs will be equal.

For example in the Cobb–Douglas example we have seen in the previous section — see equation (15.7) — that the optimal level of capital for producing output y is given by

$$k = y^\gamma \left(\frac{\beta}{\alpha} \frac{w}{r} \right)^{\alpha\gamma}$$

Hence the level of output $y(k)$ at which k is optimal is

$$y(k) = \left(\frac{\alpha}{\beta} \frac{r}{w} \right)^\alpha k^{1/\gamma}$$

If we substitute this output into our expression for long-run total cost (15.8) we obtain a value

$$\text{LTC} = \frac{rk}{\beta\gamma}$$

Equally if we substitute $y(k)$ into our expression (15.10) for the short-run total cost we obtain

$$\text{STC} = \frac{rk}{\beta\gamma}$$

Hence at this level of output LTC = STC. We can conclude that the STC does not lie below and touches the LTC curve.

It follows that

$$\text{STC} - \text{LTC} \geqslant 0$$

and is equal to zero for some output $y(k)$. If we view this difference STC—LTC as a function of y it follows that it has a minimum at $y(k)$ and thus $y(k)$ is a stationary point of this function. But the derivative of this difference is simply the difference between the marginal costs. Hence we can say that at $y(k)$

$$\text{SMC} = \text{LMC}$$

That is to say the output at which the short- and long-run (average) total cost curves meet is also the output at which the short- and long-run marginal cost curves meet. This was implicitly used in constructing Figure 15.5 and is further illustrated in Figure 15.6. ∎

The relationship between short- and long-run cost curves holds true for all levels of capital, i.e. for every k the SATC curve does not lie below and touches the LATC curve. In this way we can view the LATC curve as the 'envelope' of the SATC curves.

We can also note that the inequality

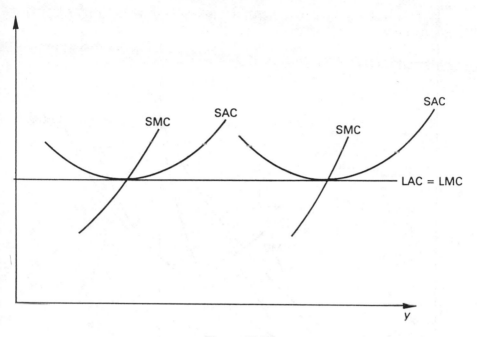

Figure 15.5

$c^s(y,w,r,k) \geqslant c(y,r,w)$

implies that $c(y,r,w)$ is the minimum value of $c^s(y,w,r,k)$ viewed as a function of k. Hence we can construct the long-run cost function $c(y,w,r)$ from the short-run cost function $c^s(y,r,w,k)$ by minimising the latter function considered as a function of k.

11.7   For example if

$$c^s(y,w,r,k) = \frac{wy}{k} + rk$$

then

$$\frac{\partial c^s}{\partial k}(y,w,r,k) = -\frac{wy}{k^2} + r$$

and

$$\frac{\partial^2 c^s}{\partial k^2}(y,w,r,k) = +\frac{2wy}{k^3} > 0$$

The second order derivative function indicates that this cost function is

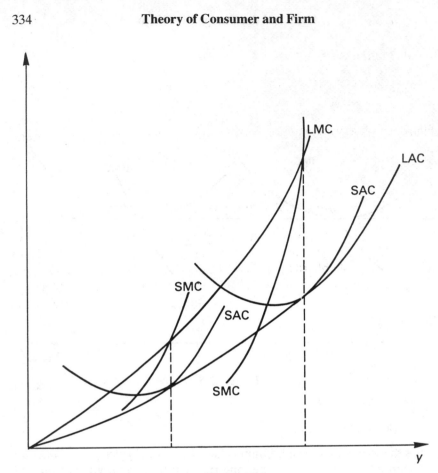

Figure 15.6

convex in k, for all y, w and r. Hence a necessary and sufficient condition for k^* to be a minimum is that it be a stationary point, hence k^* is given by

$$-\frac{wy}{k^{*2}} + r = 0$$

or

$$k^* = \left(\frac{wy}{r}\right)^{1/2}$$

If we substitute this value of k into the short-run cost function we will obtain the long-run cost function. Hence

$$c(y,w,r) = c^s(y,w,r,k^*)$$

$$= wy\left(\frac{r}{wy}\right)^{1/2} + r\left(\frac{wy}{r}\right)^{1/2}$$

$$= 2(ywr)^{1/2} \qquad \blacksquare$$

Costs and the Competitive Firm

Note that in this case

$$\text{LMC} = \frac{\partial c(y,w,r)}{\partial y} = \left(\frac{wr}{y}\right)^{1/2}$$

which declines as y increases, reflecting the presence of increasing returns to scale.

1.6 Conditional Input Demand Functions

Here we consider a firm's demand for inputs conditional on a given level of output, these being the analogy of compensated or Hicksian demands for the consumer. Shephard's Lemma (see Chapter 12) tells us that these conditional demands can be found directly from the firm's cost function. Hence the long-run conditional demands for labour and capital are given as follows:

$$k(y,w,r) = \frac{\partial c(y,w,r)}{\partial r}$$

and

$$l(y,w,r) = \frac{\partial c(y,w,r)}{\partial w}$$

The short-run conditional demand for labour will be given by

$$l^s(y,w,r,k) = \frac{\partial c^s(y,w,r,k)}{\partial w}$$

12.19 The slopes of these demand functions, viewed as partial functions of the prices w and r, are given by differentiation. For example we have

$$\frac{\partial l}{\partial w}(y,w,r) = \frac{\partial^2 c(y,w,r)}{\partial w^2}$$

and

$$\frac{\partial k}{\partial r}(y,w,r) = \frac{\partial^2 c(y,w,r)}{\partial r^2}$$

Yet we know $c(y,w,r)$ is concave in w and r (see Chapter 11) and thus these second order partial derivatives cannot be positive (see Chapter 7). We can thus conclude that the conditional demand curve for labour (capital) viewed as a partial function of wage (interest) will not slope upwards. ∎

Providing the elasticity of substitution between inputs is finite, the cost function will be strictly concave in prices and the demand functions must be downward sloping.

In the two input case there is no possibility of substitution in the short run. Hence the conditional short-run demand for labour in our examples above will be independent of wages. For example, if

$$c^s(y,w,r,k) = \frac{wy}{k} + rk$$

then

$$l^s(y,w,r,k) = \frac{y}{k}$$

which is independent of w.

1.7 A Generalised Leontief Cost Function

12.16   The cost function

$$c(y,w,r) = \phi(y)[\alpha w + \beta r + 2\gamma(wr)^{1/2}]$$

where $\alpha,\beta,\gamma > 0$ is known as the generalised Leontief Cost Function. The function has the property that it can approximate (locally) any cost function by appropriate choice of $\phi(y)$, α, β and γ. The associated conditional input demand functions are given by Shephard's Lemma. Hence

$$l(y,w,r) = \phi(y)\left[\alpha + \gamma\left(\frac{r}{w}\right)^{1/2}\right]$$

and

$$k(y,w,r) = \phi(y)\left[\beta + \gamma\left(\frac{r}{w}\right)^{1/2}\right]$$

both of which are linear in α, β and γ, this being a useful feature in applied work. In the special case of $\gamma = 0$ we have

$$l(y,w,r) = \alpha\phi(y)$$

and

$$k(y,w,r) = \beta\phi(y)$$

i.e. there is no substitution between capital and labour, as in the Leontief production function case discussed in Section 1.2 above.　■

2   The Perfectly Competitive Firm

2.1 Optimal Output

In this section we shall consider a (perfectly) competitive, profit-maximising firm. The firm takes prices as given and chooses output y to maximise its (long-run) economic profit π. Profit will be defined as

$$\pi = py - c(y,w,r)$$

where p is the price of output and w,r are the prices of labour and capital services respectively. In searching for the maximum value of π, treated as a function of output y, we face the problem that it may not be a concave function of y. Hence stationarity may not be sufficient condition for maximisation, indeed stationarity may not be necessary, i.e. if the optimal output is zero then the marginal profitability of output may well be negative. Furthermore we must recognise that there is the possibility that the function does *not* possess a maximum, this being a possibility if the firm's technology exhibits constant or increasing returns to scale.

To illustrate these problems consider the case where

$$c(y,w,r) = g(y)\phi(w,r)$$

which may arise from a homothetic production function. If $g(y) = y$, i.e. there are constant returns to scale, then

$$\pi = py - y\phi(w,r)$$
$$= [p - \phi(w,r)]y$$

If $p > \phi(w,r)$, i.e. price exceeds unit cost, then π can be increased indefinitely and thus π has no maximum value. Yet if $p < \phi(w,r)$ then π is negative for $y > 0$ and zero for $y = 0$, hence $y = 0$ is the maximum of π even though the derivative $p - \phi(w,r)$ is negative. We can note that if $p = \phi(w,r)$ then π is zero for all y and thus all output levels are optimal!

11.10   As another illustration we may take $g(y) = y^\gamma$ where $\gamma < 1$, so that there are increasing returns to scale. Here we have

$$\frac{\partial \pi}{\partial y} = \phi - \gamma y^{\gamma-1}\phi(w,r)$$

and

$$\frac{\partial^2 \pi}{\partial y^2} = -\gamma(\gamma - 1)y^{\gamma-2}\phi(w,r) > 0$$

In this case π is a *convex* function of y and thus any stationary point would be a minimum. Indeed as $\pi = y^\gamma[py^{1-\gamma} - \phi(w,r)]$ we can confirm that for sufficiently large y π will be positive and increasing indefinitely with y, i.e. there is no maximum value. ∎

In this way we can illustrate the possibility that there may be no profit maximum and the prospect of zero output being a non-stationary optimum. If we know that there is an optimal non-zero output, then we can say it is necessary that the output be a stationary point of π, i.e. that price equal marginal cost. But this stationarity will not be sufficient.

To illustrate this last possibility, consider the following case:

$$c(y,w,r) = \frac{1}{3} y^3 - y^2 + \gamma y$$

where $\gamma > 0$. Here we have put $\phi(w,r) = 1$, which we can interpret as saying we consider the output price p as being the price relative to unit cost $\phi(w,r)$. In this case

$$\pi = py - (\frac{1}{3} y^3 - y^2 + \gamma y)$$

thus

$$\frac{\partial \pi}{\partial y} = p - (y^2 - 2y + \gamma)$$

and

$$\frac{\partial^2 \pi}{\partial y^2} = -(2y - 2)$$

The stationary points of this function are given by

$$y^2 - 2y + (\gamma - p) = 0$$

therefore

$$y = \frac{2 \pm \sqrt{[4 - 4(\gamma - p)]}}{2}$$

or

$$y = 1 \pm \sqrt{(1 - \gamma + p)} \tag{15.11}$$

If $p < \gamma < 1 + p$, then this equation will yield *two* non-negative stationary points. Now taking the positive and negative square roots in turn and substituting these values of y into our expression for $\partial^2 \pi/\partial y^2$ we obtain a negative and positive second order derivative respectively. We can conclude that taking the negative sign in (15.11) cannot be a local nor global maximum of π, while $y = 1 + \sqrt{(1 - \gamma + p)}$ is indeed a local maximum. We cannot say whether this is a global maximum until we evaluate the level of profit at $y = 1 + \sqrt{(1 - \gamma + p)}$. If this is negative, then profits are maximised when $y = 0$.

11.9 A much more straightforward example arises when $g(y) = y^2$, in which case profit is

$$\pi = py - y^2\phi(w,r)$$

and is thus a concave function in y. Hence the profit-maximising output will be given by the stationarity condition, i.e.

$$p - 2y\phi(w,r) = 0$$

or

$$y = \frac{p}{2\phi(w,r)}$$

If $\phi(w,r) = 2(wr)^{1/2}$ we obtain

$$y = \frac{p}{4(wr)^{1/2}}$$

Having found the profit-maximising output, when it exists, as a function of prices we can substitute this back into our expression for profits and obtain *the profit function*. That is to say we can obtain an expression for the maximum level of profits as a function of the prices.

For example in our last example we will obtain

$$\pi = p\frac{p}{4(wr)^{1/2}} - \frac{p^2}{16(wr)^{1/2}} 2(wr)^{1/2}$$

i.e.

$$\pi(p,w,r) = \frac{1}{8}\, p^2(wr)^{-1/2} \qquad\blacksquare$$

The distinction between short- and long-run cost functions leads to a similar distinction for profit functions. Indeed it may be possible that the short-run profit function exists but the long-run function is not well defined.

11.11 For example, if the production function is $y = l^{1/2}k^\beta$ the restricted cost function is

$$c^s(y,w,r,k) = w\left(\frac{y}{k^\beta}\right)^2 + rk$$

and

$$\pi^s = py - w\left(\frac{y}{k^\beta}\right)^2 - rk$$

This function is concave in y for all β, indeed

$$\frac{\partial^2 \pi}{\partial y^2} = -\frac{2w}{k^\beta} < 0$$

for all y. Hence the maximum of π with respect to y occurs when

$$p - \frac{2w}{k^{2\beta}} y = 0$$

i.e.

$$y = \frac{pk^{2\beta}}{2w}$$

Substituting this maximum into π we obtain the short-run profit function

$$\pi^s(p,w,r,k) = \frac{p^2 k^{2\beta}}{4w} - rk$$

Just as the short-run cost function, seen as a function of k, attains a minimum value equal to the long-run cost function, so too the minimum value of the short-run profit function, if it exists, is equal to the long-run profit function. The derivatives of $\pi^s(p,w,r,k)$ in the example are

$$\frac{\partial \pi^s}{\partial k} = \frac{\beta p^2 k^{2\beta-1}}{2w} - r$$

and

$$\frac{\partial^2 \pi^s}{\partial k^2} = \frac{\beta(2\beta - 1)p^2 k^{2\beta-2}}{2w}$$

It can now be seen that if $\beta \leq \frac{1}{2}$ then π is a concave function of k, while if $\beta > \frac{1}{2}$ then it is a convex function. In the latter convex case the short-run profit function does not have a maximum. This reflects the fact that if the production function exhibits increasing returns to scale there is no long-run profit function. In the concave case with $\beta \leq \frac{1}{2}$ the maximum occurs when

$$k = \left(\frac{2wr}{\beta p^2}\right)^{1/\gamma}$$

where $\gamma = 2\beta - 1$. At this value of k, the level of profit is given by the long-run profit function

$$\pi(p,w,r) = \left(\frac{1}{2\beta} - 1\right)\left(\frac{2wr^{2\beta}}{\beta p^2}\right)^{1/\gamma} \qquad \blacksquare$$

2.2 Input Demand and Output Supply Functions

12.17 From Hotelling's Lemma (see Chapter 12) we know that the competitive firm's optimal output and inputs can be found directly from the profit function. In particular the firm's optimal output is equal to the derivative of the profit function with respect to output price, this holding both for short- and long-run supply functions. In both cases the derivative of the output supply function will equal the second order derivative of the profit function with respect to price. As the profit function is convex in output price, we can conclude that this derivative is non-negative, i.e. output supply curves do not slope downwards. Formally we have the long-run supply curve

$$y = \frac{\partial \pi(p,w,r)}{\partial p}$$

so that

$$\frac{\partial y}{\partial p} = \frac{\partial^2 \pi}{\partial p^2}(p,w,r) \geq 0$$

the expressions in the short run being almost identical. ∎

12.18 Similarly the optimal demand for each input will be equal to -1 times the derivative of the profit function with respect to the input's price. Thus we have for the long-run demands

$$l = -\frac{\partial \pi(p,w,r)}{\partial w}$$

and

$$k = -\frac{\partial \pi(p,w,r)}{\partial r}$$

hence

$$\frac{\partial l}{\partial w} = -\frac{\partial^2 \pi(p,w,r)}{\partial w^2}$$

and

$$\frac{\partial k}{\partial r} = -\frac{\partial^2 \pi(p,w,r)}{\partial r^2}$$

As π is convex in input prices, it follows that these latter derivatives are non-positive, i.e. the input demand curves do not slope upwards. Similar expressions and conclusions hold up for short-run demand function. ∎

12.14 For example if

$$\pi(p,w,r) = \frac{p^2}{4}\left(\frac{1}{w} + \frac{1}{r}\right)$$

then output supply is

$$y = \frac{p}{2}\left(\frac{1}{w} + \frac{1}{r}\right)$$

and input demands are

$$l = \frac{p^2}{4w^2}$$

and

$$k = \frac{p^2}{4r^2}$$ ∎

The elasticity of supply is defined by the following ratio:

$$\frac{\text{percentage change in quantity supplied}}{\text{percentage change in price of output}} = \frac{p}{y}\frac{\partial y}{\partial p}$$

3.3 In the above example we can write the supply function as

$$y = Ap$$

where $A = \frac{1}{2}\left(\frac{1}{w} + \frac{1}{r}\right)$. In this case the elasticity of supply is

$$\frac{p}{y}\frac{\partial y}{\partial p} = \frac{p}{Ap}A = 1$$

That is to say the elasticity of supply is 1. ∎

12.15 The short-run profit function associated with the above long-run function is

$$\pi^s(p,w,r,k) = \frac{p^2}{4w} + pk^{1/2} - rk$$

The short-run supply function generated in this case is

$$y^s = \frac{p}{2w} + k^{1/2}$$

and labour demand is

$$l^s = \frac{p^2}{4w^2}$$

Note in this case the long- and short-run demand for labour functions are equal, this reflecting the separability of the profit function.   ∎

16

Monopoly and Imperfect Competition

1 Monopoly

1.1 Demand Curve

Although there are certain industries where the assumption that the firm can sell as much as it wishes at the given price is reasonable, this will not be the case for most industries. In general we would expect a firm to have to reduce its price to sell more output. A problem then arises if there is more than one firm in the industry, because a firm contemplating changing price needs to know how the other firms will react. This is not a problem when we have a pure monopolist. In this case the industry and the firm coincide and there is no distinction between the demand curve for the industry and the firm.

A crucial concept for the monopolist is the (own price) elasticity of demand η for the product which is defined as

$$\eta = \frac{\text{percentage change in quantity demanded}}{\text{percentage change in price}}$$

If we let $y(p)$ be the demand function for output, i.e. $y(p) =$ quantity demanded at price p, then we have

$$\eta = \frac{p}{y}\frac{dy}{dp} = \frac{d\,\ln(y)}{d\,\ln(p)}$$

Note η can be expected to be negative as the demand function will have a negative derivative. We say demand is inelastic if $-1 < \eta < 0$, elastic if $\eta < -1$ and has unit elasticity if $\eta = -1$. It is useful to work with the inverse of the demand function $p(y)$ where $p(y)$ = the maximum price at which the quantity y can be sold = the *demand price* for y. The derivative of this demand price function will be the reciprocal of the derivative of the demand function i.e. $\dfrac{dp}{dy} = 1 \Big/ \dfrac{dy}{dp}$ (see Chapter 3).

3.1   If the demand price function is given by

$$p = a - by$$

for positive constants a, b, then the elasticity of demand can be found as follows:
from

$$\frac{dp}{dy} = -b$$

we have

$$\frac{dy}{dp} = -\frac{1}{b}$$

and

$$\eta = \frac{p}{y}\frac{dy}{dp} = \frac{a - by}{y}\left(-\frac{1}{b}\right) = 1 - \frac{a}{by}$$

Hence we can conclude that as $y \to 0, \eta \to -\infty$, while $\eta = 0$ if $y = \dfrac{a}{b}$ and $\eta = -1$ if $y = \dfrac{a}{2b}$. Thus a linear demand function displays all possible elasticity values (see Figure 16.1). ∎

Some demand curves have constant elasticity over all outputs.

3.2   The demand price functions for this case take the form

$$p = ay^\varepsilon$$

where ε is a negative constant. The elasticity in this case is

$$\eta = \frac{ay^\varepsilon}{y}\frac{1}{\varepsilon ay^{\varepsilon-1}} = \frac{1}{\varepsilon} \qquad \blacksquare$$

3.6   A firm's total revenue TR is defined to be the product of its selling price and the quantity sold, i.e.

$$TR = py$$

this being viewed as a function of output (= sales) if we viewed p as representing the demand price function. The marginal revenue MR is then

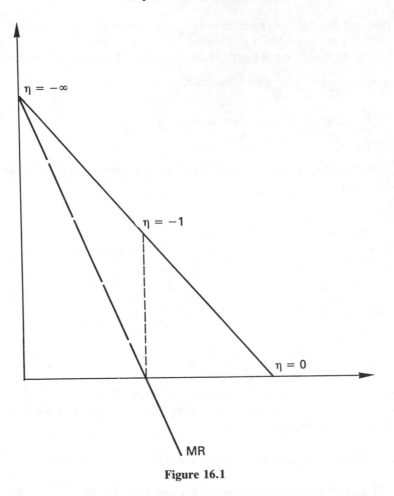

Figure 16.1

the derivative of this function, i.e.

$$\text{MR} = \frac{d\text{TR}}{dy} = p + \frac{dp}{dy}y$$

$$= p\left(1 + \frac{y}{p}\frac{dp}{dy}\right)$$

i.e.

$$\text{MR} = p\left(1 + \frac{1}{\eta}\right)$$

■

5.1 If total revenue has a maximum we would expect it to occur at a non-zero output at which point marginal revenue is zero, hence

$$p\left(1 + \frac{1}{\eta}\right) = 0$$

i.e.

$$\eta = -1$$

That is to say, a point where demand has unit elasticity will be a stationary point, and possibly a maximum, of the total revenue function. ∎

Furthermore total revenue will be rising as long as $\eta > -1$, i.e. demand is elastic and will be falling as long as $-1 < \eta < 0$, i.e. demand is inelastic.

1.2 Profit Maximisation

Maintaining the assumption that the firm aims to maximise profits, the optimal level of output will be the solution to the following problem.

maximise $\pi - p(y)y - c(y,w,r)$

where $c(y,w,r)$ is the (long-run) cost function.

The stationarity condition for this problem is

$$\frac{\partial \pi}{\partial y} = p\left(1 + \frac{1}{\eta}\right) - \frac{\partial c}{\partial y} = 0$$

this being the familiar MR = MC (marginal revenue equals marginal cost) condition. As in the case of the competitive firm, this condition may not be necessary, i.e. when zero output is optimal, nor sufficient, i.e. there may be local minima. A necessary condition for a stationary point to be a local maximum is that the second order derivative be non-positive, i.e.

$$\frac{\partial^2 \pi}{\partial y^2} = \frac{\partial MR}{\partial y} - \frac{\partial MC}{\partial y} \leqslant 0$$

which states that the MR curve has a smaller or equal slope than the MC curve, i.e. the marginal cost curve cut from below (or not from above) the marginal revenue curve.

We can also note that insofar as we expect marginal costs to be positive everywhere, then a monopolist producing non-zero output will have positive marginal revenue, which implies $1 + \frac{1}{\eta} > 0$, i.e. $\eta < -1$ or where demand is elastic.

In considering the profit function for the monopolist, i.e. the function relating prices to the maximum available profit, we must remember that the price of output is *not* a parameter of the monopolist decision. In this case the profit function will be a function of the input prices alone. If we restrict ourselves to our standard two inputs of labour and capital we seek a function $\pi(w,r)$ which tells us the maximum profits the monopolist can achieve, given w and r as the prices of labour and capital services respectively.

Thus

$$\pi(w,r) = \text{maximum value of } p(y)y - c(y,w,r)$$

11.12   In the case where

$$p(y) = y^\varepsilon \qquad -1 < \varepsilon < 0$$

and

$$c(y,w,r) = y\phi(w,r)$$

then profits

$$\pi = y^{\varepsilon+1} - y\phi(w,r)$$

which is a concave function of y, as

$$\frac{\partial^2 \pi}{\partial y^2} = \varepsilon(\varepsilon + 1)y^{\varepsilon-1} < 0 \text{ for all } y$$

Hence the stationary condition is necessary and sufficient for a maximum. The optimal output is thus given by

$$(\varepsilon + 1)y^\varepsilon - \phi(w,r) = 0$$

i.e.

$$y = \left[\frac{\phi(w,r)}{1 + \varepsilon}\right]^{1/\varepsilon}$$

At this output, profits are given by

$$\pi(w,r) = -\varepsilon\left[\frac{\phi(w,r)}{1 + \varepsilon}\right]^\gamma$$

where $\gamma = 1 + \dfrac{1}{\varepsilon}$.   ∎

As in the case of the competitive firm, the input demand functions are given by -1 times the partial derivatives of the profit function. This is readily confirmed by applying the Envelope Theorem of Chapter 12. But we must note that we no longer obtain information about output from the profit function.

1.3 Two-Part Tariffs and Price Discrimination

Our discussion above assumed that the monopolist charged a simple price per unit of output, but we can note that it may be more profitable for the firm to use more complex price schemes. A common structure found in practice is two-part tariffs where the consumer has to pay a fixed charge or rental as well as a unit price. Examples of this structure can be found in many public utilities such as telephones, electricity and gas.

12.11   To discuss this structure we need to identify the constraint on the firm's choice of fixed charge and price. Let γ denote the fixed charge and p_0 the price of the good. To simplify the discussion, we shall assume all consumers are identical and thus we proceed as if there were only one consumer. The consumer's budget constraint is complicated by the presence of the fixed charge. Let us denote by **p** the vector of prices of all other consumption goods and let m be the consumer's budget before paying the fixed charge. The maximum utility the consumer can attain if he buys the monopolist good will be given by the indirect utility function $v(p_0,\mathbf{p},m-\gamma)$. If we denote by $\bar{u}$ the level of utility that the consumer can attain if he does not buy any of the monopolist's produce, then the consumer will pay the fixed charge if $v(p_0,\mathbf{p},m-\gamma) \geq \bar{u}$. If this condition is not satisfied, then the consumer purchases a zero quantity of the good and the firm will obtain zero (long-run) profits. The question we ask then is the following. What are the maximum profits the firm can attain given the constraint $v(p_0,\mathbf{p},m-\gamma) \geq \bar{u}$? This constraint can be re-expressed as $e(p_0,\mathbf{p},\bar{u}) \leq m-\gamma$, where $e()$ is the consumer's expenditure function, i.e. the consumer has sufficient funds after paying the fixed charge to attain the level of utility $\bar{u}$. We use the constraint in this form. The problem can be expressed as follows:

maximise $\pi = p_0 y + \gamma - c(y,w,r)$

subject to $m - \gamma - e(p_0,\mathbf{p},\bar{u}) \geq 0$

where $c(y,w,r)$ is the (long-run) cost function. Forming the Lagrangian

$$L = \pi + \lambda[m - \gamma - e(p_0,\mathbf{p},\bar{u})]$$

we note that we shall treat p_0 as the decision variable and thus view y as representing the demand function. To keep matters simple, let us assume π is a concave function of p_0, so that the necessary and sufficient conditions for an optimum are

$$\frac{\partial L}{\partial p_0} = y + \left(p_0 - \frac{\partial c}{\partial y}\right)\frac{\partial y}{\partial p_0} - \lambda\frac{\partial e}{\partial p_0} = 0$$

$$\frac{\partial L}{\partial \gamma} = 1 - \lambda = 0$$

and

$$\lambda[m - \gamma - e(p_0,\mathbf{p},\bar{u})] = 0$$

We immediately conclude that $\lambda = 1 \neq 0$ hence

$$\gamma = m - e(p_0, \mathbf{p}, \bar{u})$$

It follows that $v(p_0, \mathbf{p}, m - \gamma) = \bar{u}$ and hence, from Shephard's Lemma, $y = \frac{\partial e}{\partial p_0}$. The first condition thus becomes

$$\left(p_0 - \frac{\partial c}{\partial y} \right) \frac{\partial y}{\partial p_0} = 0$$

which will normally imply

$$p_0 = \frac{\partial c}{\partial y}$$

i.e. price = marginal cost. It is to be stressed that the above expression for the solution value of the fixed charge γ implies that the level of utility of the consumer will be the same whether or not he purchases any of the monopolist's produce. That is to say, the monopolist can extract *all* the consumer's surplus in this situation. ∎

5.10 If we now allow consumers to differ in that they either have different preferences and/or different incomes, then the monopolist will wish to offer discriminating price polices, that is to say the price schemes will be contingent upon the customer. To illustrate this idea consider a situation where the monopolist faces two customers (or two types of customer) and uses a one-tariff pricing scheme for each customer.

The monopolist's profits can be expressed as

$$= p_1(y_1)y_1 + p_2(y_2)y_2 - c(y_1 + y_2, w, r)$$

where y_1, y_2 are the quantities supplied to the two customers and $p_i(y_i)$ $i = 1,2$ are the respective demand price functions. Again assuming π is concave in y_1, y_2, then the conditions for a non-trivial (i.e. non-zero) optimum will be

$$\frac{\partial \pi}{\partial y_1} = p_1\left(1 + \frac{1}{\eta_1} \right) - \frac{\partial c}{\partial y} = 0$$

and

$$\frac{\partial \pi}{\partial y_2} = p_2\left(1 + \frac{1}{\eta_2} \right) - \frac{\partial c}{\partial y_2} = 0$$

where η_i $i = 1,2$ are the customers' elasticities of demand. But we can see from the chain rule of differentiation that $\frac{\partial c}{\partial y_1} = \frac{\partial c}{\partial y_2} = $ the derivative of c with respect to total output $y_1 + y_2$. Hence we will require

$$p_1\left(1 + \frac{1}{\eta_1} \right) = p_2\left(1 + \frac{1}{\eta_2} \right)$$

and if $\eta_1 < \eta_2$ then $p_1 < p_2$, i.e. the higher price will be associated with the customer (or market) with a less elastic demand. ■

1.4 Monopoly with Durable Output

There is a large literature on the effects of monopoly on the durability of goods produced. The general results of this literature suggest a monopolist will not reduce the durability of a product, compared to a competitive supply of the good if the monopolist can rent out the product, but will reduce durability if he is forced to sell his produce.

To illustrate this result we consider a simple two-period model. As the essential feature of the argument rests upon the revenue effects of durability, we shall abstract from costs of production by assuming them to be zero. Again for simplicity, we shall consider only two forms of durability, namely a good that yields its services for one or two periods respectively.

We shall also assume that the demand price for the *services* of the good are given by

$$p = a - by$$

where y is the quantity of the good available in the respective period. Hence if we consider a firm that produces a good that lasts two years and *rents out* the services of its produce, then the profit (= revenue) from producing y_1, y_2 in the two periods will be

5.5

$$\pi = y_1(a - by_1) + (y_1 + y_2)[a - b(y_1 + y_2)]$$

Note we are assuming no time discounting here. The first order conditions for a maximum of this concave function are

$$\frac{\partial \pi}{\partial y_1} = a - 2by_1 + a - 2b(y_1 + y_2) = 0$$

and

$$\frac{\partial \pi}{\partial y_2} = a - 2b(y_1 + y_2) = 0$$

From these conditions we find

$$y_1 = \frac{a}{2b}, y_2 = 0$$

and thus the respective maximum profits are

$$\hat{\pi}_1 = \frac{a^2}{2b} \tag{16.1}$$

Should the firm produce a good of one period durability and rent out its services then profit ($=$ revenue) will be

$$\pi = y_1(a - by_1) + y_2(a - by_2)$$

which has a maximum when

$$y_1 = y_2 = \frac{a}{2b}$$

and thus has a maximum value of

$$\hat{\pi}_2 = \frac{a^2}{2b} \tag{16.2}$$

We can see the monopolist will be indifferent between the more and less durable products.

Consider now the case where the firm sells its produce. The main complication here is to identify the demand price for a good of two-period durability produced in the first period. In buying such a good the customer is purchasing the services of the good in both periods. Hence the demand price for the purchase of a quantity y_1 of the good in the first period and y_2 in the second will be given by the sum of the demand price $a - by_1$ for the *services* in the first period and the price $a - b(y_1 + y_2)$ of the *services* in the second period.

Hence the firm's profits ($=$ revenue) will be given by

$$\begin{aligned} \pi &= y_1[a - by_1 + a - b(y_1 + y_2)] + y_2[a - b(y_1 + y_2)] \\ &= y_1(a - by_1) + (y_1 + y_2)[a - b(y_1 + y_2)] \end{aligned} \tag{16.3}$$

This expression is identical to that for the rental case, hence has a maximum when

$$y_1 = \frac{a}{2b}, y_2 = 0$$

with maximum value $\hat{\pi}_1$ in (16.1). But there is a significant difference between the two cases. In the present case the firm's choice of $y_2 = 0$ is *not* an intertemporally consistent choice. That is to say, although the firm may plan $y_2 = 0$ in period 1, it will not consider this choice as optimal in period 2. In period 2 it will wish to maximise the current profits ($=$ revenue), namely

$$\pi_2 = y_2[a - b(y_1 + y_2)]$$

which has a maximum at

$$y_2 = \frac{a - by_1}{2b} \tag{16.4}$$

Now once the firm recognises that its choice of y_2 will be given by (16.4), its choice of y_1 will be that which maximises (16.3) with y_2 given by (16.4). Differentiating (16.3) with respect to y_1, remembering that y_2 is now a function of y_1, gives us the first order condition

$$a - 2by_1 + [a - 2b(y_1 + y_2)]\left(1 - \frac{1}{2}\right) = 0$$

or

$$a - 2by_1 + \frac{a}{2} - b\left(\frac{a + by_1}{2b}\right) = 0$$

that is

$$a - \frac{5}{2}by_1 = 0$$

therefore

$$y_1 = \frac{2a}{5b}$$

hence

$$y_2 = \frac{3a}{10b}$$

and the corresponding profits will be

$$\hat{\pi}_3 = \frac{9}{20}\frac{a^2}{b} \tag{16.5}$$

∎

Finally the monopolist who sells a good with one-period durability will be in the identical situation of the firm who rents out such a good and thus the ensuing profits will be given by (16.2), namely $\hat{\pi}_2 = \frac{a^2}{2b}$.

Hence we can see that a firm who sells rather than rents out his products will prefer to produce the good with lower durability as the profits (16.5) from the more durable good are lower.

In completion of this example we can note that as production costs of the two goods are zero, then a competitive market would supply the more durable good at a zero price.

1.5 Objectives other than Profit Maximising

We have assumed that the monopolist wishes to maximise profits but in
many corporations the people who run the company from day to day are not
the major shareholders. Thus the managers' preferences may dictate the
objectives of the company and they may not follow profit-maximising
objectives. Generally it involves some cost to replace a management team,
so the managers have flexibility to follow their own objectives providing the
difference between the profit they produce and the maximum feasible profit
is less than the cost of replacing them.

9.5 One possibility is that the managers are interested in maximising the
size of the company, which is probably best represented by the revenue. In
this case they would maximise $pf(k,l)$ subject to the constraint

$$pf(k,l) - wl - rk \geq \bar{r} \tag{16.6}$$

i.e. profits cannot fall below a certain level. The Lagrangian is

$$L = pf(k,l) + \lambda[pf(k,l) - wl - rk - \bar{r}]$$

and the first order conditions include (η is the elasticity of demand):

$$\frac{\partial L}{\partial l} = pf_l\left(1 + \frac{1}{\eta}\right)(1 + \lambda) - w = 0$$

and

$$\frac{\partial L}{\partial k} = pf_k\left(1 + \frac{1}{\eta}\right)(1 + \lambda) - \bar{r} = 0$$

combining to give

$$\frac{f_l}{f_k} = \frac{w}{r}$$

Therefore a firm following these objectives, even if it may be producing
more than the profit-maximising quantity, will still retain cost-minimising
combinations of inputs.

Alternatively, the management may wish to maximise the number of staff
employed by a company, i.e. they maximise l subject to (16.6). Assuming w
is greater than 1, the Lagrangian is

$$L = l + \lambda[pf(k,l) - wl - rk - \bar{r}]$$

and first order conditions include

$$\frac{\partial L}{\partial l} = 1 + \lambda p\left(1 + \frac{1}{\eta}\right)f_l - w = 0$$

and

$$\frac{\partial L}{\partial k} = \lambda p \left(1 + \frac{1}{\eta} \right) f_k - r = 0$$

combining to give

$$\frac{f_l}{f_k} = \frac{w - 1}{r}$$

Such a firm will not purchase cost-minimising combinations of capital and labour. Assuming a diminishing MRS, the firm has a lower capital to labour ratio than the cost-minimising one. ∎

2 Imperfect Competition

The perfectly competitive and monopoly models are relatively simple because they avoid our having to consider the interaction of firms' pricing policies. Nevertheless, many industries consist of a 'small' number of firms producing identical or very similar products. In such cases we must explicitly model the way firms believe their competitors will react to their price or quantity adjustments. Not surprisingly there are many competing models.

2.1 Cournot–Nash Equilibrium

5.6 It is to be stressed that we are concerned here to specify the conjectures firms make about their competitors' response to their own price or quantity adjustments. The simplest conjecture that a firm may use is that their competitors will not react to any quantity adjustment. With this conjecture the firm believes that their competitors' quantities will not change in response to the firm changing its own quantity. Hence each firm will attempt to choose its own quantity taking as given the quantity of the other firms.

The reader should note carefully that, even with this no-response conjecture, each firm's choice will be contingent upon their competitors' quantities. This has two ramifications. The first is that the firms' choices will be simultaneously determined in interaction with other firms' choices and we cannot give a simple characterisation of an optimal choice for an individual firm. Secondly, we can note that there may be a tension between the no-response conjecture and the fact that firms do respond to their competitors' quantities. This second point will not be pursued here.

In line with the first implication we introduce the Cournot–Nash concept of equilibrium. Consider a market containing *n* producers of a homogeneous good (i.e. each producer's output is a perfect substitute for their competitors' product). Each firm has to choose the quantity it will produce and sell. The demand price for the good will depend on the total output of all the n firms, hence the revenue and profits of each firm will depend upon the quantities produced by all other firms. We say a set of outputs $(q_1^*,\ldots,q_n^*)$ is a Cournot–Nash equilibrium if q_i^* $i = 1,\ldots,n$ maximises the ith firm's profits, given all other firms' output are fixed at q_j^* $j \neq i, j = 1,\ldots,n$. To clarify the meaning of this we can restate it in the case $n = 2$. Let $\pi_i(q_1,q_2)$ $i = 1,2$ denote the profits of the ith firm given outputs q_1,q_2. Hence (q_1^*,q_2^*) is a Cournot–Nash equilibrium if

q_1^* is the maximum of the partial function $q_1 \rightarrow \pi_1(q_1,q_2^*)$

and

q_2^* is the maximum of the partial function $q_2 \rightarrow \pi_2(q_1^*,q_2)$

For further clarification let us assume both firms have a cost function of the form

$$c(q_i,w,r) = \phi q_i \qquad i = 1,2$$

where ϕ is the unit cost, i.e. the firms' produce under constant returns to scale. Furthermore let us assume the demand price for the good is given by the linear function

$$p = a - b(q_1 + q_2)$$

The profits of the two firms are given by

$$\pi_1 = [a - b(q_1 + q_2)]q_1 - \phi q_1$$

and

$$\pi_2 = [a - b(q_1 + q_2)]q_2 - \phi q_2$$

Viewed as partial functions of q_1,q_2 respectively, these profit functions are concave. Thus the conditions for a Cournot–Nash equilibrium, ignoring any non-negativity constraints, will be given by the simultaneous stationarity conditions

$$\frac{\partial \pi_1}{\partial q_1} = a - 2bq_1^* - bq_2^* - \phi = 0$$

$$\frac{\partial \pi_2}{\partial q_2} = a - bq_1^* - 2bq_2^* - \phi = 0$$

We can note that the position of the two firms is identical and these two conditions are symmetric in q_1^*,q_2^* i.e. if we switch q_1^* and q_2^* in these equations we end up with the same two equations. We might anticipate that in these circumstances $q_1^* = q_2^*$. If we use this observation, or solve the equations in the usual way, we obtain the conclusion

$$q_1^* = q_2^* = \frac{a - \phi}{3b}$$

and profits will be $\pi_1^* = \pi_2^* = \frac{1}{b} \left(\frac{a - \phi}{3} \right)^2$

Before proceeding further, let us reconsider the stationarity conditions individually above which can be rewritten respectively as follows:

$$q_1 = \frac{a - \phi}{2b} - \frac{1}{2} q_2 \tag{16.7}$$

and

$$q_2 = \frac{a - \phi}{2b} - \frac{1}{2} q_1 \tag{16.8}$$

In this form the condition (16.8) tells us what quantity q_2 the second firm will choose, given the quantity q_1 produced by the competitor. (We have dropped the asterisk because we no longer wish to restrict attention to the equilibrium values.) This relationship is illustrated in Figure 16.2(a), this being known as firm 2's *reaction curve* while the function in (16.8) would be firm 2's *reaction function*. As we noted above, there is a tension here between the fact that firm 2 does react to firm 1's choice and firm 1's conjecture that there will be no such reaction. Similar terms and remarks apply to the relationship in (16.7).

Figure 16.2(b) illustrates the reaction curves of both firms and the fact that the Cournot–Nash equilibrium lies on both and is thus given by the intersection of these curves. ∎

In the general case of n firms producing a homogeneous good with identical constant returns to scale technology, and facing a linear demand price function for their product, the ith firm's profit will be

$$\pi_i = (a - bQ)q_i - \phi q_i$$

where $Q = q_1 + \ldots + q_n$ is the total output of all n firms. Again viewed as a partial function of q_i this is concave with a stationary point where

$$\frac{\partial \pi_i}{\partial q_i} = a - bQ - bq_i - \phi = 0 \tag{16.9}$$

so that

$$q_i = \frac{a - \phi}{2b} - \frac{1}{2} Q_i$$

where $Q_i =$ the sum of all outputs *other than* q_i. This is the ith firm's reaction function.

Again we can argue that as all firms are in an identical situation, their

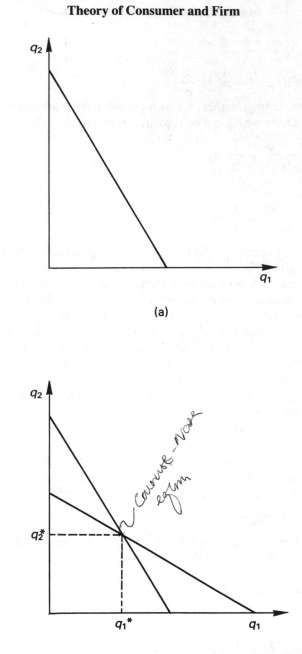

(a)

(b)

Figure 16.2

choices will be equal at the Cournot–Nash equilibrium. Let this common quantity be q^* so that the corresponding total $Q^* = nq^*$. Substituting these values for q_i and Q in (16.9) gives

$$q^* = \frac{a - \phi}{(N + 1)b}$$

Note that the total output in this case would be

$$Q^* = \frac{n(a - \phi)}{n(n + 1)b} \tag{16.10}$$

at a demand price

$$p^* = \frac{a}{n + 1} + \frac{n\phi}{n + 1} \tag{16.11}$$

yielding individual profits

$$\pi^* = \frac{1}{b} \left(\frac{a - \phi}{n + 1} \right)^2$$

We can note that a monopolist working with the same technology and facing the same demand situation would produce

$$q^m = \frac{a - \phi}{2b}$$

at price

$$p^m = \frac{u + \psi}{2}$$

and profits

$$\pi^m = \frac{1}{b} \left(\frac{a - \phi}{2} \right)^2$$

In contrast a perfectly competitive industry would supply the good at a price equal to marginal = average cost, i.e. at a price

$$p^c = \phi$$

and thus supply a quantity

$$q^c = \frac{a - \phi}{b}$$

yielding zero profits.

We can see that the Cournot–Nash equilibrium in (16.10) and (16.11) satisfies

$$p^c \leqslant p^* \leqslant p^m$$

and

$$q^m \leq Q^* \leq q^c$$

Furthermore we can note that

$$p^* \text{ converges onto } p^c$$

and

$$Q^* \text{ converges onto } q^c$$

as n tends to infinity. Note $(n + 1)/n = 1 + 1/n$ converges onto 1 as n goes to infinity.

2.2 Stackelberg Equilibrium

5.7 In discussing the Cournot–Nash equilibrium, no attempt was made to describe just how the equilibrium might be obtained. It is worthy of the description equilibrium because, once obtained, neither firm has an incentive to change its output given the no-response conjecture. Consider now a slightly different situation where there are two firms, one called the *leader* and the other the *follower*. Here the leader chooses his output and announces his choice to the follower who then chooses his output. It is to be understood that once the leader has announced his choice he is committed to it, he cannot make any subsequent changes. Hence the follower can take his competitor's choice as given when he makes his own choice. Thus the follower will choose his output to maximise his profits, given the output of the leader. That is to say, the follower's output will be given by his reaction function. The situation of the leader is less straightforward in that he has to anticipate the choice of the follower. Should the leader recognise that the follower's choice will be determined by the follower's reaction function, then the leader will embody this information in his own profit calculations.

Again assuming the linear demand price function and constant returns technology as before, the follower's reaction function will be given by (16.8) — we shall take the follower to be firm 2. Hence the leader's profits will be given as follows:

$$\pi_1 = [a - b(q_1 + q_2)]q_1 - \phi q_1$$

where

$$q_2 = \frac{a - \phi}{2b} - \frac{1}{2} q_1$$

The stationary condition for the maximum of this concave function of q_1 is

$$\frac{\partial \pi_1}{\partial q_1} = a - 2qb_1^* - \frac{a - \phi}{2} + bq_1^* - \phi = 0$$

so that

$$q_1^* = \frac{a - \phi}{2b}$$

From which we can conclude

$$q_2^* = \frac{a - \phi}{4b}$$

$$Q^* = q_1^* + q_2^* = \frac{3(a - \phi)}{4b}$$

and

$$p^* = \frac{a + 3\phi}{4}$$

Furthermore, the firm's profits will be

$$\pi_1^* = \frac{1}{2b}\left(\frac{a - \phi}{2}\right)^2$$

$$\pi_2^* = \frac{1}{b}\left(\frac{a - \phi}{4}\right)^2$$

This solution to the leader–follower structure is known as the Stackelberg equilibrium and we can note that in comparison with the Cournot–Nash equilibrium, the leader obtains more profits from a higher output while the follower obtains less profits from a lower output. Overall output will be higher and price lower in the Stackelberg equilibrium compared with Cournot–Nash. ∎

2.3 Sweezy Equilibrium

5.4 Consider a firm who conjectures that its competitors will respond in an asymmetric manner to changes in its own policy. For example, if the firms all produce the same homogeneous good, an increase in production may be viewed as an aggressive act by the competitors and thus may be expected to respond by increasing their own output. In contrast a reduction in output may not be viewed as threatening and competitors may be expected not to change their output in response. Let $\bar{q}_i$ be the current output of the ith firm and let Q_i be the output of the remaining firms. Our conjecture concerning the competitors' responses can be expressed by a (conditional) function of the ith firm's output q_i as follows.

$$Q_i = \begin{cases} \bar{Q}_i & \text{if } q_i \leqslant \bar{q}_i \\ \bar{Q}_i + \gamma(q_i - \bar{q}_i) & \text{if } q_i > \bar{q}_i \end{cases}$$

where $\gamma > 0$ and $\bar{Q}_i$ is the current output of the competitors. If the demand price for the common output is given by the usual linear function

$$p = a - bQ$$

where $Q = q_i + Q_i$ is total output then we have

$$p = \begin{cases} a - b\bar{Q}_i - bq_i & \text{if } q_i \leqslant \bar{q}_i \\ a - b\bar{Q}_i - b\gamma(q_i - \bar{q}_i) - bq_i & \text{if } q_i > \bar{q}_i \end{cases}$$

For example, if $\bar{q}_i = 50$, $\bar{Q}_i = 200$, $\gamma = 3$, $a = 450$ and $b = 1$, then

$$p = \begin{cases} 250 - q_i & \text{if } q_i \leqslant 50 \\ 400 - 4q_i & \text{if } q_i > 50 \end{cases}$$

In this case the marginal revenue MR for the ith firm will be $250 - 2q_i$ for q_i less than 50, and $400 - 8q_i$ for q_i greater than 50. Because the total revenue function is not differentiable at $q_i = 50$, the marginal revenue is not defined at this output. Figure 16.3 illustrates the demand price and marginal revenue curves in this case, while Figure 16.4 draws the profit level as a function of q_i. If the firm's cost function takes the form

$$C = \frac{1}{2} q_i^2$$

then marginal cost MC is equal to q_i. We can confirm that for $q_i \leqslant 50$, MC will be less than MR and yet for $q_i > 50$ MC will be greater than MR. Hence at no point is the first order condition MR = MC satisfied. Nevertheless we can argue that $q_i = 50$ is the optimal output. This follows from the fact that any attempt to reduce output will lead to a greater fall in revenue than in costs (because MC < MR), while any rise in output will increase revenue less than costs (as MC > MR).

Note that the marginal revenue function is not continuous and any small shifts up or down in the MC curve will leave the optimal output and prices unchanged. This sort of argument has been used to explain the apparent stickiness of prices in oligopolistic industries. ∎

2.4 Collusion

5.9 One might expect that if there is a small number of firms in an industry that they may attempt to collude. For example, they may aim to choose their produce (of a homogeneous good) jointly so as to maximise the sum of their

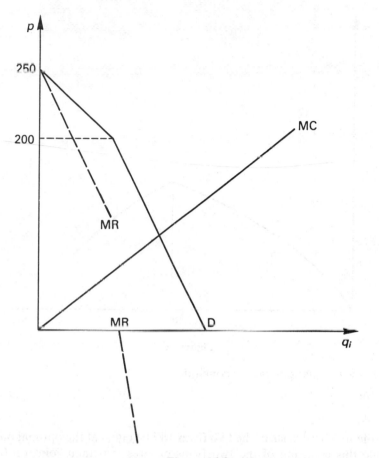

Figure 16.3

profits. Hence if $p(Q)$ is the demand price function, $Q = q_1 + q_2$ and $q_i\ i = 1,2$ the two firms' output, then their joint profits would be

$$\pi = p(Q)Q - c_1(q_1) - c_2(q_2)$$

where $c_i(q_i)$ are the two firms' cost functions.

Assuming the requisite concavity, the first order conditions for an optimum suffice and the firms' outputs will satisfy

$$\frac{\partial \pi}{\partial q_1} = p(Q)\left(1 + \frac{1}{\eta}\right) - \frac{\partial c_1}{\partial q_1} = 0$$

and

$$\frac{\partial \pi}{\partial q_2} = p(Q)\left(1 + \frac{1}{\eta}\right) - \frac{\partial c_2}{\partial q_2} = 0$$

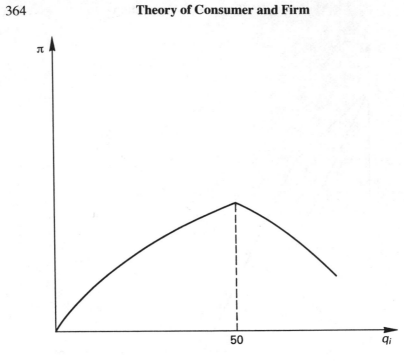

Figure 16.4

From these equations we can conclude

$$\frac{\partial c_1}{\partial q_1} = \frac{\partial c_2}{\partial q_2}$$

i.e. the marginal costs of the two firms will be equal at the optimal outputs. While this collusion of the two firms ensures that their joint profits are maximised and in general higher than if the outcome was a non-cooperative Cournot–Nash equilibrium, nevertheless the firms in general will need to come to some agreement on the distribution of these profits. In general there would need to be 'side-payments' of profits from one firm to another. ∎

3 Monopoly in the Input Market

3.1 The Conventional Trade Union Model

12.20 If a union is a monopoly supplier of labour to a firm, then we can apply the monopoly pricing model to the union's determination of the optimal wage. Suppose the union has L members and any member not employed by the firm can earn the competitive wage $\bar{w}$ elsewhere. Let us assume that the union's objective is to maximise the total income of its membership, hence writing l for the number of members employed in the industry at wage w, the objective is to maximise

$$wl + (L - l)\bar{w}$$
$$= (w - \bar{w})l + \bar{w}L$$

We can note immediately that as all members are assured of wage $\bar{w}$ elsewhere, the union must choose w to be no less than w.

Let $\pi(w)$ be the sum of the profit functions of all firms in the industry, other price variables in the function being left implicit at this stage. By Hotelling's Lemma, if w is the wage set by the union, then the demand for the labour will be given by

$$l = -\frac{\partial \pi}{\partial w}$$

Hence the union's objective is to maximise

$$(w - \bar{w})\frac{\partial \pi}{\partial w} + \bar{w}L$$

subject to $w \geq \bar{w}$ (we assume throughout this section that $\pi(w)$ is such that this objective is concave). If the optimal w is greater than $\bar{w}$ it must be a stationary point of this function and thus satisfies

$$-\frac{\partial \pi}{\partial w} - (w - \bar{w})\frac{\partial^2 \pi}{\partial w^2} = 0$$

hence

$$w = \bar{w} - \frac{\partial \pi / \partial w}{\partial^2 \pi / \partial w^2} \qquad\blacksquare$$

3.2 Contract Length

12.22 Generally labour contracts are relatively short compared to the life of capital and the union has an opportunity to fix wages when capital is fixed. If there are no binding labour contracts, the union can (re-)negotiate wages once the firm has invested in a fixed capital level. In this case the labour demand is given by the restricted profit function.

To illustrate this situation consider the restricted profit function

$$\pi(p,w,r,k) = Ap^\alpha w^{-\varepsilon}k^\delta - rk$$

where $\varepsilon > 0, 0 < \delta < 1$. We shall assume here that p is fixed and independent of w. One possible rationalisation of this simplifying assumption is that the price of the good is determined in a much larger international market. From the previous section we can conclude that the union would choose wage w where

$$\hat{w} = \bar{w} - \frac{\partial \pi / \partial w}{\partial^2 \pi / \partial w^2} = \bar{w} + \frac{\hat{w}}{\varepsilon + 1}$$

so that $\hat{w} = \bar{w}\left(1 + \dfrac{1}{\varepsilon}\right)$

We must now consider the implication of this choice of wages on the investment policy of the firm. Given that the firm recognises that the union will choose the wage in this manner, the firm will choose k to maximise $\pi(p, \hat{w}, r, k)$, i.e. it set $k = \hat{k}$ where

$$\hat{k} = \left(\frac{\delta A p^{\alpha}}{r \hat{w}^{\varepsilon}}\right)^{\gamma}$$

where $\gamma = \dfrac{1}{1 - \varepsilon}$. With this capital stock, profits will be equal to

$$\hat{\pi} = \left(\frac{1}{\delta} - 1\right) r \hat{k}$$

and employment will be

$$\hat{l} = -\frac{\partial \pi}{\partial w} = \frac{\varepsilon}{\delta} \frac{r}{\hat{w}} \hat{k}$$

Note the total income of the union's membership will be

$$\hat{Y} = \hat{l}\hat{w} + (L - \hat{l})\bar{w} = L\bar{w} + \hat{l}(\hat{w} - \bar{w})$$

$$= L\bar{w} + \hat{l}\frac{\bar{w}}{\varepsilon}$$

$$= L\bar{w} + \frac{\varepsilon}{\delta}\frac{1}{\varepsilon + 1} r\hat{k}$$

Compare this situation to that where the firm can negotiate a binding wage contract before it invests in its capital stock. In this situation the demand for labour and capital will be given by the unrestricted profit function. To generate results comparable to those above, let us consider the unrestricted profit function associated with the above restricted example, namely

$$\pi(p, w, r) = \left(\frac{1}{\delta} - 1\right) r \left[\frac{\delta A p^{\alpha}}{r w^{\varepsilon}}\right]^{\gamma}$$

where $\gamma = 1/(1 - \delta)$. Here the optimal wage $\bar{w}$ for the union will be

$$\hat{w} = \bar{w} - \frac{\partial \pi / \partial w}{\partial^2 \pi / \partial w^2} = \bar{w} + \frac{\bar{w}}{\varepsilon \gamma + 1}$$

so that

$$\hat{w} = \bar{w}\left(1 + \frac{1}{\varepsilon \gamma}\right)$$

As $\gamma > 1$ we can conclude $\hat{w} > \bar{w}$, i.e. the union sets a higher wage when there is no binding contract. Furthermore the optimal capital stock will be given by

$$\bar{k} = -\frac{\partial \pi}{\partial r} = \left[\frac{\delta A p^\alpha}{r \bar{w}^\varepsilon}\right]^\gamma$$

and $\bar{k} > \hat{k}$ as $\bar{w} < \hat{w}$, that is to say the firm will invest in less capital when there is no binding contract. The associated employment $\bar{l}$ is given by

$$\bar{l} = -\frac{\partial \pi}{\partial w} = \frac{\varepsilon}{\delta} \frac{r}{\bar{w}} \bar{k}$$

As $\bar{w} < \hat{w}$ and $\bar{k} > \hat{k}$ we can conclude $\bar{l} > \hat{l}$, i.e. there will be more employment when there are binding contracts. Similarly the firm's profits will be

$$\bar{\pi} = \left(\frac{1}{\delta} - 1\right) r\bar{k}$$

and $\bar{\pi} > \hat{\pi}$, i.e. profits are higher with binding contracts. Finally, the total income of the union's membership will be

$$\bar{Y} = L\bar{w} + \bar{l}(\hat{w} \quad \bar{w})$$

$$= L\bar{w} + \bar{l}\frac{\bar{w}}{\varepsilon \gamma}$$

$$= L\bar{w} + \frac{\varepsilon}{\delta} \frac{1}{\varepsilon \gamma + 1} r\bar{k}$$

It is not clear whether $\bar{Y}$ is less than or greater than $\hat{Y}$.   ■

3.3 A Two-Part Wage Schedule

12.21 Drawing out the analogy between the union and the monopolist selling a good to a consumer, we can anticipate that the union can extract all economic surplus, i.e. profits, from the firms in the industry by using a two-part wage structure. Let the union levy the firms in the industry a charge c as well as require a wage w for each unit of labour employed. Let $\pi(w)$ be the maximum profits the firms can attain before paying the fixed charge c, so that the firms' profit will be $\pi(w) - c$. The firms' demand for labour will be given as usual by $-\partial\pi/\partial w$. Hence the union's objective will be to choose w and c to maximise

$$Y = c + \bar{w}L - (w - \bar{w})\frac{\partial\pi}{\partial w}$$

subject to $\pi(w) - c \geq 0$ and $w \geq \bar{w}$. The first constraint arises from the fact that firms will not produce if their profits are zero.

As $\partial Y/\partial c > 0$ we can see that the unions will always choose $c = \pi(w)$ and thus leave the firms with no profits. Furthermore the wage rate will now be chosen so as to maximise

$$Y = \pi(w) + L\bar{w} - (w - \bar{w})\frac{\partial\pi}{\partial w}$$

If we take the price of the product as fixed independently of w, then $\pi(w)$ will be convex in w (see Chapter 11), hence $\pi(\bar{w}) \geq \pi(w) + (\bar{w} - w)\frac{\partial\pi}{\partial w} = \pi(w) - (w - \bar{w})\frac{\partial\pi}{\partial w}$.

In this situation

$$Y \leq \pi(\bar{w}) + L\bar{w}$$

and $\bar{w}$ is the optimal wage for the union. That is to say the optimal structure for the union is to charge the competitive wage for the labour and then levy a fixed charge equal to the ensuing 'profits' of the firms. ∎

3.4 Efficient Bargaining

12.23 In this section we shall consider a union bargaining with a monopolistic producer and we shall be concerned with efficient bargains. A bargain is efficient if it is *not* possible to increase one participant's objective without decreasing the objective of the other participant. An alternative characterisation of efficiency is that one objective function is at a maximum subject to a constraint on the value of the other objective function.

Consider the following form of the bargaining process between union and firm. The firm employs a given number of workers, l, and pays a certain sum to each worker. This sum paid to each worker can be broken down into two parts — a wage w satisfying

$$l = \frac{\partial\pi(w,r)}{\partial w}$$

and a supplement s. The bargain between union and firm determines w and

s. The firm's profit will be

$$\pi(w,r) - sl$$

i.e. the firm's objective function is

$$P = \pi(w,r) + s\frac{\partial \pi}{\partial w}$$

In modelling the preferences of the union we shall assume that it aims to maximise the sum of the utilities of its members. Assuming all members have identical preferences, and letting v be their common indirect utility function seen as a function of wages, then the union's objective function will be

$$u = lv(w + s) + (L - l)v(\bar{w})$$

Here, as before, L is the total membership of the union and $\bar{w}$ is the 'competitive' wage that members can guarantee to obtain elsewhere. An alternative form of this objective function is

$$u = Lv(\bar{w}) + l[v(w + s) - v(\bar{w})]$$

$$= Lv(\bar{w}) + \frac{\partial \pi}{\partial w}[v(w + s) - v(\bar{w})]$$

To characterise efficient bargains we can consider the problem of maximising the firm's net profit P subject to the constraint that the union's objective function being bounded below, i.e. $u \geq \bar{u}$ for some $\bar{u}$. This problem has Lagrangian

$$P + \lambda(u - \bar{u}) = \pi + s\frac{\partial \pi}{\partial w}$$

$$+ \lambda\left\{ Lv(w) - \frac{\partial \pi}{\partial w}[v(w + s) - v(\bar{w})]\right\}$$

In fact there will be further constraints on the problem, namely the non-negativity of w and s together with $w + s \geq \bar{w}$. We shall assume that these constraints are not binding, and shall concentrate on the stationarity of the Lagrangian which is as follows:

$$\frac{\partial P}{\partial w} + \lambda\frac{\partial u}{\partial w} = \frac{\partial \pi}{\partial w} + s\frac{\partial^2 \pi}{\partial w^2} + \lambda\left\{ -\frac{\partial \pi}{\partial w}v'(w + s)\right.$$

$$\left. - \frac{\partial^2 \pi}{\partial w^2}[v(w + s) - v(\bar{w})]\right\} = 0$$

and

$$\frac{\partial P}{\partial s} + \lambda\frac{\partial u}{\partial s} = \frac{\partial \pi}{\partial w} - \lambda\frac{\partial \pi}{\partial w}v'(w + s) = 0$$

Subtracting the second from the first equation we obtain

$$\frac{\partial^2 \pi}{\partial w^2} \left\{ s - \lambda[v(w+s) - v(\bar{w})] \right\} = 0$$

Assuming $\left. \dfrac{\partial^2 \pi}{\partial w^2} \right| \neq 0$ we obtain

$$s = \lambda[v(w+s) - v(\bar{w})]$$

From the second stationarity condition we obtain

$$\lambda = \frac{1}{v'(w+s)}$$

hence

$$s = \frac{v(w+s) - v(\bar{w})}{v'(w+s)}$$

If v is linear in wages then we obtain

$$s = w + s - \bar{w}$$

and thus

$$w = \bar{w}$$

i.e. the wage will be equal to the competitive wage and employment will be as if the firm was hiring in a competitive labour market.

Yet if v is concave in wages, then

$$v(\bar{w}) \leq v(w+s) + v'(w+s)[w - (w+s)]$$

hence

$$\frac{v(w+s) - v(\bar{w})}{v'(w+s)} \geq w + s - \bar{w}$$

and hence

$$s \geq w + s - \bar{w}$$

or

$$w \leq \bar{w}$$

We can note that if v is strictly concave and $w + s \neq \bar{w}$, then we have a strict inequality here. That is to say, with a concave v, wages w will be lower and employment higher with the bargain than they would be if the firm was hiring from a competitive labour market — note though that we would still have $w + s \geq \bar{w}$.

We can note that if we interpret v as a von Neumann–Morgenstern utility function embodying the union members' preferences toward risk, then the concavity of v would reflect the risk aversion of the members. We can thus interpret the last result as saying that the risk averse union members would aim to increase employment above the corresponding competitive level. ∎

Appendix

1 Introduction

The aim of this Appendix is threefold. Our first task is to offer a summary view of matrix algebra. We have been careful not to make use of matrices in the body of the text so that we could proceed relatively quickly to our major theme of optimisation and duality. Nevertheless, most economists will require some familiarity with matrix algebra and part one of this Appendix offers an introduction to the basic ideas.

In part two of the Appendix we offer a relatively formal review of differential calculus. In particular we offer a statement of Taylor's Theorem and indicate its use in discussing local optima. The reader may find it useful to read this part in conjunction with a re-reading of Part II of the text.

Part three of the Appendix summarises the ideas of trigonometric functions and complex numbers which are so useful for discussing dynamic models. It concludes with a discussion of second order difference equations.

PART ONE

2 Vectors and Matrices

A vector is an ordered set of numbers, so that one can refer to the first, second etc. elements of the vector. A *column* vector is such that we consider the numbers stacked in order vertically with the first element at the top. A *row* vector is such that we consider the numbers stacked in order horizontally with the first element on the left. Normally a vector is a column vector unless otherwise stated. Hence in this Appendix the appearance of a vector, **x** say, indicates a column vector. Given a column (row) vector **x** the *transpose* **x'** of the vector is the row (column) vector with the same elements in the same order. The *dimension* of a vector is the number of elements it contains. Hence if **x** is an n dimensional (column) vector, its transpose **x'** can be written as $(x_1, x_2, ..., x_n)$ where x_i $i = 1, 2, ..., n$ is the ith element of **x**.

A *matrix* can be viewed as an ordered set of column or row vectors. Alternatively it can be viewed as a two-dimensional array of numbers. We say a matrix A has dimensions $m \times n$ if it contains m row vectors each of dimension n or equivalently if it contains n column vectors each of dimension m. Alternatively A is $m \times n$ if it is viewed as a two-dimensional array with m rows and n columns. If we write a_{ij} for that element of A in the ith row and jth column then we visualise A as

$$\begin{bmatrix} a_{11} ..... a_{1j} ..... a_{1n} \\ a_{i1} ..... a_{ij} ..... a_{in} \\ a_{m1} ..... a_{mj} ..... a_{mn} \end{bmatrix}$$

Alternatively if we write $\mathbf{a}^j$ $j = 1...n$ as the jth column of A, so that the ith element of $\mathbf{a}^j$ is a_{ij}, then we can view A as the row of column vectors

$$[\mathbf{a}^1 ... \mathbf{a}^j ... \mathbf{a}^n]$$

Equally writing $\mathbf{a}_i$ for the ith row of A $i = 1...m$, so that the jth element of $\mathbf{a}_i$ is a_{ij}, then A can be viewed as the column of row vectors

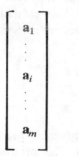

Note that both row and column vectors are examples of matrices. For example if **x** is an n dimensional vector then it is an $n \times 1$ matrix while its transpose **x'** is a $1 \times n$ matrix.

Given an $m \times n$ matrix A its transpose A' is the $n \times m$ matrix whose rows are equal to the columns of A. Hence if A has columns $\mathbf{a}^j$ $j = 1, ..., n$ then A' has rows equal to their transpose $\mathbf{a}^{j'}$ $j = 1...n$. Alternatively we have if

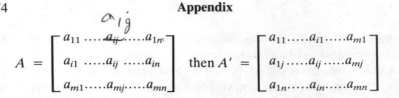

$$A = \begin{bmatrix} a_{11} \dots a_{ij} \dots a_{1n} \\ a_{i1} \dots a_{ij} \dots a_{in} \\ a_{m1} \dots a_{mj} \dots a_{mn} \end{bmatrix} \quad \text{then } A' = \begin{bmatrix} a_{11} \dots a_{i1} \dots a_{m1} \\ a_{1j} \dots a_{ij} \dots a_{mj} \\ a_{1n} \dots a_{in} \dots a_{mn} \end{bmatrix}$$

A matrix is said to be *square* if the number of its rows equals the number of its columns. In this Appendix we are primarily interested in square matrices. A square matrix A is said to be *symmetric* if it is equal to its own transpose, i.e. $A = A'$.

The following vectors and matrices are of special interest. We shall write $\mathbf{0}$ to denote the vector or matrix whose elements are all zero. Let $\mathbf{e}^{j}$ be the vector whose jth element is one and all other elements are zero, e.g. $\mathbf{e}^{1'} = (1,0\dots,0)$ and $\mathbf{e}^{n'} = (0,\dots,0,1)$. Finally we introduce the *identity* matrix I whose columns are $\mathbf{e}^{1}$ to $\mathbf{e}^{n}$. Hence we have

$$I = \begin{bmatrix} 1 & 0 \dots \dots 0 \\ 0 & 1 & \\ & & \ddots \\ 0 & 0 \dots \dots 1 \end{bmatrix}$$

An element of a square matrix lying in the ith row and ith column for some i is said to be on the *diagonal*. The elements not on the diagonal are non-diagonal or off-diagonal. A square matrix is said to be *diagonal* if all its off-diagonal elements are zero. We can see that I is a diagonal matrix with all diagonal elements equal to one.

3   Matrix Products

Given a row vector $\mathbf{x}'$ and a column vector $\mathbf{y}$ we define their (scalar) product to be the sum of the pairwise products of their elements. This product is represented simply by $\mathbf{x}'\mathbf{y}$ hence we have

$$\mathbf{x}'\mathbf{y} = \sum_{i=1}^{n} x_i y_i$$

Given two matrices A, B such that the number of columns in A is equal to the number of rows in B we define the product AB as follows:

Definition A.1: The i-jth element of AB is equal to the (scalar) product of the ith row of A with the jth column of B.

For example if

$$A = \begin{bmatrix} \alpha & \beta \\ \gamma & \delta \end{bmatrix}, \quad B = \begin{bmatrix} a & b \\ c & d \end{bmatrix}$$

then $AB = \begin{bmatrix} \alpha a + \beta c & \alpha b + \beta d \\ \gamma a + \delta b & \gamma b + \delta d \end{bmatrix}$

Note that this definition of matrix product can be applied to vectors. With a row vector $\mathbf{x}'$ and column vector $\mathbf{y}$ we need to be careful of the order in which we multiply them. For example if $\mathbf{x}' = (x_1, x_2)$ and

$\mathbf{y} = \begin{bmatrix} y_1 \\ y_2 \end{bmatrix}$ then

$$\mathbf{x}'\mathbf{y} = x_1 y_1 + x_2 y_2$$

i.e. we have the standard (scalar) product. But in contrast

$$\mathbf{y}\,\mathbf{x}' = \begin{bmatrix} y_1 \\ y_2 \end{bmatrix} [x_1 \quad x_2] = \begin{bmatrix} y_1 x_1 & y_1 x_2 \\ y_2 x_1 & y_2 x_2 \end{bmatrix}$$

i.e. this product generates a matrix, not a number. Indeed we must stress that in general the products AB and BA will differ, even if they are both defined.

We can note that the product of any (square) matrix A with the identity matrix is equal to A, i.e.

$IA = AI = A$

To see that IA is equal to A consider I as having rows $\mathbf{e}_i$ $i = 1...n$ where $\mathbf{e}_i$ has its ith element equal to one and other elements equal to zero. Now the i-jth element of IA is equal to the (scalar) product of $\mathbf{e}_i$ with the jth column $\mathbf{a}^j$ of A. But this product will be equal to the ith element of $\mathbf{a}^j$, i.e. $a_{ij} = i$-jth element of A. That is to say the i-jth element of IA is equal to the i-jth element of A. Similarly we can argue $AI = A$. It is this result which earns I the title of identity matrix.

Given a square matrix A, we say B is the *inverse* of A if its product with A is equal to the identity matrix, i.e.

$$AB = BA = I$$

We denote the inverse of A by A^{-1}. Not all square matrices have an inverse, for example $A = \begin{bmatrix} 1 & 0 \\ 0 & 0 \end{bmatrix}$ cannot have an inverse, for if $B =$

$\begin{bmatrix} a & b \\ c & d \end{bmatrix}$ then $AB = \begin{bmatrix} a & b \\ 0 & 0 \end{bmatrix}$ and $BA = \begin{bmatrix} a & 0 \\ c & 0 \end{bmatrix}$ neither of which

can be equal to I. If a (square) matrix has an inverse we say it is *invertible* or *non-singular*, if it does not have an inverse we say it is *singular*.

Consider an $n \times n$ matrix A and a n-vector $\mathbf{x}$, then the product $A\mathbf{x}$ is an n-vector whose ith element is the (scalar) product of the ith row of A with $\mathbf{x}$. That is to say the ith element of $A\mathbf{x}$ is

$$\sum_{j=1}^{n} a_{ij}x_j = a_{i1}x_1 + \ldots + a_{in}x_n$$

Hence if we consider the equation

$$A\mathbf{x} = \mathbf{b} \tag{A.1}$$

which says the elements of $A\mathbf{x}$ are equal respectively to those of $\mathbf{b}$, then one can rewrite it as

$$a_{i1}x_1 + \ldots + a_{in}x_n = b_i \qquad i = 1,\ldots,n$$

That is to say the relation (A.1) embodies a set of n simultaneous equations in the x_i's. We can immediately conclude that if the matrix A is non-singular then

$$\mathbf{x} = A^{-1}\mathbf{b}$$

This is obtained by multiplying both sides of (A.1) by A^{-1} and noting that the left-hand side becomes

$$A^{-1}A\mathbf{x} = I\mathbf{x} = \mathbf{x}$$

That is to say when we view (A.1) as a set of simultaneous equations in $\mathbf{x}$ and we know A is invertible, then we can conclude the equations have the unique solution $A^{-1}\mathbf{b}$.

To illustrate the possibilities when A is singular, consider the case where

$$A = \begin{bmatrix} 1 & 0 \\ 0 & 0 \end{bmatrix}. \text{ If } \mathbf{b} = \begin{bmatrix} 1 \\ 0 \end{bmatrix}$$

then the equation (A.1) becomes

$$\begin{bmatrix} 1 & 0 \\ 0 & 1 \end{bmatrix} \begin{bmatrix} x_1 \\ x_2 \end{bmatrix} = \begin{bmatrix} 1 \\ 0 \end{bmatrix}$$

or

$$x_1 + 0x_2 = 1$$
$$0x_1 + 0x_2 = 0$$

It follows that $x_1 = 1$ and that x_2 can take *any* possible value. That is to say there are an infinite number of solutions of the form $\mathbf{x} = \begin{bmatrix} 1 \\ x_2 \end{bmatrix}$ with x_2 arbitrary. In contrast if $\mathbf{b} = \begin{bmatrix} 1 \\ 1 \end{bmatrix}$ then the equations become

$$x_1 + 0x_2 = 1$$
$$0x_1 + 0x_2 = 1$$

but this last equation has no solution. That is to say no $\mathbf{x}$ satisfies this second equation and we must conclude there is no solution to the set of equations. This illustrates the fact that if A is singular, then (A.1) either has no solution or an infinite number of solutions.

In the light of this discussion of (A.1) we can ask the following question. Given a square matrix A, how might we decide whether A is singular or non-singular, and if it is non-singular how might we construct A^{-1}? We shall turn to this question in the next section on determinants.

4 Determinants

Given a square matrix A we can calculate a number det$A$, called the determinant of A, such that A is non-singular if and only if this determinant det$A$ is non-zero. This result is offered without proof or argument, and thus we concern ourselves primarily with indicating how this mysterious number is calculated.

Given a matrix A whose i-jth element is a_{ij}, we define the set of co-matrices as follows. The co-matrix A^{ij} associated with the element a_{ij} is the $(n-1) \times (n-1)$ matrix formed by deleting the ith row and jth column of A. For example if

$$A = \begin{bmatrix} a_{11} & a_{12} & a_{13} \\ a_{21} & a_{22} & a_{23} \\ a_{31} & a_{32} & a_{33} \end{bmatrix}$$

then

$$A^{11} = \begin{bmatrix} a_{22} & a_{23} \\ a_{32} & a_{33} \end{bmatrix}$$

and

$$A^{23} = \begin{bmatrix} a_{11} & a_{12} \\ a_{31} & a_{32} \end{bmatrix}$$

Now in defining and calculating the determinant det$A$ of a matrix A we do so recursively in that we define det$A$ in terms of the determinants of these co-matrices. Repeated use of this recursive definition will lead us to determinants of 1×1 matrices. But the determinant of a 1×1 matrix is simply equal to its unique element.

The determinant of a co-matrix is known as a *minor*, hence the i-jth minor of A is the determinant of the i-jth co-matrix. If we denote the determinant of a matrix by prefixing the term det, so that det$A$ is the determinant of A, then we can write the i-jth minor of A as detA^{ij}. To proceed we need one further idea, namely that of *co-factor*. The i-jth co-factor C^{ij} of matrix A is $(-1)^{i+j}$ times the i-jth minor, i.e.

$$C_{ij} = (-1)^{i+j} \det A^{ij}$$

With this notation and terminology we can define the determinant of A as

$$\det A = \sum_{j=1}^{n} a_{1j} C_{1j}$$

i.e. it is the sum of the products of the elements of the first row of A together with their respective co-factors. Note the determinant of a 1×1 matrix $[a]$ is simply the unique element a.

Hence if $A = \begin{bmatrix} a & b \\ c & d \end{bmatrix}$ our definition tells us

$$\det A = a(-1)^2 \det [d] + b(-1)^3 \det[c]$$
$$= ad - bc$$

An alternative notation for the determinant of a matrix is to replace the square brackets of the matrix notation by straight lines. Thus if

$A = \begin{bmatrix} a & b \\ c & d \end{bmatrix}$ we could write $\det A = \begin{vmatrix} a & b \\ c & d \end{vmatrix}$ Our definition thus says

$$\begin{vmatrix} a & b \\ c & d \end{vmatrix} = a(-1)^2|d| + b(-1)^3\, c$$

$$= ad - bc$$

Applying this notation and definition to $A = \begin{bmatrix} a & b & c \\ d & e & f \\ g & h & i \end{bmatrix}$

we obtain

$$\det A = a(-1)^2 \begin{vmatrix} e & f \\ h & i \end{vmatrix} + b(-1)^3 \begin{vmatrix} d & f \\ g & i \end{vmatrix}$$

$$+ c(-1)^4 \begin{vmatrix} d & e \\ g & h \end{vmatrix}$$

$$= a(ei - hf) - b(di - gf) + c(dh - ge)$$

We can note that we can calculate $\det A$ by 'expanding' along any row or indeed along any 'column'. For we have

$$\det A = \sum_{j=1}^{n} a_{ij}C_{ij} \quad \text{for all } i$$

and

$$\det A = \sum_{i=1}^{n} a_{ij}C_{ij} \quad \text{for all } j$$

For example if $A = \begin{bmatrix} a & b \\ c & d \end{bmatrix}$ and we 'expand' along the second row we obtain

$$\det A = c(-1)^3 \det[b] + d(-1)^4 \det[a]$$

$$= -cb + ad$$

$$= ad - bc$$

Or if we 'expand' along the first column we have

$$\det A = a(-1)^2 \det[d] + c(-1)^2 \det[b]$$

$$= ad - bc$$

as before.

For example if $A = \begin{bmatrix} 2 & 1 & 3 \\ 5 & 0 & -2 \\ -2 & 0 & 1 \end{bmatrix}$

we can expand $\det A$ along the second column to obtain

$$\det A = 1(-1)^3 \begin{vmatrix} 5 & -2 \\ -2 & 1 \end{vmatrix} = -1(5 - 4) = -1$$

From the result stated at the beginning of this section we can conclude that this matrix is non-singular, i.e. its inverse exists.

A further useful result is the following. If $j \neq k$ then

$$\sum_{i=1}^{n} a_{ij}C_{ik} = 0$$

or if $i \neq k$ then

$$\sum_{j=1}^{n} a_{ij}C_{kj} = 0$$

Note in these sums the co-factors do not match the respective elements: in the first sum we are using co-factors associated with a different column, and in the second the co-factors arise from a different row. These sums are described as expansions by *alien co-factors* and the equations above tell us that such alien expansions are always zero.

To illustrate these results consider the case where $A = \begin{bmatrix} a & b \\ c & d \end{bmatrix}$

then we have

$$\sum_{i=1}^{2} a_{i1}C_{i2} = a(-1)^3 \det[c] + c(-1)^4 \det[a]$$

$$= - ac + ac = 0$$

and

$$\sum_{j=1}^{2} a_{1j}C_{2j} = a(-1)^3 \det[b] + b(-1)^4 \det[a]$$

$$= - ab + ba = 0$$

Given a non-singular matrix A, consider the matrix B whose i-jth element is equal to the j-ith co-factor C_{ji} of A divided by $\det A = D$, say. Consider the product AB whose i-jth element is given by the (scalar) product of the ith row of A and the jth column of B, i.e.

$$[AB]_{ij} = \sum_{k=1}^{n} a_{ik}[B]_{kj}$$

$$= \frac{\sum_{k=1}^{n} a_{ik} C_{jk}}{D}$$

$$= \frac{\sum_{k=1}^{n} a_{ik} C_{jk}}{D}$$

From the above discussion we can see that if $i \neq j$, then we have an alien expansion and thus the i-jth element is zero. Yet if $i = j$ then we can see that the sum in the numerator is simply $D = \det A$, hence $[AB]_{ii} = 1$ for $i = 1 \ldots n$. We can conclude that $AB = I$. In a similar fashion we obtain $BA = I$. That is to say B is the inverse of A, i.e. the inverse of A has i-jth element equal to the j-ith co-factor C_{ji} of A divided by the determinant of A.

For example if $A = \begin{bmatrix} a & b \\ c & d \end{bmatrix}$ the determinant is $D = ad - bc$ and the

co-factors form the matrix $\begin{bmatrix} d & -c \\ -b & a \end{bmatrix}$

Hence A^{-1} is the transpose of the matrix with each element divided by D (assuming this is non-zero), i.e.

$$A^{-1} = \begin{bmatrix} d/D & -b/D \\ -c/D & a/D \end{bmatrix}$$

More specifically if $A = \begin{bmatrix} 1 & -2 \\ 3 & 4 \end{bmatrix}$ then $\det A = 4 + 6 = 10$ and the co-factor

matrix is $\begin{bmatrix} 4 & -3 \\ 2 & 1 \end{bmatrix}$ and the inverse is $A^{-1} = \begin{bmatrix} \frac{4}{10} & \frac{2}{10} \\ -\frac{3}{10} & \frac{1}{10} \end{bmatrix} = \begin{bmatrix} 0.4 & 0.2 \\ -0.3 & 0.1 \end{bmatrix}$

This can be confirmed by multiplying out AA^{-1} and $A^{-1}A$.

To complete this section we reconsider the problem of finding a solution to the equation

$$Ax = b$$

If $\det A \neq 0$ then we know A^{-1} exists and that the solution is $x = A^{-1}b$. Hence

$$x_i = \sum_{j=1}^{n} b_j [A^{-1}]_{ij}$$

$$= \frac{\sum_{j=1}^{n} b_j C_{ji}}{D}$$

But the numerator of this last expression is the determinant of the matrix obtained by replacing the ith column of A by b. Hence we can say the solution is given by

$$x_i = \frac{\begin{vmatrix} a_{11} \ldots\ldots b_1 \ldots\ldots a_{1n} \\ \vdots \qquad\qquad \vdots \\ a_{n1} \ldots\ldots b_n \ldots\ldots a_{nn} \end{vmatrix}}{\begin{vmatrix} a_{11} \ldots\ldots a_{1i} \ldots a_{1n} \\ \vdots \qquad\qquad \vdots \\ a_{n1} \ldots\ldots a_{ni} \ldots a_{nn} \end{vmatrix}}$$

This is known as Cramer's Rule.

5   Quadratic Forms

A symmetric $n \times n$ matrix is said to be *positive semi-definite* if for all non-zero n-vectors $\mathbf{x}$ we have $\mathbf{x}^T A \mathbf{x} \geq 0$. If we can replace this inequality by $\mathbf{x}^T A \mathbf{x} > 0$ for all $\mathbf{x} \neq 0$ then we say A is *positive definite*. Equally if $\mathbf{x}^T A \mathbf{x} \leq 0$ for all $\mathbf{x} \neq 0$ we say A is *negative semi-definite* while it is *negative definite* if $\mathbf{x}^T A \mathbf{x} < 0$ for all $\mathbf{x} \neq 0$.

Given a square matrix A, its principal leading minors are the determinants of the $k \times k$ sub-matrices formed by the intersection of the first k rows and k columns of A, $k = 1,\ldots,n$. Or equivalently the determinants of the sub-matrices obtained by deleting the last $n\text{-}k$ rows and last $n\text{-}k$ columns. Thus if

$$A = \begin{bmatrix} a_{11} \ldots\ldots a_{1n} \\ \vdots \qquad \vdots \\ a_{n1} \ldots\ldots a_{nn} \end{bmatrix}$$

then the principal leading minors are

$$m_1 = |a_{11}| = a_{11}$$

$$m_2 = \begin{vmatrix} a_{11} & a_{12} \\ a_{21} & a_{22} \end{vmatrix}$$

$$m_3 = \begin{vmatrix} a_{11} & a_{12} & a_{13} \\ a_{21} & a_{22} & a_{23} \\ a_{31} & a_{32} & a_{33} \end{vmatrix}$$

and

$$m_k = \begin{vmatrix} a_{11} \ldots\ldots a_{1k} \\ \vdots \qquad \vdots \\ a_{k1} \ldots\ldots a_{kk} \end{vmatrix}$$

We state without proof the following result.

Theorem A.1: A symmetric $n \times n$ matrix A is positive definite if and only if all its principal leading minors are positive. Furthermore A is negative definite if and only if its kth principal leading minor has the same sign as $(-1)^k$ $k = 1,...,n$.

For example $A = \begin{bmatrix} -1 & 1 \\ 1 & -2 \end{bmatrix}$ has principal leading minors $m_1 = -1 < 0$

and $m_2 = \begin{vmatrix} -1 & 1 \\ 1 & -2 \end{vmatrix} = 1 > 0$ and thus A is negative definite. Yet $A =$

$\begin{bmatrix} 1 & 0 \\ 0 & 0 \end{bmatrix}$ has principal leading minors $m_1 = 1 > 0$ and $m_2 = 0$ and is thus *not*

positive definite, though in fact it is positive semi-definite.

Note that if e^i is the standard vector with its ith element equal to one and all others zero then $e^{i'} A e^i = a_{ii}$, the ith diagonal element of A. It follows that A is negative (positive) definite only if all its diagonal elements are negative (positive). Equally it is negative (positive) semi-definite only if all its diagonal elements are non-positive (non-negative).

PART TWO

6 Length, Distance and Open Sets

In the case of two dimensions, it is possible to give simple geometric interpretations of a vector — indeed these are two such interpretations. For a vector can be thought of as a point and/or as a line of particular length and direction. In Figure A.1 we have plotted the point P with coordinates x_1, x_2 and this point P can be seen representing the vector $\begin{bmatrix} x_1 \\ x_2 \end{bmatrix}$ But we have also drawn the line OP from the origin to the point P and we can consider this line as representing the same vector $\begin{bmatrix} x_1 \\ x_2 \end{bmatrix}$ Most of the time we tend to identify vectors with points such as P, but the alternative view leads naturally to the idea of our discussing the *length* of a vector. In Figure A.1 we can consider OP as the hypotenuse of the right-angle triangle OQP. Now the lengths of the lines OQ and QP are clearly x_1 and x_2 respectively, hence by Pythagoras' Theorem the length of OP is $\sqrt{(x_1^2 + x_i^2)} = \sqrt{(x'x)}$ where $x =$

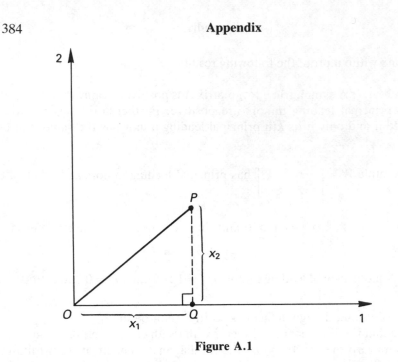

Figure A.1

$\begin{bmatrix} x_1 \\ x_2 \end{bmatrix}$. Similarly, more complex geometric arguments allow us to assert that in three dimensions the length of a vector $\mathbf{x}$ is $\sqrt{(\mathbf{x}'\mathbf{x})}$. Hence we extend these geometric ideas to the general case with the following definition.

Definition A.2: Given an n dimensional vector $\mathbf{x}$ with elements $x_i \, i = 1,\ldots,n$ the length of the vector is denoted by $|\mathbf{x}|$ and is given by the following expression:

$$|\mathbf{x}| = (\sum_{i=1}^{n} x_i^2)^{1/2} = (\mathbf{x}'\mathbf{x})^{1/2}$$

The most important use of this idea is to give meaning to the idea of the distance between two vectors (now viewed as points).

Definition A.3: Given two n-vectors $\mathbf{x},\mathbf{y}$ the distance from y to x is defined as the length of the vector $\mathbf{x} - \mathbf{y}$, i.e.

$$|\mathbf{x} - \mathbf{y}| = [\sum_{i=1}^{n} (x_i - y_i)^2]^{1/2}$$

Given a point $\mathbf{x}$, its open neighbourhood N_ε of radius $\varepsilon > 0$ is the set of all points whose distance from $\mathbf{x}$ is less than ε. Hence

$$N_\varepsilon = \{y : |x - y| < \varepsilon\}$$

For example, in two dimensions the neighbourhood N_ε of x is the set of points inside the circle of radius $\varepsilon > 0$ and centred at x, see Figure A.2.

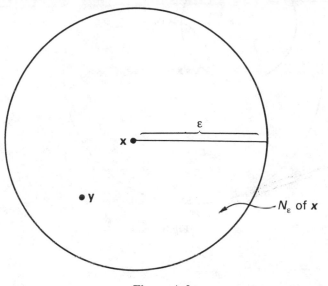

Figure A.2

A set S is *open* if for all points x in S we can find some neighbourhood N_ε of x contained in S, that is to say there is some $\varepsilon > 0$ such that if the distance of y from x is less than ε, then y is contained in S. Formally put, S is open if for all x in S there is a $\varepsilon > 0$ such that the neighbourhood N_ε of x is contained in S. The intuitive significance of openness is that if we imagine ourselves at a point in an open set, then we can move some distance in any direction without leaving the set. We note that neighbourhoods N_ε are themselves open sets, see Figure A.3. The set of points on or above the horizontal axis is not open because every neighbourhood of a point on the axis contains points below the axis, see Figure A.4.

These ideas can be used to give formal expression to the idea of a continuous function. Intuitively a function $f(x)$ is continuous on its (open) domain if there are no sharp jumps or breaks in the value of the function as x moves about the domain. Alternatively expressed, this means that for any point x in the domain we can ensure that value $f(y)$ at a point y is as close to $f(x)$ as we may desire by choosing y sufficiently close to x. Formally put, we say f is continuous at x if for any $\delta > 0$ there is a neighbourhood N_ε of x such that if y is in N_ε then $|f(y) - f(x)| < \delta$, i.e. $f(y)$ is in

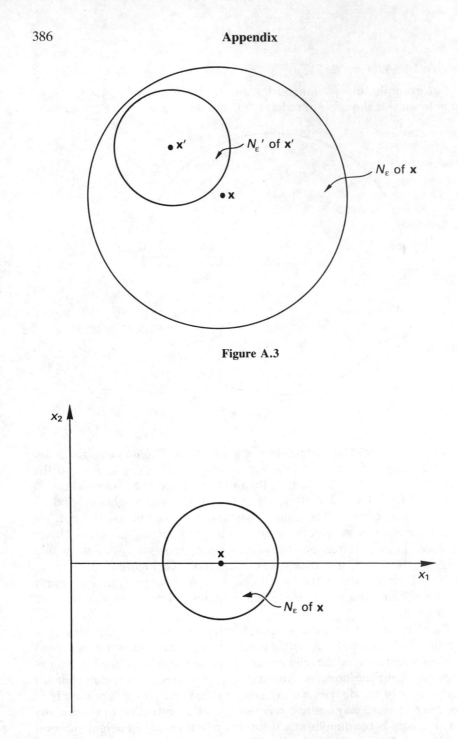

Figure A.3

Figure A.4

the neighbourhood N_δ of $f(x)$. We can note that all differentiable functions are continuous.

7 Convex Sets and Concave Functions

A set of S of vectors, viewed as points, is said to be *convex* if the straight line between any two points in the set is itself contained in the set. Formally speaking this means that for all x, y in S and all real numbers λ satisfying $0 \le \lambda \le 1$, the vector $z = \lambda x + (1 - \lambda)y$ is contained in S. Note that the ith element of the vector z is $\lambda x_i + (1 - \lambda)y_i$.

A function $f(x)$ *defined on a convex domain* is concave if for all x,y and $z = \lambda x + (1 - \lambda)y$ where $0 \le \lambda \le 1$ we have

$$f(z) \ge \lambda f(x) + (1 - \lambda)f(y) \tag{A.2}$$

(See Chapter 7.) It is to be stressed that when we speak of a concave (or convex) function we are implicitly assuming that its domain is convex.

Figure A.5(a) illustrates the standard examples of convex sets in the two-dimensional space, while Figure A.5(b) illustrates sets which are *not* convex.

A function $f(x)$ defined on a convex set is said to be quasi-concave if for all x^* in the domain of f

$$[x: f(x) \ge f(x^*)] \text{ is convex} \tag{A.3}$$

An equivalent characterisation of quasi-concavity is that for all x,y in the domain of f and all λ satisfying $0 \le \lambda \le 1$ we have

$$f(z) \ge \min[f(x), f(y)] \tag{A.4}$$

where $z = x + (1 - \lambda)y$. To show the equivalence of (A.3) and (A.4) we proceed as follows. To deduce (A.4) from (A.3) we note that for any x,y in the domain of f either $f(x) \ge f(y)$ or vice versa, and thus we can assume $f(x) \ge f(y)$ without any loss of generality. Consider now the set

$$S = [z: f(z) \ge f(y)]$$

which (A.3) tells us is convex. Furthermore, x,y are both contained in S; hence $z = \lambda x + (1 - \lambda)y$ for all λ satisfying $0 \le \lambda \le 1$ is contained in S, hence

$$f(z) \ge f(y) = \min[f(x), f(y)]$$

To deduce (A.3) from (A.4) we consider the set

$$S = [x: f(x) \ge f(x^*)]$$

for some x^* in the domain of f. If x, y are both in S then $f(x) \ge f(x^*)$ and $f(y) \ge f(x^*)$ and thus

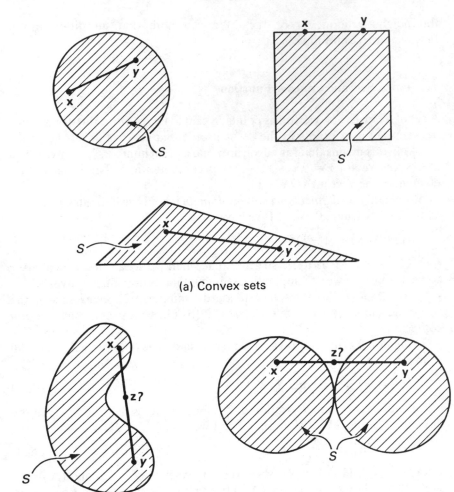

(a) Convex sets

(b) Non-convex sets

Figure A.5

$$\min [f(\mathbf{x}), f(\mathbf{y})] \geqslant f(\mathbf{x}^*)$$

From (A.4) we can conclude that for any convex combination $\mathbf{z} = \lambda\mathbf{x} + (1 - \lambda)\mathbf{y}, 0 \leqslant \lambda \leqslant 1$ we have

$$f(\mathbf{z}) \geqslant f(\mathbf{x}^*)$$

hence $\mathbf{z}$ is in S and S is convex.

Note that the concavity condition (A.2) implies (A.4) because as $\lambda \geqslant 0$

and $(1 - \lambda) \geqslant 0$, then $\lambda f(\mathbf{x}) + (1 - \lambda)f(\mathbf{y}) \geqslant \min[f(\mathbf{x}), f(\mathbf{y})]$. That is to say concave functions are quasi-concave.

It follows that the condition (A.3) is true for concave f. Hence if $F(\mathbf{x}) = g[f(\mathbf{x})]$ is indirectly concave with f concave and g monotonic then we have, for all $\mathbf{x}^*$ in the domain of F

$$[\mathbf{x}:F(\mathbf{x}) \geqslant F(\mathbf{x}^*)] = [\mathbf{x}:f(\mathbf{x}) \geqslant f(\mathbf{x}^*)]$$

because of the monotonicity of g. Hence these sets are convex and we conclude all indirectly concave functions are quasi-concave.

8   Differentiation: The One-Variable Case

In this section we consider a real valued function f of a single variable x. We shall assume f is defined on an open set of numbers, hence for any x in the domain we can decrease or increase its value without leaving the domain. For example, if we choose h sufficiently small, without necessarily being zero, we can be confident that $x + h$ lies in the domain of f. We say f is differentiable at x if the quotient $[f(x + h) - f(x)]/h$ converges to some finite number as h approaches zero. We denote this number by $f'(x)$ and it is called the derivative of f at x. To say the quotient converges to the derivative means that the difference between the quotient and derivative can be made as small as we like by choosing h sufficiently small. We can denote this by writing

$$\left| \frac{f(x + h) - f(x)}{h} \quad f'(x) \right| \to 0 \quad \text{as} \quad h \to 0$$

or

$$\left| \frac{f(x + h) - f(x) - f'(x)h}{h} \right| \to 0 \quad \text{as} \quad h \to 0 \tag{A.5}$$

Consider now Figure A.6 where we have drawn the graph of some function f together with the graph of the linear function mapping h, this being measured from x, onto $f(x) + f'(x)h$. We can ask whether we can use this linear function as an approximation to f around x? Now the error in using this approximation at $x + h$ would be

$$\text{error} = f(x + h) - f(x) - f'(x)h \tag{A.6}$$

Hence we can view (A.5) as saying that

$$\left| \frac{\text{error}}{h} \right| \to 0 \quad \text{as} \quad h \to 0$$

i.e. the error goes to zero faster than h or the *relative error*, error/h, goes to zero as h goes to zero.

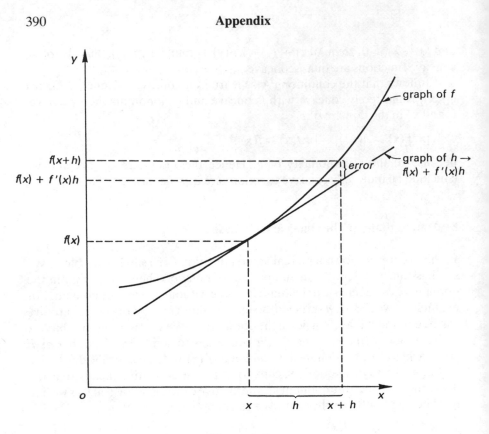

Figure A.6

Now turning (A.6) around we have

$$f(x + h) - f(x) = f'(x)h + \text{error}$$

$$= [f'(x) + \text{relative error}]h \qquad (A.7)$$

It follows that if $f'(x) \neq 0$ then for sufficiently small h we will have

$$\text{sign of } [f'(x) + \text{relative error}] = \text{sign of } f'(x)$$

and for $h > 0$

$$\text{sign of } f(x + h) - f(x) = \text{sign of } f'(x)$$

Hence if $f'(x) \neq 0$, we can deduce the sign of changes in the value of f for sufficiently small changes in its argument. It is to be stressed that we are here able to make conclusions about the value of the function in the neighbourhood of x on the basis of the single number $f'(x)$.

In answering our above question, we can conclude that if $f'(x) \neq 0$ then $f(x) + f'(x)h$ is a 'good' linear approximation of f around x. But if $f'(x) = 0$, i.e. x is a stationary point of f, this is no longer the case. Indeed in this situation (A.7) becomes

$$f(x + h) - f(x) = \text{error}$$

and the linear approximation tells us nothing. Given this it is natural to ask whether we can use a quadratic approximation to f, or indeed higher order polynomial approximations. The answer to this question is given by the following result.

Taylor's Theorem
If f has derivative of order $n + 1$ everywhere in the neighbourhood of x, then for $x + h$ in that neighbourhood we have

$$f(x + h) = f(x) + \frac{f'(x)h}{1!} + \frac{f''(x)h^2}{2!} + \dots$$

$$\dots + \frac{f^{(n)}(x)h^n}{n!} + \text{error}$$

or

$$f(x + h) = f(x) + \sum_{k=1}^{n} \frac{f^{(k)}(x)h^k}{k!} + \text{error}$$

where

$$\left| \frac{\text{error}}{h^n} \right| \to 0 \quad \text{as} \quad h \to 0$$

Here $f^{(k)}(x)$ denotes the kth derivative of f at x, while $k!$ is k *factorial* and is equal to $k(k - 1)\dots2.1$.

In particular we have if f is three times differentiable, then

$$f(x + h) = f(x) + f'(x)h + \frac{1}{2} f''(x)h^2 + \text{error}$$

where $\left| \frac{\text{error}}{h^2} \right| \to 0$ as $h \to 0$. Hence if we have a turning point, i.e. $f'(x) = 0$ but $f''(x) \neq 0$ then

$$f(x + h) - f(x) = \frac{1}{2} f''(x)h^2 + \text{error}$$

$$= \left[\frac{1}{2} f''(x) + \frac{\text{error}}{h^2} \right] h^2$$

where $\dfrac{\text{error}}{h^2} \to 0$ as $h \to 0$. Hence for sufficiently small h the term in parenthesis will have the same sign as $f''(x)$ and thus for sufficiently small h the sign of $f(x + h) - f(x)$ will be equal to the sign of $f''(x)$. For example, if $f''(x)$ is negative, then for sufficiently small h $f(x + h) < f(x)$ and x will be a local maximum.

Next we show that if f is a twice differentiable concave function, then we must have $f''(x) \leqslant 0$ for all x in the domain of f. We have seen in Chapter 7 that if f is concave then

$$f(x + h) \leqslant f(x) + f'(x)h$$

and

$$f(x) \leqslant f(x + h) + f'(x + h)(-h)$$

Adding the right- and left-hand sides of these inequalities and cancelling terms common to both sides we obtain

$$[f'(x) - f'(x + h)]h \geqslant 0$$

Multiplying by $-\dfrac{1}{h^2}$ gives us

$$\frac{f'(x + h) - f'(x)}{h} \leqslant 0$$

Letting $h \to 0$ gives $f''(x)$ on the left-hand side and we conclude $f''(x) \leqslant 0$.

If we return to Taylor's Theorem and set $x = 0$ in the nth order approximation we obtain

$$f(h) = f(0) + \sum_{k=1}^{n} \frac{f^{(k)}(0)h^k}{k!} + \text{error}$$

or with $h = x$ we obtain

$$f(x) = f(0) + \sum_{k=1}^{n} \frac{f^{(k)}(0)x^k}{k!} + \text{error}$$

This is the nth order Maclaurin expansion for $f(x)$. If we assume f has continuous nth order derivatives for *all* positive n, then we can consider what happens to this expansion as n approaches infinity. If the error goes to zero as n approaches infinity, then we can say that

$$f(x) = f(0) + \sum_{k=1}^{\infty} \frac{f^{(k)}(0)x^k}{k!}$$

and we obtain an expression for $f(x)$ as an infinite series.

A special case of this sort of series is the case where $f(x) = e^x$ in which case $f^{(k)}(x) = e^x$ for all k, hence $f^{(k)}(0) = 1$ for all k and we have

$$e^x = 1 + \sum_{k=1}^{\infty} \frac{x^k}{k!}$$

$$= 1 + \frac{x}{1!} + \frac{x^2}{2!} + \frac{x^3}{3!} + \ldots$$

this holding for all x.

Equally if we consider $f(x) = \ln(1 + x)$ then $f'(x) = (1 + x)^{-1}$, $f^{(2)}(x) = (-1)(1 + x)^{-2}$, $f^{(3)} = (-1)^2 \, 2(1 + x)^{-3} \, f^{(4)}(x) = (-1)^3 \, 3!(1 + x)^{-4}, \ldots, f^{(k)}(x) = (-1)^{k-1}(k - 1)!(1 + x)^{-k}$. Hence $f^{(k)}(0) = (-1)^{k-1}(k - 1)!$ and

$$\ln(1 + x) = 0 + \sum_{k=1}^{\infty} \frac{(-1)^{k-1}(k - 1)!x^k}{k!}$$

$$= \sum_{k=1}^{\infty} \frac{(-1)^{k-1}x^k}{k}$$

$$= x - \frac{x^2}{2} + \frac{x^3}{3} - \frac{x^4}{4} + \ldots$$

9 Differentiation: Several Variables

As before we write e^i for the n-vector with its ith element equal to one and all other elements equal to zero. Hence $x + he^i$ has the same elements as x apart from its ith which will be $x_i + h$. Given a function $f(x)$ of the n variables x we can consider the function mapping h onto $f(x + he^i)$ as the ith partial function of f at x. The ith partial derivative of f at x is then the derivative, if it exists, of this partial function at $h = 0$. The function mapping x onto the ith partial derivative is the ith partial derivative function and is denoted by f_i'. If all the partial derivative functions of f are defined and continuous in a neighbourhood of x, we say f is *continuously differentiable* at x.

We shall write $f'(x)$ to denote the *row* vector whose ith component is $f_i'(x)$. Hence if h is a column vector, then

$$f'(x)h = \sum_{k=1}^{n} f_i'(x)h_i$$

If f is continuously differentiable at x, then we have the following result:

$$\frac{f(x + h) - f(x) - f'(x)h}{|h|} \to 0 \quad \text{as} \quad |h| \to 0$$

alternatively put this says

$$f(x + h) - f(x) = f'(x)h + \text{error} \tag{A.8}$$

where the relative error $= \dfrac{\text{error}}{|\mathbf{h}|} \to 0$ as $|\mathbf{h}| \to 0$

Given a function f of n variables and a vector v such that $[f(\mathbf{x} + h v) - f(\mathbf{x})]/h$ converges as $h \to 0$, the limit is known as the directional derivative of f at $\mathbf{x}$ in the direction of $\mathbf{v}$. From (A.8) we can see that if f is continuously differentiable at $\mathbf{x}$, then the directional derivative of f at $\mathbf{x}$ exists for all directions $\mathbf{v}$ and is equal to $f'(\mathbf{x})\mathbf{v}$. To confirm this let $\mathbf{h} = h\mathbf{v}$ in (A.8), divide by h and then let $h \to 0$, in which case $|\mathbf{h}| = h|\mathbf{v}| \to 0$ also.

If we put $\mathbf{h} = h\mathbf{v}$ in (A.8) we obtain

$$f(\mathbf{x} + h\mathbf{v}) - f(\mathbf{x}) = [f'(\mathbf{x})\mathbf{v} + \frac{\text{error}}{h}]h$$

where $\dfrac{\text{error}}{h} \to 0$ as $h \to 0$. Hence if $f'(\mathbf{x})\mathbf{v} \neq 0$, then for sufficiently small positive h the sign of $f(\mathbf{x} + h\mathbf{v}) - f(\mathbf{x})$ will be equal to the sign of $f'(\mathbf{x})\mathbf{v}$. In particular if $f'(\mathbf{x}) \neq \mathbf{0}$, i.e. at least one of the partial derivatives of f is non-zero, then it is possible to choose $\mathbf{v}$ so that $f'(\mathbf{x})\mathbf{v} \neq 0$ and hence $\mathbf{x}$ cannot be a maximum or minimum. Should $f'(\mathbf{x}) = \mathbf{0}$, then this first order approximation tells us nothing about the way f varies near to $\mathbf{x}$.

Again in these circumstances we can consider a 'quadratic' approximation to which we now turn.

A function f is twice continuously differentiable at $\mathbf{x}$ if the partial derivative functions f''_{ij} of the partial derivatives f'_i exist and are continuous in a neighbourhood of $\mathbf{x}$. We say denote by $f''(\mathbf{x})$ the $n \times n$ matrix whose $i-j$th component is $f''_{ij}(\mathbf{x})$. This matrix is known as the *Hessian* of f at $\mathbf{x}$. We state without proof the following result:

Young's Theorem:
If f is twice continuously differentiable at $\mathbf{x}$, then the Hessian $f''(\mathbf{x})$ at $\mathbf{x}$ is symmetric, i.e.

$$f''_{ij}(\mathbf{x}) = f''_{ji}(\mathbf{x})$$

Furthermore we have

Taylor's Theorem (2nd order)
If f is three times continuously differentiable, i.e. the second partial functions $f''_{ij}(\mathbf{x})$ are continuously differentiable, then

$$f(\mathbf{x} + \mathbf{h}) = f(\mathbf{x}) + f'(\mathbf{x})\mathbf{h} + \frac{1}{2}\mathbf{h}'f''(\mathbf{x})\mathbf{h} + \text{error}$$

where $\dfrac{\text{error}}{|\mathbf{h}|^2} \to 0$ as $|\mathbf{h}| \to 0$

In particular if $\mathbf{x}$ is a stationary point, so that $f'(\mathbf{x}) = \mathbf{0}$, with a negative definite Hessian, i.e. $\mathbf{h}'f''(\mathbf{x})\mathbf{h} < 0$ for all $\mathbf{h} \neq \mathbf{0}$, then we can conclude that the sign of $f(\mathbf{x} + \mathbf{h}) - f(\mathbf{x})$ is negative for sufficiently small $\mathbf{h}$, i.e. $f(\mathbf{x})$ is a local maximum.

Indeed we can state the following result:

Second order conditions for a local maximum:
Given a three times continuously differentiable function $f(\mathbf{x})$, a necessary condition for a stationary point $\mathbf{x}^0$ to be a local maximum is that the Hessian $f''(\mathbf{x}^0)$ of f at $\mathbf{x}^0$ be negative semi-definite. Furthermore, sufficient conditions for $\mathbf{x}^0$ to be a local maximum is that $f'(\mathbf{x}^0) = \mathbf{0}$ and $f''(\mathbf{x}^0)$ be negative definite.

Furthermore we have:

Necessary and sufficient conditions for concavity:
If $f(\mathbf{x})$ is twice continuously differentiable, then f is concave if and only if its Hessian $f''(\mathbf{x})$ is negative semi-definite at all points in its domain. A sufficient condition for f to be strictly concave is that the Hessian be negative definite everywhere in the domain.

These results become operational when combined with the results in Section 5.

Related results hold for quasi-concavity, though we have to use the bordered Hessian. Given a twice differentiable function $f(\mathbf{x})$ defined on the non-negative orthant, i.e. where $x_i \geqslant 0$ $i = 1,...,n$, we have the following:

A necessary and sufficient condition for $f(\mathbf{x})$ to be *quasi-concave* is that $(-1)^r D_r \geqslant 0$ for $r = 1,...,n$ where

$$D_r = \begin{vmatrix} 0 & f'_1.....f'_r \\ f'_1 & f''_{11}...f''_{1r} \\ \vdots & \vdots \quad \vdots \\ f'_r & f''_{r1}....f''_{rr} \end{vmatrix}$$

We can see that D_r is the $r + 1$st leading principal minor of the bordered Hessian

$$H = \begin{bmatrix} 0 & f'_1.....f'_n \\ f'_1 & f''_{11}...f''_{1n} \\ \vdots & \vdots \quad \vdots \\ f'_n & f''_{n1}....f''_{nn} \end{bmatrix}$$

this being a $(n + 1) \times (n + 1)$ matrix obtained by adding on the row and column of first order partials as illustrated.

10   Equality Constraints

Consider the constrained problem

$$\text{maximise} \quad f(\mathbf{x}) \quad \text{subject to} \quad g(\mathbf{x}) = 0 \qquad\qquad (A.9)$$

Note the constraint takes the form of an equality. The associated Lagrangian is

$$L = f(\mathbf{x}) + \lambda g(\mathbf{x})$$

and a necessary condition for a maximum is that the partials of this Lagrangian be zero.

Sufficient conditions for x^* to be a local solution to (A.9) is that x^* be a stationary point of the Lagrangian, and that D_r have the same sign as $(-1)^r$ where

$$D_r = \begin{vmatrix} L''_{11} \ldots \ldots L''_{1r} & g'_1 \\ \vdots & \vdots \\ L''_{r1} \ldots \ldots L''_{rr} & g'_r \\ g'_r \ldots \ldots g'_r & 0 \end{vmatrix}$$

The D_r is the border preserving leading minor of order r of the bordered Hessian

$$H = \begin{bmatrix} L''_{11} \ldots \ldots L''_{nn} & g'_1 \\ \vdots & \\ L''_{n1} \ldots \ldots L''_{nn} & g'_n \\ g'_1 \ldots \ldots g'_n & 0 \end{bmatrix}$$

PART THREE

11   Trigonometric Functions

An important trio of functions which often occur in dynamic models are the trigonometric functions sin, cos and tan. In Figure A.7 we have drawn a right-angle triangle with an angle θ at the apex set on the origin. The sin, cos and tan of this angle can be defined in terms of the diagram by

$$\sin\theta - \frac{QP}{OP}, \cos 0 - \frac{OQ}{OP}, \tan\theta = \frac{QP}{OQ}$$

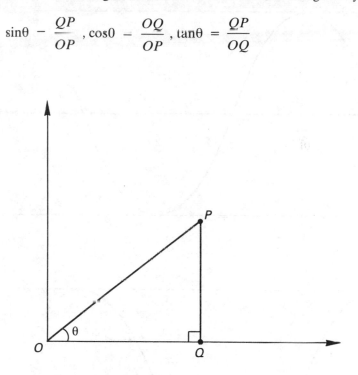

Figure A.7

We can note straight away that $\tan 0 - \frac{\sin\theta}{\cos\theta}$, that $-1 \lesssim \sin\theta \leqslant +1$, $-1 \leqslant \cos\theta \leqslant +1$, that $\sin\theta = 0$ and $\cos\theta = 1$ if $\theta = 0$, that $\sin\theta = 1$ and $\cos\theta = 0$ if $\theta - \pi/2$ or $90°$ that $\sin\theta = 0$ and $\cos\theta = -1$ if $\theta = \pi$ or $180°$ and that $\sin\theta = -1$ and $\cos\theta = 0$ if $\theta = \frac{3\pi}{2}$ or $270°$. Indeed if we plot the value of the graphs of $\sin\theta$ and $\cos\theta$ as in Figure A.8 we observe the classic 'sinusoidal' waves.

We can note that the derivatives of these functions are as follows:

$$\frac{d}{d\theta}\sin\theta = \cos\theta$$

$$\frac{d}{d\theta}\cos\theta = -\sin\theta$$

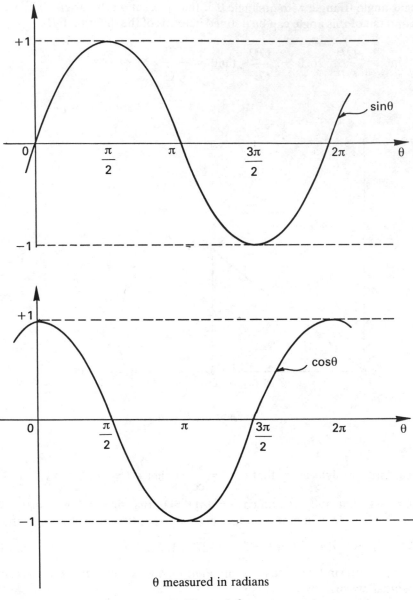

θ measured in radians

Figure A.8

The quotient rule then tells thus that

$$\frac{d}{d\theta}\tan = \frac{d}{d\theta}\left(\frac{\sin}{\cos}\right) = \frac{\cos\theta\,\cos\theta - \sin\theta(-\sin\theta)}{\cos^2\theta}$$

Now it can be checked from Figure A.7 that

$$\cos^2\theta + \sin^2\theta = \frac{(OQ)^2 + (QP)^2}{(OP)^2} = 1$$

by Pythagoras' Theorem. Hence

$$\frac{d}{d\theta} \tan\theta = \frac{1}{\cos^2\theta}$$

Repeat use of these rules of differentiation in the infinite Maclaurin expansion for cos and sin give

$$\cos\theta = 1 - \frac{\sin(0)\theta}{1!} - \frac{\cos(0)\theta^2}{2!} + \frac{\sin(0)\theta^3}{3!} + \dots$$

$$= 1 - \frac{\theta^2}{2!} + \frac{\theta^4}{4!} - \frac{\theta^6}{6!} + \dots$$

and

$$\sin\theta = 0 + \frac{\cos(0)\theta}{1!} - \frac{\sin(0)\theta^2}{2!} - \frac{\cos(0)\theta^3}{3!} + \dots$$

$$= \theta - \frac{\theta^3}{3!} + \frac{\theta^5}{5!} - \frac{0^7}{7!} + \dots$$

12 Complex Numbers

Reconsider the familiar quadratic equation

$$ax^2 + bx + c = 0 \qquad\qquad\qquad\qquad (A.10)$$

whose solutions are given by

$$x = \frac{-b \pm \sqrt{(b^2 - 4ac)}}{2a} \qquad\qquad\qquad\qquad (A.11)$$

if $b^2 - 4ac \geq 0$. Should $b^2 - 4ac < 0$, we say that the equation (A.10) has no real solutions. Now it turns out that it is possible to introduce a new set of numbers, called complex numbers, such that equations such as (A.10) always have two solutions. That is to say we can always find two complex numbers which satisfy (A.10). The set of complex numbers includes all real numbers, together with a new class of numbers called *imaginary numbers*. The basic imaginary number is the square root of minus one usually denoted by the letter i, so that we are to proceed as if $i^2 = -1$ or $i = \sqrt{-1}$. While the term imaginary is clearly appropriate, the use of this formal construct turns out to be very useful.

Using the fact that $i = \sqrt{-1}$ allows us to rewrite the solutions (A.11) when $b^2 - 4ac < 0$ as

$$x = \frac{-b \pm i\sqrt{(4ac - b)}}{2a}$$

Here we have removed $\sqrt{-1}$ from the square root sign. As $4ac - b^2 > 0$, then the term $\sqrt{(4ac - b)}$ is now a real number. Indeed the solutions can be written in the form

$$x = \alpha \pm i\beta \qquad\qquad\qquad (A.12)$$

with

$$\alpha = -\frac{b}{2a} \text{ being the } \textit{real part} \text{ of } x$$

and

$$\beta = \pm\frac{\sqrt{(4ac - b^2)}}{2a} \text{ being the } \textit{imaginary part} \text{ of } x.$$

Indeed the set of complex numbers is the set of numbers of the form $a + ib$ where a,b are real numbers and $i = \sqrt{-1}$.

It is possible to represent complex numbers much in the same way that we plot two-dimensional vectors. In Figure A.9 we have drawn two perpendicular axes in the usual way. In plotting a point to represent a complex number $z = a + ib$, it is normal to measure the real part a along the horizontal axis and the imaginary part b along the vertical axis as illustrated. As in the case of vectors, we can also think of the complex number $a + ib$ being associated with a line of particular length and direction. The length of this line would be $r = \sqrt{(a^2 + b^2)}$, i.e. the square root of the sum of squares of the real and imaginary parts. The direction would be given by the angle θ of the line with the real axis, so that $\tan\theta = b/a$ = ratio of imaginary to real parts. Note also that

$$\cos\theta = \frac{a}{r} \text{ and } \sin\theta = \frac{b}{r}$$

so that

$$a = r\cos\theta \quad b = r\sin\theta$$

and thus

$$z = a + ib = r(\cos\theta + i\sin\theta)$$

The complex number written in this way, using the trigonometric functions, is known as the *polar form* of the number.

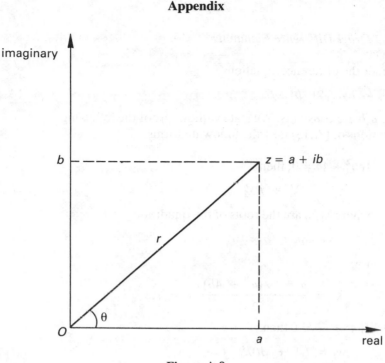

Figure A.9

We now come to one of those charming and useful results of mathematics. It turns out that

$$e^{i\theta} = \cos\theta + i\,\sin\theta$$

where e is Napier's constant. Hence any complex number $z = a + ib$ can be written in the form

$$z = re^{i\theta}$$

where r is the 'length' or absolute value of z, this being denoted by $|z|$, so that $r = |z| = \sqrt{(a^2 + b^2)}$ and $\tan\theta = b/a$.

We note that $z^t = (re^{i\theta})^t = r^t e^{i\theta t} = r^t(\cos t\theta + i \sin t\theta)$.

Finally returning to the quadratic equation with complex solutions given by (A.12), we can note that the solutions come in the form $x_1 = \alpha + i\beta$ and $x_2 = \alpha - i\beta$. A pair of complex numbers of this form, in that they differ only in the sign of the imaginary part, are called conjugate pairs. We can note that $x_1x_2 = (\alpha + i\beta)(\alpha - i\beta) = \alpha^2 + \beta^2$, recall $i^2 = -1$, and $x_1 + x_2 = 2\alpha$ are both real numbers. Hence the expression $(x - x_1)(x - x_2) = x^2 - (x_1 + x_2)x + x_1x_2$ is real, despite the presence of the two complex numbers. Note that if x_1, x_2 are complex conjugates, then their polar forms can be written as $re^{i\theta}$ and $re^{-i\theta}$ respectively.

Second Order Difference Equations

Consider the difference equation

$$y_t = ay_{t-1} + by_{t-2} \tag{A.13}$$

where a, b are constants. We state without proof the following.
   Solutions of (A.13) take the following forms:

(i)   If $a^2 + 4b \neq 0$, then

$$y_t = A\lambda_1^t + B\lambda_2^t \tag{A.14}$$

where λ_1, λ_2 are the roots of the quadratic

$$\lambda^2 - a\lambda - b = 0$$

i.e.

$$\lambda_i = \frac{a \pm \sqrt{(a^2 + 4b)}}{2} \quad i = 1,2$$

(ii)   If $a^2 + 4b = 0$ then

$$y_t = (A + Bt)\lambda^t \tag{A.15}$$

where $\lambda = \dfrac{a}{2}$

The constants A, B will be determined by initial conditions.

A major complication that arises here is the situation where $a^2 + 4b < 0$ in which case the λ_i's in (i) above are complex. As we have seen in Section 12, these pair of roots will be conjugates and thus can be written in the form $\lambda_1 = re^{i\theta}$ and $\lambda_2 = re^{-i\theta}$. Hence

$$\lambda_1^t = r^t e^{it\theta} = r_t(\cos t\theta + i \sin t\theta)$$

$$\lambda_2^t = r^t e^{-it\theta} = r^t(\cos t\theta - i \sin t\theta)$$

This allows us to complement (i) above with the following:

(i)'   If $a^2 + 4b < 0$ then

$$y_t = r^t(A' \cos t\theta + B' \sin t\theta) \tag{A.16}$$

where $r = \sqrt{-b}$

and $\tan\theta = \dfrac{\sqrt{(-a^2 - 4b)}}{a}$

Hence, in this case, the solutions tend to exhibit a 'wave' pattern. Consider the case of non-homogeneous equations of the form

$$y_t = a\, y_{t-1} + b\, y_{t-2} + c \tag{A.17}$$

where a,b,c are constants. If $a + b \neq 1$, then one can find an equilibrium value y^* of y, namely that value y^* which satisfies $y_t = y^*$ if $y_{t-1} = y_{t-2} = y^*$, so that

$$y^* = a\, y^* + b\, y^* + c$$

and

$$y^* = \frac{c}{1 - a - b}$$

If we now introduce the variable

$$x_t = y_t - y^*$$

we find that x_t satisfies the homogeneous equation

$$x_t = a\, x_{t-1} + b\, x_{t-2}$$

which we can then solve as above. Given the solution for x_t we then can find $y_t = x_t + y^*$.

In the case where $a + b = 1$ so that $a = 1 - b, b \neq 1$ then (A.17) can be rewritten as

$$y_t - y_{t-1} = -b(y_{t-1} - y_{t-2}) + c$$

Hence with

$$z_t = y_t - y_{t-1} \text{ we have}$$

$$z_t = -b\, z_{t-1} + c$$

which has solution of the form

$$z_t = (-b)^t\left(z_0 - \frac{c}{1 + b}\right) + \frac{c}{1 + b}$$

Hence

$$y_t - y_{t-1} = (-b)^t\left(y_0 - y_{-1} - \frac{c}{1 + b}\right) + \frac{c}{1 + b}$$

from which we can conclude

$$y_t = y_0 = \sum_{t=1}^{t} (-b)^t(y_0 - y_{-1} - \frac{c}{1 + b}) = \frac{ct}{1 + b}$$

or

$$y_t = y_0 + \frac{1 - (-b)^{t+1}}{1 + b}\left(y_0 - y_{-1} - \frac{c}{1 + b}\right) + \frac{ct}{1 + b} \tag{A.18}$$

If $a + b = 1$ and $b = -1$ so that $a = 2$, (A.17) becomes

$$y_t = 2y_{t-1} - y_{t-2} + c$$

or

$$y_t = y_{t-1} = y_{t-1} - y_{t-2} + c$$

hence

$$y_t - y_{t-1} = y_0 - y_{-1} + ct$$

and

$$y_t = y_0 + (y_0 - y_{-1})t + ct^2 \qquad\qquad\qquad (A.19)$$

If we start with the non-homogeneous case where $a + b \neq 1$, convert it to the homogeneous equation (A.13) as illustrated above, then we can view y_t as the 'deviation from equilibrium'. Hence if we are interested in knowing whether the equilibrium is stable, then we ask whether y_t approaches zero as t goes to plus infinity.

Viewing the solutions (A.14) we can conclude that if $a^2 + 4b > 0$, then y_t will converge to zero if λ_1, λ_2 are less than one in absolute size, i.e. $-1 < \lambda_i < +1$ where

$$\lambda_i = \frac{a \pm \sqrt{(a^2 + 4b)}}{2} \quad i = 1,2$$

Note $\lambda_1 + \lambda_2 = a$

and $\lambda_1 \lambda_2 = -b$

Now the conditions $-1 < \lambda_i < +1$ $i = 1,2$ hold if and only if

$$-1 < \lambda_1 \lambda_2 < +1$$

and

$$(1 - \lambda_1)(1 - \lambda_2) > 0$$

and

$$(1 + \lambda_1)(1 + \lambda_2) > 0$$

These three conditions can be written as

$$-1 < b < +1$$
$$1 - a - b > 0$$

and

$$1 + a - b > 0$$

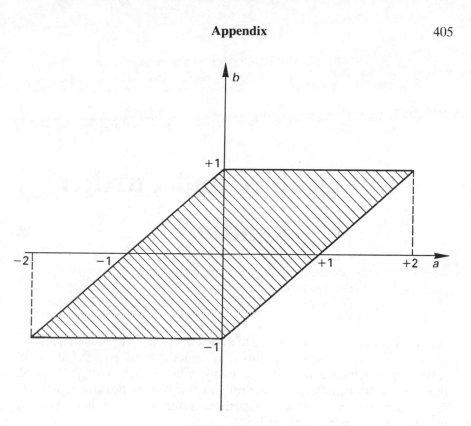

Figure A.10

The combinations of a,b satisfying these conditions are illustrated in Figure A.10.

Turning to the case $a^2 + 4b < 0$, solution (A.16) indicates that y_t will converge to zero if $r = \sqrt{-b}$ is less than one in (absolute) size, i.e. $+\sqrt{-b} < 1$. Finally when $a^2 + 4b = 0$ we can see from (A.15) that in general y_t will converge to zero if $\lambda = a/2$ is less than one in absolute size — we can assert that $t\lambda^t$ goes to zero if $|\lambda| < 1$.

Bibliography and Further Reading

As we mentioned in the Preface, a textbook at this level draws implicitly on a wide range of sources and thus it is impossible to give a full list of references which have directly or indirectly influenced its writing. We shall thus not aim for completeness, but rather present a few possible references for further reading together with those references that have directly influenced specific parts of the text.

Chapter 1: Algebra

With regard to reading on basic algebra, we make no specific suggestions. It is assumed that the student has previously studied those topics and it is thus advisable for them to refer back to their original texts.

One suggestion we can make is to have a look at

How to Solve It, G. Polya (Princeton U.P.)

which remains a valuable guide to developing a 'mathematical way of thinking'.

Chapters 2 to 5: Calculus

Students wishing to develop a deeper understanding of functions and calculus are referred to

Calculus: K. G. Binmore (Cambridge U.P.), Chapters 1–8.

406

This reference is technically quite demanding and will mainly suit those keen to develop their mathematical sophistication.

Chapter 6: Difference and Differential Equations

Again Binmore *op.cit.*, Chapters 9 to 12, offers a more advanced discussion of this general area.

A supplementary reference is

> *Economic Dynamics: Methods and Models*, G. Gandolfo (North-Holland).

Chapters 7 to 9: Concavity and Optimisation

Binmore *op.cit.* develops the requisite calculus analysis through the first eight chapters.

One author we must acknowledge as an influence is A. Dixit and we can refer the student to

> *Optimization in Economic Theory*, A. K. Dixit (Oxford U.P.)

and the Appendix to

> *Theory of International Trade*, A. K. Dixit and V. Norman (Cambridge U.P.)

The student can be referred to

> *Microeconomic Analysis*, H. R. Varian (Norton)

for a more advanced discussion of optimisation and its applications.

Chapters 10 to 12: Duality

Again the above work of Dixit, particularly Dixit and Norman, has been a significant influence and can be strongly recommended as a fine example of the application of duality ideas.

Varian *op.cit.* is again a useful if relatively advanced reference on duality.

The following offers an extended discussion of duality and its uses in the general area of consumer studies:

> *Economics and Consumer Behaviour*, A. Deaton and J. Muellbauer (Cambridge U.P.)

Chapter 14: Consumer Theory

Deaton and Muellbauer *op.cit.* is the best general reference. For further discussion of consumer surplus using indirect utility and expenditure functions see

> J. A. Hausman (1981) 'Exact Consumer Surplus and Deadweight Loss', *American Economic Review*, Vol. 81, No. 4.

The basic signalling model is given in

> Spence, M. (1974) 'Competitive Optimal Responses to Signals: An Analysis of Efficiency and Distribution', *Journal of Economic Theory*, Vol. 17, No. 3.

Chapter 15: Costs and the Competitive Firm

Varian *op.cit.*, Chapter 9, is a useful reference for further development of this topic.

Chapter 16: Monopoly and Imperfect Competition

Varian *op.cit.*, Chapter 2, is again useful. A detailed discussion of durable goods monopolist is given in

> J. I. Bulow (1982) 'Durable Goods Monopolists', *Journal of Political Economy*, Vol. 90, No. 2.

For examples of empirical analysis of production using profit and cost functions see

> *Production Economics: A Dual Approach to Theory and Applications, Vol. 2: Applications to the Theory of Production*, M. Fuss and D. McFadden (eds) (North-Holland).

Index